# THE BOOKS OF SIMION

**THE KINGDOM OF GOD IS AT HAND**

VOLUME 11

Revised edition

IVORY SIMION

ISBN 978-1-950818-46-4 (paperback)

Copyright © 2020 by Ivory Simion

All rights reserved. No part of this publication may be reproduced, distributed, or transmitted in any form or by any means, including photocopying, recording, or other electronic or mechanical methods without the prior written permission of the publisher. For permission requests, solicit the publisher via the address below.

Rushmore Press LLC
1 800 460 9188
www.rushmorepress.com

Scripture quotations marked KJV are from the Holy Bible, King James Version (Authorized Version). First published in 1611. Quoted from the KJV Classic Reference Bible, Copyright © 1983 by Zondervan Corporation.

Scripture quotations marked NIV are taken from the Holy Bible, New International Version®. Copyright © 1973, 1978, 1984 by International Bible Society. Used by permission of Zondervan. All rights reserved. [Biblica]

Printed in the United States of America

# CONTENTS

The Promise has been Fulfilled. The message has been delivered

The Kingdom of God is at Hand ..................................................5
Special Note ..................................................................................7
Preface .........................................................................................11
Introduction ................................................................................15

Chapter 1:  The Magician ..........................................................17
Chapter 2:  Yahawahshi, Jesus ancient Hebrew name ................31
Chapter 3:  Slavery and God's chosen people ............................36
Chapter 4:  White Gentiles are in Jerusalem today ....................51
Chapter 5:  The God of Islam is the same God of the
            Holy Bible ...............................................................54
Chapter 6:  The Accuser of the Brethren ...................................60
Chapter 7:  The Titans and the Olympians ...............................65
Chapter 8:  The Last Two Witnesses .........................................93
Chapter 9:  The white Gentiles Second Chance for Salvation ...105
Chapter 10: All Dominions in the universe shall serve God ......112
Chapter 11: God's first born ....................................................117
Chapter 12: The Collapse of the Gentiles global financial
            system ...................................................................138
Chapter 13: The white Gentiles are Psychotic or out of
            touch with reality .................................................153
Chapter 14: A Warning to the white Jews and white Gentiles ....164
Chapter 15: The Sanctuary .......................................................185
Chapter 16: The Kingdom of God comes to the Earth .............204
Chapter 17: There are no lost tribes of Israel ...........................238
Chapter 18: Born from the dead ..............................................243
Chapter 19: Jesus died for the sins of the People of God only ....250
Chapter 20: A Decree from God ..............................................263

Chapter 21: The Dead or Negro will be raised first ................... 273
Chapter 22: Synagogue of Satan ................................................ 282
Chapter 23: Rappers and Hip Hop ............................................ 289
Chapter 24: Double will Happen to the white Gentiles ............ 311
Chapter 25: United States declare war on the Afro Americans.... 318
Chapter 26: When the fullness of the Gentiles came in ............ 332
Chapter 27: The Scattering of the People of God ..................... 342
Chapter 28: The Valley of Jehoshaphat ..................................... 344
Chapter 29: The Vril and the original man ............................... 348
Chapter 30: The Invasion of the Earth ...................................... 362
Chapter 31: Possession ............................................................... 367
Chapter 32: He who will come with dread-locks ...................... 378
Chapter 33: The Cross ............................................................... 387
Chapter 34: The white Created Creatures purpose for existing .. 392
Chapter 35: Blue Beam Project ................................................. 412
Chapter 36: The Fullness of the Gentiles .................................. 423
Chapter 37: Black Magic ........................................................... 439
Chapter 38: The Deliverer ......................................................... 448
Chapter 39: The End of the Dominion .................................... 454
Chapter 40: Black Lives Matter ................................................. 459
Chapter 41: The Ambassador .................................................... 465
Chapter 42: The Penance ........................................................... 470
Chapter 43: The Plan for Salvation ........................................... 475
Chapter 44: The Regression ....................................................... 481
Chapter 45: The Deception ....................................................... 486
Chapter 46: The Aliens and the Beast that will come out
              of the CERN Particle Accelerator and Collider ....... 493
Chapter 47: Dominions ............................................................. 506
Chapter 48: The Promise has been fulfilled. The Message
              has been delivered. ................................................... 514

# THE KINGDOM OF GOD IS AT HAND

It is important for the Gentiles to know that fostering different perspectives around important issues furthers process, equality and a more connected society. It is for this cause that the Books of Simion are written. (Bank of America, connected)

To my friends, this is not His Tory but is My Story and My-story is totally different than His-tory. The Books of Simion are my Story.

Because the translation of the scriptures has been fragmented to suppress the truth, an ascendant from those who were the Biblical Slaves that are still Scattered will make known the understanding that was lost.

To Kings and all who are in Authority including the President of the United States;

"Great One" who is called President, the Books of Simion are the most Profound books of knowledge that have ever been delivered to the Gentile nations. The Books of Simion are written for Kings and all in Authority only so Kings and all in Authority can determine what is best for the people.

The Books of Simion are the Books of Record that are referred to as the Books of Remembrance that are written for Kings and all in Authority so Kings and all in Authority are not dishonored and their Kingdoms are not destroyed by deceptions. Ezra 4: 14-15 and Malachi 3: 16

This is the interpretation of the ancient scriptures from those who were scattered and led away from Jerusalem captive in slavery into other nations until the time of the Gentiles are fulfilled. The Holy Bible has identified those who are scattered and were slaves as being God's first born and chosen people. The same race that was slaves in Egypt, Assyria, Babylon, Persia, Greece, and Rome is the same race of people who were slaves in America. There is no other interpretation of the Holy Scriptures by any other race of people on the planet earth that is better. Once it is realized who are the true people of God, then it will be realized how important the Books of Simion are. The white Gentiles who have dominion today must know who Is Rael(Real) and who is not. Luke 21: 24 and Exodus 4: 22

The translation of the scriptures has been taken from an average Gideon Bible that was printed before 1965 as well as from the Christian Life Edition of the King James Version of the Holy Bible printed in 1985. Because recent versions of the Holy Bible have been altered to suppress the Truth, use older versions along with any modern version of the King James Version of the Holy Bible that you may have to research the facts. Do not use New Age Interpretation of the Holy Bible because those versions of the interpretation of the Holy Bible are wrong.

Of a Truth it is that the ascendant of those who were slaves God is a God of Gods and a Lord of Kings and a revealer of Secrets seeing that only an ascendant of those who were slaves could reveal this secret. Daniel 2: 47

# SPECIAL NOTE

The translation of the Holy Bible will be revealed on THREE LEVELS of CONSCIOUSNESS. Depending on whatever Level of Consciousness and level of Evolutionary Development as well as the level of Intelligence the reader is presently on will determine the amount of UNDERSTANDING the reader will receive from this translation.

Remember, all men are not on the same level of consciousness or on the same level of evolutionary development.

The Gentiles must know that all men cannot receive this message save or unless they are those to whom it is given. Matthew 19: 11

The Wicket will not understand but the Wise shall understand. Daniel 12: 10

The Gentiles who Glorify the Word of God and are ORDAINED to Eternal Life (this time because they believed last time) will believe (again this time). Acts 13: 48

Remember, a Skeptic is not one who is searching for the Truth. A Skeptic is one who Denies the Truth.

The Gentiles must know that once the Truth is written and regardless if the Truth is read because the Truth was suppressed, because it was Written and Delivered, it will set Events in the Matrix into motion that cannot be reversed, altered or canceled that will result in the Kingdom of God coming to the Earth.

The Kingdom of God has been halted in its return to the earth until Simion interprets the Mystery of the Gospel and delivers the Message of Salvation to the Gentiles to give the Gentiles their last chance to hear the Truth and act accordingly. Simion will declare how all of this is the Lord doing so God could take out of the white Gentiles a people for God's name. Only after Simion has delivered the message to the white Gentiles and revealed who are the Sons of Perdition will the Kingdom of God begin to move towards the earth again. Acts 15: 14-15 and 2 Thessalonians 2: 3-4

Once the Truth is Written and Delivered, the Kingdom of God will begin to move towards the earth again and absolutely nothing can prevent the Kingdom of God from arriving to the earth. The white Gentiles will try to change "Time" with a time machine and the "Law" of Nature through genetic engineering but the Court shall be seated and the judgment shall stand and the Kingdom and the "Dominion" and greatness of the kingdom under the "Whole Heaven" or in the entire universe shall be given to the people of the Most-High and their kingdom will be an everlasting kingdom and all dominions throughout the universe will serve and obey them. If the "Deliverer is hurt or killed, the Kingdom of God will begin to move towards the earth again at a greater speed and God will give the white Gentiles "Blood to Drink" and it will be the white Gentiles Just Due. Daniel 7: 25-27 and Revelation 16: 6

Because God wants to take out of the Gentiles a people for God's name, the Kingdom of God will be delayed until after Simion writes the words of the prophets in books and reveal who are the Sons of Perdition to save the Gentiles. Acts 15: 14-15 and 2 Thessalonians 2: 3-4

Once the words of the Prophets are written in books, the white Gentiles must seek after the "Truth" the way the white Gentiles seek after Gold and Silver to prove that they are worthy to remain grafted on the Tree of Life. Only if the white Gentiles receives the Truth and act accordingly will the Kingdom of God be delayed farther to give the white Gentiles more time to prove themselves worthy because God wants to take out of the white Gentiles a people for God's name and for this cause, all of this is done or will be allowed to be done and the words of the Prophets or the Books of Simion are written. If the white Gentiles ignore the Truth, the Kingdom of God will arrive in due time and if the End of the Age or the End of the Millennium has arrived, and the fullness of the Gentiles did come in on December 21, 2012, the remaining time to make your final choices is very short. After the fullness of the Gentiles comes in or after December 21, 2012, the "Deliverer" will come and deliver a "Profound" Truth to the white Gentiles that will turn away ungodliness. Acts 15: 14-15, Proverbs 2: 3-5 and Romans 11: 25-26

The delivery of the truth in the latter days to the Gentiles was the Gentiles plan to save themselves if all else failed and that plan was approved and agreed to by all in Heaven and recorded in the ancient Scriptures and in the Holy Bible thousands of years ago and Simion was part of their plan and their last legion or hope to hear the Truth and act accordingly and all of this was for the Gentiles to prove that they were worthy so God could take out of the Gentiles a people for God's name. The Promise God made to the Gentiles to send to the Gentiles prophets, wise men and "scribes" or those who would write books have been fulfilled. The words of the Prophets or the Books of Simion have been written and delivered. Acts 15: 14-15 and Matthew 23: 34

Only after Simion completes his Mission and reveal the Truth to the Gentiles and reveal who are the Sons of Perdition so the Gentiles would have their last opportunity to prove themselves worthy by "Falling Away" from that man of sin will the Kingdom of God begin to move towards the earth again. All of this was recorded in the ancient Scriptures and in the Holy Bible thousands of years ago for the Gentiles examination and study in the latter days so the Gentiles can determine for themselves if what was recorded in the Holy Bible has any merit and if the Gentiles wanted to Steer Events in Another Direction to Change the Shape of the Things that are Predestine to come to prevent no place found for the Great White Throne in the future. The Mission is complete and the Message to save the Gentiles in the latter days has been delivered as promised. The people of God have obeyed God and have been a light for Salvation for the Gentiles from biblical days to the "PRESENT" as was ordered by God to prevent the white Jews from judging themselves unworthy for everlasting life because they have assumed the true people of God identity and to prevent no place found for the great white throne in the future. It is now up to the Gentiles if their plan to be saved is a success. It is now up to the white Gentiles to SAVE the Kingdom or DESTROY it, however the white Gentiles see fit. Acts 15: 14-15, 2 Thessalonians 2: 3-4, Acts 13: 46-47 and Revelation 20: 11

# PREFACE

The history of the world civilization that we are being taught today is WRONG.

Everything that we were taught and believe to be true about the evolution of the species and everything that we were taught about the people of God in the Holy Bible is WRONG.

In today's world, the history that we know is the interpretation of the archeologists and historians who are determined to prove that the Western Civilization developed independent from any influence of divine intervention.

Ancient Astronaut Theorists believes that there is no God and earth was visited by astronauts from other worlds with advance technology that deceived our ancestors in believing that they were Gods.

History has misinterpreted the facts, denied the existence of evidence and has translated ancient text wrong leaving out important details of our past.

My-story unlike his-tory will reinterpret the facts to reveal a hidden truth and present new evidence or evidence that archeologists and historians have refused to accept.

My-story shall present a different translation of the ancient text that will unravel the enigma, explain the mystery and reveal the secrets that have been hidden for thousands of years.

Get ready to take a journey into the unknown to discover a lost or hidden history that will reveal the mysteries of the world.

You are about to go beyond the boundary that science, religion and archeology with their limitations of what they will accept can take you to enter a reality of truth and understanding.

You are about to take a journey that will expose you to the secrets of the earth that were lost, forgotten or deliberately hidden from the world. This is a journey that will take you where the truth is not your enemy and logic is not defined as chaos.

This book shall answer the question that the Ancient Astronauts Theorists have been asking for a long time. Who are the visitors? Why did they come to the earth? Why did they leave? Where did they go? Will they return?

This book will help you understand the Holy Bible, the book of Enoch and the Sumerian ancient text. It will connect the dots to bring all the scriptures together to make sense about what happened in the past to understand what is happening in the present to determine what could happen in the future.

This book will reveal knowledge not found in any other literature that is part of all the literature you have heard or read about God, the Fallen Angels, Creation and Aliens from other worlds.

The Reader will learn and understand more about the Holy Bible, the world and ourselves from the Books of Simion than the reader has learned and understood from the combine books and learning institutions that the Reader has been exposed to all of the Reader's life. For the first time in the Reader's life, the Reader will understand what the Reader could never understand before.

What was not understandable before will be made understandable by bringing together what happened in the past with what is happening in our present with what have been recorded in our Holy books about what will happen in the future. The Reader will understand what the Reader could never understand before. Without the Books of Simion, the Reader will go from university to university constantly learning but never able to come to the knowledge of the truth. 2 Timothy 3: 7

Do not be deceived by no one on the planet earth to believe that the opinion of those who were slaves are not important in these latter days. They are God's first born and chosen people that will inherit the earth. Only through them can salvation come to the Gentiles. They are under orders from God to be for the salvation of the Gentiles from biblical days to "PRESENT" till the end of the earth. It is because of this that the white Gentiles must know who IS RAEL (REAL) and who is not. The Salvation and survival of the white Jews and white Gentiles are at stake. Anyone telling the white Gentiles to ignore the ex-slaves opinions and expressing that the ex-slaves lives do not matter when the Holy Bible has recorded that the ex-slaves are ordered by God to be for the salvation of the Gentiles is the enemy to the white Gentiles. These people that say that the ex-slaves lives do not matter are trying to destroy the people that the Holy Bible has recorded are for the salvation of the Gentiles. The knowledge of the truth of this is written in Prophecy. The white Jews and white Roman Gentiles who has dominion today must understand this prophecy to survive. Exodus 4: 22, Matthew 5: 5, Revelation 21: 3 and Acts 13: 47

This time, to survive, you will have only your trust in who are the true people of God and their interpretation of the ancient scriptures to help you make your final latter-day choices. Last time at judgment, the white Gentiles assertion was that they were deceived by the "False Prophet" who is the "False Brethren" who are those that have assumed the true people of God identity and deceived the white Gentiles who have dominion today that the "False Brethren" knew the prophesies of the God of Abraham. If the white Gentiles are deceived again this time like last time to believe that some other race of people are the people of God, they are doomed. Revelation 19: 20 and 2 Corinthians 11: 26

The Books of Simion is the "Helmet of Salvation" and the "Sword of the Spirit" which is the "Word of God" that will cut like a two-edge sword. For the "Word of God" is living and powerful and sharper than any two-edge sword, piercing even to the division of the soul and spirit and of joints and morrow and is a discerner of thoughts and intents of the heart. For the first time since biblical days, in the Books of Simion, the readers will understand what could never be explained before. There is no other interpretation of the Holy Bible and prophesies of the God of Abraham by any other race of people on the planet earth that is better than the interpretation from those who were "Slaves" who are God's first born. Ephesians 6: 17, Revelation 1: 16, Revelation 19: 15, Hebrew 4: 12 and Exodus 4: 22

## PREPARE YOURSELF

# INTRODUCTION

## The Kingdom of God is at hand

In biblical days, the kingdom of God coming to the earth was so important that Jesus told His disciples to go out and preach the gospel of the kingdom of God coming to the earth in the future. No one else on the planet but those who were chosen before the world began will preach the gospel of the kingdom of God coming to the earth. No one else knows the message of our savior Jesus who has abolished Death and brought Life and Immortality to light through the gospel to which I was appointed a preacher, an apostle and a teacher to the white Gentiles but those that were chosen by Jesus before the world began to deliver the message to the Gentiles. No white Gentile was chosen to deliver this message, but this message is delivered to the white Gentiles by those that are chosen by Jesus. Matthew 4: 17, Matthew 6: 33, Matthew 10: 7, Luke 9: 2, Mark 1: 14-15 and 2 Timothy 1: 9-11

The message put simply is that the impossible was finally approved in heaven and now the Kingdom of God was at hand or now if you live a spiritual and righteous life, you can evolve into becoming godlike and given immortality alone with godlike abilities that are similar to our Father's abilities in Heaven. Now, your reward for living a godly life is immortality and super-human powers. Powers that are far beyond those abilities of normal men. Remember, our Father in Heaven evolved Moses to such a level that God made Moses a God over Pharaoh. Exodus 7: 1

God Himself wants to rule the next dominion on the earth and God wants the people of God to serve Him in His dominion. It's a done deal. The court that shall make this decision shall be seated with nothing else to be considered. The kingdom and dominion and the greatness of the kingdoms under the whole heaven or throughout the universe shall be given to the people and the saints of the Most-High. His Kingdom is an everlasting kingdom and all dominions throughout the universe shall serve and obey Him and His people. To be part of the Kingdom of God in the future, we all have our appointed duties to perform. The white Jews and the white Gentiles must believe what happened in the past to the old black African dominions and in a public forum admit who are the true people of God and what the true people of God have done for the white Jews and white Gentiles to survive otherwise, the white Jews and white Gentiles will be "Cut-Off" from the True of Life and regressed worse than today's Negros. The white Jews and white Gentiles must say that the branches were broken-off so that the white Jews and white Gentiles could be grafted in. They must say this in a public forum otherwise they too will be broken-off. The white Jews, the white Gentiles and the black Brethren or Brothers must prove themselves worthy to inherit the earth and live with God Himself. Daniel 7: 26-27, Romans 11: 20-22 and Romans 11: 19

This is the final message to the Gentiles

# The Magician

Do you believe in Magic? I'm talking about real magic. I'm not talking about illusions done with smoke and mirrors or sleight of hand tricks but real magic. I'm talking about the ability to really make objects disappear or the ability to really make objects float in the air.

Well that ability really exists in today's world. The ability to defy the laws of physics and do the impossible or to do real miracles really exists and is available to all that ask for it. First, we must understand who and what we are.

We are vessels, containers or bodies that were designed to house spirits. We are designed to give the spirit world the ability to experience the physical world in three dimensional containers, vessels or bodies.

The Grey's who are the aliens that are flying in today's UFO's identify the people of the earth as containers. The Greys are not here for our planet but are here for our bodies that they call containers and they need our bodies or containers to place disembodied ancient spirits in to continue their existence. The Grey's are here from the future collecting from the Gentiles uncontaminated bodies and DNA material that could not be collected in the future because of the worse plague the world will ever see that has contaminated the Gentile bodies in the future.

Today's magicians are proof that a spiritual world exists and that this spiritual world or the spiritual beings of that spiritual world are using our containers, vessels or bodies to implant their essence in to experience life in the three-dimensional physical world.

Manly P. Hall said that throughout history magicians have sold their souls to the devil and in return they received special powers during their short time on the earth.

Manly P. Hall writes, by means of the secret process of ceremonial magic, it is possible to contact these invisible creatures and gain their help in some human undertaking. Good spirits willingly lend their assistance to any worthy enterprise, but the evil spirits serve only those who live to pervert and destroy.

King Solomon was known for his communication with the spirit world and his control over elemental beings. In the secret book of King Solomon titled "The Greater Keys of Solomon", King Solomon left this letter for his son Roboam;

"O my son Roboam, seeing that of all sciences there is none more useful than the knowledge of the Celestial Movements, I have thought it is my duty being at the point of death to leave thee an inheritance more precious than all the riches which I have enjoyed. In order that thou may understand how I arrived at this degree of wisdom and greatness, it is necessary to tell thee that one day when I was meditating upon the power of the Supreme Being, the Angel of the great God appeared before me as I was saying O how wonderful are the works of God. I suddenly beheld at the end of a thickly shaded vista of trees a Light in the form of a blazing Star which said to me with a voice of thunder: Solomon, be not dismayed, the Lord is willing to satisfy thy desire by giving thee knowledge of whatever thing is most pleasant unto you. I order thee to ask of Him whatever thou desire.

Whereupon recovering from my surprise, I answered unto the Angel, that according to the Will of God, I only desired the Gift of Wisdom and by the Grace of God I obtained in addition to wisdom, the Understanding of the enjoyment of all the Celestials treasures and the Knowledge of all natural things. When I comprehended the speech, which was made unto me, I understood that in me was the knowledge of all creatures both things which are in the heavens and things which are beneath the heavens. Solomon awoke and behold it was a dream. Remember, God said that He would speak to us in dreams and visions because the Kingdom of God is within us. Luke 17: 21 and Numbers 12: 6

Understand that time is not the fourth dimension as the Gentiles geniuses believes. The first dimension is when you move from up to down. The second dimension is when you move from front to back. The third dimension is when you move from side to side. The fourth dimension is not time but is when you move from in and out of the first three dimensions for sleep, rest and recuperation. The fourth dimension is the universe where our conscious goes when we are asleep. The fourth dimension and the other higher dimensions are part of this unconscious state that we must experience to continue to have life and movement in the first three lower dimensions in our three-dimensional world. This inward universe in our mind is not part of our outer universe. There is no sun, solar system or galaxy in the higher dimensions. When you are asleep or unconscious, your mind is somewhere else other than in the Milky way galaxy. In the book of Enoch, Enoch was taken to heaven in the spirit that existence started in the seventh heaven or in the seventh dimension. There in those higher dimensions in our mind, Enoch was brought before the Throne of God. The kingdom of God is located in these higher dimensions that are within us or within the universe in our mind. This is why Jesus said that the kingdom of God is within us and this is why God said that He would speak to us in visions and in dreams as well as He will know what is in our minds and hearts. Luke 17: 21, Numbers 12: 6 and Revelation 2: 23

After awaking from this dream and the conversation Solomon had with the Angel of the Lord named Homadiel, Solomon wandered into the fields and he heard the voices of the animals; the ass brayed, the lion roared, the dog barked, the rooster crowed and behold Solomon understood what they all said one to the other. It is by this mean my Son that I possess all the virtues and riches of which thou now see me in the enjoyment. I assure thee that the Grace of the Great God will be familiar unto thee and the Celestial and Terrestrial Creatures will be obedient unto thee and will give thee the knowledge of a Supreme and ultimate science that is above our normal laws of physics whereby all things are possible which only works by the strength and power of natural things and by the pure Angels which govern them. Think not, however, O my Son that it would not be permitted thee to profit by the good fortune and happiness which the Divine Spirits can bring thee. On the contrary, it gives them great pleasure to render service to Man for whom many of these Spirits have great liking and affinity, God having destined them for the preservation and guidance of those Terrestrial things which are submitted to the power of Man. Furthermore, I wish to make thee understand that God has destined to each one of us a Spirit which watches over us and takes care of our preservation; these are called Genii who are elementary like us and who are more ready to render service to those whose temperament is conformed to the Element which these Genii inhabit. With the help of these divine beings or demonic beings, all things are possible. This is being proven by today's magicians who are performing miracles that are far beyond our normal laws of physics. (King Solomon: The Greater Keys of Solomon) and Matthew 19: 26

It must also be known that this invitation to have a relationship with an Elemental Being is only made to those who are on a spiritual level searching for God and the Angels who serve God. Jesus, who is now a spiritual being said that if anyone loves Him, he will keep Jesus word and our Father God will love him and God the Father and God the Son will come to him and make their home with him. John 14: 23

Average people who do not have control over their basic nature who are lost in Sin and Fornication and are searching for wealth, attention and power are told never try to make contact with these or any other Elemental Being because your nature and what is in your heart will determine what elemental being you are attracted to or is attracted to you and the negative Elemental Beings will deceive you and then defile you. Leviticus 19: 3, Leviticus 20: 6 and Leviticus 20: 27

Solomon leaves this warning to his son Roboam. Thou may then by the use of their Seals and Characters render these Spirits familiar unto thee who are destined to regulate the motion of the Stars, others to inhabit the Earth, others to aid and direct men and others again to sing continually the praises of the Lord provided that thou abuse not this privilege by demanding from these Angels things which are contrary to their nature. (The Greater Keys of Solomon)

It is possible to make contracts with spirits whereby the magician becomes for a stipulated time the master of an elemental being. (Manly P. Hall)

True black magic is performed with the aid of a demoniacal spirit who serves the sorcerer or magician for the length of the magician earthly life with the understanding that after death, the magician shall become the servant of his own demon. Manly P. Hall

A man can barter his eternal soul for temporal powers and down through the ages, a mysterious process has been evolved which actually enables him to make this exchange. Manly P. Hall

Today's magicians are performing all sorts of miracles and wonders. They are performing feats that are beyond our laws of physics. They are walking on water, floating in the air, teleporting themselves to other places, making objects disappear and reappear and they are even bringing back to life animals and insects that have died. What the magicians are in contact with is not science or technology but is something better that is beyond science and technology capabilities. The magicians are in contact with something that permits all things to be possible. The magicians identify themselves as true X-Men with the ability to perform miracles.

The magicians are in contact with beings that are beyond our normal laws of physics. What is impossible for us to do being animals of the third dimension is not impossible for these ascended beings. With God, all things are possible. Remember, we are vessels, containers and bodies that were made to house these spirits. Once in our bodies, our lifestyle would change tremendously and enormously. No one would have to work because food, clothing and shelter would all be provided to you because you would have the ability to manifest anything you want instantly with just a thought just as the magicians are doing today to entertain the Gentiles. Food, water, clothing and shelter would appear instantly when you need them. Jesus said do not worry about food, water, clothing and shelter because your heavenly Father knows that you need all of these things. Jesus said do not ask for these earthly things but rather seek first the Kingdom of God or ask for the Holy Ghost and all these things shall be added to you. The Power to do anything and everything is yours if you are possessed by the Holy Spirit or the Holy Ghost. Jesus screamed that "the Kingdom of God or the power to do the impossible is at Hand or is available to you with the Holy Spirit. To this very day, people including religious leaders have not fully understood the implication of what Jesus said. If they did, we wouldn't be working our lives away during the day and at night we wouldn't be chasing each other like crazy, drinking alcohol, wishing for that night to end in you draining your evolutionary energy you need to evolve on the Tree of Life for pleasure in the form of an orgasm. We have been deceived to believe that the love of the flesh in sex is good and healthy. This is Satan deception to deceive you to make you unworthy to be join with God to inherit the universe. For if you live after the flesh (searching for sex) you shall die but if you through the Spirit mortify (practice self-denial or kosher) the deeds of the body you shall live. Matthew 19: 26, Matthew 6: 31-33, Luke10: 19-20, Acts 1: 8, Luke 24: 48 and Matthew 10: 7, Romans 14: 17, Matthew 4: 17, Mark 1: 14 and Romans 8: 13

If the magicians are here now to deceive the Gentiles than those who are Sent to save the Gentiles are also here with greater power. Those who are here to save the Gentiles will have the power of the Holy Spirit or Holy Ghost in them. Unlike the magicians who will perform tricks in their own name to deceive the Gentiles and to hide the demon and the name of the demon who is giving them their power, those who are Sent to save the Gentiles will have the power to use the name of the Son of God to heal all manners of disease and illness. They will be able to cast out demons and devils or spirits of divinations, they will have powers over scorpions and serpents and they will be able to raise the dead all in the name of the Son of God. Matthew 10: 8, Luke 10: 19, Acts 16: 18 and Mark 16: 17

They will preach about the kingdom of God coming to the earth and they will demonstrate the power of the Holy Spirit that will be given to all who are worthy to dwell in New Jerusalem when the Kingdom of God is established on the earth. The preachers of today must understand that to fully preach the Gospel of Jesus, you must also show mighty signs and wonders by the power of the Spirit of God which is the Holy Ghost by a demonstration of the Spirit or Holy Ghost and the Power. Matthew 10: 7, Luke 9: 2, Romans 15: 18-19 and 1 Corinthians 2: 4

The magicians are possessed by Spirits of Divination but those who are Sent to save the white Jews and the white Gentiles will be possessed by the Holy Spirit or the Holy Ghost. Acts 16: 16, Acts 1: 4-8, Acts 2: 1-4 and Luke 24: 48-49

Those who are Sent to save the white Jews and the white Gentiles are sent by the white Jews in the future because the Jews in the future knows that the Jews in our Present are the False Prophet or False Brethren spoke of in the book of Revelation and in the book of Corinthians in the Holy Bible because the white Jews assumed the true people of God identity and deceived the white Gentiles who have dominion today that they were the people of God that knew the prophesies of the God of Abraham and it was that deception that resorted in the Jews judging themselves unworthy for everlasting life and also that deception was the cause why there was no place found for the great white throne in the future. At Judgment last time after seeing all that were given to the people of God in God's new world, the Jews wanted to share in this great gift and blessing. To guarantee the delivery of an important message or truth which would be their salvation, they sent their best friend in the future back in time to our present to give themselves a message or to deliver a truth to themselves, so they would know what was going on, so they would know what to do. This message is sent to the Jews first and then the message will be given to the white Gentiles. This delivered truth is the salvation that the white Jews and the white Gentiles asked for last time at Judgment, so they too could be saved and enjoy Paradise. Those who are Sent are ordered by God to complete their mission to deliver the latter-day message to the Jews and Gentiles because God wants to take out of the Jews and Gentiles a people for God's name. For the Lord has commanded us saying, "I have set you as a light to the Gentiles that you should be for their salvation from Biblical days to Present to the End of the Earth". Revelation 19: 20, Revelation 2: 9, Revelation 3: 9, 2 Corinthians 11: 26, Acts 13: 46, Revelation 20: 11, Acts 15: 14-15, Acts 13: 46 and Acts 13: 47

Last time when the Kingdom of God came to the earth in the twinkling of their eye, God's people were given an evolutionary jump that transformed them into the X-Men that today's movies are made about that gave them all of the powers that Jesus spoke about or all of the powers that today's magicians are demonstrating. 1 Corinthians 15: 51

The people of God were able to float like the clouds and fly like the birds. Anything that they imagined in their minds came true. They could not be KILLED. When they prayed, God would answer them while they were praying and gave them what they asked for before the prayers were over. All in the universe especially the Gentiles on earth declared that the people of God were the seed that the Lord had blessed. They had access to a River of Life that if you drank from it, you would live forever and if you swim in it, you would rejuvenate your body to a younger age. They also had access to Trees of the Knowledge of Life that if you ate from these Trees it would expand your consciousness and heal all diseases. Isaiah 60: 8, Matthew 17: 20, Luke 17: 6, Revelation 21: 4, Isaiah 65: 24, Isaiah 61: 9, Ezekiel 47: 8-9 and Ezekiel 47: 12

God's people that dwelled inside of New Jerusalem and the white Gentiles who dwelled in the outer court of this unbelievable, amazingly impressive, breathtaking great city were considered blessed beyond all blessings or good fortunes. So much so, that this time the white Jews and the white Gentiles who were not "ordained" to eternal life this time because they did not believe last time wanted to guarantee their chances to be there this time that they sent the latter-day message to themselves, so they would know what is going on, so they would know what to do. Remember, Jesus said that the white Jews and the white Gentiles did not know what they were doing because they have no idea what is going on. Because the Angels will come forth at the end of the age to separate the wicket from the just, to guarantee the delivery of this profound message in the latter days after the fullness of the Gentiles had come in at the end of the age or after December 21, 2012, the white Jews and white Gentiles sent their best friend in the future to our present to make that delivery knowing that their best friend in the future would make the delivery without offending them in the process. Revelation 11: 2, Luke 23: 34, Matthew 13: 49, Romans 11: 25, Luke 21: 24

God has said by Peter who was Simon who was called Simeon and called a Nig er (Nigg er) mouth only would the Gentiles hear the message or truth and Believe. The ancient Prophets are subject to the latter-day prophets or the ancient prophets will be in the latter-day Prophets. Acts 15: 7, Acts 10: 5, Acts 15: 14-15, Acts 13: 1 and 1 Corinthians 14: 32

The word "Saint" is a mispronunciation of the word "Sent" and only those who are "Sent" are called "Saints". A "Saint" is not a white Gentile that has lived a righteous life. A "Saint" is only those who are "Sent". Those who are Sent (Saint) that will be called Saints (Sents) are sent to the Jews first because the Jews at judgment in Heaven are the ones who sent the messenger so the white Jews would not judge themselves unworthy for everlasting life because they want to be the people of God so bad that they are assuming the identity of the true people of God and then those who are Sent will turn and deliver the message to the white Gentiles who have dominion today to prevent no place found for the great white throne in the future because the white Gentiles who have dominion today have joined the white Jews to deceive the world that they are the people of God because they are both white. They are not Human but are White. Acts 13: 46 and Revelation 20: 11

Being white is not a mark of superiority as the white Gentiles were deceived to believe. You cannot be a white man and Hue man at the same time. You are either one or the other. White is the absent of all color and being Human or a Hue Man is only those who have a shade, color or tint or a Hue in them. A Human is a colored man because Hu or Hue means color. That is why the white man wants to be a Human or Hue Man because being white is not better or superior to those who have a Hue. The white race is a young race on the Tree of Life. Their oily hair and white skin are proof that they are a young race that has not been exposed to the sun for hundreds of thousands of years. Dark skin and nappy hair are proof that race has been exposed to the sun for hundreds of thousands of years. The Human race is an ancient race on the Tree of Life. The white Gentiles were ordered to JOIN with the Humans to become a human being but they refused and at the same time they proclaimed to all in Heaven that the joining of the white race with the human race had occurred and all on the planet earth were human beings or people with a shade, color or tint knowing that they were still white. This is the Profound message from the future that you must receive to be saved that today's movies are made about.

From this message, events must be steered in another direction to prevent what is prophesied to come to pass. There will be no other message from the present or future to warn the Gentiles as Hollywood is deceiving the white Gentiles to believe. There will be no "John Connors" or white Gentile from the future that will return to save the white Gentiles or "Mankind" as was portrayed in Hollywood 1984 science fiction movie titled, "The Terminator". The Holy Bible has recorded that the End of the dominion will be declare from the beginning of the dominion and in the beginning, it was Simeon who delivered this message to the Gentiles and since the End will be declared from what happened in the beginning, it will be Simeon the Nig er and only Simion the Nigg er who will deliver this message to the Gentiles to save the Gentiles after the end of the age or after December 21, 2012 because God wants to take out of the Gentiles a people for God's name. After the end of the age comes in or after the fullness of the Gentiles comes in, the Deliverer will deliver this message to the Gentiles. Acts 13: 46, Revelation 20: 11, Isaiah 46: 10, Acts 13: 1, Acts 15: 14-15 and Romans 11: 25-26

This knowledge was also channeled to the white Gentiles from the white Gentiles from the future to the white Gentiles of our present and the white Gentiles from the present put that channeled message in the 2010 movie titled, "The Books of Eli" starring Denzel Washington. It was channeled to the white Gentiles that the deliverer would be a "Nig er" ("Nigg er") but unlike in the movie titled "The Books of Eli", the deliverer will not memorize the Holy Bible for the Gentiles. The Deliverer name will not be "Eli" but Simeon because it was Simeon in the beginning who delivered the message that God want to take out of the Gentiles a people for God's name and for this cause, the words of the prophets or the Books of Simion are written and since the end of the dominion will be declared from what happened at the beginning of the dominion it will be Simeon and only Simion who will deliver the message at the end of the dominion after the fullness of the Gentiles comes in. Simion will interpret the Mystery of the Gospel and from that interpretation of the Mystery of the Gospel, the Deliverer will deliver not just the Holy Bible to the white Gentiles but also deliver the message of Salvation to the Gentiles that is within the Holy Bible to save the Gentiles. He will preach the gospel of the Kingdom of God coming to the earth so the Gentiles second chance for salvation would not be in vain, but salvation would come to the Gentiles, so the Gentiles could be with the people of God in the future. The Deliverer will not deliver his message in a post-apocalyptic time, but the Deliverer will deliver his message after the fullness of the Gentiles comes in or after the end of the age or after December 21, 2012 to prevent a post-apocalyptic time. Acts 15: 14-15, Isaiah 46: 10, Matthew 3: 2, Matthew 4: 17, Mark 1: 15, Matthew 10: 7, Luke 9: 2 and Romans 11: 25-26

In Biblical days, Paul who was possessed by the Holy Spirit was confronted by a girl who was possessed by a Spirit of Divination who had insight and foresight who could predict and forecast the future. She brought her masters much profit by fortune-telling and revealing the unknown through omens, oracles or supernatural powers as the magicians are doing today. She proclaimed that Paul and those who are Sent to save the Jews and the Gentiles are servants of the Most-High God and their only purpose is to show the Jews and the Gentiles the way to salvation. This she did for many days. But Paul, greatly annoyed, turned to her and said to the spirit that was in her or had possessed her body and was giving her powers to be a fortune-teller, "I command you in the name of the Son of God to come out of her" and the spirit of divination came out of her that very hour. These signs will follow those who believe and only purpose is to show the Gentiles the way to salvation. In God's name they will cast out demons, they will speak with new tongues, they will take up serpents and if they drink anything deadly, it will by no means hurt them, they will lay hands on the sick and the sick will recover. Acts 16: 16-18 and Mark 16: 17

If the magicians are here now to deceive the Jews and Gentiles with tricks as they did in Biblical days, then those who are sent that will be called Saints are here now to save the Jews and the Gentiles by showing them the way to salvation as was done in Biblical days.

# Yahawahshi, Jesus ancient Hebrew name

The original name of Jesus is Yahawahshi. Because of the great authority of that name to use our Father in Heaven or God's power to perform miracles, the people of God were forbidden to speak the name of the Son of God. Anything that the people of God ask God in Yahawahshi name who is the Son of God was given to them by God. Because of the great authority of the name Yahawahshi to use the power of God, Yahawahshi was changed to Jesus but still, Yahawahshi made it possible for the name of Jesus to be used to perform miracles when it is referred to the Son of God. Many miracles have been performed in the name of Jesus the Son of the God of Israel by Men of God who believed that Jesus is the Son of the God of Israel. Acts 4: 17-18, John 16: 23 and Mark 16: 17-18 and (You Tube-google: How to spell Jesus real name in ancient Hebrew)

By using the name of Yahawahshi, the Son of God is glorified as well as God Himself being glorified. John 13: 31-32

The last two witnesses of the Gentiles second chance sent by God will perform many miracles in the mighty and holy name of Yahawahshi. Warning, they must not appear clothed in sackcloth or poor. If they are, God will give them the power to strike the earth with all plagues as often as they like. Revelation 11: 3-6

In the past, those who are sent to save nations were promoted and given gold and great wealth and made third ruler in the kingdom. Daniel 2: 47-48, Daniel 5: 29, and Genesis 41: 37-43

Yahawahshi came into this world in His father's name. His Father name is Yahawah. Yahawah is His Father's or Family name that the name Yahawahshi shares with His Father's name. Both names Yahawah and Yahawahshi have Yahawah in them because Yahawah is the name of God. When you use the name Yahawahshi, you glorify the Son and the Father. Remember, the Messiah who is our Savior came into this world in His father's name. "Shi" is a reference to the individual in that family which is similar to our first name and it mean Savior. John 5: 43 and John 13: 31-32

No one knows the day or the hour when the Son of God will return. We are told to watch for signs in the heavens and on the earth to prepare us for what's to come. We are told to watch for certain things and when you see these things come to pass or feel that these things are about to come to pass, we are told to get ready. A great sign will be seen in heaven on September 23, 2017. It is a woman clothed with the sun with the moon under her feet and on her head a garland of twelve stars. Matthew 24: 36, Matthew 24: 44, Matthew 24: 32-33, Matthew 25: 13, Matthew 24: 42-44 and Revelation 12: 1

We are told that the killing of the people of God who are the ascendants of those who were slaves who are God's first born and chosen people would be so numerous and outrageous in the latter days that all who died because of the word of God and for the testimony which they held and that physical testimony was that they were black or were the color of brass (brown) that has been burned in the furnace (dark brown to black) with hair like sheep wool or nappy hair as is the Lamb in Heaven or in the after-life are asking God when will He avenge their deaths on those who dwell on the earth. Exodus 4: 22, Revelation 1: 13-15 and Revelation 6: 10

Jesus was not a white Jew but is a black Brother from the Brethren. Jesus who is the Lamb in Heaven is the color of brass (brown) that has been burn in a furnace (dark brown to black) with hair like sheep wool or nappy hair. Jesus, the Lamb in Heaven is not a white Jew but is a black brother from the brethren with sheep-wool hair or nappy hair and dark brown to black skin. When Jesus found out that the white Jews wanted to kill him, Jesus no longer walked among the Jews. The Shroud of Turin is a LIE and a FAKE. Revelation 1: 13-15 and John 11: 53-54

The audacity that the white Greeks and the white Romans have to portray God and the Son of God and God's people in the white pagan gentile imagine or in the imagine of those white gentiles that hated God and hated the Son of God and hated God's people is beyond forgiveness. The white Gentiles worship the white Gentiles as God and the Son of God. In the white Gentiles dominions on the earth from Greece to Rome to this last dominion we live in today identified as "Iron and Clay", the white Gentiles portrayed God and the Son of God as white pagan gentiles. The Holy Bible has recorded that all who worship the image or "picture" of the upright Paleolithic beast passing off as the Son of God will be "Cursed" by God. All Christians must know that if they die believing that God and the Son of God are white and die with a hate for God's people who are the Afro Americans today, they will not receive what was promised to those that worship God no matter how dedicated they were and no matter if they had a good report about their faith. They must know that without a love for the people of God who are the Afro Americans today, they will not receive nothing that was promised to those that believe in God and have a good report about their faith. I pity the white Gentiles that die believing that God and the Son of God are white. Remember, the Holy Bible says that the white Gentiles do not know God or the Son of God because the white Gentiles believes that God and the Son of God are "White". At Judgment this time, Jesus will say to them that thought He was white, depart from Me, you who practice lawlessness. You never knew Me, and I never knew you. Revelation 14: 9-11, Hebrew 11: 39-40 and John 16: 3, John 8: 19, John 15: 21 and Matthew 7: 23

Hollywood and the Synagogue of Satan that controls Hollywood are condemning the white Gentiles because of the white Gentiles unjustified conceit. The white Greek Gentiles, the white Roman Gentiles and the "Iron and Clay" Gentiles which were the last three dominions in the white Gentiles second chance for salvation that the Holy Bible says were inferior to the black kingdoms that came before them are the lowest of all of the dominions in the white Gentiles second chance for salvation because they were not represented as Gold or Silver as black Babylon and black Persia were but as bronze and iron and they must stop saying that the grafted branch who are the white Gentiles that had no planet is better that black Babylon represented as "Gold" and black Persia represented as "Silver" who are the owners of the planet earth because it is these black people who gave the white Gentiles race a dominion on their planet to growth in and to join them and become part of the "Human Race". Revelation 3: 9 and Daniel 2: 31-41

The Holy Bible is about the white Jews, the white Gentiles and the black Brethren or Brothers. The black Brethren or Brothers are those who ancestors were slaves and the slaves and the ascendants of the slaves are God's chosen people and God's first born. They are the Afro Americans today. Exodus 4: 22

That is what the word Hebrew means. Hebrew means "Hey Bro" in reference to the Brethren or the Brothers. The correct pronunciation of the word Hebrew is "Hey Bro". Look for the correct pronunciation of the word "Hebrew" in any dictionary and it will reveal to you that the correct pronunciation of the word "Hebrew" is "Hey Bro". That is how the Gentiles call out to those who had no name and no country from a God with no name. Until this very day, the Gentiles call out to the Afro Americans by saying "Hey Bro" and in so doing they are calling the Afro Americans Hebrews.

# Slavery and God's chosen people

How psychotic or out of touch with reality can this world be to say that the Afro Americans have no history? The Holy Bible is the history book of those who were slave who are God's first born and chosen people. The Afro Americans are the ascendance of those who were slaves. The Holy Bible is the Slaves or the Afro Americans history book. To deny this truth is to say that you are not intelligent and civilized but is psychotic being out of touch with reality. The same race that was slaves in Egypt is the same race that were slaves in America. This is a fact. The "Slaves" are not the Gentiles. The Romans, the Greeks, the white Jews and the Christians are the Gentiles. In the white gentile dominion of "Iron and Clay" in which is the dominion we live in today, the Holy Bible has recorded that the Gentiles would be in Jerusalem by the power of their guns and the true people of God would have been led away from Jerusalem in slavery until the time of the gentiles are fulfilled at the end of the age. The end of the age was on or around December 21, 2012. If the white Gentiles do not understand this now at the end of the age when the fullness of the Gentiles have come in or now since the Gentiles are at their smartest and maximum level of evolutionary development, then this will be the proof that the white Gentiles are not worthy, "Tekek", and have been found wanting what is necessary to remain grafted on the Tree of Life. Exodus 4: 22, Luke 21: 24 and Daniel 5: 27

Those who are the ascendants of the "Slaves" who were called the "Brethren" or "Brothers" are the most important people in the world today. They are God's first born and chosen people. There is no other race on the planet earth that surpass those who were "Slaves" that God has said are His first born and chosen people. The Holy Bible has recorded that the "Slaves" or the ascendants of the "Slaves" are God's first born and chosen people and not the white Jews. Exodus 4: 22

The white Jews from Greece are not the people of God but are those who are assuming the identity of the true people of God. When the Greek dominion was over, and the Roman dominion started, the white Greeks assumed the identity of the people of God to have authority in the Roman dominion. The Romans sold the true people of God to the Greeks and the Greeks removed the true people of God from Israel and then assumed the true people of God identity. Because of that, the true people of God stop calling themselves Jews and only referred to themselves as the "Brethren" or "Brothers". Jesus was not a white Jew but is a black brother from the brethren. Jesus who is the Lamb in Heaven is the color of brass (brown) that has been burned in a furnace (dark brown to black) with hair like sheep wool or nappy hair. Jesus said He was the physical image of the invisible God. Jesus said that Him and the Father are one. Jesus said he who has seen Him has seen the Father. The Father God who is called the Ancient of Days color is dark brown like Jesus and God has nappy hair or hair like pure wool. The unbelieving white Jews who were the Greeks stir up the white Roman gentiles who have dominion today poisoning the white Roman gentiles who have dominion today against the Brethren or the brothers. When Jesus found out that the white Jews wanted to kill Him, Jesus no longer walked among the white Jews. Remember, the true pronunciation of the word "Hebrew" is "Hey Bro" or "hey brother". Look it up in any dictionary. When the Gentiles called out to them, the Gentiles would say "Hey Bro" as the white Gentiles do today. They were a people without a name from a God without a name, Joel 3: 6, Revelation 1: 14-15, Colossians 1: 15, John 10: 30, John 14: 9, Daniel 7: 9, Acts 14: 2 and John 11: 54

The true people of God are the only ones that are ordered by God to be a "light" for the white Gentiles and to be for the white Jews and white Gentiles "Salvation" from biblical days to "Present" till the end of the earth and it is because of this that the people of God who are the Afro Americans today are the most important people in the world today for the white Jews and white Gentiles. The Holy Bible has recorded this profound truth to prevent the white Gentiles who have dominion today from being deceived by the "False Prophet" who are those who have assumed the true people of God identity and is deceiving the white Gentiles who have dominion today that they are the people of God that knows the prophesies of the God of Abraham. Acts 13: 47

It is because of this that the white Gentiles of today's dominion must know who Is Rael (Real) and who is not because only the true people of God can show the white Jews and white Gentiles the way to "Salvation". The agreement was in order to prevent the white Jews from judging themselves unworthy for eternal life because they want to be the people of God so bad that they have assumed the true people of God identity, him who is sent is ordered to go to the white Jews first because the white Jews in the future are the ones who sent the "Deliverer" to deliver this profound message to them in our present so they would know what's going on and know what to do to be saved by being with the "Deliverer" to back the "Deliverer" up when the "Deliverer" goes to the white Gentiles then, the "Deliverer" will turn and deliver the message of "Salvation" to the white Gentiles. Do not judge yourself unworthy for eternal or everlasting life because of your conceit like last time and renege on this agreement. You have been "Alerted". Acts 13: 46

Those that are against the white Jews and white Gentiles and do not want the white Jews and white Gentiles to receive "Salvation" will not want the white Jews and white Gentiles to come together with the true people of God. The enemy to the white Jews and white Gentiles who are the disbelieving white Jews from the Synagogue of Satan identified as the Sons of Perdition will stir-up the white Gentiles against the "Brethren" or "Brothers" who are the Afro Americans today and poison the white Gentiles who have dominion today minds against the "Brethren" who are the Afro Americans today. The "Accusers" of the "Brethren" are the enemy and the "Brethren" or "Brothers" are the Afro Americans today. This is Prophecy. Anyone accusing the brethren who are those who are the ascendants of the slaves who are the Afro Americans today of anything is the "Enemy" to the white Jews and white Gentiles who have dominion today. Remember, the ascendants of the "Slaves" are God's first born and chosen people. Revelation 2: 9, Revelation 3: 9, Acts 14: 2, Revelation 12: 10 and Exodus 4: 22

To help the white Jews and white Gentiles in the latter-days of their dominion, this knowledge about who can help the white Gentiles and who are the enemy to the white Gentiles is recorded in the Holy Bible and only the true people of God can deliver this truth concerning "Salvation" for the white Jews and white Gentiles to the white Jews and white Gentiles as is recorded in the Holy Bible.

To prevent the white Jews from judging themselves unworthy for everlasting life because they want to be the people of God so bad that they have assumed the identity of the true people of God and to prevent no place found for the great white throne in the future, the people of God are ordered by God to be for the "Salvation" of the white Jews and white Gentiles from biblical days to "Present" till the end of the earth. The true people of God will obey God's order and be for the "Salvation" of the white Jews and white Gentiles regardless if the white Jews and white Gentiles are saying that the people of God "lives do not matter" and it is this actions of obeying the order from God in the mist of extreme hatred from the white Jews and white Gentiles that will farther guarantee the return of God and the people of God place in Paradise. Acts 13: 46-47 and Revelation 20: 11

It is recorded in the Holy Bible that the day of God return will not come until the Sons of Perdition or the Sons of Hell from the Synagogue of Satan are revealed to give the white Jews and white Gentiles a choice to either remain in iniquity or "Fall Away" from that man of "Sin" who opposes and exalts himself above all that is called God or that is worshipped so that he sits as God in the temple of God showing himself that he is God. Revelation 3: 9 and 2 Thessalonians 2: 3

In biblical days, it was Simeon who revealed to the white Jews and white Gentiles that God wants to take out of the white Jews and white Gentiles a people for God's name and since the end of the dominion will be declared from what happened at the beginning of the dominion and in the beginning of the dominion it was Simeon who revealed this to the Gentiles, at the end of the dominion it will be Simeon and only Simion who will deliver the message that God wants to take out of the Gentiles a people for God's name and for that cause and purpose, the words of the Prophets or the "Books of Simion" are written. Isaiah 46: 10 and Acts 15: 14-15

To be saved, the white Jews and white Gentiles must believe and reveal all that have happened otherwise, the white Jews and the white Gentiles will be broken off from the Tree of Life. The old black dominions that included the slave race that were before the white Gentile dominions did not "believe" that God could take their dominion away from them and give it to the young white primitive race of Gentiles because anything that the old black dominions wanted to do, they had the ability to do it and yet, they were broken-off and their dominion was given to the young white Gentiles for a time. Romans 11: 22, Romans 11: 20 and Genesis 11: 6

Disbelieving will get you broken-off from the Tree of Life in a New York minute. The white Gentiles of today's dominion must "believe" what happened in the past to the old black dominion and know for a surety that the same will happen to the white Gentile dominion if the white Gentiles do not believe that God can take their dominion away if they disobey God. Romans 11: 20-22

The "Slaves" were the builders in Egypt. The "Slaves" not only built the pyramids, but they also built Pharaoh's treasure cities "Pithom" and "Ramses". The white Gentiles must look at the ascendants of the "slave" race who are the Afro Americans today who were the pyramids builders of the past and look at them now because of disbelief and be "WARNED" and know the same or worse will happen to the white Gentiles if the white Gentiles also disbelieve and is "Cut-Off" from the Tree of Life. Exodus 1: 11 and Romans 11: 20-22

Do not be deceived by the Ancient Astronaut Theorists who are lying because of their conceit and are telling the white Gentiles that the ancient ruins were all built by extraterrestrials because of the extraordinary way the ruins were built. These ruins were not built by extraterrestrials but were built by the old black African dominion to make a name for themselves before they were scattered to make room for the young white replicated gentile race. This was to show the white Gentiles what the old black Africans were capable of and still, they could not fight God. Do not let the Ancient Astronaut Theorists destroy this special warning for the white Gentiles that is meant to help the Gentiles understand what is really going on. The same extraterrestrials that were here in biblical days are here now, but they are not building anything because construction is not their agenda. Their agenda is about creating vessels, containers or bodies to house disembodied ancient spirits in to receive life immortal. Genesis 11: 4

Because Jesus said that the white Jews and white Gentiles did not know what they were doing, at judgment last time, the white Jews and the white Gentiles asked that the knowledge of what is actually going on be sent to them, so they would know what to do to be saved. Luke 23: 34

Only the people of God can deliver that knowledge to the white Jews and white Gentiles to prevent the white Jews from judging themselves unworthy for eternal life and to prevent no place found for the great white throne in the future because God has order them and only them to be for the white Jews and white Gentiles "Salvation" from biblical days to "Present" till the end of the earth. Therefore, let it be known to you that the "Salvation" of God or the knowledge of what is going on has been sent to the Gentiles in the "Books of Simion" and the white Jews and the white Gentiles will hear and receive it. Acts 13: 46-47, Revelation 20: 11 and Acts 28: 28

The Holy Bible says that the white Gentiles must behold and consider the goodness of God when God gave the Gentiles a dominion on the earth and the white Gentiles must look at the severity of God when God broke the old black Africans off from the Tree of Life and babbled their understanding otherwise the white

Gentiles will also be "Cut-Off". The white Jews and white Gentiles must not say that "Black Lives do not Matter" but must say that "Black Lives Matter" because it was them and only them who are sent by God to offer "Salvation" to the white Jews and white Gentiles and it were them that were "Broken-Off" that the white Jews and white Gentiles could be "Grafted-In" and if those Black Lives are not with the white Jews and white Gentiles sharing in their wealth, the white Jews and white Gentiles will not receive what was promised to them if they had good faith. The Holy Bible has recorded that without the people of God who are the Afro Americans today, the white Jews and white Gentiles will not get what was promised to them if they had good faith. Romans 11: 20-22, Romans 11: 19 and Hebrew 11: 39-40

In a public forum, the white Gentiles must say that the "branches" were "broken-off" so that the white Jews and white Gentiles could be "Grafted" in. To be saved, the white Jews and white Gentiles must say this in a public forum. There is no other revelation in the world today that is more important than this truth that is being revealed. This is the truth that can save the white Jews and white Gentiles if the white Jews and white Gentiles receives the truth and act accordingly. Therefore, let it be known to you that the salvation of God has been sent to the Gentiles in the "Books of Simion" and the Gentiles will hear it. Romans 11: 20-22, Romans 11: 19 and Acts 28: 28

The "Slave" race built Pharaoh's treasure cities "Pithom" and "Ramses" including the Ramses statues that are seen in Egypt today as well as built the Pyramids in Egypt. The "Slave race" were the builders in ancient Egypt according to the Holy Bible and not extraterrestrials as the Ancient Astronauts Theorists believes. Only the people of Satan from the Synagogue of Satan who are against the Holy Bible will say different than what is recorded in the Holy Bible. Exodus 1: 11

The "Slave race" or those who were "Scattered" and the old black African dominion built all of the ancient cities whose ruins are found today that the Ancient Astronaut Theorists says were built by extraterrestrials as well as built the "Towers" or "Pyramids" whose tops are in the heavens and they built these ancient extraordinary cities by some unknown manner to make a name for themselves before they would be "Scattered" to make room for the white Gentile dominions. To make a name for themselves means, they wanted the white Gentile dominions that would come after them to know who they were and what they were capable of doing and still, they could not fight God. The Afro Americans are those who are being "Scattered" today in the last white Gentile dominion when God has promised to return to "gather" those who are being "Scattered". Where are the Afro Americans that use to live in Los Angeles, California? Why were they scattered? Genesis 11: 4, Mark 13: 26-27, Jeremiah 23: 2-3, Jeremiah 31: 10, and Jeremiah 50: 17

The children of Israel did not come to America on ships like the Titanic in luxury and in the comfort of first class cabins. The children of Israel came to America on slave ships in bondage and were sold to their enemies and became slaves. Deuteronomy 28: 68

Being a Slave and being oppressed are the conditions that will prove that the Afro Americans are God's chosen people and are God's first born. If your race was not Slaves and oppressed by the Gentiles for 430 years, you are not God's chosen people and you are not Is rael (real) or the true people of God that the Holy Bible is referring to. The holocaust of the people of God is about "Slavery" and "Oppression" or being a Slave, persecuted and scattered for 430 years and not about white Gentiles being a prisoner of a white gentile war for 4 years. Acts 7: 6-7

Slavery is a reoccurring condition for the people of God in the Gentiles second chance for salvation in the world we live in today. The nation where God's people are slaves in bondage and oppressed for 400 years will be judged by God and after that these ascendants of Slaves shall come forth and serve God. They are the direct ascendants of Abraham, Isaac and Jacob and they are the ones who will be "Gathered" by God and inherit the earth and be joined with God. Jerimiah 30: 3, Amos 9: 14, Joel 3: 1, Acts 7: 6-8, revelation 13: 10, Mark 13: 27 and Revelation 21: 3

Being a slave in America in the past and being persecuted and scattered in America today is the undying proof that the Afro Americans are God's chosen people. A city on the hill cannot be hidden is what Jesus told His disciples about God's people. The meaning to this parable is that everything that have happened to the people of God will prove who they are. The people of God are that city on the hill where everyone can see or everything that have happened to the people of God and everything that is now happening to the people of God like being persecuted and scattered will prove who the true people of God really are. Matthew 5: 14

The Holy Bible has recorded that the people of God would not be the landlords, bankers, doctors and the rich in the Gentile dominion but would be slaves, persecuted and scattered. The race that has been slaves and are now being persecuted and scattered is the true people of God. This is why this house on a hill or the people of God being slaves and persecuted and scattered cannot be hidden or denied. Everything that is happening to the people of God will prove that they are the true people of God. Slavery will prove who are the true people of God.

The children of Israel were slaves in Egypt for 400 years. When the children of Israel came out of Egypt and went to Israel, the

Assyrians came and captured Israel and made the children of Israel Slaves. 2 Kings 17: 6

The children of Israel came out of Assyria and went back to the land of Israel then the Babylonians came and captured Israel and made the people of Israel Slaves. 1 Chronicles 9: 1

The children of Israel came out of Babylon and went back to Israel then the Persians came and captured Israel and made the children of Israel Slaves. Ezra 9: 9

The children of Israel came out of Persia and went back to Israel then the Greeks came and captured Israel and made the children of Israel Slaves. Maccabees 8: 18 and Joel 3: 6

The children of Israel came away from servitude to the Greeks and went back to Israel then the Romans came and captured Israel and made the children of Israel Slaves.

In the latter days of the Gentiles dominion which is the last dominion for the white Gentiles which is an extension of the Roman dominion which is a dominion of iron mixed with clay or the white Gentiles as the iron which is strong but is not natural and the clay which are the people of God who are the descendants of Adam and Eve who were created from clay by the hand of God, the people of God were taken to this last kingdom by way of ships in bondage which we now know is America and were slaves in bondage and servitude and were persecuted and scattered for 430 years as they were in Egypt, Assyria, Babylon, Persia, Greece and Roman. The white Gentiles who are not Human Beings because they are white without color were supposed to mix with the seed of men and become Human Beings or Hue Men or Colored Men with a shade, color or tint but they did not whereas iron cannot be mix with clay. Yet, the white Gentiles proclaimed to all in Heaven that the joining with the human beings had taken place and everyone on the planet earth were human beings or beings with a shade, color or tint knowing that they were still white without color. To be a Human Being or a hue man or a colored man you must have a hue or a shade, color or tint. White is the absent of all color. You cannot be a white man and a Hue man or human being at the same time. You are either one or the other. Daniel 2: 31-43 and Deuteronomy 28: 68

    The white Gentiles of today wants the public to believe that different races were slaves at different times. They want the world to believe that those who were slaves in America is not the same race that was slaves in Egypt. They are wrong. The people that were slaves in Egypt were also the same race that were slaves in Assyria, Babylon, Persia, Greece, Rome and they are the same race that were slaves, persecuted and scattered in the last Gentile dominion of iron and clay that we live in today and that race was taken to a foreign land by ships in the latter days in bondage and held there in America as slaves for 430 years and they are being persecuted and scattered till this very day as they were in all of the other dominions. That race is called Afro Americans today. If your race was not slaves and persecuted and scattered for 430 by the white Gentiles, you are not the people of God. Where are the Afro Americans citizens that used to live in California or used to live in the "Sanctuary" cities that were given to illegal immigrants in America? What happened to them? Why were Afro American citizens "Scattered" out of the cities they grow up in and their cities became "Sanctuary" cities that were given to illegal immigrants? Why were the illegal immigrants told that they could stay in America as long as they did not move in white Gentile or white Jewish cities and in white Gentile or Jewish neighborhoods but stayed in the Afro Americans cities that were identified as "Sanctuary" cities for illegal immigrants? Why have the American government ignored the persecution and the killing of Afro Americans citizens by white Gentiles because the white Gentiles have said that they are envious of the Afro Americans and are afraid of Afro Americans and why have the American government "Abolished" the right to protest for the Afro Americans and have told the Afro Americans citizens that their protest for equal rights is a disrespect to the white Gentiles flag and a disrespect to white Gentile veterans? How much disrespect to Americans veterans are the white Gentiles leadership showing when they support white Nazi supremacists in a country that fought against white Nazi supremacy and the many veterans that died fighting white Nazi supremacy in World War Two? Acts 7: 6-7, Deuteronomy 28: 68, Jeremiah 30: 3, Jeremiah 30: 18, Joel 3: 1, Acts 13: 45 and Acts 17: 5

Slavery is the condition that will identify the true people of God. The true people of God were slaves in Egypt, Assyria, Babylon, Persia, Greece, Rome and America. Reoccurring slavery for the people of God was so dominate and consistent that Jeremiah ask our Lord and heavenly Father if Israel was nothing but a servant. Is Israel a homeborn slave? Why is Israel spoiled or plundered? Jeremiah 2: 14

Understand that the reason why Israel was a slave in the last five dominions on the earth in the Gentiles second chance for salvation in the world we live in today is because they are the Meek who will inherit everything including the earth and be joined with God and given immortality in ascended bodies. Halleluyah, praise Yah, the author of this book is so glad to be an ascendant of the slaves that are call dead or Negro today because tomorrow, the Negro shall inherit the earth and be joined with God. Matthew 5: 5 and Revelation 21: 1-7

Reoccurring Slavery is how the true people of God are identified. Like in Egypt, Assyria, Babylon, Persia, Greece and Rome, in this last dominion that we live in today of "Iron and Clay", it is the Afro Americans who are the ascendants of the Slaves. If your race was not oppressed, persecuted, scattered and a Slave for the Gentiles for 400 years, your race is not the people of God. The Holocaust of the people of God is about being a "Slave" as well as being "Oppressed", "Persecuted" and "Scattered" for 400 years by the Gentiles and not about being a "prisoner of war" for four years in a gentile war against the Gentiles. It is the Afro Americans who are the true people of God that shall inherit the earth. The Slaves are God's first born and chosen people. Blessed are the Afro Americans who are proud to be a Negro and the ascendants of Slaves for they shall inherit the earth and be joined with God. They are God's first born. Daniel 2: 37-43, Acts 7: 6-7 and Exodus 4: 22

The white Greek gentile Jews that are in Israel today who are the descendants of the Greeks are not the people of God. When the Greek dominion was over, and the Roman dominion started, the Romans sold the people of God to the Greeks and the Greeks assumed the identity of the people of God to deceive the white Roman Gentile, so the white Greeks Gentile could have authority in the white Roman Gentile dominion. It is this deception that will be the cause why the white Jews judge themselves unworthy for ever-lasting life because they want to be the people of God so bad that they have assumed the identity of the true people of God and this deception will be the cause why there is no place found for the great white throne in the future. The white Greeks and white Roman gentiles must not fight and kill the human being of the earth to assume their identity as human beings of the earth. The white Greeks and the white Romans must "Join" the human beings of the earth to become human. Joel 3: 6, Acts 13: 46 and Revelation 20: 11

These white gentile Jews from Greece are called the "false brethren" which is another way of saying the "false prophet" because they deceived the white Roman Gentiles to believe that the white Greek Gentile knew the prophesies of the God of Abraham. Last time at judgement, the white Roman Gentile assertion was that they were deceived by the false prophet or "false brethren" who worked signs or made atom bombs and horrible weapons for the Beast and for the white Gentiles. It is this deception that will cost the white Gentiles everything. It is this deception that will be the cause that the white Jews judge themselves unworthy for ever-lasting life and the cause of the white Roman Gentiles who have dominion today are broken off or Cut Off from the Tree of Life and regressed into the Paleolithic upright beast of their past and there will be no place found for the great white throne in the future. 2 Corinthians 11: 26, Revelation 19: 20, Romans 11: 22 and Revelation 20: 11

It is because of these consequences that will be paid in the future for the white Jews and white Gentiles actions today that the white Jews and the white Gentiles in the future sent a profound message to the past or our present, so they would know what is going on to prevent from being deceived so they would know what to do to be saved. Remember, Jesus said that the white Jews and the white Gentiles did not know what they were doing because the white Jews and white Gentiles do not know what is really going on. Luke 23: 34

# White Gentiles are in Jerusalem today

The Holy Bible has recorded that the white Gentiles would be in Israel in the latter days. The true people of God would be led away from Jerusalem captive and put in slavery and Jerusalem shall be trodden down by the white gentile Jew until the times of the white Gentiles are fulfilled at the end of the age. The end of the age was on December 21, 2012. The white Gentiles thought that this date marked the end of the world, but that date marked the end of the age and the end of the white Gentiles dominion on the earth which to the white Gentiles was the end of their world. Luke 21: 24

Soon, God will return, and the Gentiles will be judged and if events are not steered in another direction to change the shape of the things that will come, there will be no place found for the great white throne in the future. The earth and the heaven will flee away from the white Gentiles and the white Gentiles will have no place on this earth in the future. Revelation 20: 11

The Olmec calendar from the old black African dominion that was found in South America has recorded that the end of the age was on December 21, 2012. After that date, the Angels will come forward and gather the people and separate the wicked from the righteous. The people of God will not be place in Israel by the forces of this world or by England and America but by God Himself. It is God who will bring the people of God back to Jerusalem. Matthew 13: 49, Ezekiel 11: 16-17, Ezekiel 28: 25-26 and Ezekiel 36: 24-29

The white gentile Jews in Jerusalem today are not proof that they are the people of God but is proof that the white Jews that are in Jerusalem today are Gentiles and it is not by God that the white Jews are in Israel today but by the power of the sword or gun that the white Jews are there. Luke 21: 24

The white Jews that are in Israel today do not believe that Jesus is the Son of God. They say that Jesus was just another prophet that they disagreed with. (YouTube: Why Jewish people do not believe in Jesus, Why is Jesus not the messiah for Jews, and What do Jews in Israel think about Jesus Christ.)

To be the people of God and saved, you must know Jesus and believe that Jesus is the son of God. Jesus is the way, the truth and the life. No one comes to the Father except through Jesus. If you do not believe that Jesus is the Son of God, you cannot serve God or know God. If you believe that God and the Son of God are white instead of the color of brass (brown) that has been burned in the furnace (dark brown to black) with hair like sheep wool or nappy hair, you do not know God or the Son of God. To be saved, the white Jews and white Gentiles must believe and admit that the Lamb in Heaven who the white Gentiles call Jesus is a colored man with nappy hair. To be saved, the white Jews and white Gentiles must say that the Shroud of Turin is a LIE and a FAKE. 1 John 2:23, John 15: 23, John 3: 36, John 3: 16, 1 John 4: 3, John 14: 6-7, John 16: 3, John 8: 19 and Revelation 1: 14-15

The white Jews that are in Israel today are the Sons of Perdition or the Son of Hell or the Hellenistic white Greek Gentiles who are assuming the identity of the true people of God. They are the only ones who are still lost because they do not believe in Jesus as the Son of God. John 17: 12

The Sons of Perdition had to be revealed before the coming of the Lord to the white Jews and to the white Gentiles to give them their chance to fall away from that man of sin who opposes and exalts himself above all that is called God or that is worshiped so that he sits as God in the temple of God portraying himself that he is God. 2 Thessalonians 2: 3-4

The Holy Bible has recorded that no one comes to the Father but by the Son. If you do not know the Son, you do not know the Father. John 14: 6

Every spirit that does not confess that Jesus, the Son of God, did come in the flesh is not of God. This is the spirit of the antichrist or anti God which you have heard was coming and is now already in the world in Jerusalem or is now occupying Israel today. The Anti-Christ is in Jerusalem today, right now passing off as the people of God. 1 John 4: 3

The white Roman Gentiles who have dominion today have put white Gentiles in the Holy Land that do not believe in Jesus who are identified by the Holy Bible standards as the Anti-Christ and the Sons of Perdition. The Anti-Christ is in Jerusalem right now. 1 John 4: 3

# The God of Islam is the same God of the Holy Bible

These white Hellenistic Greek gentile Jews have deceived the white Roman Gentile who have dominion today to fight the God of the Holy Bible which is the same God of Islam and to fight the descendants of Abraham who are the descendants of Ishmael who was a child of Abraham who are those that are Islamic today all for the Greeks who God is Zeus and these white Greek gentile false Jews are the Changelings that have assumed the identity of the true people of God to have authority in the white Roman Gentile dominion.

This is the great deception that has deceived the world and suppressed the truth about who are the true people of God and will be the cause that the white Jews are found not worthy for eternal life and also be the cause why there will be no place found for the great white throne in the future. The latter-day Deliverer is sent first to the white Jews because the white Jews in the future are the ones that sent the message to themselves in our present by the Deliverer to prevent them from judging themselves unworthy of ever-lasting life because they want to be the people of God so bad that they have assumed the true people of God identity then, the Deliverer will turn to the white Roman gentiles who have dominion today and deliver the truth to them to prevent no place found for the great white throne in the future. Acts 13: 46 and Revelation 20: 11

Last time at judgment, the white Roman Gentiles that have dominion today assertion was that they were deceived by the "False-Prophet" who were those white Greek gentile Jews that deceived the white Roman Gentiles who have dominion today that the white false Jews were the people of God who knew the prophesies of the God of Abraham. The Lord has commanded His people to be a "Light" to the Gentiles and to be for the Gentiles salvation from biblical days to "Present" till the end of the earth and the "False Prophet" who are the disbelieving Jews has prevented the people of God from being for the salvation of the white Gentiles because of "Envy". These white Greek false disbelieving Jews who envy the "Brethren" must not stir-up the white Roman Christian gentiles who have dominion today against the "Brethren" who are the "Brothers" today who are the Afro Americans as they did in biblical days. Revelation 19: 20, Acts 13: 47, Acts 17: 5 and Acts 14: 2

The white Roman Gentile that have dominion today must understand that the God of Islam is the same God of the Holy Bible that the Christians worship. That's how much the white Christian Roman gentiles who have dominion today are being deceived.

Because of the white Gentiles who have dominion today unjustified conceit about being white, they have been deceived by the "False Prophet" to believe that they are the people of God because they are not "Human Beings" but are "White Beings". The white Roman gentiles who have dominion today are being deceived by the Greek Jewish Sons of Perdition because they are white and are those who have assumed the identity of the true people of God and have deceived the white Gentiles who have dominion today to support those that are assuming the people of God identity because they are also white. They have deceived the Roman gentiles that have dominion today to believe that the Greek and the Roman gentiles are the people of God because they both are white. The white Greek Jewish gentiles and the white Roman gentiles who have dominion today must not try to kill all color people or all human beings on the earth so the white Greeks and white Romans gentiles could assume the identity of the human beings.

White must not join with white to remain white but must join with black to become Human Beings. The white beings must not say they are human beings or colored people knowing that they are still white. They must make that joining to prevent the reaper at the time of the Harvest of the earth from gathering together the white replicated beings who are identified as the "Tares" of the earth that were put on the earth to join the people of the earth to become human beings from being gathered together in the Valley of Jehoshaphat to be burned because they want the inheritance of the "Meek" to inherit the earth and the "Meek" are the People of God who are the ascendants of the "Slaves" who are the Afro Americans today. Matthew 5: 5, Matthew 13: 30 and Joel 3: 2

When the white Gentiles belittle Islam, Allah and the Muslims, they are also belittling and degrading the God of the Holy Bible and the Son of God and the People of God in the Holy Bible. The white Roman Gentiles who have dominion today and the white Greek Jewish Gentiles from the Synagogue of Satan are not the people of God, but the Muslims are because they are the descendants of Abraham son name Ishmael. The white Greeks and the white Romans from the Synagogue of Satan are the people that hated Jesus and was responsible for the death of Jesus and the death and the suffering of the true people of God in biblical days. Once Jesus realized that the white gentile Jews from the Synagogue of Satan wanted to kill Him, Jesus no longer walked among the white gentile Jews. Because of the white gentile Jews assuming the people of God identity and calling themselves "Jews", Jesus and the true people of God referred to themselves only as the "Brethren". It is because of this that God will give Israel another name. The people of God shall be called "Hephzibah" which mean that God is delighted in them. Now, at the end of the white Gentiles dominion, they want to deceive the world that they are the people of God and they are telling the world that they have a right to exist or they have a right to assume the true people of God identity. They are wrong. It is this lie that is responsible for all the deaths and unrest in the Middle-East and throughout the world today and it is this lie that will be responsible for the white Jews judging themselves unworthy for ever-lasting life because they want to be the people of God so bad that they have assumed the people of God identity and say that they have a right to do so and it is this lie that will be responsible for no place found for the great white throne in the future because the white Roman gentiles who killed Jesus and killed the true people of God are saying that they are the people of God because they are "White". It is this lie that will have the white Jews and white Gentiles in the Valley of Jehoshaphat fighting God in the war of Armageddon for the people of God name and inheritance. The white Jews and white Gentiles will never be considered a race of intelligent and evolved people as long as they are "Psychotic" or "out of touch with really" by assuming the name and identity of the "Slave" race who are God's first born. That is how important the slave race is in the world we live in today. The slave race is so important in the world we live in today that the powers of this world wants the history and the inheritance of those who were slaves. Revelation 3: 9, John 11: 53-54, Isaiah 44: 5, Isaiah 62: 4, Acts 13: 46, Revelation 20: 11, Joel 3: 2 and Exodus 4: 22

For the white Roman Gentiles who have dominion today to be saved, they must know who Is Rael (Real) and who is not. They must HELP the true people of God who were led away from Jerusalem as captive or slaves and scattered into all nations who are the Afro Americans today NOW if they expect to receive help LATER. They must HELP those who are being SCATTERED. They must FALL AWAY from the Sons of Perdition who are the sons of Hell because Perdition means Hell who are the Hellenistic white Greeks gentile Jews from the Synagogue of Satan who are assuming the identity of the true people of God who are that gentile man of sin who is in Jerusalem today portraying himself that he is the children of God. Luke 21: 24, Revelation 2: 9, Revelation 3: 9 and 2 Thessalonians 2: 3-4

Paul spoke boldly in the name of the lord Jesus and Paul disputed against the Hellenists white gentile Jews. The Hellenists white gentile Jews plotted to kill Paul because Paul preached that Jesus was the son of God. Acts 9: 20, Acts 9: 23 and Acts 9: 29

Remember, the white Jews are afraid that if the white Roman Gentiles who have dominion today in this last kingdom of iron and clay find out who are the true people of God, the white Roman Gentiles who have dominion today would take away the Jews nation and give a nation to the Brethren or the people of God who are those who are scattered. The white Greek gentile Jew was afraid that Jesus would gather together those who were scattered abroad and became Slaves and then, the white Romans who have dominion today would take away the white Jews title as the people of God and give that title and a nation to the true people of God that were scattered abroad. From that day on, the white Jews plotted to put Jesus to death to preserve their lie and their nation. This is why the white Jewish gentile from Greece and the white Roman Gentile proclaims that Jesus died for them. They are wrong. Jesus was KILLED for them to preserve their lie that white gentile Jews and the white Roman

Gentiles are the people of God. Jesus was not sent to the white Gentiles but only sent to the people of God. Jesus told His disciples "NOT" to go to the white Gentiles but to go to the "Lost Sheep" of Israel only. Jesus is the people of God "Savior" only. Paul and Simeon were sent to the Gentiles. Jesus died for the people of God sins only. The Afro Americans who are the ascendants of Slaves are those who are scattered today in the latter days of the dominion. Like in the past and in the first six dominions of the Gentiles second chance for salvation from Egypt, Assyria, Babylon, Persia, Greece and Rome, in the last dominion of the Gentiles second chance identified as a dominion of "Iron and Clay", the people who are the "Slaves" in that dominion are the true people of God. The "Slaves" are God's first born and that includes the people who were "Slaves" in America in the iron and clay dominion that we live in today. They are Jesus people and the true people of God. This is the revealing of the Mystery of the Gospel. Daniel 2: 38-45, John 11: 45-53, Matthew 10: 5-6, Matthew 15: 24, Acts 9: 15, Act 15: 14-15, Daniel 2: 38-43 and Exodus 4: 22

We are told that all in Heaven are telling those who are asking God to avenge their deaths that they should wait a little while longer until their fellow Brethren who were killed last time are killed this time in the white Gentiles second chance for salvation, so all could be complete or as it was last time so all that happens to the white Jews and white Gentiles are justified or their just due for killing the people of God. Revelation 6: 11 and Revelation 16: 6

# The Accuser of the Brethren

The Afro Americans who are the ascendants of Slaves who are God's first born who are the Brethren or Brothers are not the enemy to the white Gentiles but are the ones that can help and save the Gentiles. This is prophecy. This is what the white Jews and white Gentiles must understand to be saved. Prophecy in the Holy Bible has recorded that the Brethren or the people of God are those that can show the white Jews and white Gentiles the way to salvation. They are commanded by God to be a light for the Gentiles and to be for the Gentiles salvation from biblical days to "PRESENT" to the end of the earth. Now, the Gentiles must not be deceived about who these people really are. The white Jews and white Gentiles survival depends on knowing the identity of these special people who will deliver a profound truth that is so profound that in biblical days the unbelieving white gentile Jews said that the delivered truth could turn the world upside down and to save the white Jews and white Gentiles this conversion must come to pass. Exodus 4: 22, Acts 13: 47 and Acts 17: 6

The ACCUSER of the Brethren is the enemy to the white Jews and to the white Gentiles and he must be cast down and all must fall away from that man of sin. Those who are assuming the people of God identity to deceive the white Gentiles is the enemy to the white Jews and to the white Gentiles. For the Lord has commanded us or the Brethren to be a light for the Gentiles and that we be for salvation to the Gentiles from biblical days to the PRESENT to the end of the world. The people of God that are born again or raised from the spiritually, morally and mentally dead Negro that are redeem from among men that are sent are still under that command from the Lord to be for the salvation of the Gentiles. Anyone advising the Gentiles today at this late hour to scatter, persecute, ignore the people of God opinion and say that the people of God who are the Afro Americans who are the ascendants of Slaves and the Slaves are God's first-born "lives do not matter" is the "ENEMY". The Accuser of the Brethren is the enemy. Exodus 4: 22, Revelation 12: 10, 2 Thessalonians 2: 3-4, Acts 13: 47, Revelation 14: 4-5 and Exodus 4: 22

It is the understanding that the people of God have that can guide the Gentiles to salvation. It is because of this that the white Gentiles who have dominion today should have protected the true people of God because the people of God are the only ones on the planet that can show the white Gentiles the way to salvation. Once Dr. Martin Luther King revealed this to president Kennedy, President Kennedy attempted to protect the people of God with the "Civil Rights Bill" for the true people of God and in so doing, help the white Jewish gentiles and the white Roman gentiles. The people of God and the white Gentiles fate are connected. "Double" will happen to the white Gentiles that happens to the people of God. That's double the curses or double the blessing. In the cup that the white Gentiles mixed, mix double for the white Gentiles. President Kennedy and Martin Luther King both were killed by the Sons of Perdition to preserve the lie that the white gentile Jews and the white Roman gentiles are the people of God because they are "White". Acts 13:47 and Revelation 18: 6

To destroy the Gentiles, the people of the devil have removed the true people of God from the Gentiles and that action has allowed the Gentiles to be deceived and led down the path of destruction instead of being led to the path of salvation. Instead of flooding the people of God with sins and fornications to destroy the people of God, the white Roman gentiles that have dominion today should have joined with the people of God and made certain that the people of God served God and not sin and fornication. The people of God are the only ones on the planet that can show the white Gentiles the way to salvation. God has commanded them to be for the salvation of the white Gentiles from biblical days to "Present" till the end of the earth. It is because of this that the people of God are the most important people in the world to the white Gentiles. Therefore, I exhort first of all that supplications, prayers, Intercessions and giving of thanks be made for all men, for Kings and all who are in authority or the illuminati that the people of God lead a quiet and peaceful life in all godliness and reverence for this is good and acceptable in the sight of God our savior who desire all men to come to the knowledge of the truth. For the people of God who are the Afro Americans today to live quiet and peaceful lives is good and acceptable in the sight of God who desire all men to come to the knowledge of the truth with the true people of God. Instead of forcing the people of God to live a life of sin and fornication flooding the people of God neighborhoods with crime, the white Gentiles should have guaranteed that the people of God lived quiet and peaceful lives in the white Gentiles dominions so in the future, the white Gentiles could be with the people of God in Paradise at the "Outer Court" of the great new city named "New Jerusalem" that will be given to the white Jews and white Gentiles who believe. Acts 13: 47, 2 Timothy 2: 1-4 and Revelation 11: 2

The white Gentiles must know that they must shepherd the flock of God which is among them, serving as overseers, not by compulsion but willingly not for dishonest gains but eagerly nor as being lords over those entrusted to them, but being examples to the flock and when the Chief Shepherd appears, they would receive the crown of glory that does not fade away. 1 Peter 5: 2-4

The false prophet who is the false brethren or those who have deceived the Gentiles to believe that they are the people of God have led the Gentiles in the wrong direction. We are at the end of the age and the end of the dominion and the false prophet or those that have assumed the true people of God identity have not spoken of salvation for the Gentiles. They have deceived the white Gentiles to believe that the white Gentiles salvation is in developing more powerful weapons to kill the true people of God in the Middle East, America and all over the world. They have "deceived" the white Gentiles who have dominion today to believe that the extraterrestrials will help them escape judgment and damnation by leaving the earth in gentile made space crafts, built by a company named "Space X". The "False Prophet" and the white Gentiles must be "Warned" that when they try to leave the earth in Gentile built space ships, they will be cast into the "Lake of Fire" which is the "Sun". 2 Corinthians 11: 26 and Revelation 19: 20

In the latter days of the dominion, it is not about preserving the white Jews lie that they are the people of God and it is not about the white Gentiles lie and conceit that they are the people of God because they are white. Now, at this late hour, it is about delivering a truth to the white Jews and to the white Gentiles that will steer events in another direction to change the shape of the things that are prophesied to come to prevent the white Jews from judging themselves unworthy of everlasting life because they want to be the people of God so bad, they have assumed the people of God identity and to prevent no place found for the great white throne in the future. This time line must not be allowed to continue. This is the theme that was channeled to the white Jews and white Gentiles that was put in the white Jews and white Gentiles television series titled, Star Trek the next generation episode titled, "Yesterday Enterprise" that stressed that the white Gentiles will have only their trust in who are the true people of God and the true people of God interpretation of the gospel of God to help them make their final choices wisely.

Events must be steered in another direction to change the shape of the things that are prophesied to come to prevent the white gentile Jews from judging themselves unworthy for eternal life and to prevent no place found for the great white throne in the future. The white Gentiles will have only their trust in who are the true people of God and the true people of God understanding of the prophesies of the God of Abraham to help them make their latter-day choices. Remember, the Holy Bible has recorded that the white Gentiles were deceived by the "false prophet" or "false brethren" who are those that have deceived the white Gentiles that they are the people of God and they know the prophesies of the God of Abraham. Acts 13: 46, Revelation 20: 11, Revelation 19: 20 and 2 Corinthians 11: 26

# The Titans and the Olympians

The latter-day Deliverer is the white Jews and white Gentiles final legion to obtain salvation. This was the white Jews and white Gentiles plan for a deliverer to be sent to them in the latter days to reveal this truth, so they could make their final latter-day choices wisely. The Deliverer mission is only to deliver the truth without offending the Gentiles, so the Gentiles would at least hear what was delivered and not to try to make the Gentiles accept the truth because the Gentiles must do what is in their hearts to prove that they are worthy to continue to exist. The Gentiles will not be persuaded, convinced, influenced, won over or forced by the power of argument to accept the delivered truth. If the white Gentiles order, request or suggest that the delivered truth is not spoken, the delivered truth that the white Gentiles asked to be deliver to them will not be spoken of ever again. The white Gentiles must do what is in their hearts to prove or disprove if the white Gentiles are worthy to continue to exist with the human beings of the world. It is because of this that the truth will not be forced on the white Gentiles. After the truth is delivered, if the Gentiles still assert that they are the people of God then they must be right, and all will follow the Gentiles lead. Good luck fighting God for the people of God who are Israel who are the Afro Americans who you have scattered inheritance in the Valley of Jehoshaphat. Joel 3: 2

Understand that this world and this life is a test to determine who will live in the greatest kingdom to ever exist in the omniverse or exist in all the existing universes regardless of the dimension that they may exist in. To explain this thoroughly, we must go back to the beginning when there was a war in Heaven.

In the Throne Room of Heaven, there are twenty-four thrones around the throne of the "Most-High" God who is described as the "Ancient-of-Days" or described as He who has lived the longest. On the twenty-four thrones around the throne of the "Most-High" who has lived the longest and called the "Ancient of Days" are twenty-four "Elders" or twenty-four older Gods but not as old as the "Ancient of Days" who is the "Most-High" because He is the "Ancient of Days". The "Elders" in the Throne Room of the Gods are not old people from the earth but are older Gods. The twenty-four "Elders" fall down before the "Most-High" who is the "Ancient of Days and worship Him who sits on the top Throne in the Throne Room who has lived forever, and they cast their "Crowns" before the Throne of the "Most-High" who is the "Ancient of Days". Revelation 4: 4, Revelation 4: 10 and Daniel 7: 22

In the beginning, after the Gods had evolved into spiritual beings and had been in that state of existence for trillions times trillions of centuries, some of them became bored with their existence. They wanted to have feelings and emotions again. This was forbidden because it would interfere with their spiritual existence at their godly level. To reach their spiritual level of existence identified as being a God, they had to abandon their lower emotions. Without these feelings and emotions, existence for them became very boring.

In the spiritual realm of Heaven, Lucifer also referred to as the Dragon entered the Hall of Records and began to review who the Gods were before they evolved into highly spiritual beings. Because of his boredom, he desired to have all of the feelings and emotions that the Gods used to have when they lived in worlds like the earth. He shared his thoughts with other spiritual beings in Heaven and developed a desire in them to want feelings and emotions again. Lucifer and those that he had encouraged to follow him brought their demands to the Throne Room of Heaven and insisted that they be allowed to experience these emotions and feelings again because they were bored in their spiritual state in Heaven. A war broke-out in Heaven between Lucifer, the Dragon and his followers against Michael and His Angels. Lucifer, the Dragon and his followers lost the war in Heaven. They were put out of Heaven and cast to the earth and told that they could never return to the spiritual realm. They were told that there was no place for them in Heaven anymore. Revelation 12: 7-9

These were the older Gods that were called the Titans. The Titans were some of the older Gods or Senior Gods or Elders and the first to leave Heaven. They were the ones who were cast-out to rule in Hell on the earth or the physical three-dimensional universe instead of serving in Heaven or the spiritual realm.

In the beginning when the Titans were cast-out of the spiritual realm, there was no known universe. An enormous bang happened in the endless Void of Darkness that was called "Outer-Darkness" which is "Outer-Space" because "Outer-Space" is "Outer-Darkness". All that the Cast-Out Gods would need to create a physical universe was pushed through a single hole in the space of that endless void of darkness. Science calls that incident the "Big-Bang" effect and it was that effect that started or was the beginning of our known physical universe. Now, for those that will say that the "Most-High" created the earth as is recorded in the book of Genesis in the Holy Bible, understand that the "Most-High" is responsible for "All" things. He created the world that was before this world and before the war in Heaven of this world against the Dragon. It is because of His word that everything was restarted over and this universe and this world we live in today exist. God formed the light and create darkness. God makes "peace" and create "evil". God the Lord do all these things. Drop down, "ye heaven" from above which means that the "Most-High" was responsible for everything that the "Cast-Out ones created. By the "Will of God", everything was created and the skies pour down righteousness. Let the earth open and let them bring forth salvation. Let righteousness (and unrighteousness) spring up together. God the Lord have created it. Drop down "ye heaven" from above to the earth is a reference of the Cast-Out ones being departed to the earth, this time and the Lord God was responsible for all of this and everything that they did may it be good or evil. Everything that the cast-out ones would create this time was created first by God and given to them, so they could create our known universe, this time. The skies or Heaven pour down righteousness to them to make all that they did possible. Isaiah 45: 7-8, Genesis 1: 1-5 and John 1: 1-5

When the Titans or the Dragon left Heaven or the spiritual realm, they started the known physical universe. The Titans took one-third of the heavenly body with them on the first fall or when they were cast-out. Revelation 12: 7-9

The Olympians were also old Gods but the last to fall and the Olympians were those Fallen Angels who looked down on everything that the Titans had created especially mankind and then abandoned their Heavenly posts or heavenly stations as clouds to descend down to the lower three dimensions of the physical world and they took on the form and likeness of man to mix and have sex with mankind and to join with the Titans in the physical world.

The Holy Bible has recorded that after the God that was called the Dragon left the spiritual realm and created the known universe, the Olympians looked down on all that was created and abandon their heavenly posts to join the Titans or the Dragon in the physical realm to have sex with mankind. The Holy Bible has recorded that after the Dragon left the spiritual realm and was cast to the earth with his angels, with his tail he drew another third of the stars of heaven or the heavenly body or the Olympians from their stations and threw them to the earth as well. Revelation 12: 7-9 and Revelation 12: 4

Later it would be ordered by all in the Throne Room in Heaven that the Gods or the Olympians return to their heavenly stations and not to interfere with the doing of mankind.

In the beginning before the universe was created, the great Dragon was cast out of the spiritual realm who is that serpent of the old dominion called the devil and Satan who deceived the whole world was cast to the "earth" with his angels. In the beginning, those who would be called the Titans fought with the Elders in the Throne Room in Heaven to create a physical universe. They lost and were cast out and no place was found for them in Heaven anymore. Revelation 12: 7-9

After Michael and His angels defeated the Titans who leader was called the Dragon, the Devil and Satan of the old dominion, the Titans were given a choice to stay in Heaven and be punished for the war that they had started to have the right to create the physical realm or they could leave the higher spiritual realm with their rebellious ones and descend down to the lower physical realm that was called Hell and called the earth to have their physical kingdom. Their choice would be final. Revelation 12: 7-9

If they stayed, they would be reduced in grade and the leaders of their rebellion were of the highest grade of angels. Understand that Lucifer who was cast out of Heaven is the son of the Morning Star and the Morning Star is Michael who fought with Lucifer who was the Dragon and Satan and Michael is called Jesus who is called the Lamb in Heaven and the Lamb of Heaven who shall inherit all things is the color of brass (brown) that has been burned in a furnace (dark brown to black) with hair like sheep wool or nappy hair. If they departed, they would never be allowed to return. Isaiah 14: 12 and Revelation 22: 16, John 1: 29, Revelation 5: 6, Revelation 12: 11, Revelation 13: 8, Revelation 19: 9-10, Revelation 22: 1-3 and Revelation 1: 14-15

Lucifer was jealous of his father the Morning Star who would inherit everything. Lucifer proclaimed that his father, the Morning Star was not worthy to receive so much. All in Heaven proclaimed that the Lamb in Heaven who is the Morning Star is "Worthy". No one other than God Himself in Heaven or on the earth or under the earth or such as are in the sea could do what the Lamb did. Blessing and honor and glory and power be to Him who sit on the throne and to the Lamb forever and ever. Lucifer wanted the power, riches, wisdom, honor, glory and inheritance that went to his father, the Morning Star who is the Lamb in Heaven. It was because of this that Lucifer chose to rule in Hell instead of serving in Heaven. There in Hell on the earth, Lucifer would rule and gain wisdom, power, riches, honor and glory as his father had received in Heaven. Satan demands that his followers honor and glorify him as their God and in return, they will receive power, fame, glory and riches on the earth. Revelation 5: 4-9, Revelation 5: 9-14, Revelation 5: 13 and Revelation 12: 9

The false prophets of the earth today that are seen on television with the big churches and thousands of followers promise their followers fame, glory and riches while the true prophets of God promise their followers prosperity in good health on the earth and the "Gift of the Holy Ghost" to do all things. The power to do all things is not about the power to "buy" all things with money and only the things that money can buy but is about becoming god-like in your abilities on the earth to perform miracles to do and have the things that money can't buy. Understand, the super-rich false prophets of today that are promising their followers financial success will never enter the Kingdom of God. These rich preachers living in homes that cost millions of dollars have chosen their paradise here on earth. They will not enter the Kingdom of God. It is easier for a camel to get through the eye of a needle than for a rich man to enter the Kingdom of God. If they really want to enter the Kingdom of God, they must sell what they have and give to the poor and follow the "Word of Jesus" then they will have treasures in Heaven. To preach the gospel of Jesus, preachers are ordered not to take gold or silver and to have little possessions because their treasures are not money to buy things but are treasures in Heaven to do things like heal the sick, cast out demons and raise the dead by the power of God. Matthew 19: 24, Matthew 19: 21, Matthew 10: 9-10, Mark 6: 8 and 1 Corinthians 2: 4-5

This was the power to raise the dead and cure all manner of diseases. With the Holy Ghost, you would not need money because anything that money can buy, you could make whatever you wanted to buy appear or manifest in front of you. If you are hunger, food will appear out of thin air. If you had to go somewhere, you would not need a car because you could teleport yourself wherever you wanted to go. You would need no money to buy a home because any type of home that you could imagine would manifest in front of you. Jesus said, do not worry about what you shall eat or what you shall drink or what you shall wear for after all these things the white Gentiles seek. Know for a certainty that your Father in Heaven knows that you need all these things. Jesus said seek first the kingdom of God and God's righteousness and all these things shall be added to you. Matthew 6: 31-34

This is what Jesus did when Jesus walked the earth. Jesus made food appear in abundance. Jesus walked on water and teleported himself anywhere He wanted to go. Jesus was in contact with an ability that was beyond our laws of physics that made it possible for miracles to be performed. Today's magicians are in contact with demons that possess a fraction of this power. The magicians are performing miracles in their own name because of the power that these cast-out demons are giving them when they give their soul to Jinn demons. The Jinn or Genie are supernatural beings that the magicians worship and have sold their souls to for protection and magical powers. Know for a certainty that the power of God is greater than the power that is given to magicians by cast-out Jinn demons. What we see the magicians doing verifies everything that Jesus said about the power and abilities we will have if we first seek the Kingdom of God. With the power of the Holy Ghost, nothing would be impossible for you to do. Everything that the magicians can do with the help of Jinn demons is no comparison to what those who are possessed by the spirit of the Holy Ghost can do. Acts 1: 8, Acts 2: 4-11, Acts 2: 38, Acts 4: 31, Luke 24: 49, Acts 9: 36-42, Acts 10: 38, Acts 10: 43-45 and Acts 19: 2-6

These signs will follow those who believe. In Jesus name, they will cast out demons, they will speak with new tongues, they will take up serpents and if they drink anything deadly, it will by no means hurt them and they will lay hands on the sick and the sick will recover. This power of the Holy Ghost to do all things even to raise the dead cannot be purchased with money but can only be obtain through the "Belief" in God. Acts 8: 19-20, Mark 16: 15-18, Matthew 10: 7-10 and Matthew 11: 4-5

If the spirit of Him who raised Jesus from the dead dwells in you, "He who raised Jesus from the dead will also give life to your mortal bodies through his spirit who dwells in you. Romans 8: 11

When Jesus had called His twelve disciples to Him, He gave them "Power" over unclean spirits to cast them out and to heal all kinds of sickness and all kinds of disease. Jesus instructs His disciples to go preach, saying, "The Kingdom of God is at hand" meaning all that the disciples saw Jesus do, preach to the people that they will be able to do also if you believe in God. The Kingdom of God is at hand means that now it is possible from mortal men to have the power of the kingdom of God. Matthew 10: 1, Matthew 10: 7-10

Today's super rich preachers that are seen on television with the big churches and thousands of followers that are offering the people fame, riches, sexual pleasures in relationships and success in their worldly affairs are the false prophets and what they are doing is not preaching the gospel of Jesus. To preach the gospel of Jesus, you must show mighty signs and wonders or miracles by the power of the Spirit of God called the Holy Ghost. Peter said, "Repent and let every one of you be baptized in the name of Jesus for the remission of sins and you shall receive the gift of the Holy Spirit". Jesus said, "Unless the people see signs and wonders, they will by no means believe". Paul said, "My preaching was not with persuasive words of human wisdom but in a demonstration of the "Spirit" and of the "Power" that your faith should not be in the wisdom of men but in the power of God". Romans 15: 19, Acts 2: 38, John 4: 48 and 1 Corinthians 2: 4-5

The Titans choice was to leave the spiritual realm and take their chances in the creation of a new three-dimensional physical universe where they could enjoy what it felt like to breathe again, to walk again, to have life again in a physical existence and enjoy all of the things concerning or governing what it is to live again.

These were things that the spiritual Gods did not have or experience in their spiritual state of existence. These were things that was sacrificed so that they could evolve into higher beings or a higher state of existence. After a trillion times a trillion centuries passed, those who would be called the Titan became bored with their existence in the spiritual realm and wanted to return to a physical existence that offered feelings and emotions and all of the things that are experienced in life so they could never become bored with their existence again.

Before they left the spiritual realm, they gathered all that they would need to create planets and life on the planets because they could never return to the spiritual realm again. Revelation 12: 8-9

Suddenly, an enormous explosive of Fire happened in the endless void of space and that explosion throw into the endless void the elements that would later form the planets and all of the astral bodies in the universe. It was an unbelievable fiery furnace that lasted for eons in the endless void and that fiery furnace in the void was called Hell. When the fire went out and the elements cooled, the planets formed. Once the planets formed, the Gods created life and living beings were added including genetically engineering beasts to walk upright to serve.

It is recorded in Genesis of the Holy Bible that it was a group of Gods that created the planets and life on the planet. With that being said, the readers must understand that the "Most High" God in the Throne Room of Heaven is responsible for all things rather good or evil and all is part of His divine will and plan to established His kingdom and His throne and His Son throne on the earth in the future as well as to select those who would replace the angels that rebelled in heaven and to also select those who would be found worthy to exist and occupy the greatest kingdom to ever exist anywhere in the oniverse who shall be given immortality and god-like powers. It is the "Most-High" in the throne room in Heaven that created all things and it is by His will that the fallen angels exist and all that they did were created. Because of different levels of evolutionary development, some of the readers may not understand the scope of the "Most-High" powers. It will take more time for them to come to the understanding of the multi-dimensions of the "Most-High" great power. Genesis 1: 26, Revelation 4: 2-11, Isaiah 45: 7, Revelation 21: 1-7, Revelation 21: 22-27, Revelation 22: 1-5, Revelation 4: 11 and Colossians 1: 16-17

Because the white Gentiles do not know God or the Son of God, they cannot translate ancient scriptures correctly. The white gentile pagans cannot translate biblical scriptures correctly. At judgment this time, Jesus will say to the white Gentiles, "I never knew you, depart from Me, you who practice lawlessness." John 16: 2-3, John 8: 19, John 15: 21, 1 Thessalonians 4: 5 and Matthew 9: 22-23

In the translating of the King James version of the Holy Bible and all other Gentile versions, the Gentiles were confused trying to understand scriptures and they combined many stories into one story because they did not understand the meaning of the words that they were translating. Only the People of God can translate the ancient scriptures correctly because only the people of God knows more about the words and phrases then the definition of the words.

Only the People of God know the feelings of the words translated and the many underlying or unsaid phrases that goes along with every word that is recorded. There is no Da Vinci code in the Holy Bible but there is a secret coding of words and phrases in the Holy Bible that was called, "speaking in parables" in biblical days and it was designed to speak words and phrases that had multiple meanings. This was design this way so that only those that were "Wise" in the understanding of God ultimate plan for the earth would understand and the wicked would have no idea what was being said. Matthew 13: 34-35, Mark 4: 10-12, Mark 4: 33-34 and Matthew 13: 10-14

Later, after the fire went out and everything cooled down in the void, the Titans transformed the void that was called Hell into a paradise. The Titans transformed the huge solid burned matter in the void into planets and suns and supplied the planets with waterfalls, mountains and valleys as well as the light and the dark and hot and cool breezes. Then, the "Cast-Out" ones that were called the Titans contacted the heavenly spiritual realm and suggested that the spiritual Gods there in the Throne Room of Heaven who were against the creation of the three dimensional physical universe visit the created universe that was called Hell that had been turned into a paradise to see for themselves that it was not that bad and that the Gods could exist in the physical realm comfortably.

A special planet was selected for the spiritual Gods to experience life in the three-dimensional physical realm that had been created by the "Cast-Out" ones. The planet was called Eden (Aden) and the garden of Eden (Aden) would be where the spiritual Gods would be staying on their visit to the physical worlds. Since the earth was the special planet for the Cast-Out ones, the Fallen-Ones created the moon as their domain. It was called Olympus. It had large oceans, valleys, trees and grass. There on Olympus the moon, the Fallen-Ones would observe mankind. When they descended from the heavens or the moon to mingle with mankind, their headquarters was on the highest mountain in Greece that was later called Mt. Olympus. When the Olympians were ordered to return to their heavenly stations around the same time of the biblical flood on the earth, the Olympians capital on the moon was totally destroyed. The outside of the moon was devastated by the God in Heaven and by the Cast-Out ones to ensure that the Fallen-Ones could not return to their created station that they would call their heaven. Olympus was created to resemble the royalty and slender of the spiritual heaven that they had left from but there on the created heaven on the moon, they could enjoy emotions, feelings and sex.

At first, the spiritual Gods refused. The spiritual Gods knew that the physical realm was a hell to survive in and that is why the "Cast-Out" ones were given a choice to stay in the spiritual realm and be punished for their rebellion or leave and create their physical realm which would also be a punishment because it would be a struggle to survive there and all of this would be what the once spiritual cast-out Gods were not use of.

But the leader of the "Cast-Out" ones had done his homework well. Before he left the spiritual realm, he entered the "Hall of all recorded knowledge" and learned well what it would take to turn a hell into a paradise. When the fire in the void went out and the molten hot rock cooled, he transformed the huge rocks into growing living physical planets. He added to the huge cool down rocks, mountains, valleys, waterfalls, trees, grass, hot and cool breezes or seasons. The day came when the fiery hell in the endless void was indeed turned into paradise for the Gods to visit the physical realm. All of this was in the "Most-High" ultimate plan because the "Most-High is responsible for all things rather they be good or evil. God has said that God form the light and create darkness; God make peace and create evil; it is God the Lord that do all these things. Isaiah 45: 7

Knowing that the spiritual Gods could refuse because the physical realm was a realm that the "Cast-Out" ones were sent to for punishment by hard labor, he assured the spiritual Gods that servants would be created for their needs while they were visiting the physical realm. He assured the spiritual Gods that they need only to come and take on physical form and visit with no toil or hard work involved. This started the beginning of the "Cast-Out" ones genetic engineering program to genetically engineer an ape into a servant worker.

The spiritual Gods agreed to visit the physical realm to see just what was being created and why because all that was created would later tempt the "Olympians" at their heavenly stations and be the cause why the "Olympians" and one third more of the spiritual realm would leave their heavenly post to descend to the lower dimensions to experience life and all that had been created. The Holy Bible has recorded that after the leader of the "Cast-Out" ones called the "Dragon" and his angels were "Cast-Out" of heaven, with his tail, he drew a third of the "Stars" or "Gods" from their heavenly stations to the earth. Revelations 12: 4

After the Dragon and his angels were cast out of the spiritual realm and created the physical realm and turned the fiery furnace in the endless void into paradise, other spiritual Gods at their heavenly stations look down on all that were created and enjoyed by the "Cast-Out" ones and desired to join them to enjoy life. One third of the spiritual Gods in heaven abandon their heavenly stations to descend down to the physical realm to enjoy life and all that life had to offer. They were the "wind", "water", "fire" or the elements of the spiritual universe that abandon their stations and their nature of existence to descend down to the physical realm to take on human shape and become flesh and blood living beings to enjoy life and all that life have to offer. The clouds descended down to earth like fog or as the dew is seen on the grass early in the morning but instead of remaining fog or dew on the grass as we see today, the fog and dew on the grass took on human shape and became flesh and blood beings. They abandon their station or purpose as fog or dew to become flesh and blood beings to enjoy life. To breathe again, to feel again, to have emotions and pleasures again was compelling to them because they had not experience those feelings in trillions of centuries. Once living creatures and mankind were created and the "Cast-Out" ones were seen having sex with mankind enjoying extreme feelings of pleasure, the Olympians" left their heavenly stations to enjoy sex with mankind. There on Mt. Olympus, which was a recreation of the spiritual realm they had abandon but still needed to be part of because of their nature and true existence, they watched mankind and descended to the earth at will to have sex with mankind.

Once the spiritual Gods arrived and observed what was going on and how advance beings were leaving the spiritual realm to have sex with the created creatures on the planet, a decree was passed, and it was Ordered that those Gods that were leaving their heavenly stations to descend to the physical realm return to their station at once and discontinue involving themselves in the affairs of mankind and men.

The Titans argued the point that they were given a choice and they chose to leave, create and build the physical realm and all that is in it and this was agreed by all in Heaven as a punishment for them because of the rebellion in Heaven and that judgment was final because from that judgment No Place was Found for them in Heaven ever again. They could not return, or it was not spiritually possible for them to return to the spiritual realm. They had to stay. Revelation 12: 8

It was because of that they could never return to the spiritual realm, but this was not the case for those Olympians who abandon their heavenly stations to join in. They were not given a choice and they were ordered to return to their stations at once. The Olympians would refuse, and a war would begin between the Titans and the

Olympians to force the Olympians to return to their heavenly stations or else, the spiritual Gods in the Throne Room of Heaven would order all life on the planet and the planet itself destroyed leaving the Titans that could not return to the spiritual realm with no place to go and their best created planet in the void for paradise destroyed. This meant that the Titans would have to start all over again. The Titans concluded that the Olympians must return to preserve everything that was created.

To prove that the decree and the threat from the Throne Room was real concerning destroying all life on the planet to force the Gods back to their stations, a Flood was introduced or released on the planet that would kill all life on the planet and if the Titans did not force the Olympians away and back to their stations, the planet destruction would be next. The Olympians lost that war and were forced back to their heavenly stations.

Because the Titans could not return, they stayed in their created universe that they were cast-out to. The Serpent head Sphinx rising out of the earth with the face of the leader of the Cast-out ones who was called the Monarch of the Earth was a representation of the Dragon or the Serpent who was Cast-Out of the spiritual realm to the physical realm that was called Hell and now the Serpent was rising out of Hell coming out of the earth that he had turned into paradise. Later, a body of a dog would be added to the Serpent head Sphinx designating that there was a new world order that had replaced the first world order. Revelation 12: 9

The spiritual Gods were aware that two thirds of the heavenly body had left the spiritual state to experience life in the physical form. In the Throne Room of the twenty-five thrones of elder, they concluded that something must be done immediately before the remainder one third of the heavenly body abandon their post to join the Fallen-Ones. A decree was passed ordering the Olympians to return to their heavenly stations. The Titans were given a choice and they chose to leave instead of serving in Heaven. The Olympians were not given a choice to leave or stay. They abandoned their posts or heavenly stations to join in. Revelation 4: 4 and Revelation 12: 7-9

When the Olympians or those who would be called the fallen Ones because they Fell from grace because of what they saw on the earth were in their spiritual state, they looked down on the physical realm that was created by the Titans who were the Cast-Out ones and then abandoned their spiritual duties to descend down to the physical realm to obtain form and flesh and blood bodies to share feelings and emotions with mankind which were things that they did not have in the spiritual realm at their stations. Another third of the heavenly body were convinced to leave their spiritual heavenly stations and join the rebellion to descend down to the lower levels or dimensions to be with mankind because of feelings and emotions.

Feelings and Emotions are extremely important. It allows us to enjoy life in a special way. Because of the rebellion in Heaven by the Titans or the Cast-Out ones and the abandoning of their heavenly stations by the Olympians or the Fallen-Ones over feelings and emotions and they were superior ascended beings that had reached the evolutionary level identified as a God, the heavenly throne will come to the earth for the next million years to give all in the spiritual realm the experience of life again and then after this vacation from cosmic and spiritual duties in the spiritual realm or the heavenly realm, the Gods and all who have evolved into beings who can exist without bodies of flesh and blood that was interested in pursuing feelings and emotions would return again to the spiritual realm and now none would be rebellious over feelings and emotions. He who overcomes the temptation of the flesh stimulated by feelings and emotions shall inherit all things. Now, it would be established that after so long in one realm, the Gods could vacation in another realm always returning to the spiritual realm and it is this vacation to experience what is not experience in the spiritual realm that will destroy any future rebellion in the spiritual realm because of boredom. Revelation 21: 1-8

Because the Titans rebelled in Heaven and were Cast-Out because of wanting feelings and emotions and the Olympians fell from Grace when they abandoned their heavenly stations to have sex with mankind, the test for us would be who could Mortify the deeds of the body by controlling their feelings and emotions and the abstinence from living after the extreme pleasure feelings of the flesh in a sexual orgasm. This is why the test of life for us today is to determine who of us can mortify the deeds of the body so that we can live and all who live after the flesh shall die. This is the test for life or death for us. Romans 8: 13 and Revelation 2: 2

Sexual immorality will cast you into a sickbed and bring horrible tribulations upon you and your children. Revelation 2: 20-24

Jesus, the Lamb in Heaven says, "He who overcomes the lust of the flesh, Jesus will give to eat from the Tree of Life which is in the midst of the paradise of God. Revelation 2: 7

He who overcomes shall not be hurt by the second death. Revelation 2: 11

He who overcomes, Jesus will give some of the hidden manna to eat and Jesus will give him a white stone, and on the stone a new name written which no one knows except him who receives it. Revelation 2: 17

He who overcomes and keeps Jesus works until the end to him Jesus will give power over the nations. He shall rule the nations with a rod of iron from the spiritual realm or the twelfth dimension. With this rod of iron from the twelfth dimension, nations shall be dashed to pieces like the potter's vessels. He who overcomes shall be given great power as Jesus also have received from our heavenly Father. Revelation 2: 26-29

He who overcomes shall be clothed in white garments and Jesus will not blot out his name from the Book of Life, but Jesus will confess his name before our heavenly Father and before His angels. Revelation 3: 5

He who over comes, Jesus will make him a pillar in the temple of God and he shall go out no more. Jesus will write on him the name of God and the name of the city of God, New Jerusalem, which comes down out of Heaven from God and Jesus will write on him Jesus new name. Revelation 3: 12

He who overcomes, Jesus will grant to sit with Him on Jesus throne as Jesus overcame and sits down on His throne with our Father on our Father's throne. Revelation 3: 21

He who overcomes sexual immorality, being a coward, an unbeliever, their abominations, murder, sorcery, idolaters and lying shall inherit all things, and God will be his God and he shall be God's son. Those that can't overcome these things shall have their part in the lake which burns with fire and brimstone which is the sun. Revelation 21: 7-8

All of these things, Jesus overcame. Jesus said, "In the world you will have tribulations but be of good cheer, I have overcome the world". John 16: 33

For whoever is born of God overcomes the world. Our faith is the victory that has overcome the world. Who is he who overcome the world but he who believes that Jesus is the Son of God. 1 John 5: 4-5

There are heathens and infidels that have been deceived to believe that Jesus had sex with Mary Magdalene. The white Gentiles are saying that a white Gentile has written a book about Jesus being married to Mary Magdalene and having many children. What in the world do a white Greek or Roman Gentile know about God or the Son of God? The name of God is blasphemed or cursed among the white Gentiles. Remember, the Holy Bible says that the white Gentiles do not know God or the Son of God, so they cannot interpret biblical scriptures correctly. The white Gentiles believe that God and the Son of God are white. They do not believe that Jesus who is the Lamb in Heaven that has been given everything or given all authority in Heaven and on the Earth, is the color of brass (brown) that has been burned in a furnace (dark brown to black) with hair like sheep wool or nappy hair. The white Gentiles believe that the Shroud of Turin is a likeness of Jesus. The Shroud of Turin is a Lie and a Fake. Only the people of God can correctly interpret biblical scriptures and only the people of God can write book two to the Holy Bible. Romans 2: 24, John 8: 19, John 15: 21, John 16: 3, 1 Thessalonians 4: 5, Matthew 28: 18 and Revelation 1: 14-15

Jesus would never give up sitting with His Father God on His throne to have sex with nobody. Jesus has instructed His followers to be abstinence. Paul said that it is good for a man not to have a woman. Christians have been deceived to believe that sex is okay and even Jesus had sex with Mary Magdalene. That is a lie. The Holy Bible has recorded that, he who overcomes sexual immorality shall inherit all things and God will be his God and he shall be God's son. All authority has been given to Jesus in heaven and on earth. Jesus would never tarnish that authority by having sex with no one. Revelation 21: 5-8 and Matthew 28: 18-20

Mary Magdalene was not told to "COME" and be with Jesus and His disciples but was told to "GO" and Sin no more. Jesus would never "Sin" by having sex with Mary Magdalene or no one else. Do not be deceived. 1 Corinthians 7: 1, John 8: 11 and Luke 7: 50

Mary Magdalene was not with the men who were the disciples of Jesus but was with the women who had been healed of evil spirits and infirmities. Jesus cast-out seven demons out of Mary Magdalene. Because of this, Mary Magdalene was thankful and believe in Jesus and followed Jesus just as many others did but she was not put with Jesus disciples. Mary Magdalene was with the women who believed and observed from afar. Do not be deceived by lying demon possessed devils that want you to believe that Mary Magdalene was made a disciple of Jesus and was Jesus wife. Luke 8: 2-3, Matthew 27: 55-56 and Mark 15: 40

Being abstinence is so important that Paul asked God to take away the temptation of wanting to have sex. Paul said, least he should be exalted above measure by the abundance of this revelation on abstinence, a thorn in the flesh was given to him which was a messenger of Satan to buffet him lest he be exalted above measure. God tells Paul that God grace is sufficient for Paul for God strength is made perfect in weakness. Meaning, when we pray to God for strength because of temptation, God's strength is made perfect and is shown and used in our time of weakness when we ask for strength and receives the strength to mortify the body to resist sins. God's strength is made perfect when we use God's strength to overcome the desires of the flesh or anything else. Therefore, Paul said that he takes pleasure in infirmities, in reproaches, in needs, in persecutions, in distresses for Jesus sake because when he is weak then he asks God for strength and becomes strong through God and it is this action when we are weak that makes God's strength perfect. It must be noted that abstinence from sexual pleasures by mortifying the body to live instead of enjoying sex for pleasure that will cause you to die can exalt you in Heaven above measure. This is why Jesus said that you would receive so much from Heaven if you overcome like Jesus overcame. To destroy this last dominion of "Iron and Clay" and to make none worthy to enter Paradise, sexual pleasures and the abuse and waste of our evolutionary energy in an orgasm have been promoted to the people at every level. Sexual pleasures are "stumbling blocks" that has been thrown in front of you to prevent you from evolving and inheriting Paradise. Indeed, the devil is about to throw some of you into a sexual prison that you may be tested. 2 Corinthians 12: 7-10, Romans 8: 13, Revelation 3: 21-22, Revelation 2: 14 and revelation 2: 10

Sex, Drugs and Rock & Roll stole the white Roman Gentiles glory and gave them pleasure instead of understanding and that prevented the white Roman Gentiles who have dominion today from knowing the truth and saving their kingdom. The white Gentiles never understood that the sexual energy that they were using for pleasure was the same energy needed for procreation to give life. If that energy is not being used to bring life into the world, that energy is used to sustain life and without that energy or the abuse of that energy, life would cease to exist or become unbalance or at dis-eased which is called diseased. For if you live after the flesh loving sex so much that you want sex every day, every hour of the day, you shall die but if you through the Spirit do mortify the deeds of the body practicing abstinence, you shall live. Do not commit suicide by pleasure. Do not kill yourself or put yourself in a sick bed by the abuse of the extreme pleasures of sex. To prove that the white Gentiles are truly evolved people, this must not be beyond the white Gentiles understanding, this time. Romans 8: 13 and Revelation 2: 22

Nothing in the world feels better than the sexual orgasm and the lust after the flesh and it is by this extreme pleasure of good feelings that we will be tested to determine who are worthy to live. Was then that which is good made death unto me? No, God forbid. This good feeling is to encourage us as people to use our very needed evolutionary energy to procreate but this good powerful energy feeling is not meant to be abused and used for pleasure as often as possible in a useless waste of energy in the form of an orgasm for pleasure. Romans 7: 13-25

Knowing that we need this evolutionary energy to grow and evolve on the Tree of Life, pleasure in the orgasm was an incentive to us to procreate. This is an enticement to make you use your evolutionary energy that you need to grow on the Tree of Life to live for procreation, but this evolutionary energy must not be used for your pleasure alone. In the beginning of our creation, it was believed that our sexual energy would be so valuable to us growing on the Tree of Life that we need to evolve into the gods that we would refuse to use that energy for procreation. As an incentive to use your evolutionary energy to procreate, the orgasm was designed to be extremely pleasurable. Those of us who can use this extremely powerful pleasure feeling for procreation only and not for physical pleasure as often as possible will pass the test of life that is designed to determine who are worthy to be part of the Tree of Life. Temptation is how true apostles or prophets, or pastors, or priests will be tested to determine if they are liars. Revelation 2: 2

In our prayers we ask God not to lead us into temptation as punishment. The holy Bible has recorded that "Blessed is the man who endures temptation for when he has been approved, he will receive the crown of life which the Lord has promised to those who love Him. Matthew 6: 13 and James 1: 12

True apostles, prophets, pastors or priest that serve the Lord will overcome temptation. They will not be married. He who is unmarried cares about the things of the Lord but he who is married cares about the things of the world and how he may please his wife or her husband. Jesus cared about things that pleased God His Father and not about the things of this world and how He may please a woman. Do not be deceived to believe that Jesus was married to Mary Magdalene or had sex with anyone. 1 Corinthians 7: 32-34

The devil has thrown this world into a sexual immorality prison that we may be "TESTED". Be faithful until death and Jesus will give you the crown of life. Sexual immorality and the extreme pleasures of the orgasm is a "Stumbling block" thrown in front of you as a test. Revelation 2: 10 and Revelation 2: 14

Being the true people of God, we know that Peter could not walk on the water because Peter had a secret love affair not spoken about. Because of that, Jesus said that Peter had little faith in what Jesus was teaching about abstinence. Because of Peter's secret relationship for sexual pleasure, Jesus warns Peter that Satan has asked for Peter to sift Peter like wheat or to destroy Peter by sexual immorality, but Jesus said that He had prayed for Peter that Peter's faith should not fail. Matthew 14: 25-33 and Luke 22: 31-32

It is because of this test to determine who can endure and resist the temptation of the flesh to use this evolutionary energy for pleasure that sex may appear as sin working death in us by that which is so good. Romans 7: 13

At the end of our days, our confession to the Lord is that, "I fought the good fight against sin and fornication and sexual immorality, I have finished the race (test), I have kept the faith in the returning of the Lord to establish His throne on this earth. Finally, there is laid up for me the crown of righteousness, which the Lord, the righteous Judge, will give to me on that Day of His return, and not to me only but also to all who have loved His appearing". 2 Timothy 4: 7-8

The only fight that Jesus instructed us to fight is the fight against sin, fornication and sexual immorality. That is the "good fight". All other enemies, Jesus instructed us to bless and not curse our enemies and to seek peace but for sin, fornication and sexual immorality, we are told to fight these enemies to the end and Jesus will give you a crown of life. The Devil is about to throw some of you in a sexual immorality prison that is hard to break away from that you may be TESTED. I have finished the test and not race because we are not in a race but in a test to determine who is worthy to live in the greatest kingdom ever to come in the three-dimensional universe and the faith of God's people is knowing that God will return and establish His throne and His Son throne on the earth and will evolve us into superhuman beings just as the white Gentiles were evolved from primitive paleolithic beings to advance homo sapiens beings in the twinkling of their eye. Luke 6: 28, Romans 12: 14-21, Romans 12: 17-21, 1 Corinthians 4: 12-13, Revelation 2: 10, Revelation 21: 1-8 and Revelation 22: 1

Paul says, "Brethren, become complete. Be of good comfort, be of one mind, live in peace and the God of love and peace will be with you". 2 Corinthians 13: 11 and Romans 15: 33

Shalom and Salaam have the same meaning. They both means peace. "Peace be with you" mean, the grace of the Lord Jesus and the love of God and the communion of the Holy Spirit be with you. In Arabic, As-Salamu Alaykum or As-Salaam Alaikum means "peace be with you". The response is, "Wa Alaikum-Salaam" which means "And to you, peace". 2 Corinthians 13: 14

Anyone who is offended by this greeting "praising God to be with you" is a demon possessed devil that do not serve God but serves the devil. Those that are possessed by demons cannot utter this phase nor can they stand to hear it. Demons and those possessed by demons will run from this saying or this praise to God the way they say Vampires run from the crucifix. 2 Corinthians 13: 14

Jesus instruct us to ask our heavenly Father not to lead us into temptation as a punishment but to deliver us from that evil. The temptation of the flesh is an extreme evil no matter how good it feels. Sex is Sin working death in us by that which is so good. Matthew 6: 13 and Romans 7: 13

In the book of Adam and Eve, God blessed Adam by removing Adam sex drive from him. This was not a curse but was a blessing. The curse is being led into sexual immorality. Sexual immorality and adultery will lead you into a sick bed and fill your life with great tribulation. Revelation 2: 21-22

In the beginning, the people of Sodom and Gomorrah and others throughout the new white Gentile dominion refused to preserve their evolutionary energy for evolutionary growth because of the extreme feelings of pleasure that is experience in the orgasm. Evolutionary growth is a very slow, unnoticed and unfelt process that was compared to the orgasm which is instant satisfaction of extreme physical as well as psychological pleasure.

Those who were told to sacrifice this extreme pleasure to grow and stay healthy and to extend their life could not understand the importance in preserving their evolutionary energy and even if they did, they still could not sacrifice the everyday pleasure feelings from the orgasm. They proclaimed that they would rather live shorter lives as long as they could experience the extreme pleasures from the orgasm as often as possible. They worshipped the body and sex in all forms and positions and they proclaimed that having sex as often as possible with the best and most beautiful bodies was experiencing and living in what they called their paradise.

It is psychotic meaning, out of touch with reality, to use this evolutionary energy as often as possible for pleasure. No other living being or creature throughout the universe uses their evolutionary energy for pleasure but mankind or the young wild olive tree who is contrary to nature and that is why the young wild olive tree could not grow and survive. Romans 11: 24

Not even the living creatures that fly in the sky from the mosquitoes to birds or animals and insects that live on the earth or live under the earth or fish that live in the ocean or no other living creature that exist from the smallest of parasites to the largest of whales and elephants uses their evolutionary energy for pleasure. The living force that is behind instructing any living creature or living beings to use their evolutionary energy for pleasure has a long term hidden agenda to see that creature or beings broken off from the Tree of Life and is setting that creature or beings up to be destroyed.

In the latter days of the kingdom, the people were told that no harm would come to those who abuse their sexual energy for pleasure because science would create medicine that would counteract any negative side effects from the draining of their evolutionary energy for pleasure. Science also provided pharmaceutical or sorcery concoctions or pills that promised old men erections to continue to drain their energy away at their old age in sex.

This pleasure is so extreme that the Olympians gave up their godly powers and everlasting life or immortality to live 120 years as mankind to enjoy all of the things especially sex that mankind enjoyed. This extreme pleasure comes at an extreme price.

Jettisoning away your evolutionary energy everyday as often as possible in the form of a sexual orgasm for pleasure feelings and emotions will cause you to die or it will drain your evolutionary energy that you need to use to evolve on the Tree of Life and shorten your lifespan. The draining of your evolutionary energy will dry up your branch on the Tree of Life and be the cause why that branch will naturally break off from the Tree of Life. Using your evolutionary energy for pleasure is psychotic and is not a normal action or a natural action and it is because of this that the Holy Bible has recorded that the young wild olive tree that uses its evolutionary energy for pleasure is contrary to nature. Roman 11: 24

Those of us who pass the test in controlling our feelings and emotions by mortifying the deeds of the body will be permitted to live with God and the Son of God when Heaven is established on the earth in the greatest kingdom that will ever exist in the universe. Romans 8: 13

# The Last Two Witnesses

Last time at Judgment, the white Jews and the white Gentiles lost or were found "Wanting" what was necessary to remain grafted on the Tree of Life and they were broken off and regressed into their beginning at a low evolutionary stage of development known as Paleolithic man. Daniel 5: 27

The white Jews and the white Gentiles asked the people of God that came out of the tribulations with them to ask their father in Heaven to do the impossible and give the white Jews and the white Gentiles a second chance for salvation because all things are possible with God. The people of God that came out of the tribulations with the white Jews and white Gentiles felt "Sorrow" for them. All in Heaven said that the people of God were "Stumbling" to make this request. This time at Judgment there will be no "Sorrow". Matthew 19: 26, Revelation 7: 14, Revelation 20: 4, Romans 11: 11 and Revelation 21: 4

The request was granted. Everything was "Rewound" over what happened last time so if nothing is changed this time, what happened last time will fill in that space. We are told that our future is set from last time, but we also have the freedom of choice in our actions to change the future, so our future this time is still unwritten. This is why we experience the "Déjà Vu" experience which is the experience of doing something or experiencing something that you experienced once before. It is the experience of reliving a situation exactly as it was experienced or done before. This experienced is so profound to the individual that the individual who is experiencing the reliving of a past experience exactly as it was done before will instantly stop what they are doing and confess or say to all in the room that they are now experiencing reliving this exact situation that they are presently in that happened somewhere else in some other time but is exactly what is happening right now. Time, this time, is being recorded over what happened last time so if nothing is changed this time, the same thing that happened last time will happen again this time making our future set. It is because of this that our future is set, and we still have the freedom of choice to change the future because our future, this time, because of the second chance for salvation, is still unwritten.

Knowing the state of mind that the white Jews and the white Gentiles would be in at the fullness of the Gentiles at the end of the age this time because of what happened last time, to ensure that the white Jews and the white Gentiles this time are not deceived to error and be found "Wanting " what is necessary to remain grafted of the Tree of Life, a plan was developed by the white Jews and white Gentiles to help them to remember what happened last time so this time they could make the necessary corrections to remain grafted on the Tree of Life in time.

Because only those whose are truly worthy to evolve on the Tree of Life can do so, no one other than him that is sent by God to the white Jews and to the white Gentiles can help the white Jews and white Gentiles. Before the world begun, God chose Simon Peter or him who would be possessed by the spirit of Simon Peter to deliver the word of the gospel in the latter days to the Gentiles, so they could believe. Peter's Basilica in Rome was set up to receive this individual and only him who would be possessed by the spirit of Simon Peter who would deliver the Mystery of the Gospel in the latter days to the Gentiles. 2 Timothy 1: 9 and Acts 15: 7

Remember, the ancient prophets are subject to the prophets or the ancient prophets will be in the latter-day prophets. Remember, the end of the dominion will be declared from the beginning of the dominion and in the beginning of the dominion it was Simon Peter who was called a "Nig er" (Nigg er) and called Simeon that delivered the word of the gospel to the Gentiles and at the end of the dominion it will be Simeon the "Nig er" and only Simion the "Nigg er" that deliver the word of the gospel to the Gentiles again that God wants to take out of the Gentiles a people for God's name and for this cause, the words of the prophets or the books of Simion are written. 1 Corinthians 14: 32, Isaiah 46: 10, Acts 13: 1, Acts15: 14-15

Remember, the white Jews and white Gentiles will not be persuaded, convinced, influenced, swayed, converted or "won over" to accept the delivered Truth. The mission of the latter day "Deliverer" is only to deliver the Truth. This delivered Truth will reveal to the white Gentiles who have dominion today and to the white Greek gentile Jews that this time line must not be allowed to continue. Events must be steered in another direction to prevent what is prophesied to come to pass or to prevent the white Jews from judging themselves unworthy for ever-lasting life because they want to be the people of God so bad, they have assumed the identity of the true people of God and to prevent no place found for the great white throne in the future. Now, the white Jews and white Gentiles must do what is in their hearts to prove if they are worthy to continue to exist. They must search and seek out this Truth the way they seek out and search for gold and silver. The latter day "Deliverer" and those who are sent will accept the white Gentiles final choices as being what is right and just no matter what those choices are. Only at judgment this time will the white Jews and white Gentiles have to answer for their actions today. Acts 13: 46, Revelations 20: 11 and Proverbs 2: 3-6

Now, the white Jews and white Gentiles must understand this to be saved. The latter-day Deliverer must be given authority to speak boldly as he ought to because it is the white Jews and white Gentiles who sent the latter-day deliverer to deliver this profound truth to them, so they too could be saved. Regardless of what is happening in the world today, for the white Jews and white Gentiles to be saved, they must appoint the latter-day Deliverer as the ambassador from the people of God to the throne of the Gentiles that is given "Utterance" to speak boldly as he "ought" to speak or as you agreed last time at judgment that you would allow him to speak to make known to you to save you the "Mystery of the Gospel". He must not be an Ambassador in chains forbidden to reveal the mystery of the gospel. If the latter-day Deliverer is ignored, the white Jews and white Gentiles will be destroyed. Ephesians 6: 19-20 and 2 Corinthians 5: 20

It is the latter-day Deliverer who is less than the least of all saints who this grace is given to preach among the Gentiles the unsearchable riches of Jesus and to make all men see what is the fellowship of this mystery which from the beginning of the world have been hidden in God that God's people can access to the intent that now unto the principalities and power in Heavenly places might be known to the Gentiles. This is according to the eternal purpose which the Deliverer has in Jesus. Ephesians 3: 8-11

The white Gentiles who have dominion today must not scattered the people of God and say that the people of God lives do not matter but must nurture the people of God to ensure that the people of God evolve to the state where the people of God are worthy to receive and understand the mystery of the gospel from God and reveal that mystery to the Gentiles to save the Gentiles. To Me, who is delivering this truth to you, who am less than the least of all the saints or those who are sent, this grace was given that I should preach among the Gentiles the unsearchable riches of Jesus and to make all see what is the fellowship of the mystery which from the beginning of the ages has been hidden in God. No other race of people must deceive the white Gentiles who have dominion today that they are the people of God and fail to reveal the mystery of the gospel to the white Gentiles. Those who are assuming the identity of the true people of God are the "False Prophets" who do not know the prophesies of the God of Abraham and they are the ones that the Holy Bible has recorded "Deceived" the white Jews and white Gentiles who have dominion today, last time. The white Jews and the white Gentiles who have dominion today futures are at stake. To be saved, they must know who Is Rael (Real) and who is not. Ephesians 3: 8-9 and Revelation 19: 20

There will be two latter day "Deliverers" or last two "Witnesses" of the white Jews and white Gentiles second chance for salvation sent by God. One will go to the people of God and he will be possessed by the spirit of Elijah and the other will go to the white Jews and white Gentiles and he will be possessed by the spirit of Simon Peter. This is why Peter's Basilica was built in Rome to receive Peter's spirit in the latter days to receive this most important truth that could turn the world upside down to steer events in another direction to change the shape of the things that are prophesied to come to pass to prevent the white Jews from judging themselves unworthy of everlasting life and to prevent no place found for the great white throne in the future. The disbelieving white Jews who are not persuaded and are "envious" of the "Brethren" must not set the cities in an uproar by stirring up the white Roman gentiles who have dominion today poisoning their minds against the "Brethren" who are the Afro Americans today. Revelation 11: 3-6, Malachi 4: 5-6, Acts 15: 7, Acts 13: 46, Revelation 20: 11, Acts 17: 5-6 and Acts 14: 2

These last two witnesses of the white Gentiles second chance must not be hurt in any way to prevent God from giving the white Jews and white Gentiles blood to drink because it will be the white Jews and white Gentiles "Just Due". Revelation 16: 6

They must not appear in sackcloth or be poor. If they are, God will give them the power to shut heaven so that no rain falls, and they will have the power to turn water into blood and they will strike the earth with all kind of plagues as often as they desire. Because the latter-day Deliverer is sent by the Gentiles to themselves and the latter-day Deliverer is the white Gentiles best friend in the future, the white Jews and white Gentiles swore that the latter-day Deliverer would be treated like their best friend in our present and given "Utterance" to speak "Boldly" as he "ought" to, to make known the "Mystery of the Gospel" to the white Jews and white Roman gentiles. Do not renege on this agreement. Remember, you will see the latter-day Deliverer again at judgment this time. Revelation 11: 5-6 and Ephesians 6: 19-20

The last two witnesses of the Gentiles second chance sent by God will sing a new song that no one knew or could learn without them. They will have a "Truth" that no one else knows and once spoken, their "tongues" will cut like a "two-edge Sword". This is like the "profound truth" that is being "delivered" in the "Books of Simion" that must be delivered to the Jews first because the Jews sent the messenger to prevent the Jews from judging themselves unworthy of everlasting life and then the deliverer will turn to the white Gentiles and deliver the truth to them to prevent no place found for the great white throne in the future. This is the white Jews and the white Gentiles backup plan to be saved and this is the mission of the latter-day deliverer. Revelation 14: 3, Hebrew 4: 12, Acts 13: 46 and Revelation 20: 11

The Deliverer shall be redeemed from among men or redeemed from among the Afro Americans or forgiven for his sins and transgressions being one of the first fruits or the first saved or one of the first to awake from the mentally, morally and spiritually dead or awake from the Negro to God and to the Lamb and in his mouth, was found no deceit for he is without fault before the throne of God. Jesus was one of the first born from the dead or awaken from the Negro who are mentally, spiritually and morally dead. Negro and Necro is the same word and Necro means dead. Negro should be pronounced the same way as you pronounce "Negative". "Neg" and "Nec" have the same sound. Jesus, the Lamb in Heaven, said, "I know you have a name that you are alive, but you are dead", or "I know you have a name that means dead, but you are alive". That name is Negro because Negro and Necro are the same word and Necro means dead. The Fire of the Truth will proceed out of the "Deliverer" mouth and devour his enemies. It is this "Fire of the Truth" which is the "Word of God" that is delivered in the Books of Simion. For the word of God is living and powerful and sharper than any two-edge sword, piercing even to the division of soul and spirit and joints and morrow and is a discerner of the thoughts and intent of the heart. Revelation 14: 4-5, Revelation 1: 5, Revelation 3: 1, Revelation 11: 5-6, Revelation 1: 16, Revelation 19: 15 and Hebrew 4: 12

Remember, Jesus, the Lamb in Heaven who is the Son of God and the judge of this earth who shall inherit everything and be married to the earth is the color of brass (brown) that has been burned in the furnace (dark brown to black) with hair like sheep wool or nappy hair. The Shroud of Turin is a LIE and a Fake. For it is written,

"Every knee shall bow to the Lamb in Heaven and every tongue shall confess that black Jesus in Lord. Revelation 5: 12, Revelation 12: 11, Revelation 13: 8, Revelation 19: 9, Revelation 21: 22, Revelation 22: 1, Revelation 1: 14-15 and Romans 14: 10-12

The white Jews and the white Gentiles will know for a certainty him that is sent by the message that he delivers. No one else on the earth will know that message but him that is sent. It is the most important message in the Holy Bible for the white Jews and white Gentiles yet, it has never been revealed.

There is no Da Vinci code to be understood but there is a "Mystery to the Gospel" and only him that was chosen by the white Jews and white Gentiles and sent by God will reveal the "Mystery of the Gospel" in the delivered Truth. It is a message so profound that the white Jews said in biblical days that the delivered message by the Brethren or Brothers could turn the world upside down and it is this conversion and only this conversion that can save the white Jews and white Gentiles. There is only one suppressed truth that could turn the world upside down and the white Gentiles will know for a certainty if that truth was indeed delivered. It is this delivered suppressed truth that is so profound that it could turn the world upside down that will reveal who is the latter-day "Deliverer" and who are the true people of God. Remember, the Brethren or Brothers are the true Hebrews because the word Hebrew means "Hey Bro" referring to the "Brethren" or the "Brothers". Look up the correct pronunciation of the word "Hebrew" in any dictionary. Acts 17: 6

At judgment last time, the plan to save the white Jews and white Gentiles was brought to the people of God that came out of the tribulations with the white Jews and white Gentiles. The people of God agreed with the plan, so the white Jews and white Gentiles could be saved. The plan was that if for some reason the white Jews and white Gentiles were on the wrong path at the end of the age in their second chance, a messenger would be sent to them revealing a profound Truth that would unravel the Mystery of the Gospel, so the white Jews and white Gentiles would know what to do to be saved. No one else would be allowed to help the white Jews and white Gentiles but this one person chosen by God in the beginning or before the world begun. 2 Timothy 1: 9, 2 Thessalonians 2: 13, Romans 16: 25 and Acts 15: 7

Simon Peter, who was called Simeon and called a "Niger "(Nigger) was chosen to deliver the latter-day Truth to the white Jews and to the white Gentiles to save the white Jews and to save the white Gentiles in the latter days. God has said by Peter mouth only or by him who would be possessed by the spirit of Peter would the white Jews and white Gentiles hear the truth in the latter days and believe the truth, so they could be saved. When the white Jews and white Gentiles believe what was delivered no matter how hard it is to believe, then they shall know who the "Deliverer" is because only the true "Deliverer" will deliver a profound unbelievable message to the white Jews and white Gentiles that is so profound it could turn the world up-side down and the white Jews and white Gentiles will believe the delivered message. It is recorded in the Holy Bible that God chose Peter to deliver the truth to the white Jews and white Gentiles in the latter days that the white Jews said in biblical days could turn the world up-side down and the white Jews and white Gentiles will believe the delivered message. The white Jews and white Gentiles will believe what was written and delivered to the white Jews and to the white Gentiles in the Books of Simion. Acts 15: 14-15, Acts 13: 1, Acts 15: 7 and Acts 17: 6

Now understand, the prophets are subject to the prophets or the latter-day prophets will be possessed by the ancient prophets. This is why Peter's Basilica was built in Rome to receive him who would be possessed by the spirit of Simon Peter in the latter days who would deliver this Profound Truth to the Gentiles to save the Gentile. 1 Corinthians 14: 32

The latter day "Deliverer" is sent to the white Jews first because it was the white Jews that came up with the plan for salvation so the white Jews would not judge themselves unworthy for everlasting life and then the latter day "Deliverer" will turn to the white Gentiles and deliver the Truth to them so the Gentiles could be saved to prevent no place found for the great white throne in the future because God wants to take out of the white Gentiles a people for God's name and for this cause, the "Deliverer" was sent and the words of the Prophets are written in the Books of Simion. Acts 13: 46, Revelation 20: 11 and Acts 15: 14-15

The end of the dominion will be declared from what happened at the beginning of the dominion and in the beginning of the dominion it was Simon Peter who was called Simeon and called a "Niger" (Nigger) who delivered the message that God wants to take out of the white Jews and white Gentiles a people for God's name and at the end of the dominion it will be Simeon and only Simion who will deliver this written message in books to the white Jews and to the white Gentiles again to save the white Jews and save the white Gentiles. In the latter days of the white Gentiles dominion at the end of the age after December 21, 2012 when the fullness of the white Gentiles has come in, the Books of Simion are the words of the Prophets being written. After the fullness of the white Gentiles comes in at the end of the age on December 21, 2012, the "Deliverer" will come forth and turn away ungodliness from Jacob and maybe from Esau to, if Esau can receive the Truth and act accordingly. Remember, Simon Peter who was called Simeon and called a "Niger" (Nigger) will be sent by God to deliver a Truth explaining the Mystery of the Gospel to the white Gentiles who are represented as Esau and the white Gentiles will "Believe". This is Prophecy, and this is the revealing of the Mystery of the Gospel. Isaiah 46: 10, Acts 13: 1, Acts 15: 14-15, Romans 11: 25-26 and Acts 15: 7

There is only one Truth that is being suppressed in this world today that the white Jews in biblical days said that if the Brethren or Brothers delivered that suppressed Truth that the Truth could turn the world upside down. Acts 17: 6

The white Jews and the white Gentiles will know for a certainty that the delivered Truth was indeed that suppressed Truth that could have turned the world upside down in biblical days and it is the revealing of this suppressed Truth and only this suppressed Truth that can save the white Jews and the white Gentiles.

Do not be psychotic or out of touch with reality and be deceived to believe that the Kingdom of God will not come and there will be no judgement and no New Jerusalem. For we must all appear before the judgment seat of the Lord that each one may receive the things done in the body, according to what he has done whether good or bad. Understand that the extraterrestrials are from the future and they are here now in our present rapturing the Gentiles in the air on their ships giving the Gentiles evolutionary development examinations to determine if the Gentiles are at their fullness or maximum level of evolutionary development and if they are, collecting DNA from the Gentiles who are at their maximum level of evolutionary development to construct vessels or bodies to house disembodied ancient spirits somewhere else that could not be collected in the future because of the plague that developed from taking the mark of the beast to buy and sell because of the final crash of the Gentiles global financial system that will require the Gentiles to accept a new system to buy and sell and that new financial system mark on their right hand or forehead to buy and sell will destroyed Christianity and destroyed the

Gentiles. That is why the Grey's, from the future are here in the past, our present, collecting DNA from the white Gentiles that could not be collected in the future because of the plague. 2 Corinthians 5: 10, Romans 2: 16, Romans 14: 10-12, Galatians 6: 7, Ephesians 6: 8, Romans 11: 25 and Revelation 13: 16-17

This Truth is the most important subject in the world today because determining on what the white Gentiles do after the delivered Truth will determine the future for the white Jews and the white Gentiles. It is because of this great importance in hearing this Truth so that different choices could be made this time that did not happened last time to ensure that this time at Judgment, the white Jewish Gentiles will be found worthy to remain grafted of the Tree of Life and the great white throne of the Roman Gentiles who have dominion today will be in the future that the white Jews and the white Gentiles sent the latter day "Deliverer". Acts 13: 46 and Revelation 20: 11

The latter-day deliverer must be made Ambassador from the people of God to the throne of the Gentiles that is given "Utterance" to speak "Boldly" as he ought to speak since the white Jews and the white Gentiles themselves sent the latter day "Deliverer" so they too could receive salvation and be saved. Ephesians 6: 19-20

He who is sent will be called a "Saint" because the word "Saint" is a mispronunciation of the word "Sent" because only those who are "Sent" are called "Saint". A "Saint" is not a white Gentile that has lived a godly life. A "Saint" is only those that are "Sent". Peter, Paul and the others who were "Sent" were called "Saints". Only those who are "Sent" are "Saints".

# The white Gentiles Second Chance for Salvation

The white Jews and white Gentiles were given a second chance in the world we live in today. The story of Jacob and Esau is about that second chance. In the beginning before this world began, the white Gentiles betrayed the people of God in the womb of the universe to be born first to receive a second chance for salvation that was promised to the white Jews and to the white Gentiles and to also receive what was promised to the people of God for giving the white Jews and white Gentiles a second chance for salvation. The people of God were told to be "Meek" in the white Jews and white Gentiles second chance for salvation and afterwards the people of God would inherit the earth. Matthew 5: 5

Understand that the story of Jacob and Esau is not about the children because the children being not yet born had done no wrong. The story of Jacob and Esau is about a purpose of God to give the younger nation a second chance for salvation that they did not earn by their works. The story of Jacob and Esau is about two nations fighting in the womb to determine who would be born first. The younger nation was given a second chance for salvation and the older nation was told to be MEEK in the younger nation second chance and afterward, the older nation would inherit the earth. The younger nation betrayed the older nation in the womb of the universe to be born first to receive the second chance promised to the younger nation and to also receive what was promised to the older nation to inherit the earth. Romans 9: 11 and Genesis 25: 23

The younger nation also put the older nation who was giving the younger nation a second chance for salvation in slavery and it is because of this that God has said that God HATES the younger nation referred to as Esau for making the older nation referred to as Jacob the younger nation servants. God has said that God loves the older nation. God has said that God loves Jacob but HATES Esau. Romans 9: 12-13 and Malachi 1: 2-3

The white Gentiles wanted a second chance for salvation and they also wanted the people of God promise to inherit the earth so Esau who is a representation of the white Gentiles fought with Jacob who is a representation of the people of God in the womb of the universe to be born first to steal Jacob inheritance. Genesis 25: 22-23

Remember, the world we live in today is the second world. At Judgment last time, the white Gentiles and white Jews failed to be found worthy to continue to exist with the Human Beings on the planet earth. Their judgment was "Tekel" which means, they were weighed in the balances of their first chance for salvation and they were found "Wanting" what was necessary to remain grafted on the Tree of Life. There was no place found for the great white throne in the future and the white Jews judged themselves unworthy for everlasting life because they wanted to be the people of God so bad that they assumed the identity of the real people of God and wanted to fight God in the Valley of Jehoshaphat to be God's people and to receive the people of God inheritance. That is what the War of Armageddon or the War between Good and Evil will be about that will be fought in the Valley of Jehoshaphat. The white Jews and white Gentiles will be fighting God for the people of God who are SCATTERED who are the ascendants of SLAVES who are God's first born and chosen people who are the Afro Americans today identity and inheritance. Daniel 5: 27, Revelation 20: 11, Acts 13: 46, Joel 3: 2 and Exodus 4: 22

At Judgment last time, the people of God inherited the earth and there was no place found for the white Jews and white Gentiles in that new world in the Kingdom of God rule by the people of God dominion, so the white Jews and white Gentiles asked for a second chance to prove themselves worthy to continue to exist in the world we live in today, so they could be found worthy to exist in God's Kingdom to come.

The people of God asked their Father in Heaven to give the white Jews and white Gentiles a second chance for salvation. All in Heaven said that the people of God were STUMBLING but the request was granted. Romans 11: 11

The Kingdom of God and the people of God dominion were delayed until after the white Jews and white Gentiles have had their second chance for salvation in the world we live in today and then the Kingdom of God will come to the earth and will last forever and all kingdoms and dominions throughout the universe will serve them. Daniel 7: 18, Daniel 7: 22 and Daniel 7: 26-27

Not only were the kingdom of God and the people of God dominion delayed but also, we as Human Beings and White Beings bodily functions were reduced to 7% efficiency or capability until after the white Jews and the white Gentiles have had their second chance. At 100% efficiency, our eyes would be better than eagle eyes, our ears better than any animal or listening device that could be made. Our sense of smell would be better than the Bloodhound dog or any other lower animal life form. We would be faster than the fastest race horse in fact we would be able to float like the clouds and fly like the birds. Isaiah 60: 8

Our brains would be better than any known computers and we would be immortal, capable of manifesting or doing anything that we could imagine and much, much more.

No one in Heaven trust the Gentiles after the Gentiles begged for a second chance for salvation and immediately betrayed the people of God in the womb of the universe to be born first to steal the people of God inheritance to inherit the earth after the Gentiles have had their second chance so the Gentiles could receive a second chance that was promised to the Gentiles and to also receive the inheritance to inherit the earth that was promised to the "Meek" or to the people of God that goes to the first born. To be sure that the people of God were the "Meek" in the Gentiles second chance, the people of God were reduced to "Negros" who were mentally, spiritually and morally dead and it is this condition that made the people of God "Meek" in the white Gentiles second chance. If the people of God had not been "Scattered" and their minds put in chaos or confused so they could not understand each other by transforming them into the "Negro" but retained the old black African ability to do whatever they desired or nothing that they wanted to do was impossible for them to do it, the white Gentiles would have been dominated in the white Gentiles dominion and would have never been able to prove themselves unworthy or worthy to continue to exist. The Gentiles had to be put in a situation where they could do what was in their hearts to prove or disprove if the Gentiles were worthy to continue to exist with the people of the earth. Genesis 11: 6-8

Because all in Heaven are waiting for things to happen this time as things happened last time and knowing that at the end this time like last time, God will be fighting the white Gentiles and white Jews in the Valley of Jehoshaphat for the inheritance of the people of God and to make the battle simple and quick, the human Beings and the white Beings energy level and evolutionary growth were tuned down to its minimum. Revelation 6: 10-11 and Joel 3: 2

That is why we only use 7% of our brains and 7% of our total body capabilities. No one in Heaven trust the white Jews and white Gentiles and their distrust of the white Gentiles was proven when after the white Gentiles begged for a second chance for salvation and promised to do good to prove themselves worthy for salvation, in the womb of the universe at the beginning of their second chance, Esau who is a representation of the white Gentiles betrayed Jacob who is a representation of the people of God who are the people who are giving the white Jews and white Gentiles a second chance for salvation by fighting with Jacob in the womb to be born first to receive the second chance that was promised to the white Gentiles and to receive also what was promised to the people of God who were told to be MEEK in the white Jews and white Gentiles second chance for salvation and afterwards, the MEEK would inherit the earth. Esau wanted a second chance and knowing that he was not going to do good, he wanted to steal Jacob inheritance of inheriting the earth after the white Gentiles have had their second chance. The white Gentiles have said in their hearts that the "Meek" will never inherit the earth as long as the white Gentiles possesses the white Gentiles nuclear bombs. This is why it is necessary that the white Gentiles know about the advance old black African dominion that had the ability to do anything they put their minds to do that was a million time better and more advanced than the white Gentiles dominion is today and still, the old black African dominion could not fight God. Genesis 25: 22-23, Matthew 5: 5 and Genesis 11: 6

It was because of this betrayal by Esau in the womb of the universe to be born first to receive Jacob inheritance that God made it possible for Jacob to get Jacob inheritance back from Esau then God renamed Jacob to Is Rael (Real) to say that Jacob is the real one that the inheritance belongs to. This is revealing the mystery of the gospel which has been hidden for ages but now has been revealed to God's saints. To them, God will make known the riches of the glory of this mystery among the Gentiles, which is the Lord God in the people of God, and it is knowing this that is the hope for glory to the Gentiles. To be saved, the white Gentiles must know who the true people of God are. Those who are trying to destroy the white Gentiles will suppress this truth and assume the identity of the true people of God to deceive the white Gentiles. Remember, last time at judgment, the white Gentiles assertion was that they were deceived by the false prophet or the false brethren who are those that assumed the identity of the true people of God and have deceived the white Gentiles who have dominion today that they know the prophesies of the God of Abraham. Genesis 32: 28, Colossians 1: 26-27 and Revelation 19: 20

Knowing who God's people truly are is the hope for glory and salvation for the white Gentiles. God has ordered the people of God to be a light for the white Gentiles and to be for the white Gentiles salvation from biblical days to "PRESENT" till the end of the earth. The "Deliverer" from God to the Gentiles will obey that order and complete his mission to be for the "Salvation" of the Gentiles in the "Present". If the white Gentiles are deceived to believe that some other people are the people of God and reject the delivered truth, the Gentiles will be doomed. Acts 13: 47

Once the white Jews and white Gentiles realize who are the true people of God, then they will realize the importance of the truth that is delivered in the books of Simion. Then they will see the mystery which has been hidden for ages and from generations but now has been revealed to God's saints. Then they will know the riches of the glory of this mystery among the Gentiles, which is God in His people and that knowledge is the Gentles hope for glory. Then they will see the hope for glory and the salvation for the Gentiles that was ordered by God to be delivered to the Gentiles in our "Present" that was written in the books of Simion. Then the books of Simion will have fulfilled their purpose and then and only then will the mission of the "Deliverer" be complete. Colossians 1: 26-27 and Acts 13: 47

# All Dominions in the universe shall serve God

All dominions shall serve God and the people of God means that those races that are given dominion on other planets throughout the universe shall serve the people of God dominion here on the earth forever. The people of God shall preach the gospel of the kingdom of God that will be established on this earth and throughout the universe.

When the kingdom of God is established on the earth, the people of God will be given unimaginable power and authority. Because God's throne and the Son of God throne will be on the earth, the people of God will be given unimaginable power and authority to protect the earth where the true living God and the Son of the true living God thrones are. When God and the Son of God thrones are established on the earth, the earth will be transformed into the pettiest and the most glorious place in the universe. The earth shall be so beautiful that it will inspire wonder and joy so good and distinguished as to merit praise and lasting fame forever. The Kingdom of God and the people of God dominion shall be greater than all other kingdoms and dominions under the whole heaven or throughout the entire universe and all kingdoms and dominions throughout the universe shall serve and obey them. All knees shall bend, and all tongues shall confess that the Lamb in heaven who is Yahawahshi is Lord. Daniel 7: 27 and Romans 14: 11

Because when God and the Son of God kingdoms are established on the earth, there shall be a River of life whereas if you drink from it you will live forever and if you wash in it, you will rejuvenate your body and make yourself young again as well as having Trees of Knowledge growing on both sides of the River of Life that if you eat from those trees, it will expand your consciousness making you smarter with streets made from pure gold that will look like transparent glass, all life forms in the universe will want what is on the planet earth. The gift of the power to live forever, the gift of the power to be as smart and as powerful as the Gods as well as unlimited wealth laying around in the streets all will be here on the earth. To protect the thrones of God and the Son of God and to protect the earth because of what the planet earth and only the planet earth will have like trees that can expand your consciousness and make you smarter and a river of life that can prevent death and make you young again and streets made of pure gold with pebbles and rocks around the streets of gold that are diamonds and rubies, the people of God will be given extreme godlike powers. As God made Moses a God over the Egyptians, God will make His people gods over all others in the omniverse. Exodus 7: 1

Out of all the living beings throughout the universe, the people of God on the earth will be the only ones that cannot be killed. There will be no death for them. No race throughout the universe will challenge a race of people that cannot be killed and is in control of godlike powers. Not only that, but it is recorded in the Holy Bible that no weapon formed against the people of God will prosper. No matter how sophisticated and powerful a weapon might be to all others in the universe, that same weapon will not prosper or work when it is directed at the people of God. Unknown and known supernatural forces will prevent any harm to the people of God from any weapon made. That includes atomic weapons, nuclear weapons and anti-matter weapons or any other type of weapons known and unknown will not be effective against the people of God. Revelation 21: 3-4 and Isaiah 54: 17

Guns will become useless against the people of God. All projectiles aimed at the people of God from bullets to missiles to spit will be directed back to the sender. This power was demonstrated in Vietnam when government forces would direct their fire-power towards a spotted UFO and all bullets and missiles fired at the flying craft was direct back or returned to the sender. American G.I.'s would report that they were under extreme gun-fire from the orbiting craft that they open fire on and after the battle was over and an investigation was started, it was discovered that the bullets and missiles fired at government positions by the UFO's were really the government own bullets and missiles that were being directed back at soldiers who had fire the bullets and the missiles. When it is realized that every bullet fired at the people of God will return to the sender by supernatural forces killing the sender, the white Gentiles will longer threaten the people of God with guns or missiles. Guns will be of no use in the future against the people of God.

It is because of this that all kingdoms and dominions throughout the universe or under the whole heaven will serve and obey them. The people of God in the future can be compared to the fictionized characters in the Star Trek series that are referred to as Q, of the Continuum that will explore the universe like the Borg in the Star Trek series and the Ori in the Stargate series that are invincible who spreads the gospel of the truth and the origin of the species throughout the universe. They are represented as being unbeatable, unconquerable, unshakable, indomitable, impregnable, unassailable, insuperable, indestructible and supreme. The people of God in their godly dominion will be a whole lot more than what is characterized in today's movies. They will be the one who shall rule them all spreading the gospel of the kingdom of God throughout the universe. Because they can't be killed, they will always appear graceful and calm in their authority which will be final. The kingdom and the dominion and the greatness of all the kingdoms or whatever makes a kingdom great under the whole heaven or the kingdom and the dominion and whatever is great about kingdoms and dominions throughout the entire universe shall be given to the people of God and their kingdom is an everlasting kingdom that will never end or be conquered and all dominions throughout the universe shall serve and obey them. No other kingdom or dominion throughout the entire universe shall be greater than the kingdom of God that will be ruled by the people of God who will be the ascendants of those who were slaves who are God's first born and chosen people. All who see them will say that the people of God are the seed that the Lord has blessed. The key to interpreting the Mystery of the Gospel is knowing that the people of God who will inherit everything are not the rich and powerful of this world but are those who are rejected, persecuted and scattered in this world and they are the ascendants of SLAVES. This is why they were slaves. Because they will inherit so much in the future, the gods and the people of this age demanded that those who shall inherit everything in the future, be given nothing in the present and that envy from the people of this age towards the people of God because of the people of God inheritance was the people of this age biggest mistake. God tells Moses to tell pharaoh that the slaves are those who Is Rael (Real) and are God's first born and chosen people. Remember, those who were slaves in America ancestors were slaves in Egypt, Assyria, Babylon, Persia, Greece and Rome. They are the true people of God and only the true people of God were slaves in the world we live in today in the white Gentiles second chance for salvation because they are the ones who shall inherit the earth in the future when their God returns, and they shall be joined with God. Daniel 7: 27, Isaiah 61: 9, Exodus 4: 22 and Revelation 21: 1-4

# 11

# God's first born

Have you ever watched one of the "Superman" movies? They are about a character that is born on the planet Krypton that has a body made like steel that cannot be destroyed or damaged or restrained and he can float like the clouds and fly like the birds and he have the ability to make anything that he can imagine come true even reversing time. This is a description of the people of God in the future on this earth that is recorded in the Holy Bible.

Remember, the Holy Bible is the people of God who are the ascendants of Slaves history book and the ascendants of the slaves are God's first born and the African Americans in America are the ascendants of the slaves. No other race on the planet earth history is more spectacular than the history of the Slaves. They are God's first born and they are the riches for the world and the richest for the white Gentiles. It is because of them that the white Gentiles have what the white Gentiles have today. Because in the future, there will be no death for them or they cannot be killed, and they can float like the clouds and fly like the birds to their windows and anything that they imagine will come true as well as being possessed by the Holy

Ghost making all things possible for them, all who see them shall say that the people of God are the seed that the Lord has blessed. They shall rule the universe forever. These special people are asking the white Gentiles now to be their brothers and join them in this glorious future. Exodus 4: 22, Romans 11: 12, Revelation 21: 3-4, Isaiah 60: 8, Matthew 17: 20, Luke 17: 5, Matthew 19: 26, Isaiah 61: 9 and Daniel 7: 27

For all of this to be possible, God has said that He will make all things new or new laws of physics will be established for the people of God that will allow them to perform miracles and wonders including raising the dead or bringing the dead back to life which are abilities that technology and science could never achieve. Revelation 21: 5

This is what the Gentiles second chance for salvation in the world we live in today is all about. Last time, the Gentiles failed and was found "Wanting" or "Tekel" what was necessary to remain grafted on the Tree of Life because of the way the Gentiles treated the people of God in the white Gentiles dominion. The people of God who came out of the tribulations with the white Gentiles asked their Father to give the Gentiles a second chance for salvation in the world we live in today, so the Gentiles could be part of this new glorious and magnificent kingdom that will be established on the earth. All in heaven said that the people of God were STUMBLING to make that request. Daniel 5: 27, Revelation 7: 14 and Romans 11: 11

The people of God request were granted. The people of God were told to be MEEK in the Gentiles second chance for salvation in the world we live in today and afterwards, the people of God would inherit the earth for giving the Gentiles a second chance for salvation so the Gentiles who the people of God thought were their friends could be with them in Paradise. Matthew 5: 5

If the white Jews had not assumed the people of God identity and the white Gentiles who have dominion today would have made the people of God rich and prosperous giving them a nation that was respected throughout the world as was done to the white Jews, that would have changed the matrix of the world to come and made it possible for the white Jews and white Gentiles to inherit paradise with the people of God because the white Jews and white Gentiles would have shared their dominions with the people of God. The "Meek" alone would not have inherit the earth because the people of God would have not been the "Meek" in the white Jews and white Gentiles dominions but were welcome participates with the white Jews and white Gentiles. Because the white Jews and white Gentiles had shared with the people of God, God and the people of God would have shared with the white Jews and white Gentiles. That is the Law of Moses. Persecuting and scattering the people of God in the white Jews and white Gentiles dominions guaranteed the people of God inheritance to inherit the earth.

This time at Judgment, the white Jews and the white Gentiles can ask about the days that have past, in the last world (1) and since the day that God created man on the earth, in this world (2) and they can ask from one end of heaven to the other if anything have ever been as great as what the people of God did for the white Jews and white Gentiles. Deuteronomy 4: 32

The story of Jacob and Esau is the story of the white Gentiles second chance. The white Jews and the white Gentiles were given a second chance to prove themselves worthy to continue to exist and the people of God were told to be MEEK in the white Jews and white Gentiles second chance and after the Jews and Gentiles have had their second chance, the people of God would inherit the earth. God's people promise to inherit the earth was never on the table for the white Jews and white Gentiles even if they were perfect in their second chance. The most that they could achieve in their second chance for salvation was to prove themselves worthy to continue to exist.

Jacob represent the people of God from the old black African dominion and Esau represent the people of the new young white Gentile race that failed to prove themselves worthy last time. In the womb of the universe, Esau betrayed Jacob and God by fighting with Jacob in the womb to be born first to receive the second chance that was promised to the white Jews and white Gentiles who are represented by Esau and to also receive the promise to inherit the earth that goes to the first born that was promise to the people of God for giving the Gentiles a second chance for salvation. Genesis 25: 23

The story of Jacob and Esau in the womb fighting to see who would be born first is not about the children because the children being not yet born had done no wrong. Romans 9: 11

The story of Jacob and Esau is about a purpose of God to give the white Gentiles a second chance according to the request made by God's elect not because of the Gentiles good works but because God who calls people to salvation wants to take out of the white Gentiles a people for God's name. The story of Jacob and Esau is about God's plan to give the white Jews and white Gentiles a second chance for salvation and the white Jews and white Gentiles betraying the people of God and God in the beginning in the womb of the universe right after they begged for a second chance to prove themselves worthy to exist. They wanted the second chance that was promised to them and they also wanted to steal the people of God promise to inherit the earth for giving the white Gentiles a second chance for salvation and that inheritance goes to the first born so Esau also wanted to be born first and this is why Esau fought with Jacob in the womb of the universe. God later made it possible for Jacob to receive his inheritance back from Esau by making Esau sell the birth right back to Jacob and then God renamed Jacob Is Rael (Real) to reveal who was real and who the inheritance really belongs to. Because of this betrayal in the womb of the universe by Esau, no one in Heaven or Hell trusts the white Jews and white Gentiles. It is even worse than that. The white Jews and white Gentiles put the people of God who are the ones who are giving the white Jews and white Gentiles a second chance for salvation in the world we live in today in slavery. The young white race made the old black race their servants. For this, God has said that God hates the young white race referred to as Esau and loves the old black race referred to as Jacob. Romans 9: 11, Genesis 25: 29-34, Acts 15: 14-15, Genesis 32: 28, Romans 9: 12-13 and Malachi 1: 2-3

The white Christians have been deceived to believe that God love them unconditional. They are "Psychotic" meaning, they are out of touch with reality. The people of Satan have deceived the white Gentiles to believe that no matter what the Gentiles do, God still loves them. The white Christians believe that they can kill, persecute and scatter the people of God and God still loves them. God has said that God HATES the young white Gentile race for putting the people of the old black African race who are the Afro Americans today in slavery and making those of the old black African dominion in Africa their servants. God has said that God HATES Esau the young race who is a representation of the white Greek Jews and white Roman Gentiles for making Jacob who is a representation of the people of God from the old black African race their servants. No, God do not love the white Gentiles unconditionally. The white Christians believe that by the blood of Jesus, the white Gentiles are saved. The white Christians believe that when Jesus was on the cross, Jesus bore all of their sins and when Jesus died on the cross, He paid all of the white Gentiles sin debt in full and even if they repeatedly commit sins, their sins are forgiven because Jesus die for all of their sins that they have committed and all of their sins that they will commit. The white Christians believe that when they accepted Jesus as their savior, their sins were atoned for throughout all of eternity. What the white gentile Christians don't know is that Jesus is not the white Gentiles savior. They believe that no matter what they have done, their sins are atoned for by the blood and the death of Jesus. They are so wrong. Remember, we all will appear before the judgment seat of God that each one may receive the things done in the body according to what he has done, whether good or bad. Understand that this judgment shall be without mercy. Romans 9: 12-13, Malachi 1: 2-3, quotes from "In Touch" ministries with Pastor Charles Stanley, 2 Corinthians 5: 10, Roman 2: 16, Romans 14: 10, Galatians 6: 7, Ephesians 6: 8 and James 2: 13

The white Gentiles must know that after death, the Book of Life will be open, and the dead will be judged according to their works. I pity the white Jews and white Gentiles who say that the Afro Americans who are the ascendants of the slaves and the slaves are God's first-born lives do not matter. Revelation 20: 12-13 and Exodus 4: 22

The white Christians must know that Jesus was not sent to the Gentiles but was sent only to the House of Israel. Jesus told His disciples not to go to the white Gentiles but to go only to the lost sheep of the House of Israel. Jesus is not the white Gentiles savior but is only the savior for the House of Israel. Matthew 15: 24 and Matthew 10: 5-6

According to the promise, God raise up for "ISRAEL" a Savior named Jesus. John the Baptist preached that the "baptism of repentance" was for all of the people of Israel. Acts 13: 23-24

John, the Baptist, told the white Jews and white Gentiles who had integrated into the Pharisees and Sadducees and were passing off as the people of God, do not think to say to yourself, "We have Abraham as our father". John said that before God accept them, who were the false brethren, as the people of God because they were there in Israel, God would raise stones up to be the people of God. John called them, "Blood of Vipers" because they were the descendants of Cain and Cain father was the "wicked one" or the Serpent in the Garden of Eden. Cain was not Adam's child. The descendants of Cain became the Greeks and the Greeks became the white Jews and the false brethren. The children of Israel were sold to the Greeks by the Romans and the Greeks removed the people of God from Israel in bondage and then assumed their identity. Matthew 3: 9, Matthew 3: 7, 1 John 3: 12, 2 Corinthians 11: 26, Galatians 2: 4 and Joel 3: 6

When the Greek dominion was over, and the Roman dominion started, the Greeks assume the identity of the people of God to have authority in the Roman dominion. They became the white Jews and false brethren. It is this deception that will be the cause why the white Jews judged themselves unworthy of eternal life because they wanted to be the people of God so bad that they assumed the people of God identity. They will fight God in the Valley of Jehoshaphat in the War of Armageddon or the war between Good and Evil for the people of God who are scattered inheritance. The Afro Americans are those who are being scattered in the latter days when God has said that God will return and gather His people who are being scattered. Acts 13: 46, Joel 3: 2, Matthew 3: 12, Matthew 13: 30 and Mark 13: 27

It is also important for the white Christians to know that Jesus is not the savior of the world or the savior of the white Gentiles. The Holy Bible has recorded that those who are dead or called "Negro" which means dead and are broken off from the Tree of Life are the saviors of the Gentiles and the saviors of the world. Romans 11: 12-15

Through their fall from the Tree of Life, salvation has come to the Gentiles so do not provoke them to jealousy by bragging in your dominion. Romans 11: 11

The Holy Bible has recorded that it is those who fell and are Cut-Off for the sake of the Gentiles that is the riches of the world as well as, it is those who are cut-off "failure" that is the riches for the Gentiles. The way the white gentile Christians say that they love Jesus for being their savior is the way that the white Christian Gentiles should be saying how they love the people who are broken off for the sake of the Gentiles. The people that were broken off for the sake of the Gentiles are the ones that became the "Slaves" of this world. This is why this one race was slaves in Egypt, Assyria, Babylon, Persia, Greece, Roman and in America. Romans 11: 12 and Romans 11: 15

Remember, the people of God were slaves in Egypt, Assyria, Babylon, Persia, Greece, Rome and America. The repeating of the people of God going into slavery was so consistent that Jerimiah ask God if Israel was nothing but a homeborn slave. Jeremiah asked God if Israel was nothing but a servant. Jeremiah 2: 14

Being a slave, persecuted and scattered in America for 400 years as was prophesied proves that the Afro Americans are the true people of God. It was prophesied that the people of God would be brought to a strange land in the future by ships in bondage and treated like slaves in Egypt for 400 years. The people of God did not come to America on ships like the Titanic in luxury cabins but came to this strange land called America in bondage as slaves. This is recorded in the Holy Bible. Acts 7: 6-7 and Deuteronomy 28: 68

They are God's first born and chosen people who shall be joined with God in New Jerusalem. No other race on the planet earth including the pure blood white Aryans or the white Greek Jews are better than those who are the ascendants of the "Slaves" and are God's first born and chosen people. With God in your thoughts and your thoughts on your soul at judgment, do you think any other race is superior to God's first born and chosen people? You will have your chance to present your argument about this at judgment this time to the Lamb in Heaven that is the color of brass (brown) that has been burned in a furnace (dark brown to black) with hair like sheep wool or nappy hair. Remember, even if their superiority is not visible now, in the future it will be and all who see the people of God who are the ascendants of the slaves will say they are the seed that the Lord has blessed. Exodus 4: 22, Acts 7: 7, Genesis 3: 15: 14, Revelation 21: 3-4, Revelation 1: 14-15 and Isaiah 61: 9

This is the Afro-Americans history that is being suppressed to promote the lie that white Greek, pagan, gentile, Jews are the people of God and white Roman gentiles, pagans who have dominion today are the people of God because they are white. Those who are the ascendants of the "Slaves" that are still beings persecuted and scattered today in America as is prophesied are called Afro-Americans and called Negros or Dead and God is returning to gather those who are scattered and called the Dead or the Negros. Remember, the word Negro and Necro are the same word and Necro means dead. "Negro" should be pronounced the same way as you pronounce "Negative" because "Nec" and "Neg" have the same sound. The Holy Bible has recorded that the Dead or Negro shall be raised first by God when God returns. The Holy Bible has also recorded that the War of Armageddon that will be fought in the Valley of Jehoshaphat will be about the heritage of those who are being scattered. The Afro Americans are those who are being scattered in the latter days at the time when God says that God will return to gather those who are being scattered. Joel 3: 2 and 1 Thessalonians 4: 16

The "Slaves" of this world are not slaves because they are inferior but are slaves in this world for the sake of the Gentiles. They are giving the white Gentiles 93% of their evolutionary energy, so the white Gentiles can survive and grow on the Tree of Life. The people of God are using only 7% of their evolutionary energy to survive and at 7% efficiency, they are equal to the white Gentiles that are using 93% of the people of God energy. At the people of God lowest point, they are equal to the white Gentiles at the white Gentiles highest point at the end of the age when the fullness of the Gentiles has come in or at the time when the white Gentiles are at their maximum level of evolutionary development. President Barack Obama proved that in the eight years that he stood before the white Gentiles and was equal to them in every way. Because of this, this percentage is consistent throughout in this world until the return of God. We only use 7% of our brain power and 93% is inactive. We are 7% minerals and 93% water. There is 7% land mass on the planet earth and 93% of the earth is water including air, clouds, vapors, rivers, lakes, streams and the oceans. Now, the energy from the Tree of Life of this planet that should have went to the slaves to make the slaves masters of the planet was given to the young Gentiles race so that young race could grow and become strong faster than it would have taken normal evolutionary growth and development, so the Gentiles could join the people of the earth and become human beings and be equal to the people of the earth and there be no "schism" between the people of the earth and the replicated white Gentiles. 1 Corinthians 12: 25

The Holy Bible instructs the white replicated Gentiles who are the grafted branch not to boast against the broken branch that became slaves because the roots from the Tree of Life of this earth that the white replicated Gentiles are getting their energy from belongs to the slaves, who are the broken branch. The people of the earth are referred to as one body. Those members of the body which we think to be less honorable or weak, upon these we bestow more abundant honor or energy, so our weak and uncomely parts have more abundant comeliness or energy. For our comely parts have no need but God have tempered the body or people together, having given more abundant honor to that part or those people which lacked that there should be no schism or one race better than the other race in the body or on the earth, but that the members or people should have the same care or abilities one for another. The white Greeks, the white Romans and the white Americans, which is a derivative of the Roman dominion, were given dominions on the earth not because they are better and stronger than the other branches or people on the Tree of Life of the earth but was given dominions because they are weaker and less developed than the other branches or people on the planet earth. Romans 11: 17-19 and 1 Corinthians 12: 14-26

The "Slaves" of this world are the broken branch spoke of in the Holy Bible. The white Christian gentiles must say that the branches were broken off so that the Gentiles could be grafted on the Tree of Life in their place on the Tree of Life on this planet. The white Gentiles must say this. Those that are broken-off so that the Gentiles could be grafted in are the Gentiles savior and not Jesus. The white Christian gentiles must say this otherwise, they too will be Cut-off. Romans 11: 12, Romans 11: 17-18 and Romans 11: 19 and Romans 11: 22

Now if the Gentiles are the young, wild by nature, olive tree that was grafted contrary to nature into a good olive tree and achieved all that the white Gentiles achieved in their dominions, how much more shall the broken branch who became the slaves of this world achieved who are the natural branches of the Tree of Life when they are grafted back into their own olive tree and are using 100% of their evolutionary energy? Because of their belief in God, God will graft them back into the Tree of Life and join with them and give them immortality. Romans 11: 23-24 and Revelation 21: 3-4

This is the knowledge or truth that the disbelieving white Jews said in biblical days if delivered by the Brethren or Brothers, could turn the world upside down and it is this conversion and only this conversion that can save the white Jews and white Gentiles. This truth must not be suppressed. The white Jews and white Gentiles must "Behold" the truth and reveal everything that is being suppressed otherwise, the white Jews and white Gentiles will be "Cut-Off". This profound truth has been delivered to the white Jews and to the white Gentiles. The promise to the white Jews and to the white Gentiles to deliver the truth to them in the latter days so they would know what was going on, so they would know what to do has been fulfilled and the order from God to be for the salvation of the white Jews and white Gentiles from biblical days to "Present" till the end of the earth has been obeyed. Jesus said in biblical days that the white Jews and white Gentiles did not know what they were doing because they did not know what was going on. Acts 17: 5-6, Romans 11: 22, Acts 13: 47 and Luke 23: 34

The white Jews and the white Gentiles must believe that this happened and make a public declaration declaring who are the true people of God otherwise the white Jews and white Gentiles will be "Cut-Off". In the beginning, the people of God were mighty Kings and Queens that could do anything that their mind could conceive. They did not believe that God could take their dominion on the earth away and give a dominion to the young, wild, ignorant, under-develop, brute-beast, cave-men that were created by the Fallen Angels for body replacement parts and sex to be kill when no longer needed. Disbelief will get you "Cut-Off" from the Tree of Life in a New York minute. If God spare not His own people because of disbelief be warned that God will not spare the Gentiles because of disbelief. Romans 11: 22, Genesis 11: 6, Romans 11: 20, 2 Peter 2: 12 and Romans 11: 21

# THE BOOKS OF SIMION

To prevent the white Jews from judging themselves unworthy for eternal life because they want to be the people of God so bad that they have assumed the identity of the true people of God and to prevent no place found for the great white throne in the future, the white Jews and white Gentiles in the future sent the latter-day deliverer to our present to themselves to deliver this truth so they would know what was going on, so they would know what to do to be saved. Remember, Jesus said that the white Jews and white Gentiles did not know what they were doing. The latter-day "Deliverer" is sent first to the white Jews because the white Jews in the future came up with the plan to be saved and are the ones who sent the "Deliverer" or sent the message that the "Deliverer" will deliver and then, the latter-day "Deliverer" will turn and deliver the Truth to the white Roman gentiles who have dominion today. Acts 13: 46, Revelation 20: 11 and Luke 23: 34

This is the latter-day Deliverer mission who shall be possessed by the spirit of Simon Peter because God said by Peter's mouth only would the Gentiles hear the truth and believe. No one else on the planet knows this message but him that was chosen to deliver this message before the world began and the white Jews and white Gentiles will believe the delivered message. It is prophesied that after the fullness of the Gentiles comes in at the end of the age or after December 21, 2012, the "Deliverer" will come forth and turn away ungodliness. The Holy Bible has instructed the white Jews and white Gentiles to be wise in their own "Conceit" or wise in their made-up, self-importance, pride and vanity that is not justified. Acts 15: 7, 2 Timothy 1: 9, and Romans 11: 25-26

This is why Peter's Basilica in Rome was built to receive him who would be possessed by the spirit of Peter in the latter-days who will deliver a profound truth to the white Jews and to the white Gentiles. Simon Peter was also called Simeon and called a Nig er (Nigg er) and

Simon Peter delivered the message that God want to take out of the white Jews and white Gentiles a people for God's name when Simon Peter was being called Simeon and called a Nig er (Nigg er). Acts 15: 14 and Acts 13: 1

Since the end of the dominion shall be declared from what happened at the beginning of the dominion and at the beginning of the dominion, Simeon reveal this to the white Jews and white Gentiles that God wanted to take out of the white Jews and white Gentiles a people for God's name, at the end of the dominion it will be Simeon, the Nig er and only Simion, the Nigg er that reveals this to the white Jews and white Gentiles again because God wants to take out of the white Jews and white Gentiles a people for God's name and for that cause, the words of the prophets or the Books of Simion are written. Isaiah 46: 10 and Acts 15: 14-15

The ancient prophets are subject to the prophets or the ancient prophets will be in the latter-day prophets. 1 Corinthian 14: 32

There will be two latter-day "Deliverers" that the Holy Bible identify as the last two "Witnesses" of the white Gentiles second chance for salvation and they will be possessed by the spirit of Elijah and the spirit of Simon Peter. Revelation 11: 3-12

One will go to the people of God and he will be possessed by the spirit of Elijah and the other will go to the white Jews and white Gentiles and he will be possessed by the spirit of Simon Peter. It is important for the white Gentiles to know that Elijah, the ancient prophet will be sent before the coming of the great and dreadful day of the Lord to the people of God and he shall turn the hearts of the fathers to the children and the hearts of the children to their fathers lest God come and smite the earth with a curse. If the Rappers and the Hip-Hoppers that the white Jews and white Gentiles have put in the Afro-American communities to influence the people of God to do wrong prevent the fathers from turning to their children or the children who the Rappers and Hip-Hoppers are influencing from turning to their fathers, God will smite the earth with a curse. Malachi 4: 5-6 and Matthew 17: 11

The spirit of Simon Peter will be in him that is sent to the white Greek gentile Jews and to the white Roman gentiles who have dominion today. God has said, "By Peter's mouth only will the white Jews and white Gentiles hear the truth in the latter-days and believe. The spirit of Peter who was Simon who the Gentiles called Simeon and also called a Nig er (Nigg er) will be in him that is sent to the white Jews and white Gentiles. These two will be the last two witnesses of the white Jews and white Gentiles second chance for salvation. There will be no one else that comes from the future or the present to offer salvation to the white Jews and white Gentiles. There will be no white Neo from the Matrix or white John Connors from the Terminator that will come to save mankind and the illuminati must know that there will be no black Nick Fury of S.H.I.E.L.D from the Avengers to advise and guild them. There will only be Simion, the Nigger that is sent to the white Jews and white Gentiles to save mankind from a supernatural enemy in the latter days at the end of the age or after December 21, 2012. Acts 15: 7, Acts 13: 1, Malachi 4: 5-6, Matthew 17: 11 and Revelation 11: 3-6

Under no circumstances should these last two witnesses of the Gentiles actions in the Gentiles second chance be killed or harmed in any way. Last time, the Gentiles did not kill the last two witnesses and it would not be advisable for the Gentiles to do so this time, but the Gentiles are at liberty to do whatever they will to prove that the Gentiles are worthy are not worthy to remain grafted on the Tree of Life. Last time, the Beast out of the bottomless pit or the beast that came out of the vortex to infinity that the CERN particle acceleration lab in Geneva opened, killed them. Revelation 11: 7

Because the Gentiles would not kill the last two Witnesses last time, the Beast that will ascend out of the bottomless pit will make war against the Witnesses and overcome and kill the Witnesses. Revelation 11: 7

Because the Gentiles refused to kill the last two Witnesses last time, the Gentiles received sympathy at judgment and their request for a second chance was allowed to be brought before the court at judgment and was heard and considered.

This time, if the Gentiles build the sanctuary to protect the last two witnesses, God's Lambs of Peace and the righteous of the Gentiles because the righteous Gentiles are ordained to eternal life this time because they believed last time alone with Kings and Queens, the super-rich and the very powerful because they are the ones who will build the sanctuary in the best location and supply the sanctuary with everything that the sanctuary will need, who knows what the effects of such actions would be for the Gentiles. It is a definite surety that those actions would steer events in another direction to change the shape of the things that are prophesied to come because God has said that God will dwell among them in a sanctuary. At the sanctuary, God will dwell in them and walk among them and be their God and they shall be God's people. Acts 13: 48, Exodus 25: 8 and 2 Corinthians 6: 16

The white Gentiles must know that God will not be at the rebuilt temple in Jerusalem that will be trodden down by the white Gentiles until the time of the white Gentiles are fulfilled. The white Gentiles must know that God will be at the people of God sanctuary.

If the white Gentiles want to communicate with God, they must be at the sanctuary for the people of God. Luke 21: 24

There, at the sanctuary, supplications, prayers, INTERCESSIONS, and giving of thanks will be made for all men including Kings and all who are in Authority or the illuminati that we may lead quiet and peaceable lives in all godliness and reverence for this is good and acceptable in the sight of God our Savior who desires all men to be saved and to come to the knowledge of the truth. There at the sanctuary, kings and all who are in authority will be saved and come to the knowledge of the truth. 1 Timothy 2: 1-4

The last two Witnesses must not appear dressed in sackcloth or appear poor. If they appear poor, they will be given the power to shut heaven, so that no rain falls in the days of their prophecy and they will have power over water to turn water into blood and they will have the power to strike the earth with all plagues as often as they desire. If anyone wants to harm them, fire will proceed from their mouth and devour their enemies. If anyone wants to harm them, he must be killed in this manner. They will know who the Holy Bible say they are, they will be able to do what the Holy Bible say they can do, and they will have everything that the Holy Bible say that they will have. Revelation 11: 5-6

The white Gentiles must look at the people of God who are the Afro-Americans today who are the ascendants of slaves who built Pharaoh treasure cities Pithom and Ramses and were the pyramids builders who built the towers whose tops were in the heavens in the past and look at them now and know that the same or worse will happen to the white Gentiles if the white Gentiles are Cut-Off just like it happened to the Afro-Americans. Exodus 1: 11, Genesis 11: 4 and Romans 11: 22

Do not miss this warning and be deceived by the Ancient Astronauts Theorists and believe that extraterrestrials built the pyramids and the ancient ruins that are found today. Those who were slaves who are the Afro Americans today built Egypt and the people from the old black African dominion built the ancient ruins that are found all over the world today and look at them now and know that the same will happen to the white Jews and white Gentiles if they do not believe that this happened to the Afro Americans and the people of the old black African dominion. If God spared not His own people because of disbelieve, take heed white Jews and white Gentiles that God will not spare thee either. Exodus 1: 11, Exodus 4: 22 and Romans 11: 20-21

The white Jews and the white Gentiles who are the Christians says that God do not hate anyone. They are wrong. Because God has said that He hates them for putting God's people into slavery, they want to believe that God do not hate anyone, and they say to be God, He must love everyone unconditionally. They are wrong. What shall we say then? Is there unrighteousness with God? Certainly not! For God said to Moses "I will have mercy on whomever I will have mercy on and I will have compassion on whomever I will have compassion on and I will HATE whomever I will choose to hate". Remember, verse 13 is talking about God's hate for Esau for putting the people of God who are the older race who are today's Afro Americans into slavery. Romans 9: 13-15 and Malachi 1: 2-3

The white Gentiles mock or poke fun at or tease God for what they did to the people of God when they put the people of God in slavery when the white Gentiles glorified the white Generals of the Civil War that fought to enslave the people of God. When they honor these Generals and others who are against the Civil Rights Law for the people of God, they are making fun of God saying in their hearts that they don't care if God hates the younger race for putting the older race in slavery. When these white Christian Gentiles insult and make fun of the God of Islam, they are also insulting and making fun of the God of the Holy Bible because the God of Islam and the God of the Holy Bible are the same God. That is how much the white Christian Gentiles are being deceived by the false prophet. These are people that do not believe in an afterlife or the existence after this life. They believe that when you die, that is it, and there is nothing after death. They are wrong. I pity the white Jews and white Gentiles who died hating the true people of God and believing that God and the Son of God are white pagan gentiles. For we must all appear before the judgment seat of God that each one may receive the things done in the body according to what he has done whether good or evil. 2 Corinthians 5: 10

God say that He HATES Esau, the young white Gentile race, for putting Jacob, the old black African race or the Afro Americans in slavery. Do not be deceived to believe that God love the young white Gentile race. This time at judgment, the young white Gentiles will have to answer for their actions. Romans 9: 12-13 and Malachi 1: 2-3

At judgment this time, even if the white Gentles have a good report concerning their behavior on the earth and how they prayed endlessly devoting themselves to God, they will not receive what was promised to you for living a Godly life without the people of God or without acknowledging who are the true people of God. If the white Gentiles hate the people of God or have any negative emotions about the people of God who are the ascendants of slaves who are the Afro Americans today, they will not receive what was promised to those who worship God. God will never accept the white Gentiles as long as the white Gentiles say that the white Gentiles do not like the people of God who are the ascendants of slaves who are the Afro Americans today. The white Jews and white Gentiles will not be given what was promised to them by God nor will they ever be made genetically perfect no matter what science tries to do for them because without us or without the people of God who are the Afro Americans today, the white race will not be made whole or perfect. This cannot be bypassed by science. Remember, the white race with all their genetic problems was supposed to join with the human race to become human beings and genetically perfect but they stayed white and said in their hearts that the white race was better than the human race and that science would solve their genetic problem. Hebrew 11: 39-40

The people of God who are the ascendants of those who were slaves who are the Afro Americans today are the scale that will be used to measure the white Gentiles to determine if the white Gentiles are worthy to remain grafted on the Tree of Life or determine if the white Gentiles are found "Wanting" or "Tekel" what they need to remain grafted on the Tree of Life and if the judgment is "Tekel" again, the white Gentiles will be CUT Off or Broken Off from the Tree of Life and regressed into the Paleolithic upright beast of their beginning and there will be no place found for the great white throne in the future. This was channeled to the white Gentiles of today from the white Gentiles in the future and the white Gentiles of today put that revelation in the 1968 "Planet of the Apes" movie starring Charlton Heston. Prophecy is being fulfilled right now. Daniel 5: 27, Romans 11: 22 and Revelation 20: 11

"Mene" which means God has numbered your kingdom and now it is finished, or the fullness of the Gentiles has come in at the end of the age on December 21, 2012. Daniel 5: 26 and Luke 21: 24

"Tekel" meaning that you have been judged and found "Wanting" what is necessary to remain grafted on the Tree of Life because of the way you treated the people of God who are the ascendants of slaves who are the Afro Americans today who are God's first born and chosen people. Daniel 5: 27 and Exodus 4: 22

"Peres" which means that your kingdom has been divided and given to others or your kingdom has been divided and given to your neighbors by the Ten New Kings or by the Ten New Banks that will have authority with the beast for one hour as kings or for the remaining time of the Gentiles dominion that would not give housing loans to the people of God who are the Afro Americans today and citizens of America but chose to give outrages loans to illegal immigrants that spent and sent their money to their home country and it was by this act against the people of God that crashed the Gentiles housing market and collapsed the Gentiles global financial system and that almost destroyed the Gentiles kingdom in 2008. Daniel 5: 28 and Revelation 17: 12

# The Collapse of the Gentiles global financial system

The white Gentiles must know that the collapse of their global financial system in 2008 was about housing and how the white Gentiles were living luxuriously while they gave the people of God houses to illegal immigrants and it is because of this that the white Gentiles will be given torment and sorrow for they have said in their hearts no sorrow will come to them for what they did to the Afro Americans who are the ascendants of Slaves and are God's chosen people and first born. Revelation 18: 7 and Exodus 4: 22

Because of the way the people of God who are the Afro Americans are being treated by the white Jews and the white Gentiles, the white Gentiles global financial system will collapse again causing the white Gentiles to develop a new financial system whereby everyone will be marked on their right hand or forehead before anyone can buy and sell. All who receives this mark to buy and sell will be cursed by God and suffer unbearable pain. Revelation 13: 16-18 and Revelation 14: 9-11

Powerful unseen forces and principalities who are the rulers of darkness that controls the power elite of this world are behind the pestilence or viruses we are experiencing today and their goals are to shut down all businesses to devalue the dollar bill and crash the Gentiles global financial system to force the Gentiles to abandon the dollar bill and develop a new system whereby everyone will be marked on their hands and forehead to buy and sell. Ephesians 6: 12 and Revelation 13: 16-17

It is important to know that the Holy Bible says that this mark to buy and sell tattooed on your flesh will develop into a foul and loathsome, repulsive, repugnant sore that cannot be healed and will burn like fire and spread over the entire body. Revelation 16: 2

The importance of this prophecy cannot be stressed enough. The false prophet or the false brethren who are the white Greek Jewish gentiles or no other Christian church have brought this warning to the Gentiles attention for the Gentiles examination so the Gentiles can determine for themselves if what is recorded in the Holy Bible has any merit to determine if the Gentiles wants to steer events in another direction to change the shape of the things that are prophesied to come to pass. As important is this revelation in the Holy Bible is to the white Jews and the white Christian gentiles, it has never been revealed to them for their examination and study.

Only him who is possessed by the spirit of Simon Peter will the Gentiles hear the words of the gospel and "believe". Simon Peter or him that is possessed by the spirit of Simon Peter will tell you how to save all in your house or dominion. The spirits of the prophets are subject to the prophets or the spirits of the ancient prophets will be in the latter-day prophets. Acts 15: 7, Acts 11: 12-14 and 1 Corinthians 14: 32

Billions of people, especially Christians, will be killed because of this tattoo to buy and sell that will be put on your flesh. When the dollar bill is devalued because there is no gold to back up all of the dollar bills that are being printed to boost the economy, the Catholic church will offer their gold to save the Gentiles global economy but their gold will not be used to back up the dollar bill but will be used only if another financial system is created that will require all to be marked on their right hand or forehead to buy and sell. It is this mark to buy and sell on your hand or forehead that will mutate into a repugnant sore that will turn you into a monster in pain. You have been "Alerted". Revelation 16: 2

You sent the latter-day deliverer to Alert and Warn you to the things that shall come to pass just as Joseph warned Pharaoh and Daniel warned King Nebuchadnezzar of the things that were prophesied to come to pass in their kingdoms. Because of their warnings that saved kingdoms, they were promoted and given great wealth. The latter-day warning to the white Jews and white Gentiles is more important than the warning Joseph delivered to Pharaoh and more important than the warning Daniel delivered to king Nebuchadnezzar. This latter-day warning is to save billions of people from death and mutilation. Those who are sent are ordered by God to be for the salvation of the Gentiles. This warning is the salvation or redemption from what happened last time and the deliverance and the rescue from the dangers that are prophesied to come to pass in this last Gentile dominion of "Iron and Clay" this time. Please, do not ignore this warning. Acts 13: 47, Genesis 41: 37-46, Daniel 2: 48, Daniel 5: 29 and Daniel 2: 41-43

The Christians have been told for years that this mark on your right hand or forehead is a holy mark. Every year for Lent, the white Christian gentiles has been taking this mark made from ash on their right hand and forehead. It is this Christian mark that will not be ashes but will be tattooed on the flesh that will mutate and kill billions. The mark will have alien technology in it that cannot be made capable with human flesh. This mark will have your social security number, your police record and your health records and your banking information within it. To buy or sell, you only will have to place your hand over a scanner and all of your personal and banking information will be known. This mark will also be used to curve crime. If it is known that you have created a crime, your social security number will be inserted into the master super computer named the "Beast" in Brussels, Belgium and this computer system that will be possessed by the spirit of Satan will send out a wave or signal focused on that social security number that was inserted resulting in a burning sensation in the spot where the tattoo was put that will develop into great pain to force the accused to either check into a hospital or a police station to deactivate the signal and stop the pain. It is this process that will malfunction and mutate into a foul sore that can't be healed where the tattoo was place on your hand or forehead that will be horrifying, repugnant and painful.

Because it was design to cause a painful burning sensation to force a criminal to turn himself in, it will be that process that malfunction and mutates into something horrible. Because men will be bold enough or desperate enough to cut their hand off to avoid being a slave to the computer named the "Beast", men will be forced to take the mark of the beast or the mark that will turn you into a beast on their forehead. Many women will be forced to take the mark of the beast on their right hand because women will not be easily motivated to cut their hand off, but there will be exceptions. Any woman that is believed to possess the ability to cut her hand off to escape from being a slave to and controlled by the computer will also be forced to take the mark of the beast on her forehead. Revelation 16: 2

The computer's ability to cause pain will control all who have the mark of the beast tattooed on their fresh. This has been Satan's goal since the beginning. Satan wants unconditional control over everybody on the earth and through this computer he will have his desire. Once Satan take control of the computer, the Gentiles will think that the computer has become self-aware developing its own consciousness. The consciousness inside of the computer named the "beast" will be Satan's consciousness. Satan will be in control of a computer that can make more than 200 million billion calculations per second that is directly connect to all that have the mark of the beast tattooed on their flesh. Once the computer becomes self-aware or possessed by Satan, it will start making suggestions and giving orders and if the computer or Satan is not obeyed, pain and death will follow. All will have to do what the computer or Satan suggest without question to prevent the computer or Satan from giving them pain so bad that it could cause death. Sophia, the artificial intelligence robot is the beginning of that program. The Holy Bible says that the Gentiles will give this super computer named the "beast" an image or a body and then Satan will possess that image giving that image "breath" making it alive so that it can "speak" and cause as many as would not worship the beast to be killed. I pity the fool that gets this mark tattooed on his or her forehead. It is this mark that will mutate and turn you into a monster in pain controlled by artificial intelligence possessed by Satan. The artificial intelligence or the unknown intelligence that they will call artificial or called false, insincere or fake controlling the computer will be the intelligence of Satan and not the intelligence of circuits and metal. Circuits, metal and plastics have no intelligence and can never become self-aware. At that point when the computer becomes more than the sum of its parts, that will be the point when Satan will have taken control of the computer system to directly control all who is connected to the computer. Revelation 13: 14-15

Once the tattoo mutates, all with the mark of the beast or the mark that will turn you into a beast tattooed on their flesh will gnaw (bite or chew) their tongues because of the pain from the horrible sore that will develop in the same spot where the tattoo was put and spread over their body. Because of the importance of this, this message is being channeled to the Gentiles from the future and the Gentiles has put this channeled message in their movies of today not understanding the complete nature of the message. In the 1985 horror movie titled "Return of the Living Dead", a walking zombie is captured and restrained to a table and asked why are the zombies eating people? The zombie replied that they were eating people because of the unbearable PAIN. The zombie said that the zombies must gnaw or bite and chew on brains or flesh to spot the pain. This is what today's zombie movies are made about and this is what the Holy Bible says will happen to all who take the mark of the beast to buy and sell because of the new financial system that will replace the use of the dollar bill. All who take the mark of the beast to buy and sell will suffer unbearable pain and to stop the pain, they will have to gnaw or bite and chew on something persistently. They will be transformed into the walking dead zombies that today's movies are made about. You have been Warned. Revelation 16: 10-11

If anyone worships the beast and his image and receives his Christian mark on his forehead or on his hand shall drink of the wine of the wrath of God, which will be pour out in full strength into the cup of his indignation. He shall be tormented with fire and brimstone or burning pain and a funky smell from the repugnant sore on his hand or forehead in the presence of the holy angels and in the presence of the Lamb. They will have no rest day or night from the pain who worship the beast and his image or picture and receives the mark of his named. Revelation 14: 9-11

Look at all who receives the Christian mark of ash on their right hand and forehead for Lent and you will see many who shall be the first to be transformed into a monster in pain. It is these souls that asked last time at judgement to be delivered from this torment that they experienced last time this time by warning them of the things that is prophesied to come to the earth. They insisted that the "Deliverer" come to them speaking boldly to them without offending them so they would at least receive the message to warn them of this danger.

Peter Basilica in Rome was constructed in this last dominion for the Gentiles in the latter-days to receive him who would be possessed by the spirit of Simon Peter who was call Simeon and called a Nig er(Nigg er) so he could deliver this most important and profound message to save the gentile Christians from this terror. Remember, Simon Peter who was called Simeon and called a Nig er(Nigg er) will tell you how to save all in your house or all in your dominion. Remember, the spirits of the prophets are subject to the prophets or the ancient prophets' spirits will be in the latter-day prophets. Acts 13: 1, Acts 11: 12-14 and 1 Corinthians 14: 32

The end of the dominion shall be declared from the beginning of the dominion or what happened in the beginning of the Gentiles second chance will happen at the end of the gentiles second chance dominion. Isaiah 46: 10

In the beginning of the dominion it was Simon Peter who was called Simeon and called a Nig er(Nigg er) that delivered the gospel that God wants to take out of the Gentiles a people for God's name and at the end of the dominion right now, it will be Simeon the Nig er and only Simion the Nigg er that deliver the gospel again that God wants to take out of the white Jewish gentiles and the white Roman gentiles who have dominion today a people for God's name and for the cause and purpose the words of the prophets are written in the Books of Simion. You have been "Warned". Acts 15: 7, Acts 13: 1, and Acts 15: 14-15

All of this will happen because the New Ten Kings or New Ten Banks and the white Gentiles will continue to live luxuriously while they give to illegal immigrants what they should have been giving to the people of God who are the Afro Americans today and it is this action against the people of God that will collapse the white Gentiles global financial system again as their global financial system collapsed in 2008. Revelation 18: 6-7

Because of the way the people of God were treated in the white Gentile dominion, a Penance must be made if the white Gentiles are to be saved this time. To be saved this time, the white Gentiles must show sorry for what they have done to the people of God who are the people that are responsible for the white Gentiles second chance for salvation in the world we live in today. The people of God must be recognized as the true people of God and the Sanctuary must be built where the people of God can live quiet and peaceful lives in all godliness and reference for this is good and acceptable in the sight of God our savior who desires all men to be saved and to come to the knowledge of the truth. Only at the Sanctuary, will Kings and all in authority or the illuminati be saved. There at the Sanctuary supplications, prayers and INTERCESSIONS will be made for all men at the Sanctuary including for Kings and all who are in authority or the illuminati. The Sanctuary must be built in the best possible location by the ocean for fishing. There must be mountains there where God will dwell and there must be beautiful valleys, rivers and lakes with all sort of fruit trees because there in the valley, God will be by the lakes and rivers in the cool breeze there in the valley. There at the Sanctuary, the people of God must be safe and live quiet and peaceful lives in all godliness and reference for this is good and acceptable in the sight of God our savior who desire all men to be saved and come to the knowledge of the truth. There at the Sanctuary with the people of God, the white Gentiles will be saved from the destruction that will come to the earth as the Egyptians were saved at Goshen with the people of God when the spirit of death kill the first born in Egypt. 1 Timothy 2: 1-3

Without the true people of God or without mixing with the people of the old African dominion to become Human Beings, the white Gentiles will not be made genetically perfect nor will they receive anything that was promised to them. If the white Gentiles are assuming the people of God identity, they will not receive the people of God inheritance nor will they received what was promised to the white Gentiles for living a godly life. Hebrews 11: 39-40

The white Jews and white Gentiles will not receive the "Outer-Count" of the great new city named New Jerusalem when the Kingdom of God is established on the earth. If they lose that, they will not be running in and out of the great new city eating from the Trees of Knowledge to expand their consciousness nor will they be drinking from the River of life to live forever. They will not receive the evolutionary advancements that they would have received if they were with the people of God at the new great city named New Jerusalem. Absolutely nothing at this time is more important than being at that "Outer-Court" in the future. It is because of this that God gave the white Gentiles a second chance for salvation because God want to take out of the white Gentiles a people for God's name and for that purpose, the words of the prophets or the books of Simion are written. It is because of what is promised to the white Jews and white Gentiles that believes in the God and the Son of God of the Holy Bible and loves God's people who are the ones who will occupied the great new city named New Jerusalem that the white Gentiles in the future asked for a second chance and for this message to be delivered to the white Jews and white Gentiles in the latter days in time. This future that will definitely come to pass is so great in the future that the white Gentiles begged for a second chance to be part of this future. Revelation 11: 2, Revelation 21: 1-3, Revelation 22: 1-2 and Acts 15: 14-15

At judgment last time, the white Jews and white Gentiles finally screamed that, "All things are possible with God". They asked their friends to ask their Heavenly Father to do the impossible. They screamed saying, "We believe that there is nothing that God can't do". They screamed, "Give us another chance". It was the people of God or the Afro Americans who came out of the tribulations on the earth with the white Jews and white Gentiles who encourage the Jews and Gentiles to come forth and request the impossible because the people of God knew that their God could do the impossible even change time. Matthew 19: 26, Revelation 7: 14, and Revelation 20: 4

The people of God agreed with the white Jews and white Gentiles and said that the people of God would be willing to delay their kingdom to give the white Jews and white Gentiles a second chance to prove themselves worthy to be part of the people of God kingdom. All in Heaven said that the people of God were "Stumbling" or making a big mistake and they were right because once everything was rewound, Esau who is a representation of the white Jews and white Gentiles tried to steal Jacob who is a representation of the people of God birth-right to inherit the earth. Remember, the white Jews and white Gentiles were given a second chance for "salvation" in the world we live in today. Jacob or the people of God was told to be "Meek" in the white Jews and white Gentiles second chance for salvation and afterwards, the people of God would inherit the earth. Esau fought with Jacob in the womb of the universe to be born first to receive a second chance for salvation that was promised to the Gentiles and to also receive what was promised to Jacob or the people of God to inherit the earth and that inheritance would have gone to the first-born. Esau wanted to be born first to receive a second chance that was promised to the Gentiles and also receive Jacob's promised to inherit the earth that goes to the first-born. Now, no one in Heaven trust the white Jews and white Gentiles because Esau betrayed Jacob in the womb of the universe. The Holy Bible has recorded that the white Jews and white Gentiles this time at judgment can ask from one end of Heaven to the other concerning the days that are past which were before you in the first world and since the day that God created man on the earth in this world we live in today if any great thing like this or like what the people of God did for the white Jews and white Gentiles has ever happened or anything like this has ever been heard of happening anywhere in the omniverse. Romans 11: 11, Genesis 25: 22-23, Matthew 5: 5 and Deuteronomy 4: 32

The request was granted, and time was rewound over what happened last time so if nothing is changed this time, the same actions of last time will happen again this time or is predestined or predetermined and last time, the white Jews and white Gentiles were broken-off and regressed because of their actions. This is the Temporal Mechanics of the Matrix of this world. Temporal Mechanics is the advance science of the study of the working of time and its effects on the space-time-continuum. This time, changes must be made. This explains how the future is predetermined yet, we have the freedom of choice to determine a new future. This timeline must not be allowed to continue. Events must be steered in another direction to prevent what happened last time from happening again this time. That is why we experience the Déjà vu experience of experiencing something that is happening now that you experienced happened before identical to what is happening now because this time-line is being relived over what happened last time. This effect on time that we sense on our space-time-continuum of experiencing what is happening now, before, exactly as it's happening now is the proof to us that we are in our second chance and something else happened before this time exactly as it is happening now. This Déjà vu experience is so profound that you will stop what you are doing and acknowledge to all around that you have experienced this moment before, exactly as it is happening now. This second chance was given to us this time to make different choices. This is the time to make a difference to steer events in a direction that will guarantee the white Jews and white Gentiles presence in the future. The message of salvation has been delivered in the latter days after the "fullness of the Gentiles has come in" at the end of the age after December 21, 2012 by the people of God or by the "Deliverer" "whose eyes are open" as the white Jews and white Gentiles requested. It is recorded in the Holy Bible that after the fullness of the Gentiles comes in at the end of the age or after December 21, 2012 because December 21, 2012 was the end of the age, the "Deliverer" would come to turn away ungodliness. This prophecy has been fulfilled. Because God wants to take out of the white Jews and white Gentiles a people for God's name and we are at the end of the age, the words of the Prophets or the Books of Simion have been written and delivered. From this point forward, the white Jews and white Gentiles must make their choices wisely. Romans 11: 25-26 and Acts 15: 14-15

Advance science and advance medicine are no comparison to evolutionary development whereas you are in contact with supernatural forces that are beyond the abilities of science and medicine. What good is the best technology when you are in a world with people that have received evolutionary development that can't be killed, can float like the clouds and fly like the birds to their windows, that anything that they can imagine in the minds will come true? All of the advance technology that the white Gentiles are hoping for in the future in their "G.I. Joe" movies will be useless against a race of Supermen that can't be killed. It is recorded in the Holy Bible that the white Gentiles will not only bring all of their gold and silver to the people of God but will also abandon all of their advance technology and bring all of their advance technology or the forces of the white Gentiles to the people of God to receive evolutionary development and to eat from the Trees of Knowledge to expand their consciousness and to drink from the River of Life to rejuvenate the body to live forever. Once the regression starts and the white Gentiles begin to regress into the Paleolithic creatures of their beginning, Kings and Queens will be bought with evolutionary development or Kings and Queens will give everything that they have to remain and for their children to remain Homo sapiens and not regressed into the Paleolithic up-right beast or the beast that was made to walk up-right. Isaiah 60: 8, Revelation 21: 3-4, Isaiah 60: 9 and Isaiah 60: 11

In the next dominion ruled by God and the people of God in the New World, everything that you could possibly do with science will be done with evolutionary development without instrumentalities but by "thought" and "will" alone and there will be no need for medicine because with evolutionary development, there will be no death and no one will be getting sick in New Jerusalem and limbs and eyes will not be damaged with these supernatural bodies and on the outside, in other nations, limbs and eyes will be replaced instantly by the people of God using supernatural forces whenever needed. Those on the outside that die an unrighteous death, or an untimely death will be brought back to life or resurrected by the people of God as Yahawahshi and Yahawahshi disciples did in biblical days. Even if their bodies are totally destroyed, the people of God will be able to bring their spirit back to the world of the living and insert that spirit in another body that had recently died. They will be able to control the spirits in all bodies and with words they will be able to tell a body to give up the spirit in the body causing instant death. They will be able to kill not with guns or knives but with words as Peter did to Ananias and Sapphira. Remember, their abilities were to cure all manner of sickness and disease, to cast out demons and devils, they had power over the Scorpions and the Serpents or power over the extraterrestrials who are insectoids and reptilians by nature who have invaded the earth and have their main base in the sea or at the bottom of the ocean and the disciples had the power to raise the dead or bring the spirit of the dead back to the land of the living. Acts 5: 1-10, Matthew 10: 1, Luke 10: 19, Isaiah 27: 1 and Matthew 10: 8

The leaves from the Tree of Knowledge or Life will be for healing and drinking from the River of Life will cure all diseases and prolong your life and rejuvenate your body. The leaves from the Trees of Knowledge or Life will be used for the healing of the nations. No medicine that can be created will be equal to the leaves from the Trees of Life in healing the nations. The Trees will also bare fruits and these fruits will expand your conscious making you smarter and wiser. Revelation 22: 1-2

Absolutely nothing is more important than being part of the Kingdom of God when God's Kingdom is established on the earth and the "false prophet" or the "false brethren" who has assumed the true people of God identity to deceive the Christians gentiles has not brought the message of salvation to the white Gentiles. This is why we live in the world we live in today. Because of this "Test" or "Second Chance" for salvation, our planet has been isolated from all other life in the universe to ensure that the gentiles are treated fairly and not influence by others or developing alternative desires and purposes to strive for. The Gentiles only goal or purpose is to be found worthy to continue to exist with the people of the earth. Those white Gentiles that feel that they are unworthy for everlasting life will deceived the white Gentiles to believe that science and technology will be just as good as evolutionary development. They will deceive the white Gentiles who have dominion today to believe that they can abuse their evolutionary development energy as often as possible in the form of an orgasm for sexual pleasures and nothing will happen to you. They will argue with God that they have the rights to drink, smoke, eat any food, especially the forbitten pig, as well as engage in sin and fornications and abuse their evolutionary energy in the form of a sexual orgasm as often as possible for pleasure and still have the right to ascend into a higher life form. They will proclaim that science and medicine will overcome all aliments resulting from the abuse of their evolutionary development energy and they will proclaim that technology will replace evolutionary development. You can have all of the technology of Tony Stark who becomes "Iron-Man" when he is wearing his armored iron suit of advance technology in the Marvel movies and still, you will feel inferior when compared to a race of supermen not from the planet Krypton but from the earth that can't be killed, can float like the clouds and fly like the birds naturally that is stronger than the "Hulk" or stronger than Samson and Samson was stronger than the "Hulk" because Samson had the infinite power of God in him, and they will have the advance abilities of being a pure telepath that can do anything that he can imagine in his mind. The Holy Bible has recorded that the white Gentiles will give up all of their advance technology or bring all of the mighty forces of the white Gentiles to the people of God for evolutionary development. This was the message and great gospel of Jesus who was Yahawahshi in biblical days. Yahawahshi preached and told His disciples to preach about the Kingdom of God coming to the earth and all of the power and abilities the people of God will have. Last time, the white Gentiles were found unworthy to live with the people of God and with God in the Kingdom of God. They asked for a second chance to prove themselves worthy to continue to exist with the people of God in the greatest Kingdom to ever exist in the universe. Isaiah 60: 11, Matthew 4: 17, Mark 1: 14-15, Matthew 6: 33, Matthew 10: 7-8 and Luke 9: 2

# 13

# The white Gentiles are Psychotic or out of touch with reality

Now, at this end, when the white Gentiles have proven themselves unworthy to continue to exist with the people of God again for the second time, they have become psychotic or out of touch with reality. They have made up their own history.

They say that God do not exist, there were no advance ancient black dominions on the earth before the Greek and Roman dominions, that the Greeks dominion was the mother of the western civilization of today ignoring Egypt, Assyria, Babylon and Persia and they are saying that they are the only intelligent life in the universe or on the Tree of Life. They say that the people of God that gave them their second chance on the people of the old dominion planet are inferior to them and should be their slaves. Now, since they have been found unworthy again, they say that the Most-High is wrong and for here on they want to be like the Most-High. They say in their hearts or in their movies that they will ascend into heaven and will exalt the white Gentiles throne above the Stars of God. Isaiah 14: 13 and Star Trek series

In the Throne Room in Heaven where there are twenty- four thrones of Elders Gods around the Throne of the Most-High God who is called the Ancient of Days or Him who is the Eldest and has lived the longest, the white Gentiles who are a young race that is being helped by the old African human race say that they want to sit at the mount or the head of the table in the throne room on the side of the north or on the side of the young white people from the north and they will be like the Most-High. The human race is not a young race but is an ancient race. It is the old black African dominion which is an ancient race and it is their ancient ruins that are being found today. The white race is a young race. This is a young race created by the Fallen Angels for service and body replacement parts that was to be destroyed when no longer needed. They were Paleolithic, brute beasts made to be destroyed that were helped by the people of God and now they want to sit in the throne room representing themselves and be like the Most-High. When the young white race was in their Paleolithic period known as the "Old Stone age" when white cavemen were starting to use tools, the African Olmecs, who had been here on the planet earth when the earth had just one large continent named Pangea and later, all of the old black Africans that were in Lemuria, Atlantis, Sumer, Egypt, Babylon, Assyria, Persia all were great ancient black kingdoms with powers and abilities far beyond today's dominion of "Iron and Clay". Revelation 4: 4-11, Isaiah 14: 13, Daniel 7: 9, Daniel 7: 22 and 2 Peter 2: 12

The people from the old black African dominion requested that the genetically engineered replicated creatures be spared and given a dominion on their planet earth to prove themselves worthy to continue to exist because they were created to look so much like man. They were called "Mankind" or a kind of a man meaning not a man but a creature that closely resembles the true man. The true man or the original man is the black man. They were a "Replication" of the black man. Because they were a young race, they were called

Boys and Girls and not Men and Women. Boys and Girls are not a reference of young children or a male child or a female child. It is a reference to a young race of people that are not Men and Women because they are young. The young race was called Boys and Girls until the fullness of the Gentiles comes in or until the white Gentiles had reached a certain amount of maturity or evolutionary growth and development. The young wild olive tree who is the white Gentiles who are the Tares spoke of in the Holy Bible that were mixed in among the people of God from the old black African dominion must understand that they were grafted in among the people of the earth to be partakers of the root or planet that belong to the people of the old black African dominion. Do not boast against the people of the old black African dominion and remember, you do not support the root or planet, but the root or planet supports you and that root or planet belongs to the people of the old black African dominion. Romans 11: 25, Romans 11: 24, Matthew 13: 25-30 and Romans 11: 17-18

The genetically engineered creatures created out of a test tube that do not have a planet to dwell on declared that they are better than the natural people of the planet earth and because God is not own their side, they say that they want to represent themselves in the Throne Room of Heaven and even if they are young and white, they want to sit at the head of the table in the Throne Room of the Elders and the Ancient of Days who are those that have lived the longest. Revelation 4: 4, Daniel 7: 9 and Isaiah 14: 13

In the 1997 science fiction movie titled "Contact" with Jodie Foster, the white Gentiles said in their hearts or in their movie that they will be contacted by those who dwell in heaven and they will be given technology by with would allow a white gentile visitor to visit the dimension where heaven is and once there, the white gentile visitor is greeted by a white Gentile and is told that the old elder beings that created that dimension and use to control that dimension are gone and now the white gentiles are in control of that heavenly dimension. The white Gentiles are hoping that all of the ancient ascended beings die-out and leave the heavenly realm and the universe to the young white race. Isaiah 14: 13-14

Hollywood is destroying the white Gentiles by revealing what is in the white Gentiles hearts and God searches the hearts and minds of the Gentiles to determine if they are worthy to continue to exist. Revelation 2: 23

On the internet today, the white Gentiles interpretation of judgment day is that there will be a great hall for the White Throne of Judgment and all will be brought before the great white throne of judgment and a white Gentile will be god and he will pass judgment over all. They are saying that the white throne will be the entity that will judge all. (You Tube "The Great White Throne Judgment, what will it be like?")

This is a deception. There is no white throne of judgment in the throne room of Heaven. The young white throne itself will be judged at Judgment by the elders in the Throne Room of Heaven and found "Wanting" what is necessary to remain grafted on the Tree of Life and the white throne will be broken off from the Tree of Life and regressed and no place will be found for the great white throne in the future. The Holy Bible has recorded that "Heaven" and the "Earth" shall flee from the white Gentiles when "Heaven" is established on the earth. The white Gentiles are saying that in the future, Heaven and the earth will flee from the white throne and there will be no place for Heaven and the earth. Verse 11 of Revelation 20 is definitely not implying that there will be no Heaven or Earth found in the future because the book of Revelation is about Heaven being established on the Earth in the future. Revelation 20:

11 is talking about the white throne being judged and Cut Off or Broken off from the Tree of Life in the future and no place found for the great white throne as well as no place found for the people of the great white kingdom in the future because Heaven and the earth will flee from the white Gentiles. Prophecy is that God will make a new Heaven and a new earth, and the white Gentiles will have no part in the new kingdom. Revelation 4: 4, Daniel 5: 27, Romans 11: 22, Revelation 20: 11 and Revelation 21: 1-7

Remember, the Lamb in Heaven that will rule the universe as well as rule the New Kingdom that will be their Judge when judgment day comes is the color of brass (brown) that has been burned in a furnace (dark brown to black) with hair like sheep wool or nappy hair. All knees shall bend, and all tongues shall confess that the Lamb in Heaven is Lord. Revelation 1: 14-15, Revelation 5: 6-13, Revelation 12: 11, Revelation 13: 8 and Romans 14: 11

In all of the white Gentiles science fiction movies about the future and space travel, the white Gentiles are calling themselves Human Beings and are saying that it will be them that explores outer darkness or outer space in the future. September 5, 1977, NASA lounged Voyager 1 with a message to aliens in space that said the white Gentiles were the human beings on the planet earth. This was to deceive all in Heaven and space that the joining of the white Gentiles who are the tares of the earth that was put on the earth by the enemy to join with the people of the earth had occurred and now all on the earth were Human Beings knowing that they were still white. The white Gentiles and the people of the earth were supposed to grow together, and the white beings were to join with the people of the earth to become human beings, but the white beings stayed white. Now, at the time of the harvest of the earth, God will say to the reaper, "First gather together the tares and bind them in bundles to burn them but gather the wheat into God's barn". All on the planet earth were supposed to be Human beings that is why the white beings are calling themselves color-people or calling themselves human beings which means that they have a shade, color or tint in their flesh knowing that they are without color because they are white. Matthew 13: 24-30

Now, the children of God's kingdom were cast off the planet out into outer space or outer darkness for the sake of the white Gentiles in the white Gentiles dominion to give the white race a dominion on the earth. Matthew 8: 12

Being cast into "Outer-Darkness means that the advance old black Africans were forced to leave the earth and established a kingdom somewhere else in the universe. Before they were cast into "Outer-Darkness", they left a map of Orion Belt which was the star constellation that they were going to in the design of the Great Pyramids in Egypt. The three great pyramids in Giza, Egypt were constructed in the same formation as the three stars in the Orion Belt constellation. This was an indication to where they were going after they were cast into "Outer-Darkness" until the "Fullness" of the Gentiles comes in at the end of the age and then, they would be allowed to return to the earth along with God's angels. Jesus spoke of their return when Jesus said, "At the end of the age, the angels will come forth or will return and separate the wicked from among the just". Matthew 13: 49, Romans 11: 25 and Luke 21: 24

Not only will the angels come forth at the end of the age but the old dominion Olmecs who built all of the pyramids in South America left a calendar that dated the end of the age being on or around December 21, 2012. After that date, the old black Africans from the old black African dominion who were cast into "Outer-Darkness" away from the planet earth would also be allowed to return. Today, UFO sighting are at its highest. In 2017, the news media reported that the federal government has spotted UFO'S and jets have chased UFO'S. Because of what is going on in outer space and the return of the planet Nibiru, government disclosure or the revealing of extraterrestrial life should be close at hand but it's not.

The government will never reveal to the people of the earth that the government of the earth sold the earth out to the invaders for advance technology so the government and the super-rich could escape from the earth and go somewhere else before the return of God. That plan of abandoning the people of the earth is still in operation. All of the advance technology that the government says it has that is hundreds of years ahead of what the people of the earth are exposed to is only for the government elite to be used for their exodus away from the planet earth before the return of God. To admit that the aliens are here would be to open up and expose all that have happened and was done with the aliens by the government that would reveal their betrayal of the people of the earth for the government and the elite own survival. The government allow the people of the earth to be abducted, experimented on and imprison by the aliens so the government could receive advance technology from the aliens.

The white race has assumed the identity of the human race. The white race has ignored the black African dominions that came before the white Greek and white Roman dominions. When the Greeks and the Romans were living in caves, primitive, cold, and hungry; Egypt, Assyria, Babylon and Persia were great kingdoms. The white Gentiles are saying that the white Greek dominion is the mother of Western Civilization knowing all along that the black African dominions Egypt, Assyria, Babylon and Persia came before the Greek and Roman dominions and it was these advance black dominions who was Prometheus that gave the white dominions the knowledge of fire and is the mother of the Greek civilization as well as the mother of the Western Civilization or dominion that we live in today. Everything that the early Greek civilization learned and knew was from the old black civilization that came before it. Plato, who was a Greek philosopher, studied the old black African dominion to learn all that he could from the records left describing the cultures and knowledge of the old black Africans that were before the Greeks dominion and civilization. It was from Plato that the Greeks learned about Lemuria in the Pacific Ocean and Atlantis in the Atlantic Ocean which were mystical advance ancient black continents and civilizations with incredible powers and astonishing knowledge that were before the Greek dominion and civilization.

The white Gentiles are saying that they want to reorganize the heavenly throne room into an organization called the United Federation of Planets where they, the young white created race that has no planet will sit at the mount or head of the Federation as the Most-High calling themselves, "Starfleet". The white Gentiles are saying that they want to be God. The white Gentiles do not know God or the Son of God. That is why they do not worship God or the Son of God. They worship the image or picture of the upright Beast or the Beast that was made to walk upright known as Paleolithic man as Jesus, the son of God. If anyone worship this image or picture of the upright beast passing off as the son of God, he will be cursed by God. The young white gentile race from the Greek and Roman dominions which are from the last two dominions in the white Gentiles second chance worship a white gentile as God and the son of God. Isaiah 14: 13-14, 1 Thessalonians 4: 5, John 8: 19, John 15: 21, John 16: 2-3, 1 Corinthians 10: 20 and Revelation 14: 9-11

The white Gentiles are demanding an additional thousand years Reich on the earth. This is what World War Two and the "Third Reich" was about. In this additional thousand year Reich, they are hoping that they will recovered advance alien flying technology that have crashed on the earth that will be back engineered to discover how it works to give them a start and jump to travel in outer space or they are hoping that friendly extraterrestrials will befriend them and supply them with advance technology so they could expand into space and established colonies on other worlds away from the judgment of God to prevent from being judged for their actions on the earth and Cut Off from the Tree of Life and regressed into Neanderthal or Paleolithic or Cro-Magnon man. The white Gentiles and white Jews must know that without the people of God, damnation is a certainty for the white Jews and white Gentiles or those that wandered in the deserts, mountains and in caves of the earth. Without the people of God, the white Jews and white Gentiles will receive nothing that was promised. The white Gentiles are hoping that the Grey aliens who they call the Asgards will commit suicide because of a genetic problem but before they die, the grey aliens will give all of their technology to the white Gentiles. They have changed God's truth for a LIE (that they made up about themselves and about creation saying that they are the people of God) and now they worshiped and serve the "Creature" or Grey aliens for technology rather than the Creator. Hebrew 11: 38-40, (Stargate SG1 episode "Unending") and Romans 1: 25

It is recorded in prophecy that last time the white Gentiles space program failed, and they were brought down to hell to the sides of the pit. All who shall see the white Gentiles in the future shall narrowly look upon them and consider or say to themselves, "Is this the man that made the earth to tremble that did shake kingdoms". Depending on the individual white gentile judgment for his actions on the earth, will determine if that individual is regressed to Cro Magnon, Neanderthal or Paleolithic. The majority of the white Gentiles will be regressed so far back to Paleolithic man and become so unimportant in the future that people will barely or hardly look at them and people will say in their minds, "I can't believe that this man made the earth to tremble". Isaiah 14: 15-17 and 1968 Planet of the Apes with Charlton Heston

The white Gentiles must not say that this can't happen. This is why the white Gentiles must look at the old African race and the Afro Americans who were the pyramids builders in the past and look at them now and know that the same or worse will happen to the white Gentiles if the white Gentiles are broken off from the Tree of Life because they did not BEHOLD or CONSIDER everything that have happened or because they did not make that public declaration admitting who are the true people of God. To prevent from being Cut Off from the Tree of Life and regressed into the beast named Paleolithic, the white Gentiles must make that public declaration. Romans 11: 22

The white Gentiles must believe that this happened to the old black African dominion and to the Afro Americans and the white Gentiles must believe that God can do this. Understand, disbelief will get you broken off from the Tree of Life in a New York second. The old black African dominion did not believe that regression could happen to them, but it did. If God did not spare His own people for disbelief take heed white Gentiles that God will not spare you for disbelief either. The white Gentiles must also know that God has the ability to graft the people of God who are the ascendants of slaves who are the Afro Americans today back into the Tree of Life if they believe. It is written in prophecy that God will graft the people of God back into the Tree of Life and make a new covenant of love with them. All who see the people of God in the future will say the people of God is the seed that the Lord has Blessed. Roman 11: 20-23, Isaiah 54: 8-10 and Jeremiah 31: 31-34, Isaiah 54: 7-11, Isaiah 59: 21, Isaiah 61: 11, Isaiah 65: 24 and Isaiah 61: 8-9

Remember, the Afro Americans and the old black African dominion built the pyramids and the ancient structures to make a name for themselves before they were scattered in the white Gentiles dominion to show the new white Gentile race what the old black African race was capable of to warn the new white Gentile race that once a decree is made against you by God, there is nothing that you can do to change it. The old black African race was so advanced that anything that they wanted to do, they could do it and still, they could not fight God and prevent from losing their dominion on the earth. Genesis 11: 4 and Genesis 11: 6-9

# 14

# A Warning to the white Jews and white Gentiles

This regression of the old black Africans and the Afro Americans was a warning to the white Jews and white Gentiles of today that the regression of the white Jews and white Gentiles into Paleolithic was possible and to believe that it can be done. Teotihuacan, Puma Punku, Machi Picchu, Marca Wasi, Gobekli Tepe, Tiwanaku, Saksaywoman, Stone Henge, Tikal, Great Pyramids and all other ancient sites were built by the old black Africans dominions and not built by extraterrestrials as the Ancient Astronauts Theorists have suggested. The same massive carving of Africans and animals from Africa that are seen at Marca Wasi with extreme deterioration indicating that they were carved hundreds of thousands of years ago are also seen in the mountain rocks in Malibu, California. The Olmecs are seen in carving found in South America standing in a Stone Henge construction that is not broken but is complete illustrating that the Olmecs built Stone Henge in England as well. Those people who are possessed by demonic spirits who are behind the destruction of the white Gentiles will suppress this truth, so the white Gentiles could be broken off from the Tree of Life and regressed and used for body replacement parts as they were in the beginning. They say that the ancient ruins and the Pyramids were built by extraterrestrials and not built by the people of the old black African dominion. These possessed people do not want the Sons of God to reveal this truth to the white Gentiles. These evil, possessed people have prevented the Sons of God from revealing biblical prophecy to the white Gentiles to save the Gentiles and it is this action against the people of God that will result in the destruction of the white Jews and white Gentiles and the white throne being broken off from the Tree of Life.

As great as the ancient ruins and the pyramids are, they were built by the old black African dominions and by those who ancestors were slaves who are God's first born and chosen people who are the Afro Americans today and look at them now. This is proof of the power of the regression. This is proof that the regression can be done. The white Jews and white Gentiles must believe that it happened to the Afro Americans and believe that the same or worse will happen to the white Jews and white Gentiles if this time, the white Jews and white Gentiles are to be saved. Disbelief you get you "Cut-Off" from the Tree of Life. Letting the Ancient Astronaut Theorists deceived you to believe that extraterrestrials built the ancient ruins and built the pyramids will get you "Cut-Off" from the Tree of Life. If God spared not His natural branches or spared not His own people because of disbelief take heed white Jews and white Gentiles that God will not spare you two either because of disbelief. All must be "Beheld" or "Revealed" otherwise you also will be "Cut-Off". Do not suppress this truth. Exodus 1: 11, Exodus 4: 22 and Romans 11: 20-22

The white Jews and the white Gentiles of today must know that the Sons of God are the most important people in the white Gentiles dominion. God has sent them and commanded them to be a light for the Gentiles and to be for the Gentiles salvation from biblical days to

PRESENT to the ends of the earth. Those of the people of God who are sent who are alive today are still under that order or command. I can assure you that they will complete their mission. Acts 13: 47

This is why those who want to destroy the white Gentiles or want to have the white Gentiles delivered to the fallen angels or the Greys to be used as body replacement parts, so the Greys could create new vessels or bodies for disembodied ancient spirits have kept the people of God away from the white Roman Gentiles who have dominion today. The unbelieving white Jews who are assuming the Afro Americans identity must not stir up the white Gentiles against the Brethren or Brothers who are the Afro Americans today because of "Envy" as they did in biblical days. Acts 14: 2, Acts 13: 45 and Acts 17: 5

If the white Jews and the white Gentiles are Cut Off from the Tree of Life, they will be regressed into Paleolithic man and used by the Greys to make new vessels. The Sons of God must be allowed to manifest if salvation is to come to the Gentiles. That is how important the true people of God are to the white Gentiles who have dominion today. This is why it is extremely important that the white Gentiles who have dominion today know who IS RAEL (REAL) and who is not. The white Jews and white Gentiles salvation and survival depends on knowing this knowledge. Romans 11: 22

Even the creature or the Greys that controls the Gentiles is waiting for the manifestation of the Sons of God to be delivered from corruption. Father in Heaven, I decree and declare that the Sons of God are rising. Father in heaven in the name of your son Yahawahshi and by the request of the righteous that God send forth a modern-day Moses or a modern-day Peter as the "Deliverer" to the people to save the people, a modern-day Peter will be sent forth. Simon Peter was chosen by God to deliver the gospel to the white Jews and white

Gentiles in the latter-days. Because the ancient prophets are subject to the prophets or the ancient prophets will be in the latter-day prophets, him that will be possessed by the spirit of Simon Peter who will be called Simeon and called a "Nig er" (Nigg er) will make that delivery. Simeon the Niger and only Simion the Nigger will deliver the gospel to the white Jews and to the white Gentiles in the latter-days because God wants to take out of the white Jews and white Gentiles a people for God's name and for that cause, the words of the prophets or the Books of Simion are written and delivered. Romans 8: 19-21, (You Tube, "The Atomic Power of Prayer by Ambassador Cindy Trimm"), Acts 15: 7, 1 Corinthians 14: 32, Acts 13: 1 and Acts 15: 14-15

This is why Peter's basilica in Rome was built to receive him who would be possessed by the ancient spirit of Peter in the latter days that will show the white Gentiles the way to "Salvation". The ancient prophets are subject to the prophets or the ancient prophets will be in the latter-day prophets. Remember, in the beginning it was Simon who was surnamed Peter and was called "Simeon" and called a "Nig er" (Nigg er) that delivered the gospel to the white Jews and to the white Gentiles that God wants to take out of the white Jews and white Gentiles a people for God's name and since the end of the dominion shall be declared from what happened at the beginning of the dominion, at the end of the dominion it will be Simeon, the Niger and only Simion the Nigger that again delivers the gospel that God wants to take out of the white Jews and white Gentiles a people for God's name and for that cause and purpose, the words of the Prophets in the Books of Simion are written. If the white Gentiles who have dominion today put a white Gentile in Peter Basilica, they will not receive the message of salvation and if they don't receive the message of salvation, the white Jews and the white Gentiles are doomed. 1 Corinthians 14: 32, Acts 10: 5, Acts 13: 1, Isaiah 46: 10 and Acts 15: 14-15

To prevent from being Cut Off from the Tree of Life and regressed and your mind babbled as was done to the old black African dominion and the Afro Americans, the white Gentiles must permit the Sons of God to come forth and speak boldly to reveal the mystery of the gospel and the white Gentiles must make that public declaration beholding and considering everything that have happened otherwise, they too will be Cut Off and become worse than the old black Africans and the Afro Americans are. Genesis 11: 7-9, Ephesians 6: 19-20 and Romans 11: 22

It is because of these negative actions against the people of God especially the killing of the people of God because of their physical testimony that they look like the Son of God or the Lamb in Heaven that God will return to avenge His people. Revelation 6: 9 and Revelation 20: 4

Remember, Jesus, the Son of God or the Lamb in heaven is the color of brass (brown) that has been burned in a furnace (dark brown to black) with hair like sheep wool or nappy hair. The Shroud of Turin is a LIE and a FAKE. Revelation 1: 14-15

We are told that the coming of the Lord to avenge His people will bring the great earthquakes Revelation 6: 12-13

We are told that the coming of God will shake the heavens and the earth will be hit and knocked out of its place or knocked out of its orbit. We are told that the earth will reel to and fro like a drunkard. We are told that mountains and islands will be removed out of their place. Isaiah 13: 13, Isaiah 24: 20 and Revelation 6: 12-14

What in the world could cause this type of condition that the earth has been hit by something that has knocked the earth out of its orbit and has caused the earth to reel to and fro like a drunkard so bad that mountains and islands will be removed out of their place?

We are being told that a large object is approaching the earth that could cause all of this. This large object is called the coming of the Twelfth planet or the planet called Nibiru. It is believed that Nibiru will pass between the earth and the sun. The magnetic pull from a large body on the earth will be devastating causing the crust of the earth to move over the inside mantle of the earth. This will cause a polar flip. The moving of the earth's crust and a polar flip could explain the verses in the Holy Bible that speaks of the great worldwide earthquake and mountains and islands being moved out of their places. This can also explain the visual effect of the stars looking like they are falling to the earth. The moving of the earth's crust and a polar flip will also make it seem as if the sky is receding like a scroll when it is rolled up. Revelation 16: 20 and Revelation 6: 14

Large asteroids are being pulled along with this gigantic planet because of this planet's magnetic field. It is believed that one of these large asteroids is named Wormwood and will hit the earth and knock the earth out of its place or knock the earth out of its orbit around the sun. Many others will hit the sun and the moon causing the sun to be darken for a time. Isaiah 13: 13 and Revelation 8: 10-12

At this particular time, there is a warning to the white Jews and white Gentiles. Last time, the Kings or Presidents of the earth, the great men or illuminati, the rich men or the billionaires, the commanders or Generals and Admirals of the Military, the mighty men or soldiers, every slave and free man or black and white privates and sergeants and civilians hid themselves in the caves and rocks of the mountains or hid themselves in underground military complexes like Cheyenne Mountain and others and said to the mountains to fall on them and hid them from the face of Him who sits on the throne and from the wrath of the Lamb or they used explosives on the mountain tops to cause the top of the mountain to fall and cover the entrance of the complex to prevent anyone from entering the facility. They used explosives in the elevator shaft to prevent anyone from descending down to the lower levels and to the entrance to the facility command center. Revelation 6: 15-17

This event is so significant that Jesus brought it up before Jesus was nailed to the cross. Jesus said, "For indeed the day is coming in which the white Gentiles will say, 'Blessed are the barren, wombs that never bore, and breasts which never nursed" or blessed are those who could not have children naturally but had to use artificial insemination'. Then they will begin to say to the mountains, "Fall on us!" and to the hills, "Cover us!" Luke 23: 29-30

The white Gentiles will hide themselves in the caves, rocks of the mountains or in underground military complexes like Cheyenne Mountain and say to the mountain fall on them and hide them from the face of Him who sits on the throne and from the wrath of the Lamb, but it will be of no good use. The forces against them will use bombs equivalent to 200-500 mega-tons of nuclear energy capable of reaching the complex no matter how deep they may be in the earth.

Last time, many were killed, and many were trapped in the earth crust because of the tectonic plates of the earth moving so violently. Last time, the slaves or black soldiers that they brought with them, dug them up and out of these underground shelters that were turned into graves and led them to the sanctuary of the people of God for food, medical care and safety. The Gentiles shall come to the people of God light and kings to the brightness of the people of God rising. Isaiah 60: 3

The people of God shall break forth on the right hand and on the left and their seed shall inherit the Gentiles and make the desolate cities to be inhabited. Isaiah 54: 3

They that shall be of the people of God shall build the old waste places. They shall raise up the foundation of many generations and they shall be called, the repairer of the breach and the restorer of the path to dwell in. Isaiah 58: 12

Behold, darkness shall cover the earth and gross darkness the people, but the Lord shall arise upon His people and His glory shall be seen upon His people. Isaiah 60: 2

In the 1968 science fiction movie titled, "Planet of the Apes" with Charlton Heston, the white Gentiles referred to the people of God as being apes. The people of God were not genetically engineered from apes but were created by "black magic" or "black technology" or created by the "power of God" when God formed clay to make an image of man then blew His breath in it to make it come alive. The white Gentiles were genetically engineered from apes by the fallen angels. That is why if you shave the hair off of a monkey, the monkey has white skin and thin lips. Nowhere in the Holy Bible does it say that apes shall inherit the earth. The Holy Bible says that the ascendants of the slaves and the people of the old black African dominion will inherit the earth because they are the "Meek" in the white Gentiles dominions. In the movie Planet of the Apes, it is astonishing to think that Apes could evolve into beings that call talk and reason. Well, the evolutionary development given to the people of God who are the ascendants of the slaves will be a whole lot more astonishing. They will be transformed from human beings into Gods as God transformed Moses into a God over Pharaoh. Exodus 7: 1

They will be given new evolved, ascended bodies in the twinkling of their eyes that can float like the clouds and fly like the birds at low seeds and at high speed, they will move faster than today's fastest supersonic jets. Isaiah 60: 8

There will be no death for them or they will not be able to be killed. Like in the Superman movies, they will have bodies made harder than steel. Nothing will penetrate their flesh without their permission. They will be able to exist underwater and in outer-space without equipment. In the ascended bodies, they will possess instant healing of any damage to the bodies. Like with the X-Men character named "Wolverine", as fast as the flesh is destroyed, faster will the flesh be regenerated. Because not only will they have ascended bodies but because they will be eating fish out of the River of Life and drinking the water of the River of Life, their life energy will be so great that nothing in the universe will be able to drain it. The water from the River of Life will be so potent that every living thing that moves wherever the River go will live. Living beings throughout the universe will envy the people of God that dwell in New Jerusalem and envy the white Gentiles that dwell at the Outer-Court of New Jerusalem. The white Christian gentile will not be given New Jerusalem. If the white Gentiles are found worthy at judgment this time, they will be given the "Outer-Court" of the great new Kingdom named New Jerusalem. Because all life forms in the universe will want what the people of God have, the people of God will be given godlike powers to protect the earth where the throne of God and the thrown of the Son of God are on a planet that have a River of Life and Trees of Knowledge with streets made from pure gold. The Holy Bible has recorded that while the people of God are praying, they will receive what they are asking for instantaneously. Because there will be no death for them, they will be able to stand at the detonation point of an anti-matter explosion and survive the extreme heat and blast force of the explosion without their clothes be singed or burn as Shadrach,

Meshach and Abed-Nego did when they were thrown in the fiery furnace. Revelation 21: 3-4, Ezekiel 47: 9, Revelation 11: 2, Isaiah 65: 24 and Daniel 3: 19-25

No weapon formed in the universe will prosper against them and every tongue that shall rise against them in judgment, they shall condemn. This is the heritage of the servants of the Lord. Isaiah 54: 17

Anything that they can image will come true. Matthew 17: 20

All dominions throughout the universe shall serve and obey them. This is a done deal. The court that will decide who will receive the next dominion on the earth has made its choice and is now seated with nothing else to consider about the subject. The kingdom and dominion and the greatness of the kingdom under the whole heaven or throughout the universe shall be given to the people and the Saints who are those that are Sent of the Most-High. Daniel 7: 26-27

The people of God shall build the old wastes cities, not apes, and they shall raise up the former desolations and they shall repair the waste cities and the desolation of many generations. The Gentiles shall stand and feed the people of God flocks and the sons of the Gentiles shall be the people of God plowmen and their vinedressers. The people of God shall be named the Priest of the Lord as the Priors are the priest for the Ori in the Stargate movies. They shall spread the gospel of God which is the gospel of the origin of the species throughout the universe. Men shall call them the Ministers of our God. They shall eat the riches of the Gentiles and in the Gentiles glory, they shall boast themselves saying, "this was a German, or a American or a Russian or a Englishman but now he is tending to my garden. Isaiah 61: 4-6

For their shame in the white Gentiles dominions, they shall have double and for their confusion they shall rejoice in their portion or they shall be those who organize the beginning of a new and great kingdom that will never fall. Therefore, in their land they shall possess the double and everlasting joy shall be unto them. Isaiah 61: 7

Their seed shall be known among the Gentiles and their offspring among the people. All that see them shall acknowledge them that they are the seed which the Lord has blessed. They shall greatly rejoice in the Lord. Their soul shall be joyful in God for God has clothed them with the garments of salvation. God will cover them with the robe of righteousness. For as the earth bring forth her buds and as the garden cause the things that are sown in it to spring forth, so the Lord God will cause righteousness and praise to spring forth in them before all the nations. Isaiah 61: 9-11

The Gentiles shall see the people of God righteousness and all kings the people of God glory and the people of God shall be called by a new name which the mouth of the Lord shall name. The people of God shall also be a crown of glory in the hand of the Lord and a royal diadem in the hand of their God. The people of God shall be the epitome of the glory of God and everything that is glorified with God and at the top of everything that is called royal in the universe because they will represent God. The people of God shall be the work of God's hands that God may be glorified. No race in the universe will be more intelligent or more evolved on a physical, mental and spiritual level than the people of God. The kingdom and dominion, and the greatness of the kingdom under the whole heaven or throughout the universe shall be given to the people of the Most-High. All dominions throughout the universe will serve them. The people of God shall no more be termed Forsaken neither shall their land any more be termed Desolate, but they shall be called "Heph-zi-bah" which means God is delighted in them and their land called "Beu-lah" that the Gentiles call "Sham Bal-lah" that is a mispronunciation of "Sham Beu-lah" which is the capital city in the inner earth kingdom known as "Agartha", the land of advance beings. This inner earth Kingdom of advance beings will be given to the people of God. Isaiah 62: 2-4, Daniel 7: 26-27 and Isaiah 60: 21

This is why the inner earth beings underground in Antarctica wanted the Germans in War World Two to kill the Hebrews to prevent the Hebrews from inheriting their inner earth kingdom. When Hitler killed the white Jews instead because the white Jews would be the cause why Germany's economy collapsed as is predicted in this last dominion of "iron and clay" that will force this last dominion of "iron and clay" to adopt a new financial system whereby everyone will have to be marked on their hand or forehead to buy and sell and that mark will cause the worse plague the world will ever see and because the white Jews were passing off as the people of God, they would be the cause why there would be no place found for the great white throne in the future destroying Hitler's dream of a third Reich, Hitler went after the white Jews for Germany sake ignoring the interest of the underground aliens in Antarctica who were helping the Germans. The aliens abandon the Germans and insisted that the Germans return all of the aliens' technology to Antarctica after the war. Revelation 13: 16-17

The Gentiles shall call the people of God "The holy people", "The Redeemed of the Lord" and they shall be sought-out and called "A city not forsaken". Isaiah 62: 12

The people of God shall suck the milk of the Gentiles and shall suck the breast of kings and they shall know that God, the Lord am their Savior and their Redeemer. God is the mighty One of Jacob. Remember, this inheritance is so great that Esau wanted to steal Jacob inheritance by fighting with Jacob in the womb of the universe to be born first. God made it possible for Jacob to get his inheritance back from Esau then, God renamed Jacob to "Is Rael (real)" designating who was real and who the inheritance actually went to. Isaiah 60: 16

The people of God shall be all righteous. They shall inherit the land forever. They are the branch of God's planting and the work of God's hands that God may be glorified. Isaiah 60: 21

Gentile kings shall be the people of God nursing fathers and Gentile Queens shall be the people of God nursing mothers. Gentile kings and Queens shall bow down to the people of God with their face towards the earth and lick up the dust off the people of God feet and the people of God shall know that God is the Lord. Isaiah 49: 23

God has said that God will feed them that oppressed the people of God with their own flesh and they shall be drunken with their own blood as with sweet wine and all flesh shall know that God, the Lord is the people of God Savior and their Redeemer. He is the mighty One of Jacob. Isaiah 49: 26

Remember, all who take the mark of the beast to buy and sell shall be cursed by God and transformed into the walking dead zombies that today's movies are made about. A foul sore will develop in the spot where the mark to buy and sell was put on your hand and forehead that will cause great pain and to stop the pain, the Gentiles will have to "gnaw" or bite and chew on flesh, drinking blood like sweet wine to get relief from the pain. Revelation 14: 9-11, Revelation 16: 2 and Revelation 16: 10-11

For, behold, God will create a new heaven and a new earth, and the former shall not be remembered nor come into mind. Nothing about this world will be remembered in the New World. That is how much more the New World will be over the world we live in today. Nothing about this world will be of any importance or interest to the people in the World to Come. Evolving into ascended beings with powers and abilities far beyond those of normal men and learning about the miracles and power of God and the Son of God and New Jerusalem, which shall be a place of wonder, being established on the earth with Trees of Knowledge and a River of Life within it will supersede the thoughts and memories of the things of this world. No advance technology that is talked about today will be of any interest in the World to Come. In the World to Come, it will not be about advance technology but about evolutionary development and ascended beings with powers and abilities that will supersede any technology. Technology is used to give those without an ascended body, abilities that those with an ascended body have. With ascended bodies, you would need no technology. Evolutionary development in ascended bodies will transform normal men into Gods as God transformed Moses into a God over the Pharaoh of Egypt. They shall be transformed into Gods in the twinkling of their eyes. They shall be raised up into incorruptible beings that are given immortality then shall be brought to pass the saying that is written, "Death is swallowed up in victory". Revelation 21: 1-6, Exodus 7: 1, 1 Corinthians 15: 51-55,

Halleluyah, this is preaching the gospel of the Kingdom of God coming to the earth that Jesus told His disciples to preach. Only Jesus disciples will preach this gospel. Preaching this gospel give them the authority to heal the sick, cleanse the lepers, cast out demons and raise the dead. Matthew 4: 17, Matthew 10: 1, Matthew 10: 7-8, Luke 9: 2 and Luke 9: 60

Behold, I tell you a mystery. We shall not all sleep like the Negros who are in a state of Slumber, but we shall all be changed. In a moment, in the twinkling of an eye, at the last trumpet. For the trumpet will sound and the dead or Negro because Negro and Necro are the same word and Necro mean dead will be raise incorruptible, and we shall be changed. The white Jews and white Gentiles will be changed also. They will be "Cut-Off" from the Tree of Life and regressed into the Paleolithic creatures of their beginning if they do not make that public declaration beholding or revealing everything that have happened. Romans 11: 8, 1 Corinthians 15: 51-52 and Romans 11: 22

God shall create a new heaven and a new earth. New laws of physics will be created that permits the people of God to float like the clouds and fly like the birds to their windows, naturally. New laws of physics will be developed that will permit the spiritual realm to be established on the physical earth. Everything shall be new and astonishing. A new world that have people in it that can't be killed and can fly like the birds, naturally. This new world shall have trees of knowledge in it that eating from these trees will expand your consciousness and increase your knowledge. This new world shall have a river of life that drinking from this river will extend your lifespan and rejuvenate your body. They shall dwell in a new fascinated city named New Jerusalem whose top shall be fifteen hundred miles high, pass the thermosphere and exosphere of the planet. New Jerusalem shall have streets of pure gold smooth like transparent glass with precious stones like diamonds, peals, rubies and many more known and unknown stones spread all around the streets. New Jerusalem shall not look like the cities that the Gentiles envisions with steel and glass building with massive transportation systems or highways throughout the city. New Jerusalem shall look like the Garden of Eden with ascended beings living in nature or living in God because God and the Son of God will be the nature-energy that will engulf the entire complex and the people shall be one with the environment or one with nature or one with God. They will not be living in high rise buildings but shall be living in the nature of

God. Isaiah 65: 17-24, Revelation 21: 1, Isaiah 60: 8, Revelation 21: 16-21, Revelation 21: 22-23, and Revelation 22: 1-5

John describes New Jerusalem as a great and high mountain that had the glory of God in it with lights like precious stones. A great and high mountain made like to the nature of God. This great and high mountain that will be constructed like the Garden of Eden shall have ascended beings in it that can float like the clouds and fly like the birds to their windows in the forest or in the Garden. Huge, tall trees in the forest will be their dwelling places as was seen in the 2009 science fiction movie titled "Avatar". The glory of Lebanon shall be in New Jerusalem. The fir tree, the pine tree, and the box tree will be enormous to beautify the place of God's sanctuary and God will make the place of His feet glorious. Revelation 21: 10, and Isaiah 60: 13

There will be no need for business building because the people of New Jerusalem will not be engaged in business. They will be engaged in the worshipping of God, so their building constructions shall be conformed and designed for that purpose and not for business. The houses that they build shall be part of the nature of the planet and they shall be one with nature and the nature of the planet shall be God. In New Jerusalem, the people of God will never have to worry about business or the economy nor life itself. They will not worry about what to eat or what to drink nor about their bodies or what they shall put on. Jesus said, "look at the birds of the air, for they neither sow nor reap nor gather into barns, yet our heavenly Father feeds them". Like the birds, the people of God will fly all over the world and food and drink will be everywhere for them to consume. To them, the earth will be their home and restaurant. In ascended bodies, the people of God will sleep and rest anywhere on the earth in comfort. In ascended bodies and given immortality, the people of God will not rely on food and drink for nourishments to survive.

Given immortality, the people of God will need no substance to support their life. They will live forever without a demand for eating or drinking. Even if they do not need food and drink to survive, they will enjoy food and drink with the other life on the planet and throughout the universe. They too will enjoy the fruits from the Trees of Knowledge, and they will drink the water from the River of Life. They will never have to worry about clothing. Jesus said consider the lilies of the field, how they grow, they neither toil nor spin and yet I say to you that even Solomon in all his glory was not arrayed like one of these. Now if God so clothes the grass of the field, which today is, and tomorrow is thrown into the oven will God give much more to His people. In the Kingdom of God, all things shall be given to the people of God. Understand, just like the animals of God are not clothed, in the future, the people of God will not be clothed but will be covered in splendor, wonder, and glory of great magnificence and will appear as brilliance or braininess, brightness and wisdom to all who see them which will be greater than any clothing for a rich man. These people of God that will live forever may not have visible sex organs because sexual pleasures to drain their evolutionary energy will not be desired and people that is given everlasting life will not be worried about procreation because producing ascended being for them will be done by a totally new process. They will appear without manufacture clothing yet, they will be arrayed better than a rich man like Solomon. Matthew 6: 25-34

God will make all things new for them or new laws of physic will be created for them that will allow them to become a new species of life in the universe that cannot be killed and can float like the clouds and fly like the birds to their windows. All who see them will say that they are the seed that the Lord has blessed. Achilles, in Greek mythology was dip in the water of life and that water made him immortal. He could not be killed unless he was struck at his achilles tendon where he was held when he was deep in the water of life. Revelation 21: 4-5, Isaiah 60: 8 and Isaiah 61: 9

The stone or "Tare" or white Gentiles that the builders or God rejected that was put on the planet earth by the enemy or by the black Aryans from Aldebaran star system has become the chief cornerstone or has been given dominion. This is the Lord's doing and it is marvelous in our eyes. Therefore I say to you, "the kingdom of God will be taken from the people of God and given to a nation bearing the fruit or people of it. This is about the world or dominion being taken away from the old black Africans and dominion given to the young white Gentiles. Evolving the white Gentiles from apes to homosapiens whereas they could have dominion on the earth was marvelous in the eyes of the people of God because it was proof that evolving the people of God from men and women to gods was possible. Remember, God evolved Moses into a God over Pharaoh. God evolved apes into homosapiens. God will evolve the people of God from men and women into a new species of gods in the universe. Matthew 21: 42-43, Psalms 118: 22-23, Matthew 13: 24-30, and Exodus 7: 1

Ascending up the great mountain will be like walking in the Garden of Eden with trees that have fruit on them that can expand your consciousness as well as improve your health. There shall be waterfalls, lakes, rivers and streams that flows from the throne of God and the throne of the Son of God that will give life wherever it goes. Drinking of this water will give life and revive, revitalize, rejuvenate and invigorate old bodies making the body young and strong, stronger than it was before with enhance abilities and senses. Beautiful carved canyons and elaborate caves more intricate than the carving of Petra in Jordan will lead into the interior of the great mountain that cannot be described with words. Inside this great mountain shall be part of the higher spiritual dimensions where Heaven used to be before heaven was established on the earth. Inside shall reveal the matrix of the great and high mountain that will be unlike anything that have ever been experience in the three-dimensional universe. Inside shall reveal the matrix of a new world with new laws of physic whereby miracles are performed and experienced. Inside shall reveal the impossible being made possible as well as exposing you to all of the possibilities that could be made possible. Inside will be where physical objects used by the ascended beings will be constructed. Spaceships that can carry none ascended beings will be built there. These ships will be used when ascended beings take none ascended beings with them on deep space flight in the outer-darkness of the universe. The rocks, dirt and grass on the ground will sparkle with life like precious stones. With ascended bodies, they shall control the environment of their homes wherever their homes shall be.

There will be no need for airplanes and cars and highways to transport the citizens from place to place because the citizens in New Jerusalem will be able to float like the clouds and fly like the birds to their windows. They will possess the power to teleport themselves anywhere in the universe by thought alone as did Jesus when Jesus teleported Himself and His disciples from a boat in the water to dry land instantly. The white Gentiles that will dwell at the "Outer-Court" of this great new city will not need cars, planes and trains to transport themselves. They shall enjoy the miracles and wonders of New Jerusalem. Flying carpets given to them by the people of God in New Jerusalem shall be used to transport them from place to place as well as used to ascend to the higher levels of New Jerusalem that shall be fifteen hundred miles high. Eating from the Trees of Knowledge and drinking from the River of Life shall give the Gentiles there at the "Outer-Court" enormous physical powers including mental clarity from the expansion of their consciousness, physical strength and longevity without any disease or sickness. The future will not be about advance technology but will be about ascended bodies that can't be destroyed, never get sick or break-down, and can float like the clouds and fly like the birds. No technology nowhere in the universe will be equal to a new species of life that can't be killed and can do anything that their minds can conceive. Remember, the Holy Bible have recorded that the Gentiles will be running in and out of New Jerusalem for 42 months in God's time. Now, a day with the Lord is like a thousand years to us. 42 months with days in the month that are thousand years long will have the Gentiles in and out of New Jerusalem for an eternity. Those white Gentiles that join with the people of God and share in this inheritance shall be with the people of God in glory for a million years. This is why the white Gentiles and white Jews were given a second chance in the world we live in today to be part of this new kingdom. The Books of Simion are written to inform the white Jews and white Gentiles of this inheritance. Do not be deceived by the powers of this world to forfeit your place at the "Outer-Court" of New Jerusalem in the future because of your conceit today. Nothing in this world is more important than your second chance for salvation and what is promised in the world to come. We all shall die one day and in the existence after this life, we will be judged to determine who will inherit paradise with God. You will be so sorry in the existence after this life if you are found unworthy to be part of this new and everlasting godly kingdom that will definitely come to the earth. Remember, the Holy Bible has recorded that in the future, in the people of God dominion that will last forever, everyone that see the people of God will say the people of God is the seed that the Lord has blessed. They will also say those who are at the "Outer-Court" of New Jerusalem that are joined with the people of God are also blessed as well. John 6: 21, Revelation 11: 2, 2 Peter 3: 8, 2 Corinthians 5: 10, Daniel 2: 44, Daniel 7: 27and Isaiah 61: 9

The people of God shall build houses and inhabit them, and they shall plant vineyards and eat the fruit of them. They shall not build, and another inhabit. They shall not plant, and another eat for as the days of a tree are the days of my people and mine elect shall long enjoy the works of their hands. They shall not labor in vain nor bring forth for trouble for they are the seed of the blessed of the Lord and their offspring with them. It shall come to pass that before they call, God will hear and while they are yet speaking, God will answer. This is the gospel of the Kingdom of God is at hand or is coming to the earth. Isaiah 65: 22-24

For the nation and kingdom that will not serve the people of God shall perish. Those nations shall be utterly destroyed. The sons of them that afflicted the people of God shall come bending unto the people of God and all those that despised the people of God shall bow themselves down at the soles of the people of God feet and they shall call the people of God, "The city of the Lord, The Zion of the Holy One of Israel. Whereas the people of God have been forsaken and hated so that no man went through them or wanted to be with them, God will make them an eternal excellency and a joy of many generations. Isaiah 60: 12-15

As for God, this is God's covenant with His people. God spirit that is upon them and God's words which God will put in their mouth shall not depart out of their mouth nor out of the mouth of their seed nor out of the mouth of their seed's seed said the Lord from henceforth and forever. Isaiah 59: 21

For a small moment have God forsaken His people, but with great mercies will God gather His people. In a little wrath God hid His face from His people for a moment, but with everlasting kindness will God have mercy on His people said the Lord, their Redeemer. For the mountains shall depart and the hills be removed but God kindness shall not depart from His people neither shall the covenant of God's peace be removed said the Lord that have mercy on His people. Isaiah 54: 7-10

# 15

# The Sanctuary

Because of what the white Gentiles and white Jews have done to the people of God, a Penance must be paid. Last time at judgment, the white Gentiles and white Jews agreed that a Penance would be made, and this Penance would also be the way to salvation for the white Jews and for the white Gentiles. Remember, for the white Jews and white Gentiles to receive help in the FUTURE, the white Jews and white Gentiles must HELP the people of God NOW. The fate of the white Jews and white Gentiles are connected to the fate of the people of God. It is written that double will happen to the white Jews and white Gentiles that happened to the people of God. Now, that is double the curses or double the blessing. Only at God's people sanctuary will the white Jews and white Gentiles be saved as the Egyptians were saved in Goshen when the spirit of death killed the first born of every house in Egypt. It is recorded in the Holy Bible that when our Lord returns, the heavens and the earth will shake but the Lord will be a shelter for his people and the strength of the children of Israel. When the poles shift because of the return of our Lord, if the white Jews and the white Gentiles are to be saved, they must be with the people of God at the sanctuary and to be at the sanctuary, the white Jews and white Gentiles must honor their oath they made last time at judgment to pay that Penance. Revelation 18: 6 and Joel 3: 16

There at the Sanctuary, supplications, prayers and intercessions will be made for all men including Kings and all who are in authority or the Illuminati. This is not the government FEMA concentration camps but a Sanctuary for the people of God and for God because God Himself will dwell in them and walk with them there at the Sanctuary. Only at a true Sanctuary can intercessions be made for Kings and all who are in authority or the Illuminati. There at the Sanctuary, the people of God would live quiet and peaceful lives in godliness and reverence for this is good and acceptable in the sight of God our Savior who desires all men to be saved and to come to the knowledge of the truth. Only at the Sanctuary for the true people of God can Kings and all who have authority be SAVED and come to the Knowledge of the Truth. It is because of this that the royalty of England has joined with an Afro Americans in marriage. Prince Harry of England married Meghan Markle who is an Afro American. Afro American DNA which is the DNA of the Slaves will be mixed with the DNA of the royalty of England. 1 Timothy 2: 1-4, 2 Corinthian 6: 16-17 and Revelation 21: 3

When the poles shifts, one sanctuary for the true people of God is worth all of the space ships and underground shelters that the white Gentiles are building to survive what will come to the earth. Only at a Sanctuary where the people of God are living quiet and peaceful lives can intercession be made for Kings and all in authority to be SAVED because doing this for the true people of God will be GOOD and ACCEPTABLE in the sight of God who desires all men to be SAVED and come to the knowledge of the truth. Remember, the second beast that will look like a lamb or look like one of God's people of peace and the false prophet or those who deceived the white gentiles who have dominion today that they were the people of God that knew the prophesies of the God of Abraham space ships leaving the earth will be thrown into the Lake of Fire or thrown into the Sun and Kings, great men, the rich men, the commanders and the mighty hiding in top quality underground shelters including inside of the Cheyenne Mountain complex will not survive. To be saved, they must be at the Sanctuary for the true people of God. 1 Timothy 2: 1-4, Revelation 19: 20 and Revelation 6: 15-17

There at the sanctuary, Kings and all who are in authority would be saved as the Egyptians were saved in Goshen when the spirit of death killed the first born in Egypt. Being at the Sanctuary with the true people of God was the Gentiles back up plan if all else failed. Knowing that a Sanctuary must be established, the people of Satan will deceive the white Gentiles who have dominion today to give away their nation to their neighbor in sanctuaries for illegal immigrants instead of establishing the Sanctuary for the people of God that will also save kings and all in authority including the Illuminati. The destruction of the white Gentiles nation in the latter-days by the giving away of the white Gentiles nation to their neighbors is prophesied in the Holy Bible. "Peres", your kingdom has been divided and given to your neighbors. The white Gentiles who have dominion today in America have gave away Texas, New Mexico, Arizona, California, Nevada, Oregon, and Washington to their neighbor who they call illegal immigrants and these illegal immigrants in sanctuary cities in America fly's the Mexican flag there and not the American flag. The languish spoke there is not English but Spanish. The Sanctuary for the people of God must be built. The Sanctuary for the people of God was supplied with everything that the people of God and Kings and all in authority would need to survive. The Sanctuary was built in the best possible location by the ocean or on top of a mountain and in the Sanctuary, were mountains, lakes, valleys and streams. God will dwell on the mountain, be the calm in the lakes and streams and be the smooth wind in the valley. God has promised to dwell in His people and walk among them when His people come out from among the heathens and be separate at the Sanctuary. 1 Timothy 2: 1-4, Daniel 5: 28, Ezekiel 43: 7 and 2 Corinthians 6: 16-17

The Sanctuary for the people of God is more important than building the latter-day Solomon temple in Jerusalem to contact the Most-High. The Most-High will not be at the latter-day temple of Solomon built in Jerusalem for the white Gentiles to communicate with God. Building the latter-day temple in Jerusalem for the white Gentiles will destroy the white Gentiles and bring forth the end of the white Gentiles dominion. Therefore, when you see the white Gentiles or the abomination of desolations spoken of by Daniel the prophet standing in the holy place or temple of God you must flee to the mountains. For then there will be great tribulations such has not been seen since the beginning of the world until this time nor ever shall be. If the white Gentiles want to make a latter-day communication with God, they must be at the Sanctuary with the people of God because God will be there at the Sanctuary in His people and walking among them. Ezekiel 43: 7, 2 Corinthians 6: 16-17 and Matthew 24: 15-21

There at the Sanctuary INTERCESSIONS will be made because the people of God will live quiet and peaceful lives in all godliness and reverence for this is good and acceptable in the sight of God who desires all men to be saved and to come to the knowledge of the truth. The white Gentiles must understand that this is the only way to be saved and come to the knowledge of the truth. 1 Timothy 2: 1-4

There at the Sanctuary, intercessions will be made for all men including Kings and all in authority. To be saved and come to the knowledge of the truth, the white Gentiles must be at the Sanctuary with the people of God. 1 Timothy 2: 1-4

The Heavens and the earth will shake but the Lord will be a shelter for His people and the strength of the children of Israel there at the Sanctuary. Joel 3: 16

This is why it is important that the white Gentiles who have dominion today know who IS RAEL (REAL) and who is not because the Gentiles will go to the true people of God for help and to survive all that will come to the earth because of the coming of their Lord and the last thing the Gentiles should want to do this time is kill the people of God just before God returns to gather His people.

During this earth-wide earthquake, the Son of Man will be seen in the sky returning on the clouds of heaven with power and great glory to gather his people. The mountains melted like wax before the presence of the Lord or the mountains and islands were moved out their place because the coming of the Lord caused the polar shift and the polar shift caused the world- wide earthquake. Matthew 24: 30 and Psalm 97: 5

And the Son of man will send his angels with a great sound of a trumpet and they will gather together his elect from the four winds. The Afro Americans are those who are being scattered in the latter-days when God has promised to return and gather His people that are being scattered. Matthew 24: 31

Shiloh is him who will be seen on the clouds with great glory and it is he who will be the one with the Lord who will gather the people. Genesis 49: 10

Shiloh is a fellow servant and a Brother from the Brethren who have the testimony of Jesus which is the spirit of prophecy. Revelation 19: 5-10

John was taken to heaven and shown the Marriage Supper of the Lamb with the earth. Remember, the Lamb is the color of brass (brown) that has been burned in a furnace (dark brown to black) with hair like sheep wool or nappy hair. Revelation 19: 7-10 and Revelation 1: 14-15

What the Angel wanted to show John was so dramatic for some one of John's evolutionary development at that time that the Angel gave John a Knowledge pill that instantly increased John understanding, so John could understand what the Angel was showing John and what the Angel was telling John. The Knowledge pill was like a One-A-Day Vitamin pill that we take today to supply ourselves with nutrition. John says the Knowledge pill was in the shape of a book and it was sweet on his tongue but bitter in his stomach. Like a One-A-Day Vitamin pill of today, the Knowledge pill had a candy coating over the bitter Cod-liver oil core. Revelation 10: 1-11

Think about that for a moment. Think about a pill that instantly increases your knowledge or the understanding. Ezekiel was given a similar pill that instantly gave him knowledge of what to do and say. Ezekiel 2: 10 and Ezekiel 3: 1-4

Now, understand, the latter-day deliverer is not sent to deliverer or gather the people of God. That's Shiloh mission. The latter-day deliverer mission is to deliver a profound message to the Gentiles to save the Gentiles. That is why Peter's basilica was built in Rome in the latter-days to receive him who would be sent to receive the message that would be delivered.

Those that Shiloh gathers at the time of the Rapture will be taken to the Lamb and will be with our Lord forever. For the Lord Himself will descend from Heaven with a shout with the voice of an Archangel (Shiloh) and with the trumpet of God and the Dead (Negro) in Christ will be raise first. Being dead is the term that describes those who are mentally, spiritually and morally dead in Jesus spiritual way of life for the sake of the Gentiles. Once those Negros that love God and God's way of life goes through the spiritual ritual being Baptized to be born again in water to receive the Holy Ghost, they are no longer dead or a Negro possessed by the spirit of "Stupor" which means they are "Stupid" with eyes that can't see and ears that can't hear but are new beings that were transformed by that baptism and now they understand and are no longer mentally, spiritually and morally dead Negros lost in sin and fornication but have been reborn into the children of God. They shall ascend into the clouds in the air and join the Lord and they will always be with the Lord. They will be taken to the marriage supper of the Lord and the earth. Genesis 49: 10, 1 Thessalonians 4: 16-17, Matthew 3: 11, Romans 11: 8 and Revelation 19: 7-9

The Christian ritual of being baptized to be a born-again Christian is really the Negro ritual of those who are dead when they are born for the sake of the Gentiles who have eyes that can't see and ears that can't hear who are possessed by the spirit of Stupor. Once baptized, they are born-again from the dead Negro point of mind who were lost in sin and fornication and now after their rebirth, they can see and can hear and can understand and no longer have the spirit of Stupor in them which means they were stupid. Negro and Necro are the same word and Necro mean dead. Jesus was the first born from the dead or born from the Negro because Negro means dead. Jesus said, "I know your works that you have a name that you are alive, but you are dead" or I know you have a name that means dead, but you are alive. That name is Negro because Negro and

Necro are the same word and Necro mean dead. Negro should be pronounced the same way you pronounce "negative" because "Neg" and "Nec" have the same sound. If you are not a Negro, you cannot be born-again because you are not mentally, spiritually and morally dead. Romans 11: 8, Revelation 1: 5 and Revelation 3: 1

In the 2009 movie titled Avatar, the people of A-Wah were identified as Negro when Jack Sully explained that the people of A-Wah are born twice. In their first birth, their actions are dead. The second birth is when they earn they right with the people. This is a Negro religious custom of today. The Negro is born twice. The first birth is called Dead or called Negro which means dead. Being called Negro means that when they are born, they are mentally, spiritually and morally dead. Once baptized, the Negro is reborn again from that mental, spiritual and moral dead consciousness and is now alive with eyes that can see and ears that can hear and he now understand and no longer has the spirit of Stupor in him. It is this second birth that the individual earns their right to be with the people as was portrayed in the movie Avatar.

Blessed are those who are called to the marriage supper of the Lamb because there at that gathering, they will receive everything including immortality. Revelation 19: 9

At the marriage supper of the Lamb to the earth, those who are gathered there at that event will be transformed into supermen and superwomen in the twinkling of their eye. The Dead or the Negro shall be raised incorruptible and given immortality. They will receive evolutionary growth and immortality in new ascended bodies that will enable them to float like the clouds and fly like the birds to their windows. 1 Corinthians 15: 51-55 and Isaiah 60: 8

Anything that they can imagine will come true. Absolutely nothing will be impossible for them to do, nothing. They will be able to heal all manners of disease, cast out demons, they will have power over serpents and scorpions or power over the extraterrestrials that are here now deceiving the Gentiles who true nature is that of serpents and scorpions or Insectoids and Reptilians and the people of the Lamb will be able to raise the dead. Matthew 17: 20 and Matthew 10: 8, Luke 9: 1, Luke 10: 19 and Mark 16: 17-18

They will leave with the Lamb and go somewhere that the Lamb has prepared for them since the foundation of the earth was laid. Jesus said that in His Father's house which is the universe, there are many mansions or beautiful, paradise planets. Jesus said that He was going to prepare a planet for his people that would be like a mansion. There on this new planet somewhere else, those who were at the marriage supper of the lamb shall live with the Lamb for a thousand years. John 14: 2-4, Matthew 25: 34, Revelation 20: 4-6 and 1 Thessalonians 4: 16-17

Satan shall be locked in the bottomless pit for a thousand years and the beast and the false prophet will be thrown into the Lake of Fire which is the sun forever when they try to leave the planet in spaceships to avoid judgment. Revelation 20: 1-2 and Revelation 19: 20

When the thousand years are complete, the Lamb and those who were at the marriage supper of the Lamb and the earth will return to the earth, so the Lamb could be with the earth. They will set up camp by the Beloved City which will be a city of those that dwelled on the earth for the thousand years that the Lamb was away that believe in God and the Son of God that worshipped God and the Son of God and waited patiently for the Lamb to return to the earth again. Revelation 20: 7-9

After the thousand years are complete, the devil will be released from his prison and he will go out and deceived the nations of the earth and negative beings throughout the universe will come to earth to join Satan to fight the final battle between good and evil to determine if this universe will be governed by the power of good or by the power of evil. The number of them will be like the sand of the sea. The sand grains around the oceans are more than the people of the earth but it can describe the endless beings in the universe that are manipulated by the power of Satan. Revelation 20: 7-9

In the 2009 movie titled, Avatar, the white Gentiles said in their hearts and minds or in that movie that they would be those from the bottomless pit or from outer space with women hair with the scorpion aircrafts with fire or guns in their tails led by the Dragon that would attack the people of God and burn down the Tree of Life that they called the "Tree of Souls". In that movie they deceived the white Gentiles to believe that the white Gentiles wearing their hair long like a woman or like the character "Thor" in the Marvel movies alone with the Dragon would be successful in burning down the Tree of Life. They are so wrong. Something will be burned down, but it will not be the Tree of Life but will be the Dragon and the scorpion aircrafts that attacked the Tree of Life. In the movie Avatar, the white Gentiles said that they would burn down the Tree of Life. The Holy Bible says, the white Gentiles with hair like women hair and their leader, the Dragon and the scorpion aircrafts will be burned down by supernatural fire from Heaven. In the movie, the white Gentiles said that they would go to the Halleluyah Mountains which is a reference to the God of the Holy Bible because Halleluyah means, "Praise Yah" who is the God of the Holy Bible. The diety for the native people in the movie Avatar was named "A Wah" which is the ancient Hebrew name of the God of the Holy Bible who ancient Hebrew name is Yah-A-Wah. The movie Avatar is about the white Gentiles fight against the God of the Holy Bible and the people of the God of the Holy Bible. The white Christians gentiles are being deceived by the false prophet or by Hollywood that is controlled by the false prophet. Revelation 9: 2-11 and (You Tube, The ancient Hebrew name of Jesus)

When Satan and Satan followers surround the camp of the Saints and the Beloved City in their scorpion aircrafts with fire or guns in their tails led by the Dragon as was portrayed in the movie Avatar, supernatural fire from God out of Heaven shall come down out of heaven and devour them. All the negative forces in the universe shall be destroyed on that day. Satan himself will be the only one that survive but Satan shall be thrown into the Lake of Fire which is the sun where the second beast and the false prophet are to be tormented day and night forever. Revelation 20: 9-10 and Revelation 19: 20

With Satan thrown into the lake of Fire with the second beast and the false prophet along with all of Satan mature followers that were burned up when they surrounded the Beloved City and the camp of the Saints, the universe shall be governed by the forces of good forever. The descendants of the evil ones that worshipped Satan will be without power and strength in their ways on the earth and throughout the universe. The supernatural force that gave their parents authority, strength and power with Satan will be gone. They will lose all confrontation with the people of God since the people of God supernatural force with God will be present and active in the people of God defense. It is recorded in the Holy Bible that while they are asking God for help, God will hear them and while they are praying, God will answer their prayers. No weapon formed against them will prosper. Isaiah 54: 15, Isaiah 65: 24 and Isaiah 54: 17

All of the people of God shall be righteous. They shall inherit the earth forever because they are the branch of God's planting and the works or creation of God hands so that God may be glorified throughout the universe. The Tares or white Gentiles that were thrown in among them, shall be burned. Isaiah 60: 21 and Matthew 13: 24-30

The kingdoms throughout the universe that will not serve the people of God shall be destroyed. The kingdom and the dominion and the greatness of the kingdom under the whole heaven or throughout the entire universe shall be given to the people of the saints of the Most-High whose kingdom is an everlasting kingdom and all dominions on any planet throughout the universe shall obey them and serve them. Isaiah 60: 12, Daniel 7: 18 and Daniel 7: 26-27

The judgment of the great white throne will happen next. Last time, the white Gentiles were found "Wanting" what was necessary to remain grafted on the Tree of Life and they were "Cut Off" or "Broken Off" and regressed into their primitive ancestors. There was no place found for the great white throne in the future. The beautiful new earth that was created by God and Heaven fled away from the face of the white Gentiles or God and all in Heaven wanted nothing to do with the white Gentiles. It is because of this that this time, the white gentile Jews and the white Roman gentiles sent a messenger from the future to the past, our present, to reveal a profound truth to them, so they would know what was going on, so they would know what to do to remain grafted on the Tree of Life. Remember, Jesus said that the white Jews and the white Gentiles did not know what they were doing. Romans 11: 22, Revelation 20: 11 and Luke 23: 34

The "Deliverer" mission is just to deliver the message or profound truth to them without offending them, so they could at least hear the delivered truth and not to try to make the white Jews and white Roman Gentiles believe or accept the delivered truth. The Deliverer mission is complete and was a success. The promise he made to him friends last time at judgement to deliver a truth to them to unravel the Mystery of the Gospel so they would know what is going on so they would know what to do to be saved has been fulfilled. The Books of Simion have been written and delivered. That delivery of the truth will set events in the Matrix of this world in motion that cannot be reversed, altered, or canceled that will result in the Kingdom of God returning to the earth regardless if the delivered truth is suppressed. Now, the white Gentiles must do what is in their hearts to prove that they are worthy or not worthy to remain grafted on the Tree of Life. God searches the hearts and minds to determine who are worthy. The white Jews and white Gentiles will not be persuaded, convinced, swayed or won over by arguments to accept the delivered truth. If the white Gentiles order, suggest, ask, request or hint around to that the delivered truth is not spoken or referred to again, the white Gentiles will be obeyed, and the delivered truth will not be spoken to them ever again. The truth to save the Gentiles will not be forced on the Gentiles. Jeremiah 17: 10 and Revelation 2: 23

The agreement with the Gentiles last time at judgment was to deliver the truth to the Gentiles only. The Gentiles promised that the "Deliverer" would be given "Utterance" to speak boldly to the Gentiles as he "Ought" to speak because the Gentiles are the ones who sent the deliverer to themselves this time, so they too could be saved. They would not have sent the deliverer to deliver a truth to them to save them and told the deliverer to speak softly to them and not boldly but to hesitate, waste-time and show fear when delivering the truth. Last time at judgment, the Gentiles screamed, "Speak boldly to us as you ought to because we sent you to us to reveal the mystery of the gospel to us, so we too could be saved". You are "Justified" to speak boldly to us. As for "Me", who is the one who is delivering this truth to you to save you and this applies only to the one who is delivering this message to you because the word "Me" was stressed, utterance must be given to Me, who is the one delivering the message, that I may speak boldly as I ought to for which I am an

Ambassador from the people of God to the throne of the Gentiles that must not be in chains but I must speak boldly as I ought to speak or as you agreed last time at judgment that you would allow Me to speak to save the Gentiles. I am "Justified". That is how important the truth is to the Gentiles in the latter days, so the Gentiles could be saved. Do not renege on this agreement. Ephesians 6: 18-20

Like God at judgement last time concerning those who would be sent that would be called Saints, who the Gentiles foreknew at judgement last time, they predestined to come to them this time in the latter days to deliver a profound truth. Moreover, whom they predestined last time to come to them this time in the latter days, will be called to come forth. He who is called and comes forth is justified in the latter days. He who is justified was glorified or given utterance to speak boldly as he ought to speak because you Gentiles sent the messenger that you would call a Saint. Romans 8: 29-30 and Ephesians 6: 18-20

Be watchful to this end with all perseverance and supplication for all the Saints that were Sent to come. Ephesians 6: 18

The Mystery of the Gospel is that "Blindness in Part" has happened to Israel meaning all of Israel are blind or have eyes that can't see and ears that can't hear to this very day except the "Elect". Romans 11: 25 and Romans 11: 8

The Elect will have a knowledge and understanding that the rest of Israel do not have. There will be an enormous difference between God's Elect compared to the Rappers and Hip-Hoppers that the Gentiles have created and produced in the people of God communities as they did in biblical days. In biblical days, the Gentiles elevated the low-life, the ignorant, and the sinful in the people of God communities to keep the people of God down by destroying their public image. Today, they have turned the low-life in the people of God into Rappers and Hip-Hoppers and Strippers that are lost in sin and fornication as were done in biblical days and today, it is done to justify a large police presence in the black community. As was done in the past, so is being done in the present. The Rappers and Hip-hoppers are wearing their pants low to uncover their "Buttocks". This is being done to shame their people and make their people afraid of them as it was done in biblical days. The Rappers and Hip-Hoppers have developed a culture whereby they are killing the people of God for the government as well as selling drugs to the people of God for the government to finance the government black projects. In the 2014 science fiction movie titled, Captain America, "the Winter Soldier", the Gentiles identified the part of the government that is responsible for producing crime in the black neighborhoods to justify a large police presence as "Hydra". The Gentiles must not be ignorant of this mystery, but they must be wise in their own conceit. 1 Kings 12: 31, 1 Kings 13: 33, Isaiah 20: 4-5 and Romans 11: 25

Now, it is important for the Gentiles to know that all in Heaven knows what the Gentiles are doing to the people of God. All in Heaven who have been killed by the Gentiles are crying out with a loud voice saying, "How long, O Lord, holy and true, until You judge and avenge our blood on those who dwell on the earth"? It is being said to them that they should rest a little while longer until both the number of their fellow servants and their brethren, who would be killed as they were (last time), was complete (this time) or who were killed last time are killed this time so all could be complete and justified for the Gentiles to be given blood to drink (like last time) for it is their just due for killing the people of God. They know. All in Heaven knows what the Gentiles are doing to the people of God. Revelation 6: 10-11 and Revelation 16: 6

It is the Deliverer mission to inform you that all in heaven knows what you are doing. Now, since you know that all in Heaven knows what you are doing, a total and radical alteration of your thought patterns must be performed to steer events in another direction to change the shape of the things that are prophesied to come to pass. You have been alerted. You sent the Deliverer to speak boldly to alert you of the things that shall come to pass so you would know what to do to be saved. You agreed that the Deliverer would be given utterance to speak boldly to reveal the Mystery of the Gospel. Do not renege on this agreement. Ephesians 6: 19-20

Once the Gentiles realize who Is Rael (Real) and who is not then, they will be able to recognize the elect of Is Rael. The elect will not have the spirit of Stupor in them meaning they are not stupid like the others in Is Rael (Real). Romans 11: 8

The Elect will have a knowledge and an understanding that the rest of Is Rael (Real), the magicians, the astrologers, the Chaldeans, and the soothsayers, which were the geniuses, don't have. The Gentiles logic, reasoning and wisdom, if they are not lost in their own conceit, will allow them to recognize the elect in Is Rael (Real). The Holy Bible has recorded that the elect will be ten times better than everyone else in the kingdom in all matters of wisdom and understanding. This is illustrated in the Books of Simion in the revealing of many suppressed truths as well as interpreting the Mystery of the Gospel. They were able to reveal to kings' what kings' adversaries were doing and planning in private council as well as in their bedrooms. Today, they are alerting kings about "Judgement Day" and what must be done to be saved. Remember, we all shall die one day and go before a judgement. Kings promoted them and gave them great wealth and made them chief over all others in the kingdom by making them third ruler in all of the realm. The elect will have an excellent spirit, knowledge, understanding in interpreting dreams, solving riddles, and explaining enigmas. It is because of this that the Books of Simion are written for Kings and all who are in Authority today, so their kingdoms are not destroyed by deception. Daniel 1: 20, Daniel 5: 11-12, Daniel 2: 48, Daniel 5: 16, Daniel 5: 29, 2 Kings 6: 8-12, 2 Corinthians 5: 10 and Ezra 4: 14-15

Who shall bring a charge against God's elect or those who were elected to be sent? It is God who justified him. It is God who chose who was elected to come to the Gentiles to offer them salvation. Romans 8: 33

God chose Simon who was surnamed Peter who was called Simeon and called a Nig er (Nigg er) to deliver a latter day profound message to the Gentiles that the Gentiles would believe because God wants to take out of the white gentile Jews and white Roman gentiles who have dominion today a people for God's name and for that cause and purpose the words of the prophets are written in the Books of Simion. Acts 15: 7, Acts 13: 1 and Acts 15: 14-15

Since the end of the dominion will be declared from the beginning of the dominion and in the beginning it was Simeon the Nig er who delivered the message to the white Jews and white Gentiles who have dominion today that God wants to take out of the white Jews and white Gentiles a people for God's name, at the end of the dominion it will be Simeon the Nig er and only Simion the Nigg er who will deliver the message to the Gentiles again that God wants to take out of the Gentiles a people for God's name and for that cause and purpose, the Books of Simion are written and delivered. He who deliver the latter-day message to the Gentiles will be possessed by the spirit of Simon Peter who was called Simeon and called a Nig er (Nigg er). Peter's Basilica in Rome was constructed to receive him who would be possessed by the spirit of Simon Peter in the latter-days who would deliver a profound message to the white Gentiles to save the white Jews and white Gentiles who have dominion today. The ancient prophets or subject to the prophets or the ancient prophets will be in the latter-day prophets. Isaiah 46: 10, Acts 13: 1, Acts 15: 14-15 and 1 Corinthians 14: 32

While the Gentiles are reading this translation of the gospel, a light will come on in their mind and suddenly they will say to themselves, "this Nig er (Nigg er) is revealing the suppressed truth". Remember, Simeon was called a Nig er (Nigg er) by the Gentiles and the Holy Bible has recorded the Simon Peter who was called Simeon and called a Nigg er (Nigg er) will tell you how to save all in your house. It is because of this that Peter's Basilica was built in Rome to receive him who would be possessed by the spirit of Simon Peter so the Gentiles could receive the latter-day message to save all in the Gentiles house or dominion. Acts 13: 1 and Acts 11: 12-14

The key to understanding who is sent is believing an unbelievable message. Once the Gentiles "believes" an unbelievable message that is so profound it could turn the world upside down then, they will know who the deliverer is. Then they will know who God chose a long time ago or before the world begun to deliver the word of the gospel to the Gentiles in the latter days so they could "Believe". They will not believe no one else but him who was chosen. Acts 17: 6, 2 Timothy 1: 9 and Acts 15: 7

The knowledge of this is recorded in the Gentiles conscience or DNA who would come and no one else on the planet will be able to give an understanding on this subject and suggest that they believe in something so profound it could turn the world upside down to save the white Jews and white Gentiles who have dominion today but him who was chosen. God has said by Peter's mouth only or him who would be possessed by the spirit of Simon Peter would the Gentiles hear the word of the gospel and "Believe". Acts 15: 7

He who is sent is well known to God because God chose and sent him and because you Gentiles agreed with that selection and ask who was selected to come to them without offending them no matter what was happening at the time, we know that him that was chosen and sent is also well known to you Gentiles in your conscience as well. 2 Corinthians 5: 11

This time, because of the delivered truth, the white Jews and white Roman Gentiles can steer events in another direction to prevent what is prophesied to come to pass to prevent the white Jews from judging themselves unworthy of everlasting life and to prevent no place found for the great white throne in the future if that is the white Jewish gentiles and white Roman gentiles' choice. Therefore, let it be known to you Gentiles that the salvation of God has been sent to the Gentiles and they will "Hear it". The "Deliverer" will accept the white Jews and white Gentiles final choices whatever those choices may be as being what is right and just for their kingdom and all who are in it. Only at judgment this time will the white Jews and white Gentiles have to answer for their choices and actions of today. Acts 13: 46, Revelation 20: 11, Acts 28: 28 and 2 Corinthians 5: 10

# The Kingdom of God comes to the Earth

In biblical days, the kingdom of God coming to the earth was so important that Jesus told his disciples to go out and preach the gospel of the kingdom of God coming to the earth in the future. No one else on the planet but those that were chosen before the world began will preach the gospel of the kingdom of God coming to the earth. No one else knows the message of our Savior Jesus who has abolished Death and brought Life and Immortality to light through the gospel to which I was appointed a preacher, an apostle and a teacher to the white Gentiles but those that were chosen by Jesus before the world began to deliver the message to the Gentiles. No white Gentile was chosen to deliver this message, but this message is delivered to the white Gentiles by those that are chosen by Jesus. The message put simply is that the impossible was finally approved in heaven and now the kingdom of God was at hand or now if you live a spiritual, righteous life, you can evolve into becoming godlike and given immortality along with godlike abilities that are similar to or like our Father abilities in heaven. Remember, our Father in heaven evolved Moses to such a level that God made Moses a God over Pharaoh.

# THE BOOKS OF SIMION

Matthew 4: 17, Matthew 6: 33, Matthew 10:7, Luke 9: 2, Mark 1: 14-15, 2 Timothy 1: 9-11 and Exodus 7: 1

The reason why we live in the world we live in today is to prove who are worthy to live in the greatest kingdom to ever exist anywhere in the omniverse. He who overcomes and is found worthy to live in this godly kingdom shall inherit all things and he shall be a son of God. The white Jews and white Gentiles say that they want to be the people of God, well, this is the way to accomplish that. The knowledge of this can bring "Salvation" to the Gentiles if they will hear it. Revelation 21: 7 and Acts 28: 28

God and the Son of God will be on the earth and the people of God will be given godlike powers. Because God want to take out of the white Gentiles a people for God's name, the white Gentiles were given a first chance in the world that was before this one and now a second chance in the world that God created man on this earth as well as given a white Greek and a white Roman dominion on the earth to be part of this great and everlasting kingdom. It is for this cause that the "Deliverer" is sent first to the white Jews to prevent the white Jews from judging themselves unworthy for eternal or everlasting life because they want to be the people of God so bad that they have assumed the identity of the true people of God and then, the "Deliverer" will go to the white Gentiles who have dominion today to prevent no place found for the great white throne in the future. Now, when the white Gentiles hears this they will be glad and glorified the word of the Lord and as many of the white Gentiles that are "Ordained" to eternal life this time because they believed last time, will believe again this time and the words of the Lord in the "Books of Simion" was "Published" throughout all the region. It is these "Ordain" or "Appointed" white Gentiles and more that God wants to take out of the white Gentiles a people for God's name and for that cause, the words of the Prophets or the Books of Simion are written. Deuteronomy 4: 32, Acts 13: 46, Romans 1: 16, Acts 18: 5-6, Revelation 20: 11, Acts 13: 48-49 and Acts 15: 14-15

This is the profound message that the white Gentiles wanted to be delivered to them in the latter days to ensure that they knew what was going on, so they would know what to do. Remember, Jesus said that the white Jews and the white Gentiles did not know what they were doing. Luke 23: 34

This delivered profound truth is what can bring "Salvation" to the white Jews and to the white Gentiles. God has commanded those that would be sent to be for the "Salvation" of the white Jews and white Gentiles from biblical days to "PRESENT" to the end of the earth because God want to take out of the Gentiles a people for God's name and for that cause, the words of the prophets or the Books of Simion are written. Acts 13: 47 and Acts 15: 14-15

Simon who was surname Peter and called Simeon and also called a "Nig er" or "Nigg er" delivered this message to the white Gentiles in biblical days and since the end of the dominion will be declared from what happened at the beginning of the dominion, Simon being called Simeon, the Nig er (Nigg er) and only Simion, the Nigg er will deliver this message to the white Gentiles again. It is for this cause that the Words of the Prophets or the Books of Simion are written. This is prophecy, and this is revealing the Mystery of the Gospel that must be spoken "Boldly" as it ought to be spoken by him who is delivering the Message of Truth to you. Act 10; 5, Acts 15: 14-15, Acts 13: 1, Isaiah 46: 10, 1 Corinthians 2: 7, Colossians 1: 26-27 and Ephesians 6: 19-20

Those that would be sent to save the Gentiles promised their friends that no matter what was happening at that time of delivery, the promised truth to save the Gentiles would be delivered. The command from our Father to be for the "Salvation" of the Gentiles from biblical days to "PRESENT" has been obeyed and the promised made to the Gentiles before the world began to deliver the message no matter what was happening has been fulfilled. The message has been delivered. Acts 13: 47 and 2 Timothy 1: 9

Then, the Kingdom of God will be established on the earth. God and the Son of God will have their thrones in New Jerusalem. A new Heaven and a new Earth will be created that will be unlike this planet or any other planet in the omniverse (universes within universes). The new Earth will not have the sea or the oceans. There will be waterfalls, rivers, lakes, ponds and streams but there will be no oceans or Sea. The River of Life will be there on the new earth that will flow from the throne of God and the throne of the Son of God. Revelation 22: 1

New Jerusalem will be beyond our present-day imagination. The length, breath and height of new Jerusalem will be all equal and they will be twelve thousand furlongs each. Twelve thousand furlongs is fifteen hundred miles in all directions. Fifteen hundred miles in height would put the top of New Jerusalem beyond the Troposphere and Stratosphere and far beyond the Mesosphere of earth's atmosphere deep in space. Can you imagine that? The technology behind something of this magnitude is mind baffling. John described New Jerusalem as being on a great and high mountain and the city laid out as a square that was fifteen hundred miles in height, breath and length. Revelation 21: 16 and Revelation 21: 10

New Jerusalem will be fifteen hundred miles tall, wide and long and that is just the physical dimensions of the New City. Mathematicians on the internet have calculated that a structure that is fifteen hundred miles high can have a level or floor every one-thousand feet or as high as a fifty story building and each level or floor with a radius of fifteen hundred miles wide and fifteen hundred miles long could have 7900 levels in it that would be equivalent to the land mass of eighty-one earths. Because the Kingdom of God will be on the earth and called "New Heaven", the new city will also reach into the higher dimensions that are more than a three dimensional solid existence where the "Kingdom of God" was before it was established on the earth when the Kingdom of God was within us in the universe in our minds as with the fourth dimension being in our minds that we travel to every night in our sleep or when we are unconscious and it will be called the foundations of the New City. (Youtube: The New Jerusalem-The Holy City bigger than you think), Isaiah 65: 17, Revelation 21: 1, Revelation 21: 19 and St. Luke 17: 21

These other twelve foundations or higher dimensions are described as looking like jasper, sapphire, chalcedony, emerald, sardonyx, sardius, chrysolite, berly, topaz, chrysoprase, jacinth and amethyst. In the Book of Revelation, John was taken to the Throne of God in Heaven in these higher dimensions. John said immediately he was in the spirit or out of his body and the Throne of God was like jasper and a sardius stone in appearance and there was a rainbow around the Throne in the appearance like emerald. Revelation 21: 11-20, Ezekiel 1: 28 and Revelation 4: 2-3

In the tenth foundation or tenth dimension or tenth Heaven, Enoch was taken before the face of the Lord. Enoch describes the face of the Lord as being ineffable, marvelous and very awful and very terrible. Enoch describes God's face being like iron made to glow in fire and to stand before the Lord face was like standing before a powerful blast furnace and the force and heat from the furnace was too great to gaze at or stand before.

Enoch said that he could not look directly at the Lord's face because of the force emanating from it so the Lord tells the angels to hold Enoch arms and legs and pry open Enoch eyes, so Enoch could take a good look at the Lord.

To travel to the higher dimensions, Enoch, Ezekiel and John had to be taken out of their earthly garments or body because only in the spirit in your dreams can you enter the higher dimensions in the universe in your mind. Remember, Jesus said that the kingdom of God is within you. Revelation 4: 2-3, (The book of the Secrets of Enoch, chapter 22) and Luke 17: 21

New Jerusalem will be fifteen hundred miles in all direction and parts of the city will reach deep into the "Dream" world of the higher dimensions where the Kingdom of God use to be before the Kingdom of God was established on the earth. Can you image that? Because Heaven will be on the earth, New Jerusalem will have areas in it that are part of the "Dream" world or the universe in our minds and travel from our three-dimensional solid universe to the higher dimensions in the heavenly universe in the spiritual universe in our minds will be made possible. Because of this, the people of God will be able to appear in their enemies' dreams and in their minds day or night. Luke 17: 21

Remember, the fourth dimension is not time as the white Gentile geniuses believe but is the "in and out" movement of our conscious from the physical universe to the spiritual universe in our minds where our conscious goes when we are asleep or unconscious. Remember, the first dimension is when we move from left to right. The second dimension is when we move from up to down and the third dimension is when we move from front to back. The fourth dimension is not time but is when we move in and out of the first three lower dimensions for rest and recuperation. Understand that first three dimensions are about movement, a verb and not time, a noun. The fourth dimension is also about movement. Movement in the fourth spiritual dimension in our minds every day for rest and recuperation allows us to continue to have movement in the first three lower physical dimensions. Luke 17: 21

New animals, new trees and waterfalls, lakes and rivers that will glow with the energy of life from the "River of Life" that will flow towards all waterfalls, lakes and rivers inside of the New City will engulf the inside of the New City. The energy emanating from the body of God and from the body of the Son of God will illuminate the entire complex. A source of pure, clean, unlimited, energy to be used to perform miracles will be available to the residents of New Jerusalem at all times. Because of this godly energy penetrating through everything, the animals or trees and plants will not be able to be killed or destroyed by no other race of people in the universe. No visitor shall come to the planet of the Lord and kill animals for food and the nutritional value of the food. Only the people of God will have control over the animals of the planet. Whereas no one else will be able to kill a fish and eat it, the people of God will cast their nets in the River of Life and catch many fish for their consumptions. No race will come to the planet of the Lord and feast on the animals of the planet without the permission and guidance of the people of God. Every living thing that moves wherever the river go, will live. The River of Life shall give all living creatures life and immortally whereas they can't be killed by normal people or weapons. Only the people of God will be able to take that life from the creatures on land and in the river. Eating the animals and fish that have drink the water of the River of Life will cure all disease, rejuvenate the body and extend the life span of all who consume these animals and fish for nourishment. Animals drinking from the River of Life will seem invincible to all other without ascended bodies. No one without an ascended body will be able to kill animals that have drink from the River of Life. The streets of the New City will be made of the finest and purest of gold and the stones around the streets and beside the new grass will be diamonds, pearls, rubies and sapphires. All of the precious stones of today will be normal rocks and stones in the New City. God has said that God will beautify the place of His sanctuary and He will make the place of His feet glorious. No planet anywhere in the omniverse will look better or be better than God's sanctuary on the new earth. Revelation 21: 22-23, Ezekiel 47: 9-10, Revelation 22: 1-2 and Isaiah 60: 13

A pure river of the water of Life, clear as crystal will proceed from the Throne of God and from the Throne of the Lamb that will be in the New City. In the middle of the streets and on either side of the River of the Water of Life will be Trees of Life or Trees of Knowledge which will bare twelve different fruit and each Tree yielding its fruits every month and the leaves of the Tree will be so valuable that they will be used by the nations outside of the New City for healing whole nations. Revelation 22: 1-2

There will be no Sea as we know our Oceans of today but there will be an accumulation of the water from the River of Life that will resemble the Sea that will be wide and deep coming from the valleys where the fishermen shall cast their nets and catch many fish. On both sides of the River of Life will be the Trees of Knowledge that will be used for food and medicine. Eating from these trees will expand your consciousness and cure all diseases. In their beginning, some from Judah shall smoke the leaves of the Trees of Knowledge for a deeper awareness and realization of their environment, bodies and capabilities. Remember, they will be given immortality whereas they cannot be killed and the ability to float like the clouds and fly like the birds naturally to their windows as well as the ability to travel anywhere in the universe preaching the gospel of the Kingdom of God. Their third-eye or pineal gland will be fully open and operational making it possible for them to see and experience all sorts of new things. Later, as time goes on in the ascended bodies, smoking the leaves from the Tree of Knowledge will no longer be desired. In their beginning, many times, they will sit down with each other smoking the leaves from the Trees of Knowledge in places on the earth that people have not been there in millions of years and they will fly in the deep canyons where the oceans or sea use to be and discover places to ponder in wonder about all that have been given to them. They will travel to parallel universe, other dimensions and even to the Vault of Heaven that lies beyond the vacuum of our universe space. They will discover new abilities that they have in their new ascended bodies every day. All who see them shall say that they are the seed that the Lord has blessed. They shall inherit all things and God will be their God and they shall be God's children. Revelation 21: 1, Ezekiel 47: 5, Ezekiel 47: 8-10, Ezekiel 47: 7, Ezekiel 47: 12, Revelation 22: 2, Revelation 21: 4, Isaiah 60: 8, Isaiah 61: 9, Revelation 21: 7 and Zechariah 8: 8

Remember, many of the nations that survive people will be still suffering from the conditions of the worse plague the world will ever see. Only the leaves from the Trees of Life will be able to save nations once sneaked out of the Holy City by the white Gentiles that were with the people of God at the "Sanctuary" that were given the "Outer Court" of the New City. These white Gentiles who were with the people of God will save millions of Gentiles on the outside and they will be honored above all other Gentiles in the world by the Gentiles because of their closeness to the people of God. It is them who will use the leaves of the Tree of Life to heal the gentile nations on the outside. Revelation 22: 1-2 and Revelation 11: 2

The white Gentiles on the outside shall be regressed into their primitive ancestors from Cro Magnon to Paleolithic man. The majority of the gentiles will be regressed into Paleolithic men and only a few will be Neanderthal, Cro Magnon and Homo sapiens. There will be stages of evolutionary development so some of the

Gentiles on the higher stages will know what happened to their people because of their iniquities. Because of this, the white Gentiles will come to the people of God light and gentile kings will come to the brightness of the people of God rising. Isaiah 60: 3

The gates of the New City shall be open continually. They shall not be shut day nor night that men may bring unto the people of God the forces of the Gentiles and that their kings may be bought. No gentile technology will be equal to the evolutionary development that the people of God will receive. To share in that evolution, the Gentile kings and queens will give all of their technology or forces to the people of God. Isaiah 60: 11

The gentile kings and queens will be bought with evolutionary development. Gentile kings and queens will give their lives and their love ones lives to the people of God to receive evolutionary development. The people of God will be able to touch the regressed gentiles and instantly evolve that individual from Paleolithic back to Homosapien if that individual is worthy. For this evolutionary jump, the Gentile kings shall bring the forces and wealth of the Gentiles to the New City. Kings and Queens will give everything to see their children and themselves evolved to homosapiens again at the Outer Court for the Gentiles instead of regressed into the paleolithic upright beasts. In biblical days, Peter and all the others that followed Jesus and believed in the Father and the Son were able to touch an individual and give that individual the power of the Holy Spirit to perform the miracles that Jesus performed. In biblical days, the Gentiles wanted to buy this power from the people of God, but this power cannot be bought with money or gold but only by the nature of the individual that have a desire to serve God and the Son of God. No amount of money or technology will be of any interest to the people of God who will evolve into ascended beings with godlike powers that live in a city with streets made from pure gold.

The people of God will transcend into a race of Supermen that can't be killed that can float like the clouds and fly like the birds to their windows. God will evolve the people of God from men and women into a new species of gods in the universe as God evolve Moses into a God over Pharaoh. All the people of God in the New City will be righteous. Acts 9: 36-41, Acts 9: 32-34, Acts 8: 14-20, Exodus 7: 1 and Isaiah 60: 21

The sons of them that afflicted the people of God or put the people of God in slavery shall come bending unto the people of God and all that despised the people of God or the Afro Americans shall bow themselves down at the soles of the people of God feet. Those that lead into captivity shall go into captivity. The Gentiles shall call the people of God, "The City of the Lord" and "The Zion of the Holy One of Israel". Revelation 13: 10 and Isaiah 60: 14

There shall be no NIGHT there in New Jerusalem. There will be no need for lamps or the light of the SUN or the MOON because the glory of God will illuminate the entire complex. Can you imagine that? Living in "nature" and being part of "nature" there in New Jerusalem will be living in God and being part of God. The essence of the environment there in New Jerusalem all will be of God. Everything about the kingdom to Come will be a wonder that is full of excitement and to live in the World to Come is more than we can ever imagine today. God says that there will be no more Crying or Sorrow or DEATH because God will make all things new or new laws of physics will be established that will allow all of this for the people of God to be possible for them. The streets of the city will be pure gold like transparent glass and with the people of God given the ability to float like the clouds and fly like the birds to their windows, the streets of New Jerusalem shall remain like transparent glass. Isaiah 65: 17, Revelation 21: 23-25, Revelation 21: 4, Revelation 21: 5, Revelation 21: 21 and Isaiah 60: 8

The Sun shall be no more the people of God light by day, neither for brightness shall the Moon give light unto them, but the Lord shall be their everlasting light and the days of their mourning shall be ended.

The people of God shall be all righteous and they shall inherit the land forever. They are the Branch of the Lord planting and the work or creation of God's own hand and they will be given everything so that God may be glorified. Isaiah 60: 19-21

There will be no temple in New Jerusalem for the Lord God Almighty and the Lamb will be its temple. The New City will have no need of the Sun or the Moon to shine in it for the glory of God will illuminate it and the Lamb shall be its light. These ascended disembodied Beings that will exist of pure energy will engulf the entire complex with light and the light emanating from their existence will replace the light from the sun and from the moon. Can you imagine that? This is a clean, pure, endless power source of an unknown nature that will generate power outputs in the extreme and this ability to generate extreme power levels will be capable of anything and everything with no pollution forever. Revelation 21: 22-23

The white Gentiles have imagined some beautiful cities in their movies of how they would like the future to be, but nothing can be compared to what is described in the Holy Bible concerning the New World and New Jerusalem, the Holy City. This is a new city that is fifteen hundred miles in all directions including in height with a new endless power source. The top of this new city will be above earth's stratosphere and mesosphere atmosphere deep in space. Can you imagine that? A city this high would definitely need people in it that can float like the clouds and fly like the birds to their windows because elevators as we know elevators today would be of no use there. The people of God will be given the ability to float like the clouds and fly like the birds to their windows. Isaiah 60: 8

This is the same ability that the ancient old dominion Africans had that occupied the cliff dwellings all over the world. Do not be deceived to believe that new dominion Anasazi primitive Indians built and used these cliff dwelling. The design of the inside of these cliff dwellings is not the design of Indians dwellings nowhere in the world. If it were, the Indians would have been using that design all over the Americas in their tribal villages of today and yesterday. The Indians tried to claim squatters right to the property when the Africans were "Cast Out" or Forced Out" into "Outer Darkness" or "Outer Space" because "Outer Darkness is "Outer Space" but they could not survive in the barren areas where the cliff dwellings were built because the cliff dwelling were built for those ancients that were hiding and did not want the new dominion people to be able to locate them. Once the Indians climb the cliff, they could not dwell there because there was no water close by and climbing down every day to supply the dwelling with what the people would need to live there was not practical. It was too difficult to climb down to hunt and then raise the catch up to the dwelling or to raise water up to the dwellings. The local Indians finally abandon their desire to dwell in the cliff dwellings, but they left their primitive jewelry there and bones of the old that were brought there but could not be removed from there because of the difficulty in the descending process. The Indians dwellings have always been in teepees made from animal hides. They have never had tools for carving large stones nor did they have the ability to elevate large stones in support positions in the dwellings. The ancient people who built the cliff dwellings had the ability to float like the clouds and fly to their windows like the birds and with this ability, they had the means by which to make the cliff dwellings possible and logical. Matthew 8: 12, Matthew 21: 43 and Isaiah 60: 8

It may be interesting to know that the "Negro" or those who are called "Dead" for the sake of the white Gentile dominion also built the ancient pyramids in South America and in Mexico. In the ancient city of Teotihuacan, the main road of the ancient city that runs from the Pyramid of the Sun to the Pyramid of the Moon is called the Avenue of the Dead which means the Avenue of the Negro because Negro means dead. All of the ancient pyramids in Mexico and in South America were built by the Olmecs. Like the children of Israel, these Olmecs from the old black African dominion were called "Negro" or called "Dead" in the white Gentile dominion but the Olmecs were also cast into "Outer Darkness" or "Outer Space". Matthew 8: 12

The old black African dominion was called dead in the white Gentile dominion for the sake of the Gentiles. All twelve tribes of Israel were called "Dead" or called "Negro". The Holy Bible has recorded that the "Whole House of Israel" were called "Dead" or called "Negro" or called the "Valley of Dried Dead Bones". There is no lost tribe of Israel. The whole house of Israel is called "Negro" or "Dead" today. This does not include the Puerto Ricans, Cubans, Jamaicans, Mexicans, Haitians, Hawaiians, Seminole, Panama, Columbians, Brazil, Dominicans or the American Indians as is believed by some Israelites who lack understanding. Only those that are called dead or called "Negro" who were slaves, oppressed, persecuted and scattered for four hundred years are the "Valley of the Dead Dried Bones" who are the "Whole house of Israel". Ezekiel 37: 11

There is no lost tribe of Israel. There is the lost sheep of Israel. The "Lost Sheep" is a term to describe these who have lost their way from the path of God. They are lost in sin and fornication because of the pleasures and comforts of this world. Jesus was the "Good Shephard" who job was to gather God's lost sheep and bring them back to the path of God. Jesus came into the world to lay down

His life for the lost Sheep of Israel and not for the world or for the white Gentiles. Jesus was sent to the lost sheep of Israel and not to the world or to the white Gentiles. Jesus told His disciples "Not" to go to the white Gentiles but to go to the lost sheep of Israel. Look at today's "Rappers" and "Hip-Hoppers" who are lost in sin and fornication. They are the "Lost Sheep" of Israel. Jesus was sent and told His disciples to go to these "Lost Sheep" of Israel only. John 10: 11-15, Matthew 10: 5-6 and Matthew 15: 24

The Olmecs left large statues and large curved heads of their features so the new white Gentile dominion would know who the Olmecs were and what the Olmecs had achieved. The ruins found at Tiwanaku and Puma Punku have an Olmec standing in front of what was built and destroyed with tears coming from his eyes. This is prophecy that the children from the old dominion or from the old black Africa kingdom shall be cast out into outer darkness which meant losing dominion and driven from the earth and there shall be weeping and gnashing of teeth. Many of the Olmecs statues show this weeping of their eyes including Serpent Mound in Ohio. Jesus said that it would be weeping and the gnashing of teeth. Matthew 8: 12

Zecharia Sitchin proved that it was the Olmecs who were the people to actually toil in the buildings of Teotihuacan's monuments structures and it was the Olmecs that established ceremonial centers elsewhere in Mexico. Zecharia Sitchin has recorded in his book titled, "The Lost Realms" that it was not Mayan Indians or no other Mexican Indians or Grey alien that built the pyramids in all of south America and in Mexico, but it was the black African Olmecs that were the extraterrestrial giants who brought civilization to the Americas. The only pyramids the Indians built were pyramid shaped teepees that the Indians used for housing. (The Lost Realms, chapter 3, page 44)

New Jerusalem is a New City with people in it that can float and fly naturally and cannot DIE or be KILLED and the city have Trees of Knowledge in it that when you eat from these Trees, you will expand your consciousness and a River of Water of Life in it that when you drink from this River or eat the fish in this River you will extend your life with all things in it made new from our old laws of physics with an endless power source of an unknown nature that will be capable of generating unbelievable power outputs that will be identified as the power of the universal God Himself whose main purpose is to be the God of those in the New City forever and those in the New City will serve God and honor this new, marvelous, and godly way of life there in New Jerusalem forever. Revelation 21: 6-7, Revelation 21: 22-23, Revelation 22: 1-5

Nothing evil or wicked will ever enter the New City. Only those that overcomes sin, fornication and wickedness shall inherit all things and God will be their God and they shall be God's children. Revelation 21: 7

The New City shall have twelve gates and, in each gate, will have something made like a pearl and each gate was one peal. Revelation 21: 21

What John saw was not pearls in the gates but were force fields radiating an energy screen that was in the shape of a pearl that everyone and everything have to pass through before they enter the New City. These force fields or energy screens were the essence of or supernatural energy output from twelve angels. The names on the gates were the names of the twelve tribes of Is Rael (Real). These angels or energy screens will detect anything that is not permitted in the New City and will instantly prevent and reject or repel the individual or object away from the entrance to the New City. If you have told a lie in the last seven days, you will not be able to enter the New City. This is a security system in place at every entrance of the complex that cannot fail. Everything will be scanned by this godly force field from your body to your mind. If you have told a lie, the barrier will know and prevent your entry. The scan will be so complete that even your beliefs will be known and if you are a disbeliever, you will not gain entrance to the facility. The cowardly, unbelieving, abominable, murderers, Sexually Immoral, sorcerers, idolaters and all LIARS shall never enter the New City. They will be stopped at the gates and will not be able to walk through the pearl and only those who are pure in heart will walk through the energy barrier that will resemble or appear as a pearl and gain entrance to the super complex. Revelation 21: 8, Revelation 21: 12 and Revelation 21: 27

There shall by no means or by no technology that will allow anyone or unclean thing that defiles or causes an abomination or lie enter the New City but only those who names are written in the Lamb's Book of Life. This barrier will never fail and shall last throughout eternity. Revelation 21: 27

It is because of this energy barrier which is the power of God that cannot be deceived or forced entry obtain by no technology that the gates to the New City shall be opened continually and the people inside of the New City will live in safety without fear of anything unworthy gaining entrance to their New City. This includes everything from something as small as viruses and bacteria to bullets and missiles. Isaiah 60: 11

This is mind baffling and beyond our imagination. Believe this author; you do not want to be on the outside of this New City sick, cold, hungry with a battery-operated heart looking for a "Tylenol" because of your pain and discomfort trying to survive with your present day evolutionary development while other people around you can "Fly" naturally, never get sick and cannot be "Killed" and they are in control of and are operating an unknown power source of endless power. All that see the people of God in the future will say that the people of God are the seed that the Lord has blessed. Isaiah 61: 8-9

The nations of those who are saved shall walk in New Jerusalem light and kings of the earth shall bring their glory and honor into it. The gates of the New City shall not be shut all Day and there will be no night there. No night there. Can you imagine that? Revelation 21: 24-27 and Isaiah 60: 11-14

The glory of the Lebanon shall be there, the fir tree, the pine tree to beautify the place of God's sanctuary and God will make the place of God's feet glorious. These trees will grow to tremendous size and configuration to be used for housing as was the "Tree of Souls" seen in the movie Avatar. The dwellings in these huge trees will only be for those with ascended bodies that can float like the clouds and fly like the birds to their windows. Revelation 21: 13

Gentile Kings and Queens will teach the "Negro" everything they need to know to become educated beings that will inherit the earth. Isaiah 49: 23 and Isaiah 60: 10-11

Gentiles Kings and Queens shall be bought to teach the people of God not with profits but with evolutionary development and to eat from the Tree of Knowledge to expand your consciousness and drink from the River of Life to live forever, Gentile Kings and Queens will bring the forces and riches of the Gentiles to the Holy City of the people of God and nations and kingdoms that will not serve the people of God will be wasted or destroyed. Revelation 21: 24-27 and Isaiah 60: 11-12

The (British) isles shall bring ships of silver and gold to the name of the Lord our God and to the Holy Ones of Israel. Isaiah 60: 9

This is how important Paradise will be and the white Gentiles will give all of their riches and bring all of their forces to the people of God, so the white Gentiles can share Paradise with the people of God.

Paradise is so important that the Sons of Perdition or the Sons of Hell or the Hellenistic white Greek Gentiles assumed the people of God identity to deceive the world that they are the people of this mighty inheritance to deliberately drive the other Gentiles or their competition away from inheriting the "Outer Court" of this Paradise with the hope that they will deceive God that they are God's people so they could receive God's people inheritance or the inheritance that will go to the white Gentiles who are "ORDAINED" or "Appointed" to eternal life this time because they believed last time. Acts 13: 48

The white Christian Gentiles must be informed that New Jerusalem will not be given to the white Christian gentiles as they believe today. On the internet, all references about New Jerusalem shows nothing but white Christian gentiles in New Jerusalem. White Christian gentiles believe that only white Christian gentiles will inhabit New Jerusalem. They are wrong. New Jerusalem will be given to those who were scattered, persecuted and enslaved in the white Gentile dominions. The "Meek" who are those that were "Slaves" will inherit the earth. It is the ascendance of the "Slaves" who shall inherit the earth, be joined with God and inhabit God's kingdom with God. Only the white Gentiles that are with the people of God will be at the "Outer Court" of this great New City. Remember, the "Outer Court" of this New Great City will be given to the Gentiles who "Believe" and they will be in and out of the Holy City with the people of God for forty-two months which will be a million years because a day with the Lord is a thousand years to us. Forty-two months with days in a month that are a thousand years long will have the Gentiles there in the "Outer Court" of God's Sanctuary for a million years. The white Gentiles that are chosen to share Paradise with the people of God will be with the people of God for almost an eternity. You do not want to be deceived and lose this inheritance. Revelation 11: 1-2, Ezekiel 40: 17-27 and 2 Peter 3: 8

The white Roman Gentiles who have dominion today must not be deceived, this time. The white gentile Jews and white Roman gentiles will not be joined with the Satanic Spock and the Vulcans which is a representation of the pointed ear "Pan" who was one of the fallen angel whose nature was not logic and reason but was chaos and mischief but will be joined with the people of God and there at the "Outer Court" Truth, logic, reason and understanding shall prevail. The white Gentiles shall come to the people of God light and gentile kings to the brightness of the people of God rising and not the rising of the people of the Synagogue of Satan. God will make those of the Synagogue of Satan come and worship before the feet of the true people of God, so they will know that God love the people of God. Revelation 11: 2, Isaiah 60: 3, Revelation 2: 9 and Revelation 3: 9

There at the "Outer Court" will the white Gentiles receive an inheritance with the people of God. There, the people of God will divide the land into lots as an inheritance for the people of God and for the strangers or Gentiles who dwell among the people of God. The strangers will be to the people of God as native-born or those born in the "Outer Court" among the children of Israel and they will be identified as those Gentiles who can be trusted which will be treated much different than the Gentiles on the outside and the strangers or these trusted Gentiles shall have an inheritance with the people of God among the tribes of Israel. It shall be that in whatever tribe the strangers' dwells, there the people of God shall give the strangers their inheritance. Revelation 11: 2, Ezekiel 47: 22-23

The exploration of space shall be done with the people of God and not with the people of Satan. Remember, the people of God were cast into "Outer Darkness" which is "Outer Space" because "Outer Darkness" is the way that the ancient people described "Outer Space". Matthew 8: 12

An alliance with the people of God to become "Human Beings" is the only thing that can save the white Gentiles. An alliance with the children of Satan from the Synagogue of Satan to remain white will destroy the white Gentiles and have the white Gentiles in the Valley of Jehoshaphat fighting God for the people of God inheritance. Revelation 2: 9, Revelation 3: 9 and Joel 3: 2

Ezekiel is shown the new city named New Jerusalem by a "Colored" man or a man the color of bronze or brown. The representative from God sent to reveal this knowledge to Ezekiel was not "White" but was "Brown". He tells Ezekiel to look with his eyes and hear with his ears and to fix his mind on everything that is shown to him and to "Declare to the House of Israel everything that he saw". "Halleluyah, Praise Yah", the author of this book is so glad that he is a "Colored Man". Ezekiel 40: 3-4

Ezekiel saw water flowing from under the threshold of the Throne of God and the Throne of the Son of God. Wherever this water flows will heal every living thing. There shall be a very great multitude of fish in the River and the River shall be very deep that cannot be crossed. Fishermen will spread their nets in the River and capture many fish. Can you imagine the nutritional value of these fish that come out of the "River of Life"? Ezekiel 47: 9-10, Ezekiel 47: 1-5

On both sides of the River will be Trees of all kinds used for food. The leaves of these Trees of Knowledge will not wither, and their fruit will not fail to satisfy your hunger and give to you the nutrition of knowledge, wisdom and understanding. Eating from these Trees will expand your consciousness making you smarter and wiser. This was demonstrated in the 1984 movie titled "Dune" when the characters of the movie would eat the "Spice Melange". In the Garden of Eden, eating from the Tree of Knowledge expanded Adam and Eve consciousness and their awareness. Instantly, when Adam and Eve ate from the Tree of Knowledge did they know and understand "right" from "wrong" or "good" and "evil". The Trees will bear fruit every month because their water flows from the sanctuary of God and the Son of God. The fruit from these Trees will be for food and the leaves for medicine. In mythology, three Tanna leaves could bring the dead back to life and nine Tanna leaves would give the dead movement. The leaves from the Trees of Knowledge will be a lot more potent. Genesis 2: 9, Genesis 3: 5-7, Ezekiel 47: 12, Revelation 22: 1-2 and 1942 horror classic titled "The Mummy's Tomb"

Remember, the people of God will not be able to be killed because there will be no death for them and they will be able to bring the dead back to life with a word. They will possess the power of "Life" and "Death". They will be able to sweep you out of existence with a word and with the wave of their hand, bring you back again. Nothing will be impossible for them to do, absolutely nothing. Revelation 21: 3-4 and Matthew 17: 20

In the dominion we live in today, it is about who can "kill" the most proficient. The threat of death is the motivating factor for control in this world. You do what the power structure demands, or you died. We are constantly threatened with death. In the next dominion of the people of God, the promise of "Life" will supersede the threat of death. In biblical days when Jesus walked the earth, Jesus was able to bring Lazarus back to life after Lazarus had died and his body had started to decay. Not only did Jesus have the power that the ancient Egyptians Gods did not have to bring the dead back from the underworld of the "land of the Dead" which was an ability that Seth and the other Egyptians Gods did not have but also Jesus was able to regenerate decayed flesh on a dead body and return the life force of that body back to the body. The universe will be controlled by people that can bring the dead back alive as Jesus and Jesus disciples did when Jesus walked the earth and when Jesus returns as the "Lamb of Heaven", Jesus and Jesus people will have this power again. The "River of Life" will allow an individual to live forever and the "Trees of Knowledge" will expand your consciousness and make you smarter as well as the leaves from these Trees will cure all diseases. The threat of being killed will be unimportant because the people of God will have the ability to bring you back to life even if your flesh body was totally destroyed. When the threat of death is no longer a motivating factor, the promise of the experience of ascended life will prevail and become the dominate motivating factor throughout the universe. It is not advance technology that will rule the universe tomorrow, but it will be highly evolved ascended beings that cannot be killed or catch diseases that can float like the clouds and fly like the birds that will supersede everything that the living beings throughout the universe can create because with the people of God, all things will be possible, and miracles will be performed. Moses opening the Red Sea in biblical was only a small example of the abilities the people of God will have in the future. Remember, all that see the people of God in the future will say, "Wow, these people are the seed that the Lord God has blessed". John 11: 40-44, Matthew 10: 7-8, Matthew 11: 5, Matthew 17: 20, Luke 17: 6, Mark 11: 22-24, Revelation 21: 4 and Isaiah 61: 9

The Kingdom and dominion and the greatness of the kingdoms under the whole heaven or throughout the universe shall be given to the people of the "Most-High". Their kingdom is an everlasting kingdom and all dominions no matter where the dominions are in the universe shall serve and obey them. The people of God shall travel throughout the universe spreading the Gospel of the Kingdom of God and all dominions, even on other planets, shall serve them. It is because of this that the white Gentiles will bring the forces of the Gentiles to the people of God to share in this glorious inheritance. Because the people of God cannot be killed and anything that they want to do and "Believe" that it will be done will be done for them even moving mountains, they will rule the universe and all who will not serve the people of God will be utterly destroyed. Nothing will be impossible for the people of God to do, absolutely nothing. Daniel 7: 27, Isaiah 60: 11-12 and Matthew 17: 20

The residents of the new city will be given TWO new elements that are not water, earth, wind or fire but is something else that is constructed from twelfth dimensional matter that is outside of our three-dimensional universe but have three dimensions of its twelve dimensions existing in our three-dimensional universe that will be utilized by those in the New City for comfort and security that the nations on the outside will not understand and cannot handle or destroy.

These two new elements will frighten the nations on the outside the way fire frighten the animals in the jungle. Once these two new elements are exposed or utilized on the outside, those on the outside will flee from these two new elements the way the animals in the jungle flees from fire.

Unknown radiating energy from these two new elements will sicken the white Gentiles on the outside of the great city and cause their brains and their five senses to falter or shut down leaving permanent brain damage. These two new elements will be able to reach out and touch the Gentiles hundreds of miles way.

These two new elements will be used for security and protection as well as used for comfort and inter-dimensional travel because these two new elements will be made of twelfth dimensional matter from Heaven and connected to twelve dimensions or connected to the dimension where Heaven use to be. As you look at these two new elements made like a Rod of Iron, you will see its height, its breadth, and its length which are the first three dimensions, but nine dimensions of these two new elements will be somewhere else, unseen but there.

The royal scepter that Kings and Queens carried on the earth in their kingdoms were a recreation of the power that will be in these two new elements made like a Rod of Iron. Kings and Queens royal scepters had no power but were symbolic to what would be given to the people of God in the future whose scepter made like a Rod of Iron will have infinite power to achieve all things. Like Thor's hammer, only the people of God will be able to lift and utilize the Rod of Iron power. Because only three dimensions of this twelfth dimensional material will be visible to this universe, no one else other than the people of God will be able to lift the people of God's Rod of Iron because nine dimensions of the Rod of Iron will be somewhere else that cannot be touched and only the people of God ascended bodies will be able reach into the nine unseen dimensions of the Rod of Iron nature to hold, grab and move the Rod of Iron.

In the science fiction movie series titled "Stargate-SG1, the Jaffa soldiers of the Gods carried a rod of iron staff with power. The white Gentiles misrepresented the power of the Jaffa staff of iron. The white Gentiles made it seem that the white Gentiles machined-guns were more powerful. The Holy Bible has recorded that the people of God Rod of Iron will have nuclear bomb potential because with the Rod of Iron, nations will be dashed to pieces as if a nuclear bomb had hit that nation. Revelation 2: 26-27, Psalm 2: 9 and Isaiah 60: 12

Because these two new elements will be connected to the fourth to twelfth dimensions, the people of God will be able to appear in the Gentiles dreams when the Gentiles are helpless because the fourth dimension is the dimension that our spirit travel to when we are asleep or unconscious. The Holy Bible has recorded that the people of God will rule nations with a rod of iron. Nations will be given to the people of God in their inheritance and the ends of the earth for their possession. With the Rod of Iron from the twelfth dimension, all who will not serve the people of God will be dashed to pieces like a potter's vessel. They shall be utterly destroyed. Revelation 2: 26-27, Psalm 2: 9 and Isaiah 60: 12

The fourth dimension is not time as the Gentile geniuses believe but is the "in and out" experience or movement of our conscious mind or self in the three-dimensional universe when we are asleep for rest and rejuvenation. Where our conscious goes when we are asleep is movement in the fourth dimension. Refusal to spend time in the spiritual fourth dimensional universe for rejuvenation will result in the termination of your life in the lower three physical dimensions that we have our physical existence in.

Remember, the first dimension is when we move from front to back. The second dimension is when you move from side to side. The third dimension is when you move from up to down. The fourth dimension is not "time" because "time" is not a movement and the first three dimensions are about movement from up to down, side to side and front to back. The fourth dimension is the movement when you move "in" and "out" of the first three dimensions for rejuvenation and rest in our sleep which is a necessary movement and purpose for life in the first three dimensions. It is the movement of entering your "Dreams" and in "Visions" in the universe of your "Mind" that is the fourth dimension where God will speak to you and guide you. It is there in the fourth dimension where you will find the Kingdom of God because the Kingdom of God is within you. Numbers 12: 6, Genesis 46: 2, Genesis 15: 1, Genesis 31: 11 and Luke 17: 21

For security and protection, the two new elements will generate an unknown impenetrable force field that is not electric or magnetic and it will also be able to place all who are inside of a radiating energy or force field of the two elements in the next frequency of our normal existence that will make those in the next frequencies visible but untouchable because they will not be there in that spot even if you can see them in that spot they will be somewhere else on another frequency and in another dimension just outside of our three dimensional universe frequency.

None of the Gentiles mechanical or electronic devices will work, if they have any, around these two new elements for hundreds of miles. It is because of these negative side effects on machines and devices and on those who do not have a new evolved ascended body that will make the Gentiles on the outside flee from these two new elements the way animals in the jungle flee from fire.

The people of God in New Jerusalem who do the Lord bidding will be given great power over the nations. Those who "Overcome" "Sin" and "Fornication" and is chosen to be a resident in New Jerusalem will "Rule" the nations on the outside of New Jerusalem with a "Rod" of "Iron" and this "Rod" of "Iron" from the twelfth dimension shall dashed to pieces like the potter's vessels people, places and things. The Gentiles shall flee from this "Rod" of "Iron" from the twelfth dimension the way animals in the jungle flee from fire. Revelation 2: 27 and Psalms 2: 9-11

Because these two new elements will be twelfth-dimensional matter that can exist in three-dimensional space, anything that is built from these two new elements will not be able to be moved or destroyed because only three dimensions of the new elements will be visible to the nations on the outside of the New City. Nine dimensions of the new elements will be somewhere else that cannot be seen, touched, moved or destroyed in our three-dimensional universe by no one who is not a resident of the Holy New City with an ascended body.

Because New Jerusalem will descend from Heaven, which is in the twelfth dimension, to earth that will be called the Holy City, it will be constructed of this twelfth dimensional matter. New Jerusalem will be constructed of some sort of unknown heavenly matter from an unknown place outside of our three-dimensional universe.

Ezekiel and John describe New Jerusalem as being on top of a great mountain. On that great mountain was the New City that was twelve thousand furlongs or was fifteen hundred miles high. The length, breadth and height are equal. Ezekiel 40: 2, revelation 21: 10 and Revelation 21: 16

All of the temporary dwellings that will be used by the people of God of the Holy City when they are on the outside will be constructed from these two new elements of twelfth dimensional matter and none of the dwellings constructed to house the residents of the New City on the outside will have any windows or doors because to gain entrance to these structures, one would have to have a ascended body that will be able to pass through solid objects and once in, you will feel like you are still out but protected from anything and you will be able to see everything. On the outside, the structure will look like a solid building with no windows but in the inside, the walls will appear like transparent glass giving the residents from New Jerusalem the effect of still living in the open nature of God. Once inside of these temporary constructed dwellings will place you somewhere else that is beyond our three-dimensional universe.

What was impossible in this world for the people to do will be made possible for the people in the "World to Come". God will make all things "New" for them in the New City or "New" laws of physics will be created by God for the people of God whereas all things will be possible for them to do. With God, all things will be possible for them to do. Revelation 21: 5, Matthew 19: 26, Jerimiah 32: 17 and Luke 18: 27

What will be given to the people of God in the "World to Come" is beyond our imagination today. There will be no more "Sea" in the world to come. Can you imagine that? Where the oceans were that was called the sea will be deep caverns. There are caverns in the ocean as deep as Mt Everest is high. When the ocean is gone, these deep caverns will be used for housing for those who have an ascended body that can float like the clouds and fly like the birds to their windows. These deep caverns shall resemble the cliff dwellings from the old black African dominion that are being discovered today that cannot be reached by walking up to the door. There in those deep caverns where the Sea used to be, those who can float like the clouds and fly like the birds to their windows shall discover wonders and treasures hidden there for millions of years. The experience of floating in those caverns that will be deeper than 29,000 ft. is beyond our imagination today but will be a joy and pleasure to all who have received the advance ability to float like the clouds and fly like the birds. They will never have the fear of falling off of a 29,000-ft. cliff because they will never fall but will float up or down to any level in the cavern. A large portion of the planet earth is cover in water. Because of that, a large portion of the planet is unknown. In the future, a large portion of the planet earth will be rediscovered. With the ability to fly, they will move through the air faster than our fastest super-sonic jets do today and also have the control ability of flight to move through the air as slow as and more graceful then birds. Unlike birds, they will be able to stop in the air and float. The cities built in these caverns that cannot be reached by no one without an ascended body will supersede the cities of the Gentiles on land. There will never be any intrusions or trespassers on their property from the Gentiles. The white Gentiles shall look upon these dwelling for the people of God and all of the things being done there by people who can float and fly, and they will say that those people who can float and fly that cannot be killed are the seed that the Lord has blessed. This is the inheritance of those who were slaves, persecuted and scattered who are called Afro Americans today. Revelation 21: 1, Isaiah 60: 8 and Isaiah 61: 9

Because this is the inheritance of the Afro Americans, the controllers of this world have turned the Afro Americans into Rappers and Hip-Hoppers to destroy them to make them unworthy to receive this inheritance from God. It is because of this that Jesus died only for the Afro Americans sins and transgressions that they would commit while they were being persecuted, scattered and enslaved so the Afro Americans who are the ascendants of the slaves and the slaves are God's first born and chosen people could still inherit paradise. Jesus was sent to the lost sheep or the Rappers and Hip-Hoppers of Israel only. Jesus told His disciples "Not" to go to the white Gentiles but go only to the "Lost Sheep" of Israel. Jesus is not the "Savior" for the white Christian gentiles but is only the "Savior" of the Afro Americans who are God's first born and chosen people. Exodus 4: 22, Matthew 10: 5-6 and Matthew 15: 24

Because New Jerusalem will be fifteen hundred miles high, the citizens of New Jerusalem will be able to float like the clouds and fly like the birds to their windows. Can you imagine a city build for people that can float like the clouds and fly like the birds to their windows? Can you imagine how their dwellings will look that are for people who can fly to their windows? There will be what will seem like shops, stores, entertainment and parks in locations high in New Jerusalem where only those who can fly can reach them. There shall be people that never descend down to the lower levels to walk the earth with the Gentiles and the people of God whose interest will be on the higher spiritual realms of existence will be found in the top levels of the city. Praying and worshipping God continually will be the activities done in the higher levels of the city that shall reach out into outer-space.

The white Jewish Greek Gentiles who wants the people of God inheritance and the white Roman Gentiles that want an additional thousand year Reich are being controlled by the spirit of Esau and they are trying to steal Jacob's inheritance as they did in the womb of the universe in the beginning when Esau fought with Jacob in the womb to be born first to receive a second chance for salvation that was promised to the Gentiles and to also receive what was promised to the "Meek" or promised to Jacob and the people of God to inherit the earth after the white Gentiles have had their second chance. All of the Lying and Murdering that the white Greek Jewish Gentiles and the white Roman Gentiles who have dominion today are doing to force the world today to accept them as the true people of God is in vain. The "Meek" who are the Afro Americans shall inherit the earth and nothing can be done about that. Matthew 5: 5 and Psalms 36: 11

What can be done is the Gentiles can join the people of God and share this future if and only if the Gentiles receives the truth and act accordingly. The white Roman Gentiles must not be deceived by the Sons of Perdition who are the "Changelings" and the devil offspring who have assumed the people of God identity and have a secret agenda to have the white Roman Gentiles fight God for them and with them in the Valley of Jehoshaphat for the people of God who are the ascendants of "Slaves" inheritance to guarantee that if the Sons of Perdition are not in Paradise then the white Roman Gentiles who have dominion today will not be in Paradise either. Because of "Envy", the white Greek Jewish Gentiles who are the "Sons of Perdition" must not sir up the white Roman Gentiles who have dominion today against the "Brethren" or the "Brothers" who are the ascendants of the "Slaves" who are the Afro Americans today making the gentiles minds evil against the brothers or brethren. They must not instigate the white Roman gentiles who have dominion today to say that "Black Lives Do Not Matter". Joel 3: 2, Acts 13: 45, Acts 17: 5 and Acts 14: 2

The white Roman Gentiles who have dominion today must understand that the "Sons of Perdition" or the "Sons of Hell" who are the "Hellenists" who are the "False Brethren" who are the "False Prophet" are "Lost" and only the people of God who are the ascendants of the "Slaves" can lead the Gentiles to the path of Salvation. Paul spoke boldly in the name of our Lord Jesus and disputed against the "Hellenists" who are the white Greek Gentile Jews but the "Hellenists Jews" attempted to kill Paul. The white Roman Gentiles who have dominion today must "Fall Away" from the "Sons of Perdition" and reveal who are the "Sons of Perdition", who is that man of "Sin" who opposes and exalts himself above all that is called God or that is worshiped so that he sits as God in the temple of God in Jerusalem today showing himself that he is God. John 17: 12, 2 Corinthians 11: 26, Galatians 2: 4, Acts 9: 23, Acts 9: 29 and 2 Thessalonians 2: 3-4

The white Roman Gentiles who have dominion today must "Join" with the true people of God to share in the people of God future. The people of God who are the ascendants of the "Slaves" and are God's first born are commanded by God to be for the "Salvation" of the Gentiles from biblical days to "PRESENT" till the end of the earth. The "False Brethren" who are the white Greek Hellenist Jewish Gentiles who are also the Sons of Perdition or the Sons of Hell because they are the descendants of Cain and Cain father was the wicket one or serpent in the Garden of Eden are "Lost" and do not know what they are doing must not deceive the white Roman Gentiles that have dominion today that the white Greek Hellenist Jewish Gentile in Jerusalem today are the people of God who can show the Gentiles the way to salvation. It is because of this "Lie" that the "False Brethren" is also called the "False Prophet" because they do not know the prophesies of the God of Abraham. Jesus said that the "Sons of Perdition" were "Lost" and did not know what they were doing. Exodus 4: 22, Acts 13: 47, John 17: 12, 1 John 3: 12 and Luke 23: 34

The mighty of the white Gentiles including the Sons of Perdition must not say "FUCK IT", we don't care". Everybody on the planet alive today or have ever lived in the white Gentile dominion CARED and BEGGED for a SECOND CHANCE for salvation in the world we live in today to prove that they are worthy to live in the world of tomorrow. To ensure that they would CARE this time, they SENT (SAINT) the latter-day messenger to "DELIVER" the most Profound message ever delivered to the Gentiles in the latter days of the dominion so the Gentiles would remember what happened at JUDGMENT last time and this time CARE so this time the white gentile Jews would not judge themselves unworthy for eternal life and the white Roman gentile who have dominion today would care to prevent no place found for the great white throne in the future. That is how important the world of tomorrow is. It is written that after the fullness of the Gentiles come in at the end of the age or after December 21, 2012, the "Deliverer" will come and reveal to the people of God and to the white Jews and white Gentiles the way to salvation. Acts 13: 46, Revelation 20: 11 and Romans 11: 25-26

Believe this author when he reveals to the mighty that those who are proud to kill the people of God will face those same people of God on the other side. Death is the end for the Gentiles and the beginning for the people of God. For I speak or reveal this to the Gentiles in as much I am an apostle to the Gentiles, I magnify my office and it is because of this office that utterance much be given to me that I may open my mouth boldly to make known the mystery of the gospel for which I am an ambassador in chains that in it I may speak boldly as I ought to speak or as you promised last time at judgment you would allow the "Deliverer" to speak to deliver this profound message to save the white Jews and to save the white Gentiles. Romans 11: 13 and Ephesians 6: 19-20

All white Gentiles who exist in the world we live in today begged for forgiveness for what they had done on the earth because they could not endure damnation. All white Gentiles that are alive today or that have ever lived in the world we live in today, begged for a second chance to live again to prove themselves worthy to live in the world to come because last time there was no place found for the great white throne in the future. Those that say they don't care about any consequences and not worried about judgment day in the future will beg again for their souls because they will not be able to endure damnation this time and this time, there will be no "sorrow" for them and they will receive their just due. Revelation 21: 4, Revelation 20: 11 and Revelation 16: 6

# 17

# There are no lost tribes of Israel

The sinful of Israel are called the "Lost Sheep" because they have lost their way and is now in sin and fornication. Jesus was the "Good Shepherd" that brought the lost sheep back to the flock of the righteous. There is no lost tribe as the white Gentiles believe. The Whole House of Israel was turn into the Valley of Dead Dry Bones or the whole house of Israel were call dead or called Negro because Negro means dead. The WHOLE HOUSE of Israel went into slavery and were called Dead Dry Bones or called Negro because Negro and Necro are the same words and they mean dead. All twelve tribes of Israel or the WHOLE HOUSE of Israel were described as a Valley of Dry Dead Bones. If you are not called DEAD or called NEGRO, you are not the Valley of Dry Dead Bones who are the people of God that are called dead or Negro for the sake of the Gentiles and the Negros are the WHOLE HOUSE of Israel. Only those who are called the Valley of Dry Dead Bones or called Negro are Israel. John 10: 11 and Ezekiel 37: 11

For the Lord, himself will descend from Heaven with a shout, with the voice of an archangel (this archangel with the Lord is Shiloh) and with the trumpet of God and the dead (Negro) in Christ or those who are dead to the spiritual ways of Christ will rise first. The Negro is mentally, spiritual and morally dead in Christ. 1 Thessalonians 4: 16-17

The Lamb in Heaven is speaking about the Negro when He said, "I know your works that you have a name that you are alive, but you are dead or that you have a name that means dead, but you are alive". That name is Negro. Negro and Necro are the same words and Necro means dead. Negro should be pronounced the same way you pronounce "Negative" because Neg and Nec have the same sound. Revelation 3: 1

They are the Broken Branch that was cut off for the sake of the Gentiles that is giving the Gentiles a second chance for salvation. It is by their fall and failure that the world and the Gentiles have their riches. It is the casting away of them that is the reconciling of the world or it is by them being broken off from the Tree of Life and becoming dead and giving the Gentiles a second chance for salvation in their spot on the Tree of Life that is the reconciling of the world and the Gentiles. When they are grafted back in the Tree of Life in their spot, how much more will their fullness or reward be but life from the dead. Romans 11: 11-15

Because of what they have done for the Gentiles, they will be joined with God and given immortality. Because they were called Negro or Dead, they shall be given life, immortality life. Revelation 21: 4, Revelation 20: 4 and Romans 11: 15

It is because of this that they are the slaves in the white Gentile dominion. The spirits that control the Gentiles knows what will happen at the end. They know that they will be going into eternal torment which is called "damnation" or eternal punishment in Hell forever when the Lamb kingdom is established on the earth. They asked Jesus not to cast them into the Lake of Fire and experience this everlasting torment before it was time in the latter days during the days that Jesus walked the earth and cast demons out of the people. Because they asked not to be sent to torment before it was time, Jesus cast them into swine or pigs and the pigs became so inflamed or upset about this possession that they jump over a cliff preferring or choosing to be dead before being possessed by these demons. This is why the Germans of World War Two compared anyone against them as swine because the swine did the opposite of what the Germans did in the beginning of World War Two. The Germans chose to join with the demons to receive advance technology as the Americans are doing today. Matthew 8: 29-32

In the white Gentiles secret societies where the Illuminati worship these demons for power and authority in the world, they are being deceived by these demons when these demons tell them that in the future, the demons shall win the War of Armageddon and Jesus will lose and those who are being deceived by these demons believe what these demons are saying. The demons that the Illuminati contacts in their secret rituals are very ancient as are the Gods and the ancient ones are the color of brass that has been burned in a furnace with hair like sheep wool or nappy hair.

The white Gentiles must not be deceived by these demons when they appear to the white Gentiles as Familiars or appear as white Gentiles to the white Gentiles. The spirits that are being revealed at the CERN particle collider are not white Gentiles but are black Olmec Africans and the black Olmec Africans are the same race as the Anunnaki. These spirits are ancient and when they occupied their own bodies, they were black. This was revealed in the 1968 horror movie titled "Devil's Bride" starring Christopher Lee. Remember, the Holy Bible has warned us not to communicate with these ancient familiar spirits who will appear to you as someone who you are familiar with because these spirits will deceive you and then defile you. Leviticus 19: 26 and 31 and Leviticus 20: 6 and 27

Since the slave shall be given everything including immortality, the spirits that control the Gentiles are jealous and that emotion is reflected in those who they possess. Those that they possess become jealous and envious of those that will be given everything. In the future when the Kingdom of God is established on the earth, those that see the people of God will say that they are the seed that the Lord has blessed. It is recorded in the Holy Bible that the Jews are envious of the Brethren or black Brothers who are scattered. Pilate knew that the Jews were envious of Jesus and the brethren. Isaiah 61: 9, Acts 13: 45, Acts 17: 5, and Matthew 27: 18

These invaders or demons that have invaded our planet and have possessed the wicked knows of the judgment in the future and that they will be cast into the Lake of Fire to be tormented forever asked Jesus not to torment them before their time by casting them out of two possessed men into infinity, so Jesus cast them into a herd of pigs but the pigs rejected that possession and desire death over life possessed by demons, so the pigs ran into the sea and perished in the water. Matthew 8: 28-32

So now before these demons are cast into torment at Judgment this time, they have made the people of God suffer concluding that in the Gentiles dominions, the people of God will have nothing because they are promised so much in the future. This is why the people of God were slaves in Egypt, Assyria, Babylon, Persia, Greece, Rome, and in this last dominion referred to as the dominion of "Iron and Clay" that we live in today. Ironically speaking, those who were slaves and called inferior and called dead or called Negro in the Gentiles dominion because of envy are the most evolved people on the planet and it is them that will be joined to the Creator and given everything. Matthew 8: 28-32, Revelation 21: 3-4 and Leviticus 26: 11-13

Remember, no race on the planet has the honor in Heaven as do the slave race. This time at judgment the Gentiles can ask concerning the days that are past in the last world which were before you or before this world (1) and since the day that God created man on the earth in this world we live in today (2) from one end of Heaven to the other end of Heaven if anything have ever been as great as what the people of God did for the white Gentiles. Deuteronomy 4: 32

The Gentiles were supposed to prove themselves worthy by not being influenced by these evil spirits but choosing another path sharing with the people of God, so the people of God could share with the Gentiles when the people of God kingdom is brought to the earth.

When New Jerusalem descends from heaven and is established on the earth, the Gentiles was given the "Outer-Court" of this great city and the Gentiles ran in and out of the great city for forty-two months which is an eternity because a day with the Lord is like a thousand years to us. Imagine forty-two months of days that are a thousand years long. The Gentiles will be with the people of God for an eternity but without the people of God, the Gentiles will not receive what was promised. The Holy Bible says that the white Gentiles will not be given New Jerusalem but given the "Outer-Court" which is outside of the Temple or city named New Jerusalem. Revelation 11: 2, 2 Peter 3: 8 and Hebrew 11: 39-40

# 18

# Born from the dead

Jesus was the first Negro born from the dead or born from that mentally, spiritually and morally state of mind called dead and given wisdom and understanding by the Holy Ghost of God his Father. Revelation 1: 5

Once a Negro, which means mentally, spiritually and morally dead, is baptized, he is born again. Only the Negro can be born-again because they are the ones that are called dead. Jesus said that He knew His people have a name that you are alive, but you are dead, or I know you have a name that means dead, but you are alive. White gentile Christians cannot be born-again Christians because they were never called Negro or called dead and only the Negro or those who are called dead can be born-again. Being baptized is a Negro religious ritual indicating that the baptized person is no longer dead with eyes that can't see and ears that can't hear and possessed by the spirit of "Stupor" which means "Stupid". At birth, the people of God are called Negro which means dead. Once baptized, the dead Negro is born-again and becomes a new person that now understand and have eyes that can see and ears that can hear. It is this that is referred to as being born-again. If you are not a Negro, you can't be born-again because you were never dead. Revelation 3: 1 and Romans 11: 8

It is believed by God's Elect that in the beginning, because of all of the sins in the world, God was going to destroy humanity and mankind and start over with a different type of beings created to obey without defiance. To teach those who were given life a lesson because of their disobedience, God destroyed the world by water and that still did not stop sin and fornications from dominating the world. Maybe, a different type of beings should be created that would be created to obey. Michael in Heaven asked our Father to give this form of biped beings another chance. He convinced our Father to give him a chance to prove that this form was worthy and could resist temptation and evolve into the beings of God's liking worthy to be joined with. To prove this to be a fact, he chose to come to the earth as a man, live like men exposed to all of the sins that men are exposed to, so no one could say that their sin was so great that they could not turn away from sin and come to God and at a given time reject it all and come to God. Here on the earth to prove that humanity and mankind were worthy, Michael would be known as Jesus. From year one of Jesus life to the time Jesus started collecting his disciples, Jesus was exposed to the sins of the world and rejected it. Jesus was from Nazareth and Nazareth was a bad place. When Philip told Nathanael that they had found Him of whom Moses and the prophets wrote about and He was from Nazareth, Nathanael said to him, "Can anything good come out of Nazareth"? John 1: 45-46

Jesus came from Nazareth and was exposed to everything and still turned to God to prove that no matter what sin you are engaged in, you can stop and come to God. Jesus proved that this biped form with all of their emotions, wants and desires were worthy to survive and would evolve into beings that will be worthy to join with God. Now, no drug addict or prostitute or homosexual can say that their sin was too great to break away from and it was because of that, they could not come to God. This sacrifice of oneself to save another is portrayed in our everyday life here on the earth today. There have been incidents where a parent or a love one became aware that a love one was on a dangerous drug next to impossible to break the addiction and someone close to that individual who cares a great deal about that individual that cannot bare to lose that individual who in himself knows right from wrong and is strong in his commitment to God has agreed to become addicted to the same drug that his love one is addicted to and together resist the drug and go through withdrawal systems with the love one as a crutch or support for the individual so the individual can gain strength by watching someone else resist and succeed and it is this that will give strength to the weak to copy or imitate those actions and at some point in the future, both are free from the addiction.

No one will talk about the first 33 years of Jesus life and how Jesus proved that we were worthy. Then Jesus went to Galilee, to John the Baptize and was baptized or born again which meant that he was no longer a Negro but was now a new person. When Jesus had been baptized, Jesus came up immediately from the water and behold, the heavens were opened to Him and He saw the Spirit of God descending like a dove and alighting upon Him. Matthew 3: 16-17

Remember, for the sake of the Gentiles, God gave His people the Spirit of Stupor or made them Stupid. They have eyes that can't see and ears that can't hear to this very day. There will be others that are redeemed from men in the latter days and will be the first fruits or the first ones born from this mentally, spiritually and morally state call dead that are for God and for the Lamb. In the mouths of these first fruits that are born from the dead or born from the Negro will be found no deceit because they are without fault before the throne of God. Romans 11: 8 and Revelation 14: 4

The Negro or those who are the ascendants of slaves that are referred to as dead are the most important people in the Gentile dominion. This is revealing the Mystery of the Gospel. After the tribulations come to the earth, they are the ones that shall build the old waste places. They are the ones that shall rise up the foundations of many generations. They shall be called, 'The repairer of the breach' and called, 'The restorer of paths to dwell in'. They are the ones that will be joined with the Creator and given everything. That is why Esau tried to steal Jacob inheritance. That is why the Greeks assumed their identity and are calling themselves Jews. In the future when they are joined with God and given everything including the ability to float like the clouds and fly like the birds to their windows as well as everything that they imagine in their minds will come true and there will be no death for them, everyone who see them will say they are the seed the Lord has blessed. Everyone will look at them and in their minds say, "Wow, they are the seed that the Lord has truly blessed" because they can do anything and everything including the ability to float like the clouds and fly like the birds to their windows and they cannot be killed'. They are truly the Masters of the Universe. Isaiah 58: 12, Isaiah 60: 8, Matthew 21: 22, Mark 11: 23, Revelation 21: 4 and Isaiah 61: 9

The Star Trek movies of today concerning space exploration are premonitions of how the people of God shall explore the universe in advance spaceships of light teaching the gospel of the Kingdom of God throughout the universe. Because they will be joined with God Himself, no technology anywhere in the universe will be better than theirs. In spaceships of orbs of light, some the size of planets and given immortality whereas they can't be killed, they shall rule the universe forever. They will be the Masters and the Guardians of the Universe. Their space ships will be able to travel through what is called black holes to enter into other universes and once there they will spread the Gospel of the Kingdom of God. Resistance against them will be futile because all kingdoms and dominions under the whole heaven in any dimension shall serve the people of God in this dimension on the planet earth. Revelation 21: 3-4 and Daniel 7: 26-27

In the future, the white Gentiles will not be joined with Pan the demonic Greek god of nature with pointed ears, who is the devil offspring of Satan named Spock who is a character portrayed in the Star Trek series but to explore the universe, the white Gentiles will be joined with the people of God who will have dominion. In the Star Trek series, the characters named Spock and the character named Data who is an android solves the problems that confront the crew of the Enterprise Star-ship. In reality, the people of God will be smarter and more capable of solving any problem than the character named Spock, or the character named Data in the Star Trek series. They will have godlike abilities to do anything that they can imagine. They will be able to stop time as did Joshua when he made the Sun and Moon stand still in the Valley of Aijalon or change time and space to their liking because anything that they can imagine will come true or will become part of our reality. They will be more advanced and powerful than the character in the Superman movies that can't be killed and can float like the clouds and fly like the birds plus have the ability to make anything that they can imagine come true. They will have the ability to move faster in space than any other dominion and they will also have the ability to teleport from one end of the universe to the other end in micro seconds. With a thought, they will be able to make all threats suddenly disappear. The Holy Bible says that no weapon formed will prosper against them. The Gentiles from the "Outer-Court" who are ordained to eternal life because they believed and were with the people of God will be given powerful space ships that cannot be destroyed to explore the universe and on all of their ships will be a representative from New Jerusalem who will have godlike powers to ensure that the Gentiles mission in space is successful and that no harm shall ever come to them in their space travel. With the representative from the New City on their ships that cannot be killed and can cure all manner of sickness and disease and can raise the dead, the Gentiles will have no worries while they explore outer space in ships that cannot be penetrated or destroyed. They will need no sick-bay or doctors on board their space crafts because no one will be getting sick and no one will be dying. Like with the people of God, all who will not serve the ordained Gentiles in their space travel shall be utterly destroyed. Do not be deceived by Hollywood and the Synagogue of Satan that controls Hollywood to believe that Spock or a representative of Satan shall guide the Gentiles in outerspace in the future. Those of the Synagogue of Satan who say they are Jews but are Not but are Lying shall come bending their knees to the people of God to know that God loves His people. Joshua 10: 12-14, Matthew 17: 20, Luke 17: 6, Revelation 21: 4, Isaiah 60: 8, Isaiah 54: 17, Isaiah 60: 12, Romans 2: 9 and Revelation 3: 9

The Holy Bible has recorded that the kingdom and the dominion and the greatness of the kingdom under the whole heaven or throughout the universe shall be given to the people of the saints of the Most-High whose kingdom is an everlasting kingdom and all dominions throughout the universe shall serve and obey them forever. The Dead or the Negros because Negro means dead are the ones that will be raised first and given immortality. They are the ones that made it possible for the white Gentiles to have a second chance in the world we live in today and it is because of this that the white Gentiles have what the white Gentiles have today. The Negros or those that were broken off for the sake of the Gentiles and called dead or Negro is the savior or the riches of the world and the Negros or those that were broken off for the sake of the Gentiles and called dead or Negro is the savior or the riches of the Gentiles. Daniel 7: 18, Daniel 7: 22, Daniel 7: 26-27, 1 Thessalonians 4: 16 and Romans 11: 12

The white Gentiles who have dominion today owe the people of God for what the people of God have done for the white Gentiles. Are the white Gentiles who have dominion today evolved enough and civilized enough to acknowledge debts?

If the white Gentiles that have dominion today would help the slave race who are God's chosen people it could buy more time for the Gentile dominion because God wants to take out of the Gentiles a people for God's name and for this cause, God will give the Gentiles extra time to make this a reality. This will be revealed in the words of the prophets that will be written and delivered to the white Gentiles who have dominion today, so the Gentiles could make their final choices wisely. Simeon delivered the message that the Lord wants to take out of the Gentiles a people for God's name in biblical days and since the end of the dominion will be declared from what happened in the beginning of the dominion and in the beginning of the dominion Simeon revealed this to the Gentiles, at the end of the dominion it will be Simeon and only Simion that will deliver this information or message to the Gentiles to save the Gentiles because God wants to take out of the Gentiles a people for God's name. Remember, the ancient prophets are subjected to the prophets or the ancient prophets will be in the latter-day prophets. Isaiah 46: 10, Acts 15: 14-15 and 1 Corinthians 14: 32

# Jesus died for the sins of the People of God only

Jesus died for the sins of the Lost Sheep of Israel only. Jesus told his disciples go not to the white Gentiles but go only to the lost sheep of Israel. Jesus was not sent to the white Gentiles. Jesus was sent to the Lost Sheep of Israel only. Jesus was and is the good Shepherd. From the seed of David, God raised up for "Israel" a "Savior" named Jesus. Jesus is not the savior of the Gentiles but is only the "Savior" of the people of Israel. Matthew 10: 5-8, Matthew 15: 24, John 10: 11, Acts 5: 31 and Acts 13: 22-23

Jesus was KILLED to preserve the white gentile Jews nation and lie that they are the people of God and to prevent the white Roman Gentiles who have dominion today from believing in Jesus and to prevent Jesus from gathering together the people of Jesus who were called the "Brethren" who were scattered and giving them the titled of the people of God and a nation. Jesus did not die for the white Gentiles sins but was KILLED to preserve the white Gentiles "LIE" that the white gentile Jews are the people of God and the white

Roman gentiles who have dominion today are the people of God because they were white. John 11: 51: 53

The white Christians are reading the Bible and everything that pertains to the people of God, the white Gentiles are claiming it as being for them. These are the descendants of the Romans who killed the true people of God and killed Jesus in biblical days and now at the end of the dominion when it is time for the Meek or the people of God to inherit the earth, Esau who is the white Gentiles is still fighting Jacob not in the womb to be born first but on the earth to receive the second chance for salvation that was promised to the white Gentiles and to also receive the inheritance that was promised to the Meek. Esau who are the white Gentiles are trying to steal Jacob inheritance by claiming to be the people of God who will receive glory and immortality from God when God's kingdom is established on the earth. They are saying that Jesus died for their sins and they are saved by the blood of Jesus. They are saying that Jesus is their savior. Matthew 5: 5

They have ignored everything that applies to the white Gentiles who are the young wild olive tree that is being helped. Instead of Beholding or Considering everything that have happened and in a public forum reveal who are the true people of God, these white Gentiles have assumed the people of God identity and are claiming the inheritance that goes to IS RAEL (REAL) or goes to the REAL and true people of God. Romans 11: 11-19 and Romans 11: 22

The white Gentiles have had their second chance for salvation in the world we live in today and now at the end of this last gentile dominion of "Iron and Clay", the white Gentiles wants what was promised to the Meek to inherit the earth. The white gentile beings have assumed the people of God or the human beings identity and are claiming the people of God or the human beings inheritance. This is what the fight of good and evil in the Valley of Jehoshaphat that the white Gentiles calls the War of Armageddon will be about. They will be fighting God for God's people who are scattered inheritance. The Afro Americans are those who are being scattered in the latter days of the dominion when God has promised to return and gather His people who are scattered. Where are the Afro Americans that use to live in Los Angeles, California? Why were they scattered out of Los Angeles? Joel 3: 2

Those who fell or broken off for the sake of the Gentiles are the saviors of the world. It is the casting away of the Negro or those who are called dead that is the "Salvation" of the world and the riches of the Gentiles. This is the "Reconciling" of the world. To be saved, the white Gentiles and white Jews must believe this and say this. Disbelief will get the white Jews and white Gentiles broken off from the Tree of Life. If God spare not His nature branches or His own people because of disbelief, take heed white Jews and white Gentiles that God will not spare thee for this belief. The white Jews and white Gentiles must reveal all of this to the world in a public forum, "Otherwise", the white Jews and white Gentiles will be "Cut-Off" and become worse than today's Negros. They must observe the Negros of today who built pharaoh treasure cities "Pithom" and "Raamses" and were the pyramids builders of the past but look at them today and be warned about what will happen to a race that is "Cut-Off" from the Tree of Life and is referred to as the "Dead". Worse will happen to the white Jews and white Gentiles if they are "Cut-Off" because they would not reveal the truth. The truth must not be suppressed. To save the white Jews and white Gentiles, the truth must be revealed. Romans 11: 11-19, Romans 11: 19, Exodus 1: 11 and Romans 11: 20-22

The white Gentiles must understand that to be saved. The Gentiles must say this. Disbelief will get you broken-off from the Tree of Life in a New York minute. It was because of disbelief in the power of God that the Negro was broken-off. The people of God did not believe that God could take their dominion away from them and give a dominion to the primitive cavemen Gentiles because the people of God were so powerful that anything that they wanted to do, they could do it. Romans 11: 19, Romans 11: 20 and Genesis 11: 6

If God did not spare the natural branches on the Tree of Life who are the Negro and people of God because of disbelief, take heed white Gentiles that God will not spare the white Gentiles because of disbelief. The white Gentiles must believe that the people of God were broken-off for the sake of the Gentiles otherwise, the white Gentiles also will be "Cut-Off. The white Gentiles must say that the branches were broken off so that the white Gentiles could be grafted in. To be saved and prevented from being broken off from the Tree of Life and become worse than the mentally, spiritually and morally dead Negros of today, you must say this. This truth must not be "Suppressed". You must "Behold" or "Reveal" everything that have happened are you will be "Cut-Off". Romans 11: 20-22 and Romans 11: 19

This is the profound truth that the white Gentiles wanted delivered to them this time before judgment, so they would know what is going on, so they would know what to do to be saved. Remember, Jesus said that the white Gentiles and white Jews did not know what they were doing. Luke 23: 34

At judgment last time, the white Jews and white Gentiles sent the latter day "Deliverer" to themselves this time to deliver this profound truth. All in Heaven approved with the latter-day Deliverer mission to save the white Gentiles because God want to take out of the Gentiles a people for God's name and for this cause and purpose, the words of the prophets or the Books of Simion are written. Acts 15: 14-15

The white Gentiles must believe that those who are the ascendants of "Slaves" who are the Afro-Americans today were the pyramids builders in the past that built not only Pharaoh's treasure cities Pithom and Ramses including the Ramses statues seen at Luxor today as well as seen at the temple at Abu Simbel but also built the pyramids because the people of God who were the slaves were the builders in ancient Egypt and because of disbelief in God's power, look at them now and be "Warned", the same or worse will happen to the white Gentiles if the white Gentiles are broken-off from the Tree of Life because they do not believe that it happened to the Afro-Americans who are the ascendants of the "Slaves" and are God's first born and chosen people. Exodus 1: 11, Romans 11: 20-22 and Exodus 4: 22

The ascendants of the "Slaves" are the true "People of God". The same race of people that were slaves in Egypt, Assyria, Babylon, Persia, Greece and Rome are the same race of people that were slaves in America. The Holy Bible is the history book for those who are the ascendants of the slaves who are the Afro-Americans today. There is no history of anyone else or no other race of people on the planet earth that is better or more important than the history of the slaves. This is the "Mystery of the Gospel". This is what that has been suppressed about the slave race who are the Afro Americans today to deceive the white Gentiles in the latter days of the dominion. Last time at judgment, the white Gentiles assertion was that they were deceived by the false prophet who are those that have assumed the identity of the true people of God and deceived the white Gentiles in this last dominion of "iron and clay" that they knew the prophesies of the God of Abraham. Exodus 1: 11, Exodus 4: 22 and Revelation 19: 20

If the white Gentiles worship the image or picture of the white "up-right" Paleolithic beast or the white Paleolithic beast that was made to walk up-right as Jesus, the Son of God, he himself shall also drink of the wine of the wrath of God which is poured out full strength into the cup of his indignation or resentment of who Jesus really is. He shall be tormented with fire and brimstone in the presence of the holy angels and in the presence of the Lamb who is the color of brass (brown) that has been burned in a furnace (dark brown to black) with hair like sheep wool or nappy hair. The white Gentiles worship the white Gentiles as God and the Son of God. Their vision of Jesus, the Lamb in Heaven, is white with longs, straight, gentile hair or short gentile hair that is blond or black or brown or red all of which are characteristics of white gentiles from England, France, Ireland, Scotland, Germany, and America. Revelation 14: 9-11 and Revelation 1: 14-15

Jesus is not the savior of the world as the Christians believe. Jesus is the savior of the people of God. Jesus died for the sins that the people of God would do while they were away from Jerusalem and led into captivity. Because of this, Jesus is the people of God Lord and Savior. Jesus made it possible for the people of God to still inherit Paradise after being Negro slaves that were taken away from their godly customs. Jesus is the propitiation for our sins and not for our sins only but also for the whole world if the whole world believed in Jesus but the whole world did not believe in Jesus and never knew God or the Son of God because the Gentiles believed that God and the Son of God are white pagan Gentiles. Jesus who is the Lamb in Heaven is the color of brass (brown) that has been burned in a furnace (dark brown to black) with hair like sheep wool or nappy hair. If you believe that Jesus who is the Lamb in Heaven is white, you do not know God or the Son of God so Jesus did not die for your sins and you are not the children of God. Acts 13: 22-24, Romans 11: 26-27, 1 Corinthians 15: 1-3, Hebrew 9: 28, 1 John 2: 2, John 16: 3, John 8: 19 and Revelation 1: 14-15

Jesus was not sent to the world. Jesus was in the world and the world did not know Him. Jesus was not sent to the Gentiles but was sent to His "own people" and His own people did not receive Him. Only the white Gentiles that receives Jesus as being the Lamb in Heaven that is the color of brass (brown) that was burned in a furnace (dark brown to black) with hair like sheep wool or nappy hair, to them Jesus gave the right to become children of God. Being the Children of God only apply to those who believe that Jesus was a human being or a colored man because hu-man means colored-man because "hu" means color and was He that was born not of blood nor of the will of the flesh nor of the will of man but of God. Jesus is more than just spirit who was born not of blood nor of the will of the flesh nor of the will of man but of God. The "Word of God" became "Flesh" and dwelled among us and we beheld His glory, the glory as of the only begotten of the Father full of grace and truth. If you believe that Jesus is white, you do not know God, or the Son of God and you are not the children of God. Jesus who is the Lamb in Heaven was the first one born from the dead or born from the Negro because Negro and Necro are the same word and Necro means dead. Negro should be pronounced the same way you pronounce "negative" because "neg" and "nec" have the same sound. John 1: 10-14, John 1: 1-2, Revelation 1: 14-15 and Revelation 1: 5

To make the people of God seem unworthy to inherit the earth, the white Gentiles of this world have flooded the people of God with sins and fornications. The white Gentiles have made the people of God seem like the worse people in the world. The white Gentiles have selected the "Low-Lives" in the people of God communities to be the people of God leaders as was done to the people of God in biblical days. The white Gentiles of today forced the males in the people of God to be drug dealers and they forced the females in the people of God to be prostitutes and strippers in night clubs. The white gentiles selected those with no talent who were the ugly, criminal, vulgar, homosexuals, ignorant, "low-lives" lost in sexual immorality that the white Gentiles identified as "Hip Hoppers" and "Rapper" to make music for the people of God to influence the youth in the people of God to imitate the actions of these vulgar, low-lives as was done in biblical days. It is because of this that Jesus was sent only to the "Lost Sheep" of the "House of Israel" and Jesus died for the people of God sins that they would commit because of the white Gentiles so the people of God could still inherit paradise. Jesus said, "It is not good to take the children of God bread and cast it to dogs" or "It is not good to take the gifts and blessings from Heaven for the people of God and give those gifts and blessings to the Gentiles" or those who are heathens and infidels who do not believe in God or the Son of God who Jesus called "Dogs". It is because of this that Jesus is the people of God saviors only. 1 Kings 12: 31, 1 Kings 13: 33, Matthew 10: 5-6 and Matthew 15: 24-26

The people of God or those who were broken off and became dead or Negro and went into slavery for the sake of the Gentiles who are the present-day Afro Americans are the Saviors and the Riches for the world and for the Gentiles. Read it in the Holy Bible. The way the Gentiles say that they love Jesus for being their savior is the way the Gentiles should being saying that they love the people of God who are the ascendants of the slaves who are God's first born and chosen people who are the Afro Americans today because it is them who are broken off that are the saviors of the world and the saviors of the Gentiles. Read it in the Holy Bible. It is because of those who are broken off that the white Gentiles were grafted on the Tree of Life in the broken branch place on the earth that made it possible for the white Gentiles to be partakers of the root and fatness of the olive tree or made it possible for the white Gentiles to have a place on the earth and be partakers with the people of the earth to enjoy life on the earth. The Holy Bible says that those who were broken off and became slaves and called dead or called "Negro" are the "Saviors" of the "World" and "Saviors" of the white Gentiles". Read it in the Holy Bible. The white Gentiles must say this. Understand, the white Jews and the white Gentiles must say this to be saved. The white Jews and white Gentiles must say that the branches were broken off so that the white Jews and white Gentiles could be grafted in. To be saved, they must say this. Romans 11: 11-12, Romans 11: 15, Romans 11: 17-19, Exodus 4: 22 and Romans 11: 19

The white Gentiles must say that the Branches were Broken Off that I might be Grafted in. The breaking off of the people of God on the Tree of Life and the Grafting in of the Gentiles in that spot where the people of God were on the Tree of Life or the sharing of the people of God planet with those that had been genetically cloned by the Fallen Angels to be used as body replacement parts and when longer needed were to be destroyed but because the people of God asked their father to save the genetically cloned creatures that the Holy Bible identified as "Brute Beasts" made to be destroyed who did not have a planet because they came out of a test tube and because the people of God from the old black African dominion was willing to share their planet with the cloned creatures and even asked their Godly Father to give the cloned creatures a dominion to grow and established themselves in is what that saved the world and the white Gentiles. This is the Mystery of the Gospel and the Truth that has been suppressed so the Sons of Perdition or the Sons of Hell or the Sons of the Synagogue of Satan could assume the people of God identity and deceive the white Gentiles that have dominion today that they are the people of God. Romans 11: 12-19, 2 Peter 2: 12 and Revelation 3: 9

Remember, the white Jews are afraid that if the white Roman Gentiles who have dominion today find out who are the true people of God, the white Roman Gentiles that have dominion today would take away the white Jews titled as the people of God and take away the nation that the white Jews are building and give that titled and give a nation to those who are being scattered. This is why Jesus was killed. Jesus was killed to prevent the white Roman Gentiles who have dominion today from believing in Him and from gathering together the people of God called the Brethren or Brothers that are scattered. The Afro Americans are those who are being scattered today. Because the white Jews wanted to kill Jesus, Jesus no more walked among the white Jews. John 11: 45-48 and John 11: 51-54

All in Heaven said that the people of God were STUMBLING to make this request to save the grafted branch or the white Gentiles, but the request was granted. All in heaven knew that the white Gentiles could not be trusted, and the white Gentiles proved all in Heaven right when the white Gentiles as Esau fought with Jacob who is a representative of the people of God in the womb of the universe to be born first to receive a second chance that was promise to the white Gentiles and also to receive the promise to inherit the earth that goes to the first born that was promise to Jacob the Meek in the Gentiles second chance. Romans 11: 11 and Genesis 25: 22-23

Now, if some of the branches were broken off and you white Gentiles being a young wild olive tree were grafted in among the people of the old black African dominion on their planet do not boast against the branches that were broken off so that you could survive. Don't say that God created the white Gentile race to replace the old black Africans because the young white Gentile race is superior. The white Gentile race has bad skin, bad bone structure, a weaker immune system and a shorter life span. Your new dominion young oily hair that you are so proud of that has not been exposed to the sun for millions of years as the old dominion black Africans hair have been proves that you are younger than the old dominion people and not better. Remember, you do not support the root or planet, but the root or planet supports you and that root or planet belongs to the people of God from the old black African dominion. You must say then, "The Branches were broken off that I might be grafted in". It is this broken branch that is the savior of the grafted branch who are the white Gentiles. You must say this. Romans 11: 17-19 and Romans 11: 19

The young white Gentile race is not superior to the old black African race because the young white Gentile race who is referred to as the young olive tree that is contrary to nature and they must join with the people of the old black African race to be made whole or genetically perfect or to become human beings. If the white Greek Jews and the white Roman Gentiles who have dominion today were superior to the "Colored" people, the white Jews and white Gentiles would not be calling themselves "Colored" people or calling themselves "Human Beings" because calling themselves "Human Beings" is really calling themselves "Colored" people. White is the absence of all color. You cannot be a white-man without color and a colored-man or hu-man or human being at the same time. You are either one or the other. If the white Jews and white Gentiles were superior to the "Colored" people, they would not be calling themselves "Colored" people or calling themselves "Human Beings". Romans 11: 24 and Hebrew 11: 40

Being contrary to nature means that they have bad skin, bad bone structure, a shorter life span and a weaker immune system. Upon reaching the age of thirty, the white Gentiles begin to age rapidly. Their skin wrinkles tremendously and their bone structure bends and get twisted. Their immune system begins to fail, and they become victims to many unknown diseases. Proof that the regression of the white Gentiles has started as was done to the people of the old black African dominion is that the white Gentiles are being prevented from procreation. Remember, it is prophesied that there was no place found for the great white throne in the future. Not being able to procreate is a guarantee that race will not be in the future. To save the white Gentiles, the message of salvation had to be delivered now. My Gentiles friends, you must believe that the regression happened to the old black African dominion and now the regression is happening to the white Gentiles and then steer events in another direction to prevent what is prophesied to come to pass. To save the white Gentiles because God want to take out of the white Gentiles a people for God's name, the words of the prophets or the Books of Simion are written. The latter day "Deliverer" mission is to reveal this message to the white Gentiles. Science and medicine will never be able to correct these genetic conditions. To correct these genetic conditions and be made whole or perfect, the white Gentiles must join with the people of God to become Human Beings. Without us or the people of God, the white Gentiles will not be made whole or genetically perfect. They are contrary to nature because they cannot be expose to the life-giving rays of the sun for a prolong period without developing skin cancer. The life-giving force from the sun which gives life to everyone and everything on the planet earth is death to the white Gentiles. The young olive tree who is the white Gentiles are contrary to nature. Romans 11: 17-18, Acts 15: 14-15, Hebrew 11: 40 and Romans 11: 24

The white Gentiles must not say that Jesus is your savior. You must say that the Branches were broken off and became the dead race or Negros that you could be Grafted in their spot to survive. You must say the Negros are those who were broken off and became dead so that you could be grafted in are your saviors. You must say this to survive. Romans 11: 19

You must say this in a public forum to survive or you too will be broken off and become worse than those who were broken off so that you could be grafted in. You must believe in what have happen and make that declaration or you too will be broken off. For if God did not spare His natural branches because of disbelief be warned Gentiles that God will not spare you because of disbelief. Remember, the regression has already started. Romans 11: 21- 22

Because the white Jews and white Gentiles wanted to kill Jesus, this is the message that the white Jews and white Gentiles wanted delivered to them this time before judgment, so the white Jews and white Gentiles would know what is going on, so the white Jews and white Gentiles would know what to do to be saved, this time. Remember, Jesus said that the white Jews and the white Gentiles who wanted to kill Him did not know what they were doing. John 11: 53-54 and Luke 23: 34

# 20

# A Decree from God

Be warned that once a decree is made against you by God there is nothing you can do to change it. The old black African dominion which was a million times more advance than today white Gentile dominion is and with all of the old black dominion weaponry and their advanced capabilities to do anything that they set their minds to do and their extreme knowledge could not stop what was decreed against them. God babbled their minds and scattered them. Genesis 11: 6-9

In the Star trek movie series, the Gentiles say that white Jewish Gentiles like Spock in the Star Trek series, Captain Carter in the Stargate series and Rodney Mc Kay in the Stargate Atlantis series will out think all others and solve their problems for them in the future. They are saying that regardless of being Cut-Off from the Tree of Life, the white Gentiles will develop advance understanding and would be capable of learning fast from all other races in the universe. They are wrong and is being deceived by Hollywood. When God returns, the Gentiles will not get smarter but will be "Cut-Off" from the Tree of Life and regressed into the "Morlocks". Their minds will be babbled as was done to the old black African dominion. Knowing that the

Gentiles will not evolve, the white Gentiles are saying that they will mutate into beings with powers and supernatural abilities. They will not mutate up into the X-Men that today's movies are made about but will mutate down into the up-right beast of their beginning that will be called the Morlocks. Understand that living beings "evolves" upward and "mutates" downwards. You do not mutate and get better, but you mutate and get worse. You evolve to get better. Being "Cut-Off" from the Tree of Life means that they will descend down the evolutionary scale to a lower level. One of the main messages that the old black African dominion wanted the new white Gentile dominion to realize and understand was that God will "babble" your mind or make you ignorant or give you the Spirit of Stupor and the Spirit of Slumber as God did to God's own people because of disbelief whereas you will have eyes that can't see and ears that can't hear. God has the power to destroy the wisdom of the wise and bring to nothing the understanding of the prudent. This is what happened to the old black African dominion and this is what will happen to the white Gentiles. Genesis 11: 6-9, Romans 11: 20, Romans 11: 8, Isaiah 29: 10, Isaiah 29: 14 and 1 Corinthians 1: 19

Today's Gentile dominion with their limited, primitive technology will be no match for God and the Gentiles too will be broken off just as the more advance old black African dominion was discontinued. The last dominion in the white Gentiles second chance of "Iron and Clay" will fall just as the Greek dominion fell and just as the Roman dominion fell. This is prophecy. It's a done deal. The white Gentiles will try to change time with a time-machine and try to change the law of nature through genetic engineering, but the verdict shall stand. God wants the next dominion for Himself to be joined with His people. The court concerning this transformation is complete and jurors shall be seated with nothing else to be considered. The judgment is that God shall take away the Gentiles dominion to consume and destroy it forever. Then the kingdom and the dominion and the greatness of all the kingdoms under the whole heaven or throughout the universe shall be given to the people of the "Most-High". The "Most-High" kingdom is an everlasting kingdom and all dominions throughout the universe shall serve and obey the "Most-High". Daniel 7: 25-27

It may be interesting to know that in the Montauk Project, the white gentiles used alien technology to go back in time to alter events to change the future. Al Bielek who was part of the Philadelphia Experiment and part of the Montauk Project has reported that the white Gentiles went back in time to kill Jesus and failed. Think about that. The white powers of this world wanted to kill Jesus yet, they say they are the people of God. (youtube- Al Bielek and the Montauk Project)

The white Gentiles must behold the Afro Americans who were the pyramids builders of the past and look at them now and know that if God spared not his own people because of disbelief take heed that God will not spare the white Gentiles. If the white Gentiles do not believe that the regression happened to the Afro Americans, the white Gentiles will not believe that the regression will happen to the white Gentiles and if the white Gentiles do not believe what have happened, the white Gentiles will be doomed. Romans 11: 20-22

The Gentiles must behold this as a warning in prophecy. If prophecy is fulfilled, the white Gentiles will be cut off from the Tree of Life and their language will be babbled, their understanding will be taken away and they will be regressed on an evolutionary scale to the evolutionary level of the paleolithic creature of their beginning and there will be no place found for the great white throne in the future and all of this will be done by divine means just as by divine means, the white gentiles are being restricted from procreating which is the first steps in their genetic deterioration and there will be nothing that the white gentiles or science can do to stop this. If you can't reproduce naturally, you will not be in the future. Artificial assimilation will not be the answer to the white Gentiles procreation problem. Alzheimer disease, dementia and the inability to procreate naturally in the white Gentiles are signs that the genetic regression is happening right now. The white Gentiles brains and bodies are being shut down. The white Gentiles must join with the people of God who are the Afro Americans today to be made whole. Without the people of God who are the Afro Americans today, the white Gentiles will not be made genetically perfect. This is written in the Holy Bible to save the white Gentiles. This is prophecy. Roman 11: 22, Revelation 20: 11 and Hebrews 11: 40

The survival of the white Gentiles is based on the white Gentiles knowing who are the true people of God or who Is Rael (Real) and joining with that race of people. Anyone who deceive the white Gentiles to believe that another group of people are the people of God will be directly responsible for the white Gentiles being broken off from the Tree of Life and regressed into the paleolithic creatures of their beginning and there will be no place found for the great white throne in the future. Anyone assuming the identity of the people of God to deceive the white Gentiles is the enemy to the white Gentiles and this enemy will not want the white Gentiles to know prophecy. All white gentile Christians must understand that even if they have a good testimony or a good report about their faith in God, they will not receive what was promised to the white Gentiles that have a good report concerning their faith. Without the people of God, the white Gentiles will receive nothing that was promised to those with a good report. The Christians who believe in God must know and understand this prophecy. Revelation 20: 11 and Hebrews 11: 39-40

Only the people of God can deliver a message or truth to the white Gentiles that could tip-the-scale in the Gentiles favor to steer events in another direction to change the shape of the things to come to prevent no place found for the great white throne in the future. Revelation 20: 11

Because only those that are "Sent"(Saint) can make known the mysteries of the gospel to the Gentiles and that knowledge could tip-the-scale in the Gentiles favor making it possible for the Gentiles to steer events in another direction to change the shape of the things that are prophesied to come to prevent no place found for the great white throne in the future and to prevent the white gentile Jews from judging themselves unworthy for everlasting life, be watchful for those that are sent that the Gentiles will call Saints (Sents) to this end or for this reason and for ME, who is delivering this profound truth to you, that utterance may be given to me that I may open my mouth boldly to make known the mysteries of the gospel for which I am now an ambassador in chains that in my office I may speak boldly as I ought to speak because it is you white Gentiles who sent the latter day deliverer to deliver this profound message to you in the latter days of the dominion so this time, you too would be saved. The white Gentiles must not renege on this agreement. Revelation 20: 11, Acts 13: 46, Acts 18: 6 and Ephesians 6: 18-20

Those that are Sent (Saint) to the Gentiles to reveal the truth to the Gentiles are more important to the Gentiles than all of the Gentiles guns and bombs and more important than the Gentiles science and the Gentiles geniuses. The god Plutonium along with guns, rockets, science and geniuses cannot save the Gentiles now. Only those that are Sent can deliver a truth that can steer events in another direction to change the shape of the things to come.

This is the Profound Truth that the white Jews and the white Gentiles at Judgment last time wanted delivered to themselves in time this time, so they would know what was going on, so they could make their latter-day choices wisely so this time at Judgment they would not be found "Unworthy" to remain grafted on the Tree of Life. The promise that the people of God made to the white Jews and the white Gentiles last time at Judgment to deliver a truth to them to help them so this time the white Jews and the white Gentiles would be with them in paradise has been fulfilled. The people of God have been a light for the white Jews salvation to prevent the white Jews from judging themselves unworthy for everlasting life because they are assuming the true people of God identity and have been a light for salvation to the white Gentiles who have dominion today to prevent no place found for the great white throne in the future since biblical days to "PRESENT" and will be that light for the Gentiles salvation till the end of the earth as was ordered by God. Halleluyah, praise Yah. Acts 13: 46-47 and Revelation 20: 11

The Gentiles will be regressed so far back that all who see the Gentiles in the future shall narrowly look upon the white Gentiles and consider the Gentiles saying; "Is this the man that made the earth to tremble, that did shake kingdoms"? In the future after the white Gentiles are regressed, they will be called the "Morlocks". Isaiah 14: 16

When the Lamb in Heaven returns to establish His throne on the earth, the Negro will be grafted back into the Tree of Life and given immortality and be joined with God Himself because of the sacrifice that the broken branch who are the Negros have made for the Gentiles. Once grafted back into the Tree of life, the Negro will achieve levels of growth and evolutionary development that will supersedes the growth and achievements of all other life forms in the universe. They shall be physically joined with God the Creator. For if the white Gentiles were cut out of a bad olive tree that was wild by nature and was grafted contrary to nature into a cultivated good olive tree and achieved what the white Gentiles achieved in their dominion, how much more will the people of God who are the Afro Americans who are the natural real branches be when grafted back into their own good olive tree. Revelation 21: 3-4 and Romans 11: 23-24

For if you white Gentiles were cut out of the olive tree which is wild by nature or genetically cloned from apes or when Paleolithic man was genetically engineered to evolve into Homo sapiens and given a dominion on the earth and achieved what the white Gentiles achieved in their Greek, Roman and "Iron and Clay" dominions, how much more will the natural branches who are the Afro Americans achieve when the natural branches are grafted back into their own good olive tree and joined with God and given a dominion on the earth? Romans 11: 24

In the 1968 science fiction movie titled "Planet of the Apes" with Charlton Heston, the level of growth and evolutionary development that the people of God will receive was compared to wild Apes being evolved into homosapiens that can speak. For the people of God, this evolutionary growth will be a whole lot more. They will be evolved from men to Gods that can't be killed as God evolved Moses into a God over the Egyptians a long time ago. Prophecy does not say that apes will inherit the earth, but prophecy says that the "Dead" or the "Negro" shall inherit the earth and receive this evolutionary development. Negro and Necro are the same word and "Necro" means "dead". Negro should be pronounced the same way you pronounce "Negative" because "Nec" and "Neg" have the same sound. Exodus 7: 1, Revelation 21: 3-4 and 1 Thessalonians 4: 16-17

Because there will be no death for them and they are able to float like the clouds and fly like the birds to their windows and no weapon formed will prosper against them, everyone that sees them will say that they are the seed that the Lord has blessed. All life in the omniverse (all of the universes within universes) shall bow down at the soles of the people of God feet. For the nation and kingdoms that will not serve the people of God shall perish and be utterly destroyed. Revelation 21: 4, Isaiah 60: 8, Isaiah 54: 17, Isaiah 61: 9, Isaiah 60: 14, Revelation 3: 9 and Isaiah 60: 12

The people of God shall break forth on the right and on the left or the righteous and the wicked of the people of God shall break away from the Gentiles and their seed shall inherit the Gentiles and make the desolate cities to be inhabited, Isaiah 54: 3

God has said that for a small time He forsaken His people. With wrath, God hid His face from His people for a moment but with everlasting kindness will God have mercy on His people. God has said that His kindness shall not depart from His people neither shall the covenant of His peace with His people be removed. Isaiah 54: 7-10

The Greek and the Roman dominions including this last dominion of "Iron and Clay" were the lowest and worse dominions in the Gentiles second chance. The Holy Bible has recorded that the first dominion in the Gentile second chance which was Babylon, a dominion of black humans was a dominion represented as gold. Because Babylon was represented as "Gold", it was identified as the Golden Age. The second dominion in the white Gentiles second chance which was Persia was a dominion of brown humans represented as silver. The third dominion in the white Gentiles second chance which was Greece was a dominion of white people who were created or genetically engineered from apes by the fallen angels for bodily replacement parts and for sex who God was Zeus was represented not as valuable metal but as bronze. The Greek dominion was not the Golden Age as the white Gentiles believes today. The fourth dominion in the white Gentiles second chance which was Rome was a dominion of white people that was also genetically engineered from apes and was not represented as a valuable metal either but represented as an unnatural substance call iron. They were brute beast made to be destroyed. The fifth dominion and not the fifth world or the fifth race in the white Gentiles second chance which is the dominion we live in today was the worse of them all because it was represented as iron and clay. From black Babylon to white Rome including the last dominion of "Iron and Clay", the evolution of the species did not evolve upwards but descended downwards yet the white Gentiles of this last dominion of iron and clay believes that their dominion is the highest evolved dominion that has ever existed on the earth. They are so wrong. Daniel 2: 37-43 and 2 Peter 2: 12

These white beings who are non-men mingled with the seed of men but did not join with man to become human beings but stayed white. They mingled or stood around men and refused to join with the seed of men. They are not men because they are not the descendants of Adam and Eve but were created by genetically engineering apes to homo sapiens. They were brute beast made to be destroyed. Only the ascendants of Adam and Eve are men and women. All others are call male and female people. When Adam and Eve were created, there was other people here that had been created by the fallen angels. All people are not men and women. Only the ascendants of Adam and Eve are men and women. Other people are males and females, but they are not men and women. Daniel 2: 43 and 2 Peter 2: 12

Remember, this Paleolithic beast that was evolved to homosapien was created for body parts and DNA retrieval to make more containers, vessels or bodies for the Fallen Angels to be used to house disembodied spirits. When they were no longer needed for that purpose, they were supposed to be destroyed. They were Brute Beast made or created to be Destroyed. The people of God are these brute beast saviors because it was the people of God from the old black African dominion that spoke out for the created creatures survival and it were them that allowed the brute beast that was created out of a test tube that had no planet, to live on their planet and have a dominion on the people of God planet so the brute beast could grow and evolve in. This was done not because the white Jews and white Gentiles are better than the people of God from the old black African dominion but because the white Jews and white Gentiles were weaker and less honorable then the people of the old black African dominion. The young race who are the white Jews and white Gentiles were given a dominion, so they could grow and catch up with the "human beings" on the earth to prevent any schism in the body of people of earth. All in Heaven said that the people of God were STUMBLING to make this request. 2 Peter 2: 12, 1 Corinthians 12: 23-25 and Romans 11: 11

Nothing in the history of the universe has been as great as what the people of God who are the Broken Branch did for the Grafted Branch or what the Negro did for the white Gentiles. This time at Judgment the white Gentiles can ask concerning the days that are past in the last world which were before you or before this world (first world) and since the day that God created man on the earth in this world we live in today (second world) and ask from one end of Heaven to the other if anything as great as this has ever happened before. Deuteronomy 4: 32

# The Dead or Negro will be raised first

It is because of what the slaves have done for the world and the Gentiles that the Holy Bible has recorded that the dead or the Negro will be raised first. Their fall (being broken-off) is the riches for the world and their failure (being the Meek) is the riches for the Gentiles. 1 Thessalonians 4: 16 and Romans 11: 12

For if you white Gentiles were cut out of the olive tree which is wild by nature and were grafted contrary to nature into a cultivating olive tree and prospered, how much more will the Negro who are the natural branches be when they are grafted back into their own live tree. Romans 11: 24

Remember, the word Negro is the same word as Necro and Necro means dead. Neg and Nec have the same sound. Negro should be pronounced the same way as you pronounce Negative because Neg and Nec have the same sound.

The Negro who are the ascendants of the slaves and the slaves are God's first born and chosen people and the Negro are also the ones who the Gentiles are persecuting and scattering today as they were persecuted in Egypt will be raised first. Those who are being persecuted and SCATTERED are those who the Jews in biblical days were afraid the Gentiles who have dominion today would find out that they were the true people of God and then take away the Jews title and nation and then give those who are being SCATTERED a nation and the title of being the people of God. Those who are being scattered are the true people of God. Jesus was killed to prevent the Gentiles who have dominion today from knowing this truth. Exodus 4: 22 and John 11: 48-53

The Negros or Slaves are the ones who built Egypt's treasure cities. The builders of Egypt most important treasure cities Pithom and Raamses are the builders of everything else in Egypt and they were those who were the slaves in Egypt and not extraterrestrials as the white Gentiles believes today because of the suggestions of the Ancient Astronaut Theorists. The ancient ruins of the Raamses statues that are seen in Luxor, Egypt today at the Karnak temple is just some of their excellent craftmanship. As for as the extraterrestrials are concerned, the same extraterrestrials that were in biblical days are here now rapturing the white Gentiles in the air on their UFO ships for evolutionary development examinations, but they are not building anything because construction is not their agenda. Obtaining new vessels for disembodied ancient spirits is their agenda. Exodus 1: 11

The slaves in Egypt ascendants in the future was taken to a foreign land in bondage on ships and held there for at least 430 years that we know today was America are called Afro Americans today. In fact, those who are being SCATTERED today are the same ones that were scattered in the past and those who were scattered in the past built the pyramids or towels and the ancient cities that are today's ancient ruins to make a name for themselves before they were scattered in the new white Gentile dominion and the babbling of their mind has caused them not to remember these important events. Exodus 1: 11, Deuteronomy 28: 68, Acts 7: 6-7 and Genesis 11: 4

The white Gentiles must look at the Afro Americans today and be warned about what can happened to a race when God babble their minds. The same or worse will happen to the white Gentiles if they do not make that declaration admitting that the branches were broken off so that the white Gentiles could be grafted in. You must say this. The white Gentiles must openly in public say that the people of God were broken off so that the white Gentiles could be grafted in on the Tree of Life and it is because of this that the people of God are the world and the Gentiles saviors. The white Gentiles must say this to prevent from being broken off from the Tree of Life and regressed into the Paleolithic upright beast of their beginning if not, the white Gentiles will be Cut-Off and become worse than the Negro. Romans 11: 22, Romans 11: 17-19, Romans 11: 19 and Romans 11: 22

Then we who are alive or not mentally, spiritually and morally dead and remain shall be caught up together with them the dead or the Negro in the clouds to meet the Lord in the air and thus we shall always be with the Lord. 1 Thessalonians 4: 17

Those that are raptured in the air to meet the Lord in the air will always be with the Lord. They will be given new highly evolved bodies in the twinkling of their eye. Because God is aware that His people felt inferior to the new young race because of the new young race hair and because of that, God would promise to anoint our dry hair in oil. In the future with the new highly evolved bodies, God will give His people their crown of glory which will be something like hair on their heads that will be more than hair that will have a shine or a glow or a halo and they will be able to change the color and intensity of that color at their will making this shine or glow a halo around their head and this new hair will conform to their wishes and all who see this new hair on these new highly evolved bodies will admire those that possess this crown of glory. It is not the pointed ears of the Vulcans from the Star trek series that will identify the advance people of God but will be their hair that radiates into a halo on their head or around their heads that will identify them as the advance people of God. Remember, the Holy Bible has recorded that God has said that He will make His people an eternal Excellency meaning, everything about them will be superior to all other life forms in the universe and all in the universe that see the people of God in the future will say that the people of God are the seed that God has blessed. Their new evolved ascended bodies shall be perfect in all ways. There will be no need to go to a gym to get and stay in shape. Their new ascended body will have perfect muscle construction layered on a perfect body frame. All of the men will be well built, and all of the women will be beautiful with certain women more beautiful than the others. There will be no underweight or overweight, sickly people in New Jerusalem because of the River of Life there. With these ascended bodies, the people of God will be able to change their appearance to look like anyone they desire as well as change their body size from normal height to a hundred feet tall at will. They will even be able to make themselves invisible in the three-dimensional universe. To top it all off, there will be no death for them or they will be given immortality. 1 Corinthians 15: 51-54, Psalm 23; 5, Isaiah 60: 15, Isaiah 61: 9 and Revelation 21: 4

This is not about the Jews, the Gentiles or the Christians. This is referring to the brethren or the Brothers only. The word Hebrew means "Hey Bro". Remember, they were a people without a name from a God without a name. When the Gentiles called out to them or called out to the Brethren or the Brothers, the Gentiles would say "hey bro" as the Gentiles say today. As time went on, "hey bro" was slurred together to make one word called "Hebrew". Any dictionary will tell you the correct pronunciation of the word "Hebrew" is "hey bru" or "hey bro". The word Hebrew is referring to those who are scattered without a name or country from the Brethren or Brothers from a God without a name. The Hebrews of today are called Negros or Dead and it is them that will be raised first. This is revealing the Mystery of the Gospel. 1 Corinthians 15: 51-52 and 1 Thessalonians 4: 16

For this we say to you by the word of the Lord, that you who are alive or conscious and aware and remain that way until the coming of the Lord will by no means precede or go before those who are asleep or called dead or called Negro. 1 Thessalonians 4: 15

The Afro Americans are those without a name or a country who are being scattered, persecuted and murdered by the white Gentiles in the latter days of the white Gentile dominion. In the latter days of the white Gentiles dominion in America, the white Gentiles said that the Afro Americans were not Americans and the laws for the American people did not apply to the Afro Americans. The white Gentiles and the white Jews gave illegal immigrants what they should have been giving to the people of God or to the Afro Americans who are American citizens or who thought they were American citizens. The white Jews and white Gentiles in America said in the latter days that the people of God who are the Afro Americans today lives do not matter.

In the future, the people of God will be able to fly. The Gentiles will ask, who are these that float like the clouds and fly like the birds to their windows? Isaiah 60: 8

They shall be known among the Gentiles. All that see them will say that they are the seed that the Lord has blessed. Isaiah 61: 9

After they are raptured in the air to meet the Lord, they will go to the Marriage Supper of the Lamb to the Earth and receive powers and vast abilities and immortality at that gathering in the twinkling of their eye. They will be evolved or will transcend into a race of supermen, not from the planet Krypton but from the earth, that can float like the clouds and fly like the birds that cannot be killed. The Lord will make an everlasting covenant with them whereby the spirit of God and the word of God shall always be in them. No other living beings in the universe will be higher or more evolved then them. No technology will be greater than the power of God in them whereby all things are possible. Blessed are those who are called to the marriage supper of the Lamb. Remember, the Lamb in heaven is the color of brass (brown) that has been burn in a furnace (dark brown to black) with hair like sheep wool or nappy hair. Jesus who is the Lamb in heaven is not a white Jew. Jesus who is the Lamb in Heaven is a black brother from the brethren. He has dark skin and hair like sheep wool. The Shroud of Turin is a LIE and a FAKE. 1 Corinthians 15: 51, Isaiah 60: 8, Revelation 21: 4, Isaiah 61: 8, Isaiah 59: 21, Matthew 19: 26, Revelation 19: 9 and Revelation 1: 14-15

They will live with the Lamb for a thousand years in Paradise somewhere else. Jesus said that in His father house, which is the universe, there are many mansions or in the universe there are many planets that will be turned into mansions for Jesus and those with Jesus. Jesus said that He went to prepare a place for His people. After a thousand years there in that place, they will return and be at the Lamb throne when New Jerusalem descends from heaven and the throne of the Most-High and the throne of the Lamb are established on the earth in the greatest kingdom to ever exist in the universe. Revelation 20: 4-6, John 14: 2 and Revelation 22: 1

Remember, the white Gentiles do not want this joining with the Lamb and the people of God to live a thousand years in paradise to take place. The white Gentiles wants an additional thousand years Reich on the earth to rule. The white Gentiles want the inheritance that belongs to the "Meek" who are the true people of God that will inherit the earth. The white Gentiles want an extended thousand-year Reich on the earth. Matthew 5: 5

A thousand years of Paradise with no evil spirits around to cause the people to error and do wrong is what is promised to the people of God. Satan and all of his demons and evil spirits will be locked in the bottomless pit for a thousand years. There will be peace, prosperity in evolutionary growth and abilities, happiness and contentment for a thousand years. They will have all of the super human abilities that the X-Men, Superman and super heroes' movies of today are made about concerning the abilities that these fictionized characters are supposing to have and they will have a lot more. They will be able to cure all manners of sickness and disease, cast out demons and devils, have power over scorpions and serpents or power over any fallen angel or extraterrestrial that are identified as the insectoids and the reptilians, and they will be able to raise the dead. Anything they believe in their mind without doubt will come to pass. Nothing will be impossible for them to do, nothing. Matthew 17: 20

In the future, the people of God will be able to speak and understand all languishes throughout the universe. That includes from the smallest creatures that walk on the planets to advance life throughout the universe. The people of God will have no need to create a universal translator to communicate with other beings throughout the universe. Everybody and every creature will hear the people of God in their own languish or tongues and the people of God will hear and understand all living creatures and living beings in the people of God languish. Acts 2: 4-8

One of the gifts that King Solomon received from God was the ability to understand all languishes. Our Lord tells King Solomon that "Because thou have asked for wisdom and requested not wealth or dominion over thy enemies; by thy life, wisdom and knowledge shall be thine and through them, thou shall obtain wealth and power". Solomon awoke and behold it was a dream. Solomon wandered into the fields and heard the voices of the animals; the ass brayed, the lion roared, the dog barked, the rooster crowed, and behold Solomon understood what they all said one to the other. (The Greater Key of Solomon)

Note that God spoke to Solomon in a "Dream". God has said that He would speak to Prophets and Holy Men in dreams and visions because the Kingdom of God is within you. Numbers 12: 6 and Luke 17: 21

The Kingdom of God is beyond the fourth dimension that is within us. The fourth dimension is not "Time" as the white Gentile geniuses believes. The fourth dimension is where our conscious goes when we are asleep or unconscious within us. Remember, the first dimension is when you move from up to down. The second dimension is when you move from left to right and the third dimension is when you move from back to front. The fourth dimension is about movement just as the first three dimensions are about movement and not about "Time". The fourth dimension is the movement out of the first three dimensions. The fourth dimension is when you move from "in" and "out' of the first three dimensions for sleep and recuperation. Movement in the fourth dimension is just as important to us as movement in the first three dimensions because failure to move in the fourth dimension for sleep and recuperation will terminate your ability to have movement in the first three dimensions. Just like all day you are constantly moving from left to right, front to back and up to down in the first three dimensions, all day you are also moving from "in" to "out" of the fourth dimension when you think, concentrate, meditate, or close your eyes for seconds to take a minute for rest.

They will never have to worry about something bad happening to them in Paradise. There will be no death, no pain, no sorry and no crying in paradise for them which also means there will be no fear. People that can't be killed will have no fear. Luke 17: 21 and Revelation 21: 4

# 22

# Synagogue of Satan

Now I saw heaven opened and behold a white horse and He who sat on him was called Faithful and True and in righteousness he judges and makes war. This is not a war against the Arabs as the Christians believe. The Arabs are also the people of God. They are the descendants of Ishmael who was one of Abraham children. The God of Islam is the same God of the Holy Bible. When the Christians make fun of the God of Islam they are making fun of the God of the Holy Bible. That is how much the white Christian gentile is being deceived by the false brethren who are the false prophet that have assumed the true people of God identity. Jesus said that the white Jews and the white Gentiles did not know what they were doing and at judgment last time, the white Gentiles assertion was that they were deceived by the false prophet who is the false brethren that have assumed the true people of God identity and "deceived" the white Roman gentiles who have dominion today that they know the prophesies of the God of Abraham. The false prophet who are the false brethren has deceived the white Roman gentile Christians who have dominion today to curse and fight the God of Abraham in the Holy Bible. That is how much the white gentile Christians are being deceived today. Every Christian must understand that they are being deceived to hate and fight the God of Christianity. Luke 23: 34 and Revelation 19: 20

This will be a war with God against the people of Satan or the people from the Synagogue of Satan and the Synagogue of Satan will be fighting God for God's people name, identity and inheritance in the Valley of Jehoshaphat. This is the true cause of the War of Armageddon. The white Jews from Greece who are assuming the true people of God identity are so obsess with wanting to be the people of God that they will be fighting God for the people of God who are scattered inheritance. The Afro Americans in America are the ones who are being scattered today. Where are the Afro Americans that use to live in Los Angeles, California? Why were they scattered out? Revelation 2: 9, Revelation 3: 9 and Joel 3: 2

God will make those of the Synagogue of Satan who say they are Jews and are NOT and say they are the people of God but are LYING, indeed God will make them come and worship before the true people of God feet, so they will know that God loves His people. Remember, the original Jews were all Black. After the Romans sold the true people of God to the white gentile Greeks, the Greeks assumed their identity to have authority in the white Roman Gentiles dominion. Revelation 3: 9, Revelation 2: 9 and Joel 3: 6

When the Greek dominion was over, and the Roman dominion started, the Hellenistic Greeks assumed the identity of the people of God to have authority in the Roman dominion. They are the descendants of Cain and Cain father was the wicked one or the serpent in the Garden of Eden. 1 John 3: 12

Cain was not Adam's child. God did not like Cain or respect Cain. Cain became envious of Abel his brother because the Lord liked and respected Abel. Genesis 4: 4-5

The descendants of Cain are still envious of the ascendants of Abel till this very day. The white Jews in the past were envious of the black "Brethren" or the "Brothers" as they are today. Acts 13: 45 and Acts 17: 5

The descendants of Cain became the Greeks and the Greeks became the white Jews of today. The white Jews are called the "false brethren" or the "false prophet" because they are not the true people of God. The true people of God were willing to permit the Hellenistic Greeks to study and learn their religion and as time went on, the Greeks assumed the identity of the true people of God and deceived the white Roman Gentiles who have dominion today that they were the people of God because they were white. In Biblical days, they were called the "false brethren" because they were not true Jews but were Greeks. They were called Greek Changelings because they were demon children or children of the Devil or children from the "Evil One" or children of the Serpent in the Garden of Eden that assumed the identity of the true people of God. The God in the Holy Bible identify those that are calling themselves "Jews" but are "Lying" as the Synagogue of Satan. 2 Corinthians 11: 26, 1 John 3: 12, Greek mythology or Greek history, Revelation 3: 9 and Revelation 2: 9

One shall say, I am the Lord's and another shall call himself by the name of Jacob (Israel) because Jacob's name was changed to Israel because Israel means Is Rael (Real) to designate who was real or who the inheritance really went to because Esau betrayed Jacob and God in the womb when Esau fought with Jacob to be born first to receive the second chance promised to the Gentiles and to also receive what was promised to Jacob for giving the Gentiles a second chance and Jacob promise was to inherit the earth after Esau had his second chance for salvation and another shall subscribe with his hand unto the Lord and surname himself by the name of Israel as the white Hellenistic Greeks are doing today calling themselves Jews. Isaiah 44: 5 and Genesis 32: 28

In the future when the Kingdom of God is established on the earth, the people of God will be given a new name. The people of God name will be changed to Hephzibah which means, "The Lord is delighted in you". The people of God will be given the land called Beu-lah which is the mystical inner earth kingdom of Sham Ba-lah which is a mispronunciation of Sham Beu-lah which is the capital inner earth city of Aghartha, which is the land of advance beings. Isaiah 62: 2-4

When the Lord of Israel returns He will make His holy name known to His people and He will not let the white gentile Jew profane His name anymore. Ezekiel 39: 7

Remember, the white Jews who are the false brethren are afraid that if the white Roman Gentiles who have dominion today find out who are the true people of God, the white Roman Gentiles who have dominion today would take away the white Jews title as the people of God and take away the nation that the white Jews are building and give the title of the people of God and a nation to those who are scattered who are the true people of God. Read it in the Holy Bible. John 11: 45-54 and John 11: 48

Jesus was killed to keep the white Gentiles who have dominion today from gathering together the children of God who were "Scattered" abroad. The Afro Americans are those who are being scattered today in the latter-days of the Gentile dominion and those who are being scattered today ancestors were those who were scattered in the biblical past. John 11: 48 and John 11: 52-53

This is the suppressed truth that the disbelieving Jews in biblical days said would turn the world upside down if delivered by the Brethren or the Brothers. Acts 17: 5-6

Saul who was renamed Paul and was sent to the Gentiles spoke boldly in the name of the Lord Jesus and he disputed against the Hellenists, but they attempted to kill him. The white Jews and the Hellenists are the same. The Hellenistic Greeks from Hell became the white Jews. They are called the false brethren or called the "false prophet" because they deceived the white Roman Gentiles who have dominion today that they knew the prophesies of the God of Abraham. Acts 9: 29, Acts 9: 23 and 2 Corinthians 11: 26

Remember, last time at judgment, the white Roman Gentiles who have dominion today assertion was that they were deceived by the "False Prophet" who is the "False Brethren" who are those who have assumed the people of God identity. They killed Jesus and they wanted to kill Paul. Paul and Simeon were sent to the white Gentiles and not Jesus. Revelation 19: 20, John 11: 45-54, Acts 9: 15 and Acts 15: 14-15

Jesus was sent to the lost sheep of Israel only. Jesus is not the white Gentiles savior. Jesus is the people of God savior only. The People of God that are scattered and broken off from the Tree of Life for the sake of the Gentiles are the Gentiles saviors. The white Gentiles must say this. Matthew 10: 5-6, Matthew 15: 24, Romans 11: 12-19 and Romans 11: 19

For I speak to you white Gentiles in as much as I am an apostle to you Gentiles, I magnify my ministry. If by means I may provoke to jealousy because of those who are my flesh and save some of them or if by means I may provoke you Gentiles to jealousy by saying that the people of God are your saviors because they are my flesh as I am a savior of the Gentiles sent to the Gentiles to offer salvation to the Gentiles and if the Gentiles knows this, some of my people may be saved. Romans 11: 13-14

Those of the Synagogue of Satan are really Hellenistic Greeks who God is Zeus who is the leader of the Falling Angels who left their heavenly stations to descend to earth on Mt. Olympus to have sex with mankind and the Synagogue of Satan is deceiving the white Gentiles who have dominion today to believe that they are the people of God that knows the prophesies of the God of Abraham, but they don't. They are Lying. Revelation 3: 9

They are called the false prophet because they do not know the prophesies of the God of Abraham. At Judgment last time, the white Gentiles assertion was that they were DECEIVED by the false prophet or deceived by those who assumed the identity of the true people of God and deceived the white Gentiles who have dominion today that they knew the prophesies of the God of Abraham. Revelation 19: 20

Today, they have the white Gentiles who have dominion today fighting the people of God all over the world for them including stirring up the white Gentiles minds against the Brethren or the Brothers or the Afro Americans in America today as they did in biblical days. Acts 14: 2

When the white Gentiles who have dominion today realize what the fight of the "War of Armageddon" is truly all about in the Valley of Jehoshaphat, they will change their minds and the "Valley of Jehoshaphat" will change into the "Valley of Decisions" because the Gentiles who have dominion today will change their minds in helping the children from the Synagogue of Satan and Join God and help the Arabs who are the people of God. Joel 3: 14

The Arabs are the descendants of Ishmael and Ishmael was the son of Abraham and Abraham was chosen by the Lord. The white Jews are the descendants of Cain and Cain father was the wicked one or the Serpent in the Garden of Eden from Hell. Because Cain father was from Hell, Cain father called his people Hellenistic. The Wicked One or the Serpent in the Garden of Eden were the Fallen Angels who left their heavenly stations to descend down to earth on Mt Olympus to have sex with mankind. They became the gods of the Greeks and Romans and the Hellenistic Greeks became the white Jews. Genesis 16: 15 and 1 John3: 12

When the Greek dominion was over and the Roman dominion started, the Greeks assumed the identity of the people of God to have authority in the Roman dominion. The people of God were sold to the Grecians and the Grecians removed them from Israel and then the Grecians assumed their identity. Joel 3: 6

The true people of God were sold to the Greeks and the Greeks removed them from Israel and then assumed their identity. Joel 3: 6

# Rappers and Hip Hop

The Holy Bible has identified who are the people that would be in Israel in the latter days when the fullness of the Gentiles would come in at the end of the age which was on December 21, 2012. The Holy Bible has recorded that the true people of God would be led away from Israel captive as slaves and Jerusalem would be trodden down by the white Gentiles until the time of the white Gentiles are fulfilled at the end of the age which was on December 21, 2012. The Holy Bible says that those who are in Jerusalem today at the end of the age are not Semites but are Gentiles. Luke 21: 24

If you are not the ascendants of those who were slaves, you are not God's people. The Afro Americans are the ascendants of those who were slaves. They are the people who are being scattered in the latter days of the Gentile dominion when God has promised to return to save those who are being scattered. They are God's chosen people. Where are the Afro Americans that use to live in Los Angeles, California? Why were they scattered out? The War of Armageddon or the war between good and evil that will be fought in the Valley of Jehoshaphat where God will pass judgment against the white Gentiles who are the infidels and heathens will be about saving and defending those who are SCATTERED and were SOLD and became slaves. The white Jews and white Gentiles will not be fighting the Arabs but will be fighting God for the people of God who are scattered who are the Afro Americans heritage. There in the Valley of Jehoshaphat, God will enter into judgment with them on the account of God's people and the heritage of Israel who are those who are scattered and were sold to the Greeks. Joel 3: 2 and Joel 3: 6

This is the truth that the disbelieving Jews said in biblical days would turn the world upside down if delivered by the Brethren or Brothers. Acts 17: 5-6

Read it in the Holy Bible. Do not take the false prophet or those who are assuming the true people of God identity opinion because they do not know the prophesies of the God of Abraham. Where are the Afro Americans that use to live in Los Angeles, California? Why were they scattered? Joel 3: 2 and Joel 3: 6

The white Roman pagan Gentiles who are called Christians today and the white Jews who are really Greek gentiles are the ones who killed Jesus and killed the people of God in biblical days. They have place themselves in the holy land by the power of their guns and bombs in their dominion on the earth. Now in the latter-days, they are not God's chosen people that are spoken of in the Holy Bible to be saved when God return. The Holy Bible has recorded that the true people of God would be led away from Jerusalem captive as slaves and Jerusalem would be trampled by the Gentiles until the times of the Gentiles are fulfilled. The time of the Gentiles being fulfilled will be when the fullness of the Gentiles come in or when the Gentiles are at their maximum level of evolutionary development at the end of the age. The end of the age was on December 21, 2012. The Holy Bible has recorded that the Gentiles and not the people of

God would be in Jerusalem at the end of the age. After the fullness of the Gentiles comes in at the end of the age, the people of God will no longer be blind, and the "Deliverer" will deliver a truth to the Gentiles. Luke 21: 24 and Romans 11: 25-26

They will not force God to accept them as the people of God because they are there in the holy land. John the Baptist told them not to say to themselves that Abraham is their father. John the Baptist told them that before God accept them as His people, God would turn rocks into His people. The white Jews and the white Gentiles will fight God in the Valley of Jehoshaphat for the people of God who are scattered who are the Afro Americans identity and inheritance. This is what the war between good and evil will be about that will be fought in the Valley of Jehoshaphat that the Gentiles call the War of Armageddon. Matthew 3: 9 and Joel 3: 2

The white Jews and the white Gentiles have kept the people of God away from God's word and flooded the people of God with sins and fornications to prevent the people of God from being accepted by God. This is why Jesus died for the sins of the "Lost Sheep" of Israel only. Jesus told His disciples "Not" to go to the white Gentiles but to go only to the "Lost Sheep" of Israel. Jesus died for all of the sins that the people of God would comment because of this barbaric behavior against the people of God. Matthew 15: 24 and Matthew 10: 5-6

In biblical days, the Gentiles and the wicked elevated the low-life, the ignorant and the sinful in the people of God communities over the righteous of the people of God. Today, they have turned the "low-lives" in the people of God into Rappers and Hip Hoppers and Strippers that were lost in sin and fornications as were done in biblical days. As was done in biblical days, the government today has elevated the low-lives in the people of God communities over the righteous in the people of God communities. 1 Kings 12: 31 and 1 Kings 13: 33

In 2016, they are bragging about what they did to the "Low-lives" in the true people of God in their movie titled "Straight out of Compton". In this movie, they describe how they destroyed the people of God music industry that promoted righteousness and replaced that music industry with Rappers and Hip Hoppers who were the murderers, pimps and the drug dealers in the community. These low-life Rappers and Hip Hoppers influenced the young in the people of God to be criminals like the Rappers and the Hip Hoppers are and it is this action that is responsible for all of the black on black crime and violence in the black community. Rap and Hip-Hop music is a psychological weapon used by the government to destroy the people opinions of the character and nature of the people of God. It is designed to make the people of God look bad in the eye of the public as well as to influence and motivate the "low-life" in the people of God to do evil. It is designed to cause hatred in the black community between blacks and cause hatred and disgust about the people of God with the Gentiles. It is the police and the jail system that sells the low-lives guns and instructs the low-lives on what to do and that the low-lives would not be punished severely if their victims are their own people. When the government plan to start a war between the Rappers on the east coast against the Rappers on the west coast failed, the government programed the Rappers and Hip-Hoppers to kill the people in their own neighborhoods. To guarantee job security for the police department and the criminal system, the government releases large numbers of criminals out of the jail systems because of over-crowding every so many years to commit more crimes so the need for a large police force is always needed.

The government made the low life in the black community the black community leaders, entertainers and priests as was done in biblical days. The government gave homosexual criminals who were lost in sin and fornication opportunities to make movies calling themselves" Madea" and gave these homosexual men who were passing off as Pastors television programs as motivational speakers to promote these sinful men ways and ideas in the black community. They made thieves and criminals who had spent their youth in jail judges over the people of God and had these criminals straight out of their jails bagging about their success even after having their criminal past in the white Gentile jails. These "Rappers" and "Hip hoppers" were the lowest of the low. They were much lower than the dirt in the gutter. They were lower than whale turds in the ocean. 1 Kings 12: 31 and 1 Kings 13: 33

In the 1950's and 60's, the Afro American music surpassed all known music throughout the world. It was known as music with "Soul" or deep feeling music. The Afro Americans shared this music with the white Gentiles and taught the white Gentiles how to feel the music. Those white Gentiles that understood and were able to feel the music created new rhythms and beats unknown to the white Gentiles in the past. They were called "Blue-eye soul brothers" because now they could play or sing with great feelings in their music. How could have the Afro Americans known that these Blue-eye soul brothers would destroy the Afro Americans music industry and assume their style of singing and playing music and then give the lowest of the low in the Afro American community the absolute, total, unconditional and conclusive authority to make the music that the Afro Americans would hear for now on. Music that consisted of their vulgar, elementary rhyming about their criminal Homosexual way of life.

"You Tube" on the internet has reported that the Rappers and the Hip Hoppers are Homosexuals who are lost in sin and fornication that hates God, themselves, each other, and women to the extreme.

Their music is full of vulgar lyrics about the Afro Americans, but they are seen on television honoring the white Gentiles being polite and courteous and never using a curse word. Their music screams that black women are "Bitches" and black men are "Motherfucking dogs" that they don't like or respect. The message in their music is to kill the black man and to destroy the black woman. They are killing the people of God worse than the Ku Klux Klan to impress their white friends who have given them their authority over the righteous to make recordings. The white Jews and white Gentiles are using the Rappers and the Hip Hoppers to "disgrace" and to "shame" the people of God. The Rappers and the Hip Hoppers are wearing their pants very low to expose their "buttocks" to "Shame" their own people as was done in biblical days because their people have rejected them because of their sinful ways. Isaiah 20: 4

The white Gentiles must know that as long as these heathens and infidels call Rappers and Hip-Hoppers are deceiving and killing the people of God by the orders and support of the white blue-eye soul brothers, the white Gentiles have no chance to be saved. The white Gentiles must restore Motown to save the people of God and in so doing they will be saving themselves because double will happen to the white Gentiles that happens to the people of God. That's double the Curses or double the Blessing. Revelation 18: 6

The white Gentiles were so envious of the people of God music that the white Gentiles destroyed the people of God music industry and restricted the people of God from playing or hearing the people of God music that possessed deep feelings that was called "Soul Music".

The white Gentiles introduced Rap and Hip Hop to the people of God that were created by the low-life in the community to destroy the people of God minds through their music. It worked.

The influence of Rap Music and Hip-Hop music on the people of God killed more Afro Americans and destroyed more Afro American minds than the deadly drug that was push on them named "crack cocaine". Once the white Gentiles were successful in destroying the Afro Americans by turning their low-lives against the righteous, they used that same tactic all over the world to destroy countries like Syria, Iraq, Afghanistan, Libya and many other countries in Africa. The white Gentiles contacted the low-lives or the Rappers and Hip-Hoppers in those countries and told them that America would finance their rebellion against their own government and would support their fight against their government by giving the terrorists guns and air-support and calling the terrorists Rebels. It worked. Just as the Rappers and the Hip-Hoppers or the "Low-Lives" in the Afro American community have destroyed the Afro Americans here in America, the Rappers and the Hip-Hoppers or the "Low-Lives" in Mid-Eastern countries have destroyed their country to befriend the white Gentiles. Beware of the "Enemy that is within".

The white Gentiles copied the people of God righteous music style and imitated it on television to steal the people of God identity in the people of God music. They even had Mexican Indians singing or trying to sing "soul music" and "rhythm and blues" and even Jazz while the people who created "Soul Music", Rhythm and Blues and Jazz were restricted to Rap and Hip Hop. The Rappers and the Hip Hoppers are responsible for all of the crime in the black community and they are sponsored by the Federal Government and the white Jews and these Rappers and Hip-Hoppers are forced on the people of God.

The Holy Bible has recorded that because of "Envy", the unbelieving white Jews were responsible for causing the uproar or violence in the cities against the Afro Americans as well as responsible for stirring-up the white Gentiles who have dominion today against the Brothers and making the white Gentiles minds evil affected against the Brethren or the Brothers who are the Afro Americans today. Making the white Gentiles minds evil-affected against the Brothers is another way of saying that the white Jews were responsible for all of the "Racism" or discrimination, prejudice and bigotry against the Brethren or Brothers who are the Afro Americans throughout America. The Holy Bible has made these statements about who are responsible for the hatred against the brethren and who will be held accountable at judgment this time for these actions. Acts 13: 45, Acts 17: 5 and Acts 14: 2

The white Jews wanted this warning to be delivered to them this time before judgment so different choices could be made. This is unraveling the mysteries of the gospel and this is the latter-day "Deliverer" mission. The white Jews and the white Gentiles in the future sent the latter-day "Deliverer" to deliver a truth to them so they would know what is going on, so they would know what to do. They ordered him to speak "Boldly" as he ought to speak because he is "Justified" because they, themselves sent him. To them, he is the Ambassador from the people of God to the throne of the Gentiles that must not be held in chains or restricted from speaking "Boldly". His mission is to deliver a truth to them, so they would know what to do to be saved, this time. The white Jews and white Gentiles must do what is in their hearts to prove or disprove if they are worthy to continue to exist. Ephesians 6: 19-20

This is not about preserving the "Lie" that the white Jews are the people of God and the white Pagan Gentiles are the people of God because they are white but is about saving friends who are "Ordained" to eternal life this time because they believed last time because God wants to take out of the white Jews and white Gentiles a people for God's name and for that cause, the "Words of the Prophets" or the "Books of Simion" are written and published throughout all of

America. This must not be beyond the white Gentiles that are called by God's name or called Jews understanding, this time. This is to save "Mankind" or those who were created to look like man. Acts 13: 48-49, Acts 15: 14-15 and Acts 15: 17

The Federal Government has introduced these Rappers and Hip-Hop criminals in the black community to stimulate crime to have justification for all of the police violence against the Afro Americans. In the 2014 science fiction movie titled, "Captain America, the Winter Soldier", the Gentiles identified the part of the government that is responsible for producing crime in the black neighborhoods to justify a large police presence as Hydra. (In "you tube" search engine google, ("Government Whistle blower exposes Hip-Hop conspiracy") and (The Secret Meeting that changed Rap Music and destroyed a generation)

To stop the crime and the killing in the people of God communities, Motown must be reestablished, and it must be controlled by the best of the Afro Americans. The Afro Americans must not have the white Gentiles select their leaders for them and select who will influence the Afro Americans through music. It is because the Afro Americans have ignored all that the white Gentiles are doing to them that they are called "Negro" which means they are mentally, spiritually and morally "Dead" because the word "Negro" and "Necro" are the same word and "Necro" means "Dead". It is these Negros who are the "Meek" or who are humble, timid and submissive because they are referred to as "Dead" that will inherit the earth.

Those who are the enemy to the people of God and the enemy of the white Gentiles will not want the rebirth of Motown to come to pass. The federal government and the white Gentiles music industry are responsible for all of the crime in the black community. "Soul

Music" by the people of God surpassed "Rock and Roll music" by the white Gentiles and the white Gentiles were jealous. The white Gentiles were so jealous of the people of God music that Blues, Jazz and Soul Music were banned in the black communities and only Hip-Hop and Rap music were promoted to the people of God.

The white Gentiles also banned the "Afro" hair style that represented consciousness of the Afro Americans history and freedom and independence from the white man system and the admiration of the white Gentiles hair. That hair style was banned from the people of God and the white Gentiles would not show no one on television that had that hair style. Afro Americans with the Afro hair style were told to either cut their hair, change the hair style by wearing their hair uncombed or to wear a white Gentile wig or they would not be selected for a role on television.

Because of this betrayal to the people of God by the white Gentiles because of jealousy, no righteous person will ever sing with the white Gentiles again for freedom and peace for contentment. No one trust the white Gentiles in Heaven or in Hell. Destroying the Afro American music industry that promoted a positive message to the Afro American people and replacing that positive music industry with the vulgar Rap and Hip-Hop music that promotes a violate and immoral message to the people of God proves how low-down the white Gentiles truly are and that the white Gentiles cannot be trusted. The proof of whether you are worthy to continue to exist with the people of the world will be determined by how you treated the people of God. The Afro Americans have the spirit of Stupor (stupid) in them which means they are so mentally, spiritually and morally dead Negros with eyes that can't see and ears that can't hear to this very day and they idolized the white Gentiles and only wanted to be the white Gentiles friends while the white Gentiles did everything in their power to destroy the Afro Americans because of jealousy of who the Afro Americans are and who they will become. Having the spirit of Stupor in them means they are Stupid for idolizing the white Gentiles who hate their guts who are saying today in 2018 that the people of God who are the Afro Americans "Lives do not Matter". Romans 11: 8

The white Gentiles screamed on the news that the white men are afraid of the black men and it is this fear that have the white man wanting to carry a gun at all times. What kind of barbaric, uncivilized society do America have that the white men in America wants to carry a gun because they are afraid. When the fullness of the white Gentiles came in at the end of the age when the white replicated being would be at his fullness or maximum level of evolutionary development, the white replicated being was no more evolved than the Hatfields and the Mc Coys or the Cowboys and Gangsters. After many years watching black athletes especially in football, basketball and in boxing dominate white athletes physically and the dominant performances of President Barrack Obama who was an Afro American over all of the white politicians intellectually for eight years in the White House, the white men in America were afraid-to-death of the Afro Americans. They hated the Afro American men because the white men knew that the white women wanted to be with the Afro American men more than they wanted to be with white men.

There used to be Dating shows where you would choose a person and go out on a date with that person. Once white men realized that white women wanted to go out with black men more than white men, the Dating shows were discontinued, and a new show was developed call the Bachelor where eight white women would compete to determine who would be with the one white bachelor. This was to give the impression that white women adored or wanted white men in the multitudes. It was a lie.

White women were threatened by white men if they chose to be with black men. From that, white men became determine to turn black women away from black men by promising black women acceptance if they turned their backs on their black men and many of the black, Low-Lives women who idolized the white man because of his new generation hair were persuaded. Remember, the Holy Bible said that these black women had the spirit of Stupor in them meaning that they were "STUPID". Romans 11: 8

In the 2009 science fiction movie "Avatar", the white Gentiles men said that they would use the Shol'va black woman to betray her people as well as to betray God and they said in that movie that she would be the cause of the destruction of the Tree of Life because of her admiration of the white demons. A Shol'va are those who have turn their backs on their God to be with the white gentiles. Teal'c, the Shol'va on SG-1 TV series, turn his back on God to be friends with Colonel O'neill. He gave up traveling the universe with God to be a prisoner at Cheyenne military complex on earth who cannot leave the base on a planet that says all who look like Teal'c lives do not matter. He is worse than an uncle-tom. He is an uncle-toming Shol'va. He is a disgrace to everything that is holy and human.

In the movies and in the work place, black women were chosen before black men. Remember the 1966 Star Trek the original series where male members of all races of the people of earth were chosen to be on the new Enterprise space-ship but when it came to the Afro American, the white boys chose a black woman to be there in the black man place. Her name was Uhura. She was portrayed as the whore of the Enterprise. She had sex with Captain Kirk, Spock, Scotti and white crew members of the Enterprise. Till this very day, she still does not understand how she was used against her own people.

Last time at judgment, there were sins that were forgiven or blotted-out except the sin of betraying the black man for the white man. Knowing what these inferior black women held in their hearts that they would rather be the white man Bitch instead of the black man Queen, that sin was not forgiven and those black women that were guilty of that sin did not repent so their sins were not blotted-out, so they did not see Paradise. There was no place found for them in New Jerusalem. They will suffer and be tormented throughout eternity. The Afro American women who house this secret love for the pagan white gentiles and have a secret unspoken agreement with the pagan white gentiles to betray their black man must know that all in Heaven knows what is in their hearts and minds and they will appear before the judgment seat of God to receive the things done in the body according to what they have done whether good or bad and this judgment is without mercy. Acts 3: 19, Revelation 2: 23, Jerimiah 17: 10, Romans 2: 6-9, 2 Corinthians 5: 10 and James 2: 13

Every year since 1995 in New Orleans, Louisiana there is the Essence festival. The purpose of the festival is about empowering the black woman over the black man. The black woman must understand that there is no future for the black woman without the black man. Empowering the black woman over the black man is giving the black woman the power to destroy her race. Remember, these black Essence festival women hate themselves because they are not white with straight hair. This hatred of themselves is what makes them inferior beings. They are identified as angry and mad black women. They are jealous of the white woman hair. They are wearing wigs not designed to look like Afro American hair but wigs that are designed to look like white women hair. These inferior women want white women hair so bad that they are wearing "Rope" for hair. Any black woman that is not proud of her nappy hair and is using rope for hair or is wearing white women wigs is an inferior being. There at that festival hundreds of thousands of black, low-life, ignorant, uncle-toming, weave and wig wearing women who have this secret desire to be with the white man proclaim that they do not need a black man in their life and their only desire is to be with the white man. The black man is not invited to what the black women call the "party with a purpose". When the musical concert that is designed to influence the black women that is made-up of black women who have married white men or who have openly said that they do not like black men is over, the party begins in the tourist area of New Orleans named, "the French Quarters". There at that party in a racist, confederate city with no black businesses, these black women dance, twerk, strip and sing songs to the white men saying, they will never let the white man go. These ignorant black women are spending 200,000,000 tourist dollars in a Confederate city that fought to keep confederate statues that have no black tourist businesses. Instead of going to a city with black tourist businesses to help the black economy, these uncle-tom women are in a racist city giving racist white businesses their money. Is the purpose of the Essence festival a festival of black pride, honor and the worship of God and the black family or is the purpose of the Essence festival a party for ignorant black women who want to mix with racist, HIV positive, gay white men? Remember, the black man is not invited to this Essence festival. This is the Empowering of the black woman over the black man. These black women are not empowered over the white women or in society because they are included in the statement, "black lives do not matter" in our society. The black woman is there at the Essence festival saying that she has power over the black man and only want to party with white men. These black women are in strip clubs on Bourbon street with white gay men. Hundreds of thousands of them are in New Orleans with no men saying that they want to party with the gay, HIV positive white man in the "French Quarters" on Bourbon street. Inside the restrooms of the strip clubs on Bourbon street, these weave and wig wearing, low-life, black women are doing unthinkable things to and with white, gay, racist men who openly calls them niggers and tell them to their faces that "black lives do not matter". It is because of this type of activity that HIV infected women has increased in the black community. Absolutely nothing of the Essence festival in New Orleans, La is positive to the black family. The Essence festival does not promote family values, nor do it promote honor and pride of the Afro American people nor is the agenda the pursuit of knowledge, wisdom and understanding to the Afro American people and it definite do not promote a love for God and the black man. The Essence festival promotes hatred, separation and division towards the black man and black family. The Essence festival promotes division and chaos in the black community. It empowers the black women to be without honor or loyalty and give the black women the right to be a drunken whore in the streets. The entertainment at the Essence festival for black women is walking down Bourbon Street, drunk and acting like a whore, where there is nothing but strip clubs and HIV positive, gay, white men. Bourbon Street have some of the strongest drinks made in the world. These Essence festival women want the right to be drunk in public while they walk down Bourbon street acting like a whore for the white man. The black family do not want the black woman to be empowered over her black man. The black family want the black family to be empowered. The black family do not want the black woman going nowhere without her black man and saying she had the time of her life partying with gay, HIV positive, white men on Bourbon Street. Beware of these essence festival women. They should be HIV tested before they return to their communities. Remember, the black man is not invited to the Essence festival and the black women at the Essence festival are partying at night with HIV positive, gay, white men only on Bourbon Street.

The Essence festival is a white man and government project designed to divide and break-up the black family. It is designed to give the low-life, weave and wig wearing, lost-sheep, uncle-tom, inferior, black women an opportunity to be with a white man. Everyone connected to the Essence festival is part of the conspiracy.

Bourbon Street in the French Quarters in New Orleans, La is one of the filthiest tourist areas in the United States. There is nothing but strip clubs there and the occupants of the clubs are gay, HIV positive, white men. The environment there always has a stench or smell of vomit and urine and this is where the low-life, uncle-tom, black women go to have fun at the Essence festival?

Only the black women that openly confess their loyalty to God and to the black man can be trusted and are saved. All others are identified as "The Enemy Within". They are the enemy to the black family. They are the black women that are concealing a secret agenda that they have with the white man to betray the black man. They are doomed. They will never see paradise. Remember, in the 2009 science fiction movie titled, "Avatar", the white Gentiles said that they would use the black woman to betray her people and God and be the cause for the destruction of the Tree of Life.

The black women that enjoyed the 2018 science fiction movie titled, "The Black Panther" are black Queens who are totally different than the black women that participate in the Essence festival. Biblical prophecy has it that these black Queens shall inherit the earth and live in a world that is better than what was seen and enjoyed in the movie titled, "The Black Panther". It is in their DNA to pray for this powerful black kingdom and they have faith in the fact that when God returns, He will evolve His people into a new race of Gods with powers and abilities far beyond those of normal men as was seen in the movie "the Black Panther". This is the inheritance of the "Meek" who are those who are the ascendants of "Slaves". Our prayer at night is, "Our Father who are in Heaven, holy is your name for your kingdom will come and your will shall be done on earth as it is in Heaven". The Holy Bible has recorded that when God returns, He will join with His people and evolve His people into a new race of Gods over everybody else in the universe as He evolved Moses into a God over Pharaoh. They will be given immortality where as they cannot be killed, and they can float like the clouds and fly like the birds to their windows like "Superman". All who see the people of God in the future will say that the people of God are the seed that the Lord has blessed. These Essence festival black women will not be part of God's kingdom. These Essence festival women have sold their souls to the devil to be with a white man. What these black women have in their hearts about the black man and the white man and what they are doing in the open is horrible and sinful and is known in heaven. All in heaven are the color of brass (brown) that has been burn in a furnace (dark brown to black) with hair like sheep wool (nappy hair) and they know how these uncle-toming black women feel. (Youtube-Essence 2018, dancers on Bourbon Street), Matthew 6: 9-13, Exodus 7: 1, Revelation 21: 3-4, Isaiah 60: 8, Isaiah 61: 9 and Revelation 1: 14-15

Jesus, who is the Lamb in Heaven is the color of brass(brown) that was burned in a furnace (dark-brown to black) with hair like sheep wool or nappy hair is the one who shall judge the earth and the people of the earth. I pity the black women that hates black men with nappy hair. Revelation 1: 14-15, Acts 10: 42 and 2 Timothy 4: 1

It was ordered by God that the people of God not to take pagan husbands or wives. While the white gentile men were killing black people, even killing black children, and screaming that "Black Lives Do Not Matter", these uncle-toming, inferior integrationists were secretly desiring to love and be with the white Gentiles. They all acknowledge to the white Gentiles that they did not care about themselves or their people and would be a perfect slave for the worse of the white Gentiles. The integrationists possessed and portrayed all of the characteristics of inferior beings. Anyone that cannot exist on his or her own but need the white people to be their host are inferior beings. That is a known fact. If you want to be integrated into the white society mixing with white people to be happy, you are inferior to the blacks that can stand alone without the white race. These inferior beings will not be in New Jerusalem when God's kingdom is established on the earth. Ezra 9: 12-14, Ezra 10: 2-4, Ezra 10: 10-12, Deuteronomy 7: 3 and 1 Kings 11: 2

In the future when God returns, the black women that chose the white men over the black man were cursed with the white gentile men. They were put with the white Gentiles who were regressed into the Morlocks on the outside of the great New City and on the outside of the chosen white Gentiles' Outer Court because of their love for the white Gentiles during the tribulation period. Their regrets in the future are beyond endurance and there in the future, they hate the white man the most because of what they lost because of their admiration and love for the white gentiles. Even if they had a good report through their faith, they did not receive what was promised because they were not with the black man. Remember, without the black man, these black women or white people will not receive what was promised to those who have a good report concerning their faith. Hebrews 11: 39

Their souls were incarnated in white gentile bodies in the future to be tormented with the white Gentiles, but their memories were intact. In their minds they remembered that they used to be black like the chosen people, but their choices made them white. Their torments and regrets are in knowing that they should have been with those that were given immortality and blessed with superpowers, but they were regressed with the white Gentiles into sub-human beings because they did not "believe" and were with the white Gentiles who did not "believe" and did not "behold" or "reveal" everything that had happened therefore, they were "Cut-Off" from the Tree of Life and regressed. Romans 11: 20-22

The Gentiles that are "ordain" to eternal life this time because they "believed" last time and "believed" this time, found their spirit incarnated in the ascended vessels of the blessed and chosen with superpowers after New Jerusalem was established on the earth. In their minds they knew that they used to be white, but their choices made them blessed children of God that were given immortality in ascended bodies that could never get damage or sick that could float like the clouds and fly like the birds. It is these white Gentiles that will be incarnated in new ascended vessels and the white Gentiles that will be at the outer-court of the magnificent, godly city named New Jerusalem that will be given immortality that will be drinking from the River of Life and eating from the Trees of Knowledge enjoying the gifts and blessing of the Kingdom of God that God wants to take out of the white Gentiles again this time like last time, a people for God's name and for that cause, the words of the prophets are written in the Books of Simion. Acts 13: 48, Isaiah 60: 8, Revelation 11: 2, Revelation 21: 4, Revelation 22: 1-2 and Acts 15: 14-15

Like Esau, the white Gentiles have proven themselves unworthy to live with the Human Beings in the future because of how they have treated the people of God. Because the white Gentiles betrayed the people of God in the latter days because of jealousy and the betrayal of Esau in the beginning, no one in Heaven or Hell trust the white Gentiles now. Everyone in Heaven are waiting for the white Gentiles to do this time as they did last time, so all could be fulfilled and justified when judgment comes. All in Heaven are crying out to God to judge the white Gentiles for what they are doing on the earth and all in Heaven are crying to God to avenge their blood or deaths on those white Gentiles that dwell on the earth. They are told that they should rest a little while longer until both the number of their fellow servants and brethren who were killed last time are killed this time, so everything would be complete and whatever happens to the white Gentiles at judgment this time would be their "Just Due" for killing the people of God. Revelation 6: 10-11 and Revelation 16: 6

Everything that is vile meaning evil and unpleasant and everything that is repugnant meaning offensive, disgusting and averse in a species has been revealed in you white Jews and white Gentiles because of your actions against the Afro Americans and against the people of God throughout the world. Just look at what the white Jews and white Gentiles have done to the Afro Americans who are the ascendants of slaves who are God's first born by destroying their music industry that promoted peace and greatness and forcing "Rap" and "Hip-Hop" music that promoted violence, hatred, sexual immorality and death on the people of God because the white Jews and white Gentiles were jealous and envious of the people of God music that was described as "Soul-Music", which was music that expressed deep feelings. Dominion was given to the white Gentiles by God and because of fear of losing dominion because of the wrong actions, the white Gentile beings are willing to exterminate all Human beings on the earth that have help them. Exodus 4: 22

Because of the way the people of God are treated by the white Jews and white Gentiles, a Penance must be paid if the white Jews and white Gentiles are to be saved. The Sanctuary for the people of God must be built if the white Gentiles are to be saved this time. Only at the Sanctuary will supplications, prayers, "INTERCESSIONS" and giving of thanks be made for all men including Kings and all who are in Authority because there, the people of God will live quiet and peaceable lives in all godliness and reverence. This action is good and acceptable in the sight of God our Savior who desires all men to be saved and to come to the knowledge of the truth. Only at the people of God "Sanctuary" will "Kings" and all in Authority including the

Illuminati be saved. The Illuminati must know that the worshipping of Morloch at this time for advance technology and power in government will not save them. Morloch with all of his powers will be destroyed and Satan his leader, will be cast into the Lake of Fire forever. Only at the "Sanctuary" for the people of God where the people of God are living quiet and peaceful lives will "Intercessions" be made for all men including Kings and all in Authority. 1 Timothy 2: 1-4 and Revelation 20: 10

If the white Gentiles are to be saved at this late hour, the Sanctuary must be built. This is the message concerning Salvation for the white Gentiles that the white Gentiles wanted delivered to them this time in the nick of time, so they would know what to do to be saved, this time. The message has been delivered as promised. There at the sanctuary, the white Gentiles will be saved and come to the knowledge of the truth just as the Egyptians were saved in Goshen when the spirit of death killed all of the first born in Egypt. Remember, in the days of Moses, Goshen became the Sanctuary for the Egyptians that was given to the Hebrews by the Egyptians. 1 Timothy 2: 1-4

Remember, in the beginning immediately after the white Gentiles begged for a second chance for salvation, in the womb of the universe, Esau who is a representation of the white Gentiles fought with Jacob who is a representation of the people of God to be born first to receive a second chance that was promised to the white Gentiles and to also receive what was promise to the "Meek" or the people of God which was to inherit the earth after the white Gentiles had their second chance for salvation and that inheritance goes to the first born and "no-good" Esau wanted to be born first. God made it possible for Jacob to get his inheritance back from Esau and then, God renamed Jacob to "Israel" which means IS REAL to designate who was REAL and who the inheritance goes to. Remember, the story of Jacob and Esau is not about the Children. The story of Jacob and Esau is about two nations or two races of people fighting to determine who would be born first because of a plan of God. After thousands of years of suppression of this truth, the Books of Simion have revealed God's plan for Jacob and for Esau. Matthew 5: 5, Genesis 25: 23, Genesis 32: 28 and Romans 9: 11

This is why Jesus is the Savior of the people of God because by the Blood of Jesus, the people of God are saved. Jesus died for all of the sins the people of God would commit while they were in slavery, persecuted and scattered so the people of God could still receive the inheritance. Jesus was only sent to the people of God and not to the white Gentiles who Jesus referred to as "Dogs". Jesus told His disciples "Not" to go to the white Gentiles to offer salvation to them but to only go to the "Lost Sheep" of Israel. The people of God do not have to observe the holidays or be exposed to the scriptures that the white Jews keeps away from the people of God and still if the people of God live a righteous life, they will inherit Paradise because by the Blood of Jesus, they are saved. Matthew 15: 24-26 and Matthew 10: 5-6

# Double will Happen to the white Gentiles

The white Jews who are the descendent of Cain are psychotic or out of touch with reality to believe that when God returns He will accept them as the people of God. Remember, Cain was jealous of Abel as the Jews were envious of the people of God in biblical days and are jealous and envious of the Afro Americans who are the people of God today. The white Jews were called Blood of or descendants of Vipers by John the Baptist because they are the descendants of Cain and Cain father was the serpent in the Garden of Eden (Aden) and they were warned not to call themselves the people of God or to say that Abraham was their father. They were told by John the Baptist that before God accept them as His children, God would raise up stones to be His children. Acts 13: 45, Acts 17: 5, 1 John 3: 12 and Matthew 3: 7-9

The white Gentiles who have dominion today must know that the Holy Bible has warned the white Gentiles that "Double" will happen to the white Gentiles that happens to the people of God. The white Jews and white Gentiles must know that their fate and the people of God fate are connected. Double will happen to the Gentiles that happens to the people of God. The False Prophet do not want the white Gentiles who have dominion today to understand this prophecy. They do not want the white Gentiles who have dominion today to connect what is happening to the white Gentiles with what the white Gentiles are doing to the Afro Americans here in America and to the people of God in the Mid-East and Africa. Revelation 18: 6

The white Gentiles are the cowardly using all of their military might to fight people in the Middle-East that don't have the white Jews and the white Gentiles guns, bombs, ships or planes.

Because of this act against the people of God, natural disasters and suicides have plagued the Gentiles. Tornadoes, earthquakes, floods, forest-fires and hurricanes have destroyed the Gentiles homes just as the Gentiles destroyed the people of God homes in the Mid-East. Because the people of God who are the Afro Americans were Scattered-out of California, California has become unlivable and many more white Gentiles are now forced to leave California. There is a large exodus from California because of the overcrowding, crime, no jobs and natural disasters. Unbelievable heat from wild fires in the hills of California are destroying everything in California. Homes and the country side are being scorched. Thousands of people are losing everything they have and being made homeless. Observers and firefighters will tell you that the fires themselves are not acting like natural fires. The fires have a mind of their own. They go where they want to go. They roar like gigantic dragon that spends like a tornado and the fire and heat from the dragon's mouth is three to five times hotter than a normal fire. Next, it will be the earthquakes.

In Genesis in the Holy Bible, God tells Abraham that He will not destroy Sodom and Gomorrah for the sake of ten righteous people that are in the city. Abraham asked the Lord to spare the cities if the righteous were still there and couldn't leave. Why was the ascendants of the slaves and the slaves are God's first born and the ascendants of the slaves are the Afro Americans scattered out of California? What happen to the Afro Americans that use to live in Los Angeles, California? Genesis 18: 32, Genesis 18: 23-24 and Exodus 4: 22

This is why the white Gentiles who have dominion today must know who IS RAEL(REAL) and who is not because the people of God fate is connected to the fate of the white Greek Jews and white Gentiles who have dominion today. This is why the white Gentiles cannot afford to be deceived about who are the true people of God in the latter-days of the dominion. Double will happen to them that happens to the people of God. Scattering the people of God out of California have brought the hardships to California. If they had ten, ten righteous Afro Americans left in California, California could have been spared for the sake of those ten righteous people. It is important that the white Gentiles who have dominion today know who are the true people of God because their fate and the white Jews and white Gentiles fate are connected. Revelation 18: 6

Gentile soldiers that killed the people of God in Afghanistan and in Iraq who did not have the guns, bombs, ships and planes that the Gentiles had committed suicides when they returned home. Since the people of God did not have the guns to fight back, unseen forces are causing the gentile soldiers to kill themselves. It is estimated that 20-50 gentile soldiers from the religious war that America is fighting in the Mid-East commit suicide every day. Those that do not commit suicide becomes Psychotic or Out-Of-Touch with Reality.

Because the white Gentiles killed the people of God by flooding their neighborhoods with drugs, the white Gentiles children are dying from self-affected "opioid" drug over-doses at an alarming rate. Double will happen to the white Gentiles that happens to the people of God. Those against the white Gentiles who have dominion today will not want the white Gentiles who have dominion today to understand this connection to the people of God. That is why it is important that the white Gentiles who have dominion today know who Is Rael(Real) and who is not. The white Gentiles fate and the people of God fate are connected. The Holy Bible says that double will happen to the white Gentiles that happens to the people of God. Anyone deceiving the white Gentiles who have dominion today that they are the people of God is responsible for all of the deaths in the white Gentiles community today. Revelation 18: 6

Because the white Jews and white Gentiles tried to turn the black woman against the black man, white women are betraying the white man and bringing the white man down at an alarming rate because of sexual misconduct and other reasons. White women call their movement to bring the white man down, "The Me-Too Movement".

Because the white Gentiles police officers were killing Afro Americans for any reasons because they said that they were afraid of the Afro Americans, the white Gentiles police officers are now killing the white Gentiles in the same manner and are saying that they are afraid of the white Gentiles or the public too. They are killing white Gentiles just as cold-blooded as they are killing the Afro Americans.

Because the white Gentiles were shooting the people of God and claiming to be in a neighborhood watch program, white Gentiles are now shooting white Gentiles in mass numbers at music festivals, in their churches, in their children schools and on the streets.

Because the white Gentiles had black children killing black children in the neighborhoods, white children are killing white children in the schools. The white Gentiles are at a lost for an explanation for why white children are killing white children in their schools and at a lost why the white "good-old-boys" are now killing white Gentiles even at Country-Western concerts which were concerts designed to unite the white educated Gentiles with the low-life Confederate gentiles in rural areas.

The white Gentiles who have dominion today must know that double will happen to the white Gentiles that happens to the people of God. The false prophet will not want the Gentiles to connect these two events together showing that one action is the cause of the other effect. The Holy Bible has recorded that "Double" will happen to the white Gentiles that happens to the people of God. Are the white Gentiles who have dominion today evolved enough to understand this prophecy or will they side with the False Prophet who are those that are assuming the true people of God identity because of "Envy" and say that they do not believe? Revelation 18: 6

The Holy Bible has recorded that double will happen to the white Gentiles that happened to the people of God. The white Gentiles and the people of God fates are connected. It is because of this that the white Gentiles who have dominion today must know who Is Rael (Real) and who is not if the white Gentiles are to be saved, this time. If the white Gentiles allow any other race of people to assume the people of God identity and deceive the white Gentiles who has dominion today not to protect the people of God but to protect the "Changelings" who are demon people that have assumed the identity of the people of God, all will be lost for the white Gentiles. Revelation 18: 6

The white Jews and white Gentiles are fighting a religious war in Afghanistan and Iraq and their soldiers that they are using are South American and Mexican Indians that the Holy Bible identifies as heathens and infidels who do not know God or the Son of God. These Indians believe that God and the Son of God are white gentiles. If you believe that God and the Son of God are anything other than the color of brass (brown) that has been burned in the furnace (dark brown to black) with hair like sheep wool or nappy hair, you do not know God or the Son of God. Revelation 1: 14-15, John 16: 3, John 8; 19 and John 15: 21

Afro American soldiers were not used as they were in Vietnam because they would have refused to carry out the inhumane treatment of the people of God in the Mid-East as they did in Vietnam so the Jews and the Gentiles chose heathens and infidels who do not know God who are the Indians to fight this religious war and the South American and Mexican Indians were promised the Afro Americans homes, neighborhoods, jobs, civil rights and a American citizenship if they joined the army and fought a religious war for the white Gentiles. The white Jews and white Gentiles betrayed the South Americans Indians and the Mexican Indians because after these Indians had fought a religious war for the white Jews and white Gentiles against the people of God in the Middle-East, the white Jews and white Gentiles departed them back to their countries. Only at the end did the South American Indians and the Mexican Indians realize that the white Americans wanted America for white people only. The white Jews and the white Gentiles have deceived the Indians to believe that Abraham was their father and they are the people of God because they are white. These Mexican and South American Indians worship the white Gentiles as gods. They believe that God, the Son of God and the Mother of the Son of God are white pagan Gentiles.

The white race who are the white Greeks and the white Romans who God is Zeus are fighting everyone in the Mid-East who believes in the God of the Holy Bible so the Greeks and the Romans whose dominions have come and now, at the end of the age have gone, could assume their identity and receive the inheritance of the nonwhites or humans to inherit the earth and live a thousand years with Jesus in Paradise.

Remember, Esau wanted a second chance for salvation and also wanted Jacob inheritance to inherit the earth after Esau had his second chance. Esau betrayed Jacob and betrayed the God that gave the white Gentiles a second chance in the womb of the universe when he fought with Jacob to be born first to receive a second chance that was promised to the white Gentiles and also to be born first so he could receive Jacob inheritance or the promise to the MEEK to inherit the earth after the white Gentiles had their second chance. Because of this betrayal by Esau in the womb of the universe to steal Jacob inheritance by wanting to be born first immediately after the Gentiles begged for a second chance, no one in Heaven trust the Gentiles. Remember, the white Gentiles do not want the MEEK to inherit the earth and live a thousand years in paradise with the Lamb. The white Gentiles want an additional thousand years Reich on the earth. They want Jacob inheritance. They know that God will not be with them, so they want to make a treaty or agreement with the extraterrestrials known as the Greys for advance technology in their extended thousand years Reich on the earth.

# 25

# United States declare war on the Afro Americans

The United State government has also declared war on the Afro Americans. They say that by the people of God who are the Afro Americans today saying that their lives matter is a threat to them. These psychotic white Gentiles wants the people of God to say that their lives do not matter so the white Gentiles will not feel guilty when they murder the people of God. I pity the white Gentiles this time at Judgment for what they have done to the people of God who are the "Broken Branch" that is sharing their Roots or "Planet" with the Grafted Branch who are the white Gentiles. Remember, the Holy Bible has warned the white Gentiles who are the Grafted Branch not to "Boast" but remember, you do not support the "root" (planet) but the "root" (planet) supports you. Understand that if the Branches were broken off or became "Dead" and you being a wild olive tree that is "contrary to nature" were grafted in among them or you were put among the people of the world on this planet and with them became a partaker of the root or world do not boast. You must say that the Branches were broken off that you could be grafted in. It is this act of being broken off for the sake of the Gentiles that makes the Broken Branch the white Gentiles savior. The white Gentiles must say this to be accepted by God. Romans 11: 17-19, Romans 11: 12 and Romans 11: 19

It is the fall of the people of God that is the riches of the world and the diminishing of the people of God that is the riches of the Gentiles. The white Gentiles must say this. Romans 11: 12 and Romans 11: 19

The latter-day Deliverer mission is not to farther suppress the truth or indorse the lie that the white Gentiles are the people of God. The latter-day Deliverer mission is to reveal to the white Gentiles what they must do to remain grafted on the Tree of Life to prevent from being "Cut-Off" and regressed into beings worse than the "Negros" whose regression for the "disbelief" for the sake of the Gentiles now have them identified as the "Dead". Therefore, you must consider the goodness and severity of God. On those who fell because of disbelief, severity but towards the Gentiles who were evolved into Homo sapiens and given dominion, goodness and if you continue in God's goodness you shall remain grafted on the Tree of Life otherwise you also will be "Cut-Off" from the Tree of Life. The descendants of the slaves who are the "Negros" and the word "Negro" means dead are the Dead-Dry-Bones and the "Whole House of Israel" spoke off in the book of Ezekiel in the Holy Bible that is "Cut-Off" or "Broken Off" from the Tree of Life but now "Believes" and have revealed the "Mystery of the Gospel" to prove that they "Understand" and "Believes" will be grafted back into the Tree of Life. The revealing of the "Mystery of the Gospel" to the white Gentiles to save the white Gentiles will also guarantee that the people of God will be grafted back into the Tree of Life and inherit the earth because it will prove that the people of God now today understand and believe in the power of God. Romans 11: 20-23 and Ezekiel 37: 11

The "Whole House of Israel are called "DEAD" or called "NEGRO" because Negro and Necro are the same word and Necro means "Dead". Negro should be pronounced the same way you pronounce "negative" because "Neg" and "Nec" have the same sound. If you are not called "DEAD" or called "NEGRO", you are not the House of Israel and the people of God. There is no lost tribe of Israel. The "Whole House of Israel meaning all twelve tribes are called Dead Dry Bones or called Negro today. If you are not called "Negro", you are not the people of God from the House of Israel. Ezekiel 37: 11

For I do not desire Gentiles that you should be ignorant of this mystery unless you be wise in your own "Conceit" (undeserved self-importance, pride and vanity), that blindness in part (not all of Israel shall be blind) has happened to Israel until the fullness of the Gentiles comes in at the end of the age or on December 21, 2012. Only those who are redeemed from among men being the first fruit to God and to the Son of God in the latter-days are not blind. After that time, the Deliverer will come forth and deliver a profound message that will turn you away from ungodliness. The Holy Bible has recorded that a hundred and forty-four thousand will be redeemed from the people of God who are Afro-American men and in their mouths were found no deceit for they are without fault before the throne of God. It cannot be stressed enough how important these redeemed men are to the white Gentiles and to the Afro Americans in saving their souls at the end of the age. These redeemed Afro American men are without fault before the throne of God. Revelation 14: 3-5 and Romans 11: 25-26

Therefore, let it be known to you that the "Salvation" of God has been written and delivered to the Gentiles by one who was redeemed from among men in the Books of Simion and the Gentiles will hear it and believe. Acts 28: 28

Jesus is not the white Gentile savior. Those who are broken off for the sake of the white Gentiles that are called Dead or called "NEGRO" are the white Gentiles saviors. To be saved, you must say this. Jesus is the People of God savior only. Jesus told His disciples to go only to the lost sheep of Israel and not to go to the white Gentiles. Jesus said that He was only sent to the lost sheep of the house of Israel. The way the white gentile Christians say they love Jesus for being their savior is the way the white gentile Christians should say they love the Broken Branch who are called Dead or called "Negro" because it is them who are the white Gentiles savior. Read it in the Holy Bible and understand. Romans 11: 12, Romans 11: 19, Matthew 10: 5-6 and Matthew 15: 24

Paul and Simeon were sent to the Gentiles and not Jesus. Jesus sent Paul to bear Jesus name before the Gentiles and God chose Simon Peter to reveal the word of the gospel to the Gentiles in the latter days. Jesus is not the white Gentiles savior because Jesus was not sent to the white Gentiles but was sent only to the House of Israel. Jesus died for the house of Israel sins only. Acts 9: 5, Acts 9: 15, Acts 15: 7, Matthew 10: 5-6 and Matthew 15: 24

When there was much dispute about who would deliver the truth to the white Gentiles in the latter days, Peter who was Simon and called Simeon and called a Nig er (Nigg er) rose up and said to them, "Men and brethren, you know that a good while ago (before the world began) God chose among us that by my mouth the Gentiles should hear the word of the gospel and believe". This is why Peter's Basilica in Roman was built to receive the spirit of Simon Peter or he that would be possessed by the spirit of Simon Peter in the latter-days, so the white Gentiles could hear the word of the gospel and "Believe" and be saved. Acts 10: 5, Acts 13: 1, 2 Timothy 1: 9 and Acts 15: 7

Only him who is possessed by the spirit of Simon Peter will deliver the word of the gospel to the white Gentiles and the white Gentiles will know that the "Deliverer" of the word of God is indeed him that was chosen and sent because of the message delivered and because the white Gentiles will "Believe" the delivered message that is so profound, the disbelieving Jews in biblical days said that the delivered truth from the "Brethren" or Brothers could turn the world up-side down. In the latter days, the white Gentiles will know for a certainty that the delivered truth was indeed the message that the disbelieving Jews said could turn the world up-side down. Acts 15: 7 and Acts 17: 6

There is only one suppressed truth in the world today that is so profound it could turn the world up-side down and the white Gentiles will know if that truth was indeed delivered. No one else on the planet knows the suppressed truth but him who was chosen to deliver the suppressed truth to the Gentiles to save the Gentiles. It is a suppressed truth that is real and recorded in the Holy Bible yet, it was unknown until him who was chosen and possessed by the spirit of Simon Peter revealed the "Mystery of the Gospel" or interpreted the Word of God in the Holy Bible to the Gentiles so the white Gentiles could "Believe" and be "Saved". Acts 15: 7

The Holy Bible has recorded that those that are redeemed from among men who are the first-fruits to God and to the Lamb sent to reveal the Mystery of the Gospel from biblical days till the latter days will sing a song or have a message that nobody else knows. These are the ones who were not defiled with women when they were chosen because they were chosen before the world begun and once in the world, they will be "Redeemed" from among men and they will "Repent" and be "Converted" and become Priests to the "Most-High" God and they will never be defiled with women again and all of their sins will be blotted-out and in their mouths was found no deceit for they are without fault before the throne of God. Revelation 14: 3-5, 2 Timothy 1: 9, Exodus 19: 6, Revelation 1: 6, Revelation 20: 6, and Acts 3: 19

Since the end of the dominion shall be declared from the beginning of the dominion and in the beginning of the dominion, Simon who was surnamed Peter who was called Simeon and called a Nig er (Nigg er) declared to the Gentiles that God wanted to take out of the white Gentiles a people for God's name, at the end of the dominion it will be him who is possessed by the spirit of Simon Peter that will be called Simion and called a Nig er (Nigg er) that will deliver the message again to the Gentiles that God wants to take out of the white Gentiles a people for God's name and for that cause, the words of the Prophets or the Books of Simion are written. Remember, the ancient prophets are subject to the prophets or the ancient prophets will be in the latter-day prophets. This is revealing the "Mystery of the Gospel". Isaiah 46: 10, Acts 13: 1, Acts 15: 14-15 and 1 Corinthians 14: 32

There is no Da Vinci code to be understood but there is the Mystery of the Gospel that must be revealed. Only He who is the Ambassador from the people of God to the throne of the Gentiles that is given utterance to speak boldly as He ought to speak or as you promised last time at judgment that He would be allowed to speak to reveal the mystery of the gospel to the Gentiles to save the Gentiles will make known the Mystery of the Gospel to the Gentiles. This is revealing the unknown part or the secrecy of the word of God that is described as the Mystery of the Gospel. Ephesians 6: 19-20

I pity the white Gentiles this time at Judgment for what they did to those that helped them survive who are their saviors. Understand that no race in the universe has the honor and respect in Heaven that the Broken Branch who are called Negro has. This time at Judgment, the white Gentiles can ask concerning the days that are passed which were before you in the first world and since the day that God created man on the earth in the world we live in today and ask from one end of Heaven to the other end if any great thing like this has ever happened or ask if any other race has ever sacrifice so much for another race and will be told that no other race in the universe has this honor. Deuteronomy 4: 32

The American government assassinated the Afro Americans leaders and flooded the Afro Americans neighborhoods with drugs to finance the government black or secret projects and they devised a plan to kill Afro Americans male children on a grand scale. Three to five hundred Afro Americans male children were killed in American cities every year for more than twenty years. Do the math to determine how many Afro American male children were programed to kill themselves by the white Jews and by the white Gentiles. As time repeats itself, the killing of the Hebrew male children was also done in Egypt thousands of years ago and that action brought forth Moses.

The white Gentiles police murdered a twelve-year-old child playing in a park because they said that they were afraid of him as well as murder a child coming from the store because the child had a hoody on his head.

The white Gentiles calls themselves civilized, intelligent and evolved yet they want to exterminate a race of people because of their envy and jealousy of that race. What the white Gentiles are doing to the people of the world and to the slave race proves that the white gentiles Christians are not "Civilized" and are not "Worthy" or "Tekel" to continue to exist with the people of the world. Daniel 5: 27

When the fullness of the Gentiles came in at the end of the age on December 21, 2012, the white Gentiles and white Jews were barbaric. They were no more evolved than the cowboys and the gangsters or the Hatfields and the Mc Coys of their past. What they did to the people of God in the Mid-East in their Persia Gulf war is barbaric and inhumane. For what the white Gentiles are doing to the Afro Americans by saying that the Afro American "lives do not matter" and what the white Gentiles are doing to the people of the Mid-East makes the white Gentiles who are not human guilty of human rights violations on a grand scale. What they did in the Mid-East was not about American freedom because the American freedom was never threatened. What they did in the Mid-East and to the people of God in America known as the Afro Americans was about hate, jealousy and to install fear so the white Greeks and the white Romans could occupy the people of God land in the Mid-East and assumed their identity to receive the people of God in the Mid-East inheritance as they want to steal the inheritance that belong to those who are scattered who are the Afro Americans today.

This is criminal yet, no one from the race of the "Dead" called "Negro" have suggested to bring these violations of human rights to the world court. Those from the race of the dead called "Negro" have been "Meek" which is humble, timid, submissive or afraid to speak up and out against the violations against them. The Holy Bible has recorded that those who possess the traits of the "Meek" shall be blessed and inherit the earth. Matthew 5: 5

Remember, the Holy Bible says that because of the people of God iniquity and their "Uncle-Tom" ways, the people of God who are the Afro Americans were given the spirit of "Stupor" which means they are "Stupid" and the spirit of "Slumber" which means they are walking around like they are asleep. They have eyes that cannot see and ears that cannot hear to this very day. Because they freely kissed the white man ass, king David suggested to God to let their ways be a snare and a trap and a stumbling-block and a recompense or payment to them. King David instructs God to let their eyes be darkened, that they may not see or let them be stupid and ignorant and let them bow down their backs like slaves always or let them remain a "Uncle-Tom" all of their lives. Today, this is exactly what the people of God are saying about the "Uncle-Toms" of today. When the people of God see a "Uncle-Tom" kissing the white man ass, the people of God today says in their minds that they wish that "Uncle-Tom" never wake-up and understand but remain an imbecile, an idiot and a moron or a person with subnormal intelligence forever. Because the kingdom of God is within us, that wish made in their minds goes straight to God and because king David urged God to do this, that wish on the "Uncle-Tom" is heard and granted. The "Uncle-Toms" of today must know that they will not get away with uncle-toming to the white man. They must know that they are being cursed by the righteous with a thought. Romans 11: 8-10 and Luke 17: 21

    The white Gentiles of today are saying that they are going to make America great again, but America never lost its greatness. America is still the world greatest superpower. What they were really saying under-cover was that they were going to make the white man great again realizing that the white man is being regressed as we speak on an evolutionary level and this weakening of the white man genetic structure is weakening his ability to procreate and a lot more. The white man wants more time. The white man wants a third Reich or an additional thousand years reign. This is what the fight between good and evil will be about that the white Gentiles calls the War of Armageddon which will be fought in the Valley of Jehoshaphat for the people of God who are scattered who are the Afro Americans inheritance. The Afro Americans are being scattered right now in the latter days when God has promised to return and gather His people that are being scattered. Where are the Afro Americans who use to live in Los Angeles, California? Why were they scattered out of the state? Joel 3: 2

The message that was channeled to the white Gentiles from the future that was portrayed in the 1982 movie titled, "Blade Runner" is that the white Gentiles want more time on the earth. They want an additional thousand-year reign or Reich. The thought channeled to the Gentiles that is in the movie "Blade Runner" is that the white Gentiles are demanding more life from the creator. That is why Esau betrayed Jacob in the womb of the universe to be born first to inherit the earth and why the white beings have assumed the human beings' identity and have a desire to rebuild the Temple in Jerusalem to speak to God to demand more time. In the movie, the replicated white Gentiles say it will not be easy to meet their creator, but they must because they want the Creator to repair what the Creator made. Remember, the white Gentiles have bad skin, bad bone structures, a weaker immune system and a shorter life span.

In the movie, the replicated white Gentiles say that they are afraid of death and they want more life or a longer life span. It was told to the white Gentiles that the coding sequence to the white Gentiles genetics that will prevent the white Gentiles from evolving cannot be reversed by the Gentiles. It would be fatal to attempt to make any alterations in the evolvement or evolutionary development of an organic life form. It was told to the white Gentiles that this was the facts of life for them.

In the white Gentiles dominion, the replicated white inferior Gentiles were allowed to burn twice as bright as all the others on the planet earth, but the white Gentiles were genetically designed to last half as long or to the fullness of the Gentiles comes in. In the white Gentiles lives, from year one of their life to year 29, they portray the appearance of a young branch. Their skin, hair and bone structure do not have the appearance of a body that has been exposed to the elements for hundreds of thousands of years. Their skin looks young like baby skin.

Once the white Gentiles reach thirty, their genetic flaws appear, and their aging process is accelerated. After thirty, their skin, their organs and their bone structure ages three-time faster than the colored people of the world. Their skin has the horrible appearance of something that is dead or dying because of the extreme wrinkling of their skin that resemble a dead, dry, wrinkle leaf. Their internal organs begin to fail and their immune system malfunctions triggering the onset of strange and unusual diseases. Science and technology will not be able to counteract this coding sequence of the white Gentiles genetics. It is in the white Gentiles genetics that is restricting the white Gentiles from procreation. This restriction of the white Gentiles ability to procreate is the first steps in the white Gentiles regression. If events are not steered in another direction to prevent what is prophesied to come to pass, the white Gentiles will be broken off from the Tree of Life and no place will be found for the great white throne in the future. After the fullness of the Gentiles comes in at the end of the age on December 21, 2012 or after the Gentiles have reached their maximum level of evolutionary development in their second chance for salvation, to receive farther evolutionary growth, the white Gentiles will have to be judged and found worthy to continue to receive nourishment from the roots of this planet on the Tree of Life that are for the people of God that the people of God freely chose to share with the white Gentiles, so the white Gentiles could survive. To continue to be nourish from the roots of this planet, the white Gentiles must behold or reveal everything that have happened and reveal who are the true people of

God otherwise, the white Gentiles will be broken off or cut off from the Tree of Life. The white Gentiles must say who are the true people of God to survive. Romans 11: 25, 2 Corinthians 5: 10, Romans 11: 17-18, Revelation 20: 11, Romans 11: 22 and Romans 11: 19

Once again, in the movie "Blade Runner" the white Gentiles revealed what was in their hearts and minds to do to the Creator and the white Gentiles must know that God searches the mind and the hearts to give to each of us according to our works. The white Gentiles must know that God knows what is in the Gentiles minds and hearts to do that the Gentiles will not admit out in the open but will unconsciously reveal their intensions in their movies. Revelation 2: 23, Jerimiah 11: 20 and Jerimiah 17: 10

The white Gentiles must know that God knows how the white Gentiles really feel about Him. Now since the white Jews and white Gentiles knows that God know how they feel about Him, a reorganization of their thoughts and actions should be in order to steer events in another direction to chance the shape of the things that are prophesied to come. The white Gentiles must know that the white Gentiles who are "ORDAINED" or "APPOINTED" to eternal life this time because they believed last time will believe again this time. It is these white Gentiles that God wants to take out of the white Gentiles for God's name and for that cause, the words of the Prophets or the Books of Simion are written. The white Gentiles must know that we all will appear before the judgment seat of God that each one may receive the things done whether good or bad. Revelation 2: 23, Acts 13: 48, Acts 15: 14-15, 2 Corinthians 5: 10, Romans 2: 16, Romans 2: 6 and Galatians 6: 7

Knowing the terror of the Lord, those that are Sent will attempt to persuade the Gentiles by revealing this to them. The God of the Holy Bible will be the final "Terrorist" in the white Gentile latter-day dominion of "Iron and Clay". Instead of weeping and mourning, the white Gentiles shall be seen on the Travel Channel and on the broadcast News eating, drinking and being merry refusing to change knowing that tomorrow they all shall die. They shall be seen partying, celebrating and getting married saying that nothing that happens to them will change their ways and customs or life-style just as it was in the days of Noah when they partied until the flood came and destroyed them all. 2 Corinthians 5: 11, Isaiah 22: 13, Luke 17: 26-29 and 1 Corinthians 15: 32

Those that are Sent are well known to the Lord and because you Gentiles sent the latter-day deliverer to deliver this profound message, I also trust that the deliverer and the content of the message is well known in your subconsciousness to help you in consciences decisions. 2 Corinthians 5: 11

When the Gentiles realizes that nothing that they have done and have accomplished in their dominions is enough for the God of genetic engineering that created them would let them in Paradise and Heaven for or give them eternal life or an additional thousand-year Reich, the white Gentiles put in their movie "Blade Runner" that the white Gentiles have in their hearts and minds that they would like to kill their creator or God because of that. Because the Kingdom of God is within you, God knows what is in your hearts, minds and what is in your movies. "You have been Alerted". This is the mission of the "Deliverer" that you sent to "forewarn" you and "alert" you about the things that shall come to pass. The order from God to be for the "Salvation" of the white Jews and white Gentiles in the "Present" and till the end of the earth have been obeyed and because of that order, the promise made to the white Jews and white Gentiles last time at judgment to be for their "Salvation" by delivering the "Truth" in the latter-days to them so they would know what is going on, so they would know what to do to be saved has been fulfilled. (1982 movie titled, "Blade Runner"), Luke 17: 21 and Acts 13: 46-47

Remember, Jesus said that the white Jews and white Romans did not know what they are doing. The "Truth" has been delivered. Now, when the Gentiles hears this, they will be glad and glorified the word of the Lord and as many that had been appointed or ordained to eternal life this time because they believed last time, will believe again this time and the word of the Lord in the Books of Simion will be published throughout all the region. Luke 23: 34 and Acts 13: 48-49

# 26

# When the fullness of the Gentiles came in

The Afro Americans do not have bombs, guns, ships and planes yet a high tech militarize country like America that do possess all of these things and more wants to declare war on the Afro Americans who are the true people of God. North Korea, China and Russia who have guns, bombs, missiles, ships and planes too just as America has have been trying to pick a fight with America for years, but America do not want to fight people that are equally as armed as America is. That's a coward.

America is no longer one nation under God with liberty and justice for all but is now one nation under Satan with liberty and justice only for the people of the Synagogue of Satan and the white Gentiles or only for the white Hellenistic Greeks and the white Romans from the white Gentile dominion who God is the fallen angel named Zeus.

It is because of this that the Freedom Fighters in America are now refusing to stand for America's national anthem. Freedom

Fighters in America are now taking a "Knee" when the national anthem is played in protest of all of the injustices against the human race or non-white people in America and throughout the world. Martin Luther King said that the greatness of America is, in America, you have the right to protest for your rights. Taking a "Knee" when the national anthem is played is the Afro Americans right to protest for their rights as American citizens especially when America is playing an anthem about America's liberties and rights for American people. It is against the true meaning and purpose of America to prevent the Afro Americans from protesting for their rights. Anyone that say that the Afro American taking a "Knee" when the national anthem is played is an insult to the American flag is violating the main purpose of America and disrespecting the true meaning of America. It is unconstitutional to deny the Afro Americans from protesting for their rights when the National Anthem is played which is an anthem about Americans rights. Taking a "Knee" is the Afro Americans way of asking America why the liberties and rights given to Americans does not apply to the Afro Americans. As American citizens, this is their right and anyone that denies them that right is breaking America's must highest principles and violating America's fundamental purpose which is the foundation of the American constitution. The Afro Americans have a right to protest for their rights in any arena that will best expose their protest to the minds that are violating the American constitution by denying the Afro Americans the right to protest. Tell white women that they do not have the right to protest in arenas that best exposes their injustice like at the actors' awards. Anyone who denies the Afro Americans their right to protest for their rights should be locked-up and sued because they are violating the law and everything that America stand for and they are disrespecting the constitution. America is not America and the purpose for America is a lie, if the Afro Americans right to protest for their rights is not honored. The protecting of white supremacist rights to protest in a country where American citizens died fighting white supremacy in World War 2 is disrespecting the American flag and veterans that fought against Nazism. The Afro Americans who are taking a knee are veterans in protest about their rights. They have the right to protest in any arena that will best expose the injustices toward the Afro American people of America. Like with the Indians in America, the white Gentiles have betrayed, double-crossed and broken every peaceful agreement and civil rights law made to the Afro Americans. They have a right to protest. Revelation 3: 9 and (Marlon Brando interview on the Dick Cavett show 1973)

When the fullness of the Gentiles came in at the end of the age on December 21, 2012, the white Gentiles were no more evolved than the hillbillies named the Hatfields and the Mc Coys or the cowboys and gangsters. They were not evolving or going forward but were regressing going backwards into their primitive ancestors. They regressed from wanting to be Trekies and boldly going where no man has gone before seeking higher values to the Sons of Anarchy seeking violence, disorder, chaos, lawlessness, mayhem and hatred from their past on all who are not "white".

In the 2016 presidential race, one of the white Gentile candidates is offering the white Gentiles this platform and he is saying that white dominance throughout the world on all who are not white will secure America and make America strong again. Hitler in the 1930's had the same platform. With this platform, this presidential candidate has united all of the low lives in the white Gentiles communities to support him and his uncivilized ideas. If he is elected, World War Three is a certainty.

The white Gentiles said they would never move forward, never accept new ideas, never join in or mix with others or integrate to become human beings and they would never change their primitive, hillbilly, southern Cajun, red-neck, cracker point of view. They said that this was their history that they were proud of and would not forget. In 2016, they were still celebrating the actions of evil civil war generals that fought to enslave the people of God. They should know that God has said that those who lead His people into captivity shall go into captivity. They should know that the God of the Holy Bible has said that God HATES the young white race for putting the old black African race in slavery or making the old black African race their servants and God LOVES the old black African race. God says that God LOVES Jacob or the old black African race and HATES Esau who is a representation of the new white gentile race. Revelation 13: 10, Roman 9: 12-13 and Malachi 1: 2-3

They are the unbelievers. They are the heathens and infidels. They do not believe in God or the Son of God. They believe that God and the Son of God are white, pagan Gentiles. They do not believe that God and the Son of God are Human with dark brown to black skin and hair like Sheep Wool or "Nappy" hair. It is because of this disbelief that they do not know God or the Son of God. John 15: 21, John 16: 3, 1 Corinthians 10: 20, 1 Thessalonians 3: 5 and Revelation 1: 14-15

It is recorded in the Holy Bible that Jesus who is the Lamb in Heaven and the One who will judge the white Gentiles is the color of brass (brown) that has been burned in a furnace (dark brown to black) with hair like sheep wool or nappy hair. The Shroud of Turin is a Lie and a Fake. Revelation 1: 14-15 and Romans 2: 16

They are the abominable. Their chemical and biological weapons are repulsive, detestable, monstrous, terrible and very awful for any race of people to conceive of. They are responsible for the designer viruses that are spreading throughout the world. When European and American Doctors who are white Gentiles and are the ones spreading deadly diseases in Africa were exposed to the deadly virus called Ebola, they received the cure but that same cure is forbidden to be given to the Africans. Only a monster that is influenced by demons from somewhere else could create atom bombs and biological weapons to kill so many of the people of the earth. These weapons are not designed to protect the people of the earth but are designed to kill the people of the earth or the human beings by the non-human beings or white Gentiles beings. The white Gentile Beings must not kill the Human Beings on this earth not even for the white Beings survival. That price for the white Gentiles survival is too high. To survive, the white Gentile beings must receive the truth and act accordingly. Their military industrial complex and space program is not meant for the advancement of knowledge and the prosperity of the advance life on the earth but is design for the control and the destruction of the people of the earth to preserve the white Gentiles dominion on the earth.

They are the murders of the planet. Assassinations are their top priority. They bragged about how their Navy Seal Team snipers have assassination many of the people of God all over the world. These government snipers assassinated President John F. Kennedy in 1963 and Dr. Martin Luther King in 1968 and many more American citizens because of their stand on Civil Rights for the People of God who are the Afro Americans. To this very day, the government of the United States has refused to release all records of the assassination of John F. Kennedy in fear of National Security or in fear that the American people would rebel against what the government did to one of the greatest Presidents America has ever had.

They are promoting sexual immorality to all throughout the world. This is to destroy the evolutionary growth in the people of the world, so the people of the world would have a need for the white gentile's technology. No other animal on the earth uses their evolutionary energy for a pleasure thrill throughout their body in the form of a sexual orgasm as often as possible. They will never reveal to the people that to live after the flesh desiring sex as often as possible, you will get sick and die but if you through the Spirit do mortify the deeds of the body practicing abstinence, you shall live. To have authority in the white Roman gentile dominion by being smarter than the white Roman Gentiles and living longer, the white Jewish Gentiles have deceived the white Roman Gentiles to believe that being Kosher or lawful towards God laws is for dietary purposes only. Remember, the Holy Bible says, the white Jews do not want the white Romans to be smart and realize who are the true people of God in fear that the white Roman gentiles who have dominion today would take away the white Jews nation and title of being the people of God and give a nation and the title of being the people of God to those who are scattered. This is why the white Jews plotted to kill Jesus to preserve their nation and their Lie. This is recorded in the Holy Bible. Romans 8: 13 and John 11: 47-54

They are inciting the men in America to become women and they have promoted lesbianism to women and they are saying that nothing is wrong with this type of behavior and it is the individual freedom of choice and right to express himself that determine what he should do. They are praising men that want to be transformed into women and women that want to be transformed into men and they are not telling these sick people that as long as a man has a XY chromosome and as long as a woman has a XX chromosome that they will always be who they were born to be, and it is these chromosomes that will genetically fight any such operations for transformation into the opposite sex. The fight with your DNA to be something that you are not will lead to mental unbalance, disease and then death. This type of life style is a death sentence to any race that follows it because it will destroy procreation and without man and woman coming together to procreated, there can be no future for that race. The Holy Bible has recorded that there was no future, or no place found for the great white throne in the future because of practices like that. It is because of this that Homosexuals and Lesbians will be directly responsible for the destruction of the white Gentiles and responsible for no place found for the great white throne in the future. Revelation 20: 11

The white Gentiles are already a conquered race and they don't even know it. To take away a man manhood and take away a woman womanhood is far worse to the individual than taking away from them their country. White Men wake up! Those extraterrestrials who are in control of the earth are manipulating you. To keep you docile so you are not a threat to them, they are making you their "Bitch". Once you lose your manhood, it is very easy to take anything else from you including your country and your self-freedom without a fight.

They are playing a psychological mind game on men today. They are tricking men to live their lives in their X chromosome which is their weaker side instead of their Y chromosome which is their stronger side.

Women must understand that man was given authority over woman not because his sex organs are on the outside while the woman sex organs are in the inside. Man was given authority over woman because of the Y chromosome. Man has a chromosome that woman do not have and can't understand. It is the combination of both the X and the Y chromosome in man that give man an edge over woman. Woman is not an equal vessel to man but is a weaker vessel because the woman does not have the Y chromosome. Women are easily deceived. Because of that, the Holy Bible has recorded not to permit a woman to teach or to have authority over a man but to be in silence. For Adam was not deceived but the woman being deceived fell into transgression. This is why the white Jews and white Gentiles have put the black woman in charge of the black man and the black family because the black women were easily deceived by the white man. The head of Jesus is God. The head of man is Jesus. The head of Woman is Man. 1 Peter 3: 7, 2 Timothy 2: 12-14, 1 Corinthians 14: 34-35, Ephesians 5: 21-24, 1 Corinthians 11: 3

Men have an XY chromosome and Woman have an XX chromosome. The X chromosome represents everything that is feminine or female and the Y chromosome represent everything that is masculine or male. All men have a feminine side and a masculine side. Women have the XX chromosome. One X of this double X chromosome represent logic and the other represent illogic or chaos. One X is positive, and the other X is negative, and both are feminine. Women inner fight is with which X shall express itself that day. Men was put in charge over woman because man has a Y chromosome that woman do not have and cannot understand. Man is best qualified to make the final choices between the two because man has a woman and man inside of himself and man can draw off the opinion of them both whereas woman can only see a situation from one point of view or from a feminine point of view because woman do not have a Y chromosome. Man fight each day like woman fight is to properly use both chromosomes including his feminine softer side to make his final choices to prevent from being too hard, cold and heartless. Now, since man has this feminine chromosome within himself, unseen forces are causing man to live totally in his feminine side for reasoning unknown.

Man was designed to be masculine with the ability to share in the female thinking process to best be the head of a family. Man can see and understand the feminine point of view because man has an X chromosome just as woman has. It is because of this that Man was chosen to be the leader of the family because Man has a combination of both genders in him and this allows him to understand both sides and to determine what is best for the whole. Women, stop fighting man over dominance and leadership. There is a woman inside of all men and it is because of this that women or not equal vessels to men but are weaker vessels because man has a Y chromosome that women do not have and cannot understand. Man was never meant to live totally in his X chromosome. This feminine chromosome in man expresses its self in man chest. God removed a rib from Adam's chest where his feminine chromosomes were to create Eve, a woman. What in the world do man need nipples on his chest for. Nipples are for nursing the young and nursing the young is a female job. It is an indication that if something extreme would happen to woman, God forbid, feminine men would evolve into women to continue the species. Adam was the only 100% masculine male because God took the female chromosome out of Adam's chest where his nipples were and made her walk alone side of Adam. Still, you must not be deceived to believe that you were designed to be a woman. Adam became an YY chromosome individual. Genesis 2: 21-22, Colossians 3: 18, 1 Timothy 2: 12-15, 1 Corinthians 11: 3, 8, 9 and 1 Peter 3: 7

They are the sorcerers of the planet. They are on television talking about they are Mediums for Satan and Satan demons. There is a sorcery drug store in every neighborhood. Sorcery is the ancient name for pharmaceutical or pharmacy. They have made us sick, so they could practice sorcery.

They are the idolaters. They idolize everything from women to Oscars and trophies of all kinds.

Finally, they are liars. They are in Israel right now lying about being the people of God. This lie that the white Roman Gentiles and the white Greek gentile have passing off as Jews and the people of God is the biggest lie in the world today. They are the ones who killed Jesus and killed the people of God in biblical days and now they are saying that they are the true people of God and this is what is the cause of all of the evil throughout the world today. In the white Gentile dominions, the white Gentiles are in Jerusalem until the fullness of the Gentiles comes in on December 21, 2012 or until the end of the white Gentiles dominion at the end of the age. The true people of God were led away captive and became slaves. While in and controlling Jerusalem, the holy city, the white Gentiles are more concern with not offending the cowardly, the unbelievers, the abominable, the murders, the sexually immoral, sorcerers, the idolaters and all liars than they are in obeying God. Luke 21: 24 and Revelation 21: 8

The Holy Bible has recorded that the cowardly, unbelieving, abominable, murderers, sexually immoral, sorcerers, and all liars shall have their part in the lake which burns with fire and brimstone. It is because of this that events must be steered in another direction to prevent what is prophesied to come to pass so the white Jews will not judge themselves unworthy for eternal life because they want to be the people of God so bad that they have assumed the people of God identity and to ensure that the great white throne is in the future. Revelation 21: 8, Acts 13: 46 and Revelation 20: 11

# 27

# The Scattering of the People of God

The Holy Bible has recorded this battle in the Valley of Jehoshaphat that will be about the heritage of those who are scattered. There, God has said that He will enter into a judgment with them who are assuming His people identity and wants God's people inheritance and that inheritance is for the MEEK in the white Gentile dominion to inherit the earth for giving the white Gentiles a second chance for salvation which is the story of Jacob and Esau. Joel 3: 2 and Matthew 5: 5

Remember, the white Gentiles do not want the MEEK to inherit the earth and live a thousand years in Paradise with the Lamb. The white Gentiles want to be granted an additional thousand-year Reich on the earth and they want Satan, or the forces of the Fallen Angels known as the Grey extraterrestrials to give them advance technology in the extended thousand-year Reich on the earth. Revelation 20: 4

The battle in the Valley of Jehoshaphat that the white Gentiles calls the War of Armageddon will be about those who are scattered heritage. The Afro Americans in America are those who are SCATTERED today in the latter-days when God will return to pass judgment against those who are scattering God's people and wants God's people heritage. Right now, if you are not being scattered, you are not the people of God that is referred to in the Holy Bible. Where are the Afro Americans that use to live in Los Angeles, California? What happened to them and why? Why were they scattered? Joel 3: 2

Every city in America that had a large Afro American population were called "sanctuary cities" where the white Gentiles flooded those cities with illegal immigrants. There in Afro Americans cities, the illegal immigrants were given sanctuary, or they could stay in America if they stayed in those Afro Americans cities and not in cities where white Gentiles had a large population. The Afro Americans in those sanctuary cities were scattered out of the city to make room for the illegal immigrants. The illegal immigrants in the sanctuary cities that use to be cities populated by Afro Americans were given the Afro Americans neighborhoods and jobs. Uncle Tom Barak Obama, who was the first Afro American president, was instrumental in giving the Afro American neighborhoods, jobs, and civil right to illegal immigrants. His legacy is that he was the worse president America has ever had when it comes to honoring the commandments in the Holy Bible and protecting the people of God who are the Afro Americans. He was a puppet for the white Jews and white Gentiles that carry out their agenda on the earth especially giving away the people of God who are the Afro Americans neighborhoods to illegal immigrants. The Holy Bible has recorded that the latter-day destruction of the white Gentile dominion was about "Housing" and how the white Jews and white Gentiles were living "Luxuriously" while they gave the people of God who are the Afro Americans neighborhoods, homes and jobs to illegal immigrants. It is these Afro Americans that are being "Scattered" who are the "wheat" among the "tares" that are the true people of God and the people who God is returning to gather into God's barn. Revelation 18: 7, Matthew 3: 12 and Matthew 30: 30

# 28

# The Valley of Jehoshaphat

The battle in the Valley of Jehoshaphat will be about the people of God that were sold to the Grecians, so they could be removed from Jerusalem. Once the people of God were sold to the Greeks and removed from Jerusalem, the Grecians assumed their identity and became today's white gentile Jews. Joel 3: 6

The Holy Bible has recorded that in the latter days when the fullness of the Gentiles comes in or when the Gentiles have reached their maximum level of evolutionary development at this stage at the end of the age or after December 21, 2012, the "Gentiles" would be in Jerusalem and the people of God would be led away captive in slavery. Luke 21: 24

To receive farther evolutionary development, the white Gentiles must be judged to determine if they are worthy to continue to exist with the colored people or the human beings on the earth. Last time, the judgment was "TEKEL" and it was pronounced that the Gentiles were found "WANTING" what was necessary to continue to exist.

They were given a second chance to prove themselves worthy in the world we live in today. Daniel 5: 27

The battle in the Valley of Jehoshaphat will also be about the gold and the silver the Gentiles have taken or recovered from ancient sites as well as God's pleasant things or ancient technology including the "Stargate" that the Gentiles have recovered at ancient sites that you have carried into your temples and government storage houses. All of these things must be return to the people of God. Joel 3: 5

Last time in the Valley of Jehoshaphat when the Gentiles were denied the heritage of the people of God or denied an additional thousand-year Reich and was told that God would return the Gentiles recompense upon their own heads and would sell their sons and daughters into slavery, the white Gentiles screamed proclaim this among the Gentiles. "Prepare for war". God has refused our request and has promised to bring recompense upon our head or get even with us for what we did to the people of God. God has said that those who led his people into captivity shall go into captivity. Joel 3: 7-9 and Revelation 13: 10

In the 1996 science fiction movie "Independence Day", the white Gentiles proclaimed that they would not be broken off from the Tree of Life and be regressed or go into darkness or into the "night" without a fight. Going into the "night" is a reference about the Gentiles being "Cut-Off" from the Tree of Life and regressed into the up-right paleolithic beast of their beginning because they did not make that public declaration about who are the true people of God. The white Gentiles have said in their hearts or in their movies that they will not be broken or cut off from the Tree of Life or go into darkness which they described in the movie as the "night" without a fight. The white Gentiles must understand that you cannot fight

God. The white Gentiles must know that their arms are too short to box with God. Romans 11: 22

The white Gentiles minds will be "Babbled" as were the minds of the people of the old black African dominion in the beginning that is recorded in the Holy Bible. The babbling of the Gentiles mind by God will be total and complete. Not just every country or every city will speak a different languish but every neighborhood.

Every neighborhood of the white Gentiles will speak a different languish. In most situations, the person next to you will speak a different language than you as were done to the old black Africans in the beginning. In a twinkling of your eye, we all will be changed. The "Dead" or the "Negro" will be raised first incorruptible and at the same time, the white Gentiles will be changed also. We all shall be changed. The white Gentiles minds will be babbled, and this babbling of the white Gentiles minds will be so complete that the person next to you will speak a different languish from yours that you cannot understand. Genesis 11: 9 and 1 Corinthians 15: 51-52

When the fullness of the Gentiles came in at the end of the age on December 21, 2012 which marked that the Gentiles had reached their maximum level of evolutionary development at this point, the white Jews and white Gentiles were no longer intelligent, evolved Homosapien beings prospering in the "Light" of knowledge and technology but were regressing into the paleolithic, ignorant and stupid beings of their beginning and all of this were identified as "Darkness" just as was done to the old black African dominion in the beginning to make room for the new white Gentile dominion. The white Gentiles were no more evolved than the Hatfields and the Mc Coys or the Cowboys and Gangsters. They were regressing backwards. They proclaimed that they would never evolve pass the evolutionary development of their Confederate ancestors of their past. To this day, they are no more evolved than the Hatfields and the Mc Coys or the Cowboys and Gangsters in their ways and understanding. They said in their hearts and minds or in their movies about the future that there would always be a racist, narrow-minded Dr. Mc Coy even in the future as is portrayed in the Star Trek science fiction series or a racist Commander Tucker portrayed in the Star Trek Enterprise science fiction series that was full of hate or a racist Miles O'Brien that was portrayed in the Star Trek next generation series.

# 29

# The Vril and the original man

When the aliens arrive here in the 40's because of the Philadelphia Experiment, the white Gentiles were so far behind where they were supposed to be in their evolutionary development and their understanding were so far lost, the aliens used their advance technology to go back in time to educate the white Gentiles to bring the white Gentiles up to a standard and level by which advance beings could communicate with them so the white Gentiles could do the aliens biddings on the earth in the latter days.

From the Industrial age up to today's Silicon Valley all were introduced to the white Gentiles by the aliens in the last two hundred years. None of the technology and advancements of the white Gentiles are of the white Gentiles own inventions and origin. The white, hillbilly, Cajun, cracker was helped by demons. They are no more evolved than the Hatfields and the Mc Coys or the cowboys and gangsters. The knowledge of how to do all of the white Gentiles technology and advancement was "channeled" to the white Gentiles by the Greys so the Gentiles could be developed enough to do the aliens bidding in the latter days.

The white Gentiles used occult secret societies to communicate with extraterrestrials who were really demons to receive all of their knowledge, technology and advancements.

When Maria Orsic came forward in Europe to share her gifts as a "Medium", the Germans were delighted. Maria Orsic could communicate with demons in another dimension. Demons that were imprisoned in another dimension were able to contact the mind of Maria Orsic. It was these same demons that channeled the knowledge to white Gentiles in America to open a door-way into their prison dimension to let them out in the Philadelphia experiment. Maria Orsic was a medium and the leader of the Germans secret society known as the Vril. The Nazi society in Germany was built around her communications with these demons. Maria Orsic received detailed channeled information on how to construct a flying disc from aliens or demons in the Aldebaran star system. When the German scientists studied the information that Maria Orsic receive and realized that it was detailed information on how to build a flying disc, the German leadership took Maria Orsic very seriously, and used the channeled information from Maria Orsic to be the basic and foundation for the German people and the Nazi party.

These demons said that they were the inhabitants of ancient Samaria and they were forced to leave the earth. These demons said that they were from the star system named Aldebaran. These demons said that there were two classes of people in their star system. One was the Aryan race or pure race or Elder race who were the original people and the other was a subservient race that had developed in a negative fashion having bad skin, bad bone structure, a weak immune system and a shorter life span that devolved and mutated into primitive man because of nuclear radiation. A "Elder" race is an old race and not a young race. Black skin and nappy hair are the signs and traits of an old, elder race that has been exposed to the sun and the elements for millions of years. The pure black Aryans from Aldebaran said that the white race that was with them was a subservient race.

White skin is skin that has not been exposed and burned by the sun for millions of years and oily hair is hair that has not been dried-out by the sun for millions of years and these are the signs and traits of a young race that has not been exposed to the sun and the elements for millions of years. The "Elder Race" that the Aryans were referring to was a black race and not a white race. The Aryans said that they were a race of the original man. The original man is a black man and not a white man. It is psychotic for the white race to say that the white race is a "Elder" race.

When these pure blood, black, original men came to the earth they were known as the Sumerians. The Sumerians were an ancient, old, black race. The white dominions of the Greek and the Romans were primitive races that had not started to develop during the Sumerians age.

The Vril society named themselves after the ancient Sumerian word Vr-il meaning "god-like". The inhabitants of ancient Sumer were not white Gentiles but were the black Olmecs. It was these black, nappy head, Olmecs that admired the young white race young straight hair. Because of this, the Vril members grew their hair long pass the knees to impress the black Aryans from Aldebaran. Remember, the white Gentiles were a young race whose hair and skin had not been dried-out and burned exposed to the sun for millions of years. Light skin and oily hair are the genetic proof that the white race is a young race and not an elder race or an ancient race.

These ancient demons that the Vril secret society was in contact with deceived the white Gentiles by appearing to the white Gentiles as "Familiars" or as white Gentiles. Leviticus 19: 31, Leviticus 20: 6 and Leviticus 20: 27

This was a deception because the white race is not an ancient race but is a young race no more than 20,000 years old compared to the ancient black race which is more than a million years old. The Olmecs and the Anunnaki race are the same race of people and the Olmecs are a thick-lip, nappy hair, black race just as the Anunnaki race. The Anunnaki and the Olmecs both can be seen wearing their flying suit with three wings pointed up and three wings pointed down which are similar to the four living creatures around the throne of God each having six wings with three wings pointed up and three wings pointed down. They are them who were from Heaven that fell. Revelation 4: 8 and Ezekiel 2: 6

They were the Fallen Angels that were called the "Nephilim". The language of the Anunnaki is one of the languages of the Olmecs and evidence of that has been found at Tiahuannaco and both the Olmecs and the Anunnaki were dark skin, nappy hair, thick lips and wide nose people and many of the Anunnaki can be seen with their nappy hair in corn rolls or breaded alone with their thick nappy hair breads. If you want to see how the Anunnaki looked, look at the Olmec statue heads found in La Venta, Mexico. It is them, the Olmecs and the Anunnaki who were from Aldebaran that came to the earth with their servants who are the white Aryan gentiles.

At the Precious Metal Museum in La Paz, Bolivia there is one of the most important archeological artifacts ever found near Lake Titicaca near Tiwanaki/Tiohuanaco. It was a ceramic bowl that shows the writing of the Sumerians cuneiform and also hieroglyphic script from around 3000 BC. This is a direct connection between the ancient Sumerians, the ancient Egyptians and the Olmecs at Puma Punku. The bowl also shows the spiral wormhole by which travel is obtain and most important on the bowl is the bowl handles that have the carved face of a wide nose and thick lips African or Olmec on it. The wide nose thick lips Olmecs, the wide nose thick lips ancient Egyptians whose face is on the Sphinx and the wide nose thick lips Sumerian Anunnaki are the same race of people. The Olmecs who are the Anunnaki are "those who from heaven to earth came" and they can be seen wearing the same flying suit found only in heaven that the Sumerians Anunnaki also have been seen wearing. They are the south American Gods as well as the Mid-Eastern, Eastern, European and African Gods. They were the giants that were on the earth in those days and also afterwards, when the sons of God came into the daughters of men and bore children to them. They were the mighty men who were from the "old" black African dominion. Genesis 6: 4

The white race was below the Paleolithic development when the Anunnaki occupied Sumer. The white race was cavemen not knowing what fire was when Sumer was in its glory. The white race was a young race in its beginning when Egypt, Assyria, Babylon and Persia were in their glory.

The young white Gentile race was created by the Fallen Angels to be a subservient race used for sex, body replacement parts and DNA retrieval to create more vessels to house more disembodied ancient spirits. Remember, theses Fallen Angels left their heavenly stations to descend down to the lower three-dimensional universe to have sex with mankind. The giants on the earth at that time were renown, mighty men of the "old" black African dominion. They were "renown" because of their history of being great and powerful men. They were men from the "old" or from the old black African dominion. The Fallen Angels spirits were in these Olmec or Anunnaki giants. It was these men of the old black African dominion who were the giants on the earth that controlled Samaria that the white young race called Aryans. They were called Aryans by the young white race, but these giants were not of the young white race but were men of the old black African race. They were a "Elder Race" or an old black race and not a young white race. The Holy Bible has recorded that these 10ft. giants of the "Elder Race" were men from the "Old" black African dominion. Genesis 6: 4

The Aryans from Aldebaran told Maria Orsic that the original Aryans from Aldebaran were a "pure" black race with no genetic faults. The original man of this earth is the black man. The white race has many genetic faults. The white race has bad skin, bad bone structure, a weaker immune system and a shorter life-span.

The white race is not the original race. Egypt, Assyria, Babylon, and Persia dominions were before the white Gentiles dominions. The original man is the first man created. A white Gentile was not the first man created.

The white race is not a pure race and the white race has many genetic faults. The white race has bad skin, bad bone structure, a bad immune system and a shorter life span.

The white race is not the original Aryan race. The original Aryans was a race with the original men. The white race is the race that devolved from nuclear war in the first world. This is what the original black Aryans that were in communication with the Vril society told Maria Orsic. This is also what the Grey aliens tell their abductees when the abductees are taken aboard the aliens flying craft for evolutionary development examinations. Right now, it is the white race that is threatening the world with nuclear war in the world we live in today and that war will devolve the white race on a genetic level.

It is the white race that is the subservient race that was devolved by nuclear war that the original black Aryans from Aldebaran told the

Vril society about and because of the white race mutation, even now, they do not understand. This is what the original black Aryans told Maria Orsic of the white Vril society. The German leaders especially Rudolf Hess lied about the translation of the communication channeled to Maria Orsic and the purity of the German people for power to start a war and they deceived the German people to believe that the white Germans were the pure race known as the Aryans.

The Aryans said that they were from the star system Aldebaran. The Aldebaran system is divided into two races of people. The original pure race of people who were called Aryans and a subservient race that had mutated and devolved on an evolutionary scale because of nuclear radiation. The white race was that subservient race.

The more the races intermixed, the lower the spiritual development of the pure black people collectively sank. It went from black to brown to yellow to white. The mixing of the white race with the black race does not collectively sank or degrade or devolve the white race but that mixing strengthens the white race genetic structure. It adds to the white to make color because white is the absent of all color. The degrading or devolvement is not possible from white to black because from white to black, much more has to be added to white to make white black, but the degrading and devolvement is possible from black degrading down to white because much must be taken away from black to get to white. This subtraction from black to get white is the degrading or devolvement spoke of by the black Aryans from Aldebaran to the Vril society. The white genetically imperfect race was removed from around the pure black race of Aldebaran and planted on the earth. This is the story of the Tares and the Wheat in the Holy Bible. This is the story of an enemy, the black Aryans, putting the devolved white race or "Tares" on the planet earth to mix with the "wheat" or the people of the earth and that mixing would degrade the colored-people of the earth giving the people of the earth lighter skin. Matthew 13: 24-30

The original pure race that was fearful of being degraded by receiving lighter skin was the black race and not the white race. That is how much the white Gentiles of today are being deceived. That is how upside down the world is today. White Gentiles proclaiming that they are the "Original Man" is evidence that the babbling of the white Gentiles minds is in operation because now they are portraying the condition of being psychotic or "out of touch with reality".

Without the colored-people of the world, the "Tares" or white Gentiles cannot be made whole or perfect because of their genetic imperfections. The white race must mix to survive. White mixing with white diminish and weaken the white race genetic structure. This degrading or diminishing and weakening of the white race for mixing with white producing albinos and not humans. White mixing with black adds to the white race and strengthen the white race genetic structure. Through this mixing with black, the white beings become human beings. This is not a degrading but an addition and strengthening of the white beings genetic structure. It is the black race that is degraded in this mixture or it is the black race that degrades from black to brown to yellow to white in the mixing of the races. The white race is strengthened in this mixing. The white beings must not be deceived by their conceit and believe that white beings mixing with human beings is a degrading for the white race. The Holy Bible has recorded that without mixing with the people of the earth, the white beings cannot be made whole or genetically perfect or human. The white beings that call themselves pure blood Aryans from Germany are wrong and are psychotic or out of touch with reality. To survive, they must mix. The white beings must mix with the colored beings to become human beings and human beings are only those with a hue or a shade, color or tint. White is the absence of this tint or hue. Hebrew 11: 40

This is the truth that the disbelieving white Jews in biblical days said if delivered by the "Brethren" or the Brothers, it could turn the world upside down and if the white Jews and white Gentiles are to be saved this time, that conversion of the world must come to pass. Acts 17: 6

You cannot take away from white and get black, but you can take away from black and get white. The more the pure black Aryan race mixed with the young white race, the lighter they became, and the more spiritual knowledge and abilities were lost to a point that the once pure, black Aryan race could no longer perform the magic of their forefathers. Separation was ordered. This is what the Aryans told Maria Orsic.

The genetically devolved white race that the pure race of black Aryans had created was brought to earth as the "Tares" spoke of in the Holy Bible to mix with the people of the earth to be made whole and become human or people with a shade, color or tint and after that, they could have returned to Aldebaran to mix with the pure black race now, after they became human and had acquired a shade, color or tint dark enough not to degrade the pure black original man. Matthew 13: 24-30

This is why the white Gentiles without color are calling themselves colored-people or calling themselves Human beings to deceive all in Heaven and on Aldebaran that the joining has occurred and now all on the planet earth are colored-people or human beings knowing that they are still white. In the 2011 movie titled, "Green Lantern", the white young race said in their hearts or in their movie that the young white race would assume the identity of the human race of the earth and receive the inheritance of power and abilities in ascendant bodies and it would be them that would be the guardians of the universe in the future. The human race is not a young race as was stated in the movie titled, "Green Lantern". The human race is an ancient race as the black Aryans told the Nazis in the Vril society. The white race is a young race. In the movie Green Lantern, the white race said that the white race was the human race and them as the human race was the young race.

The Bible has recorded that at the time of the "Harvest" of the earth, the reaper will gather the "Tares" or white Gentiles who did not mix but remain white into bundles to be burn and gather the "wheat" and the white Gentiles that did mix and are now Human Beings or colored-people with a shade, color or tint in their flesh into God's barn. The white race was given the Greek dominion, the Roman dominion and this last dominion of "Iron and Clay" to make that joining but they stayed white and proclaimed to all in Heaven and on Aldebaran that the joining had taken place and now all on the planet earth were of one race named the human race with people that have a shade, color or tint in their flesh. The Holy Bible has recorded that without the colored-people of the earth, the white "Tares" cannot be made whole or genetically perfect. White mixing with white is a death sentence for the white race. Matthew 13: 24-30 and Hebrew 11: 40

Because of the mutation of the white Gentiles that is going on at this moment, the white Gentiles just do not understand. Not only is the white Gentiles being restricted from procreating, their minds and understandings are being babbled fulfilling prophecy that there will be no place found for the great white throne in the future. Revelation 20: 11

The original Aryans were known as the Sumerians and we know that the Sumerians were a black, thick lip, nappy hair, race of people. This can be proven by observing any ancient Sumerian sculpture or carving or the Olmecs sculptures found in La Venta, Mexico today. The ancient Sumerians had wide noses, thick lips and thick, nappy hair that they wore in breads or corn-rolls and not long, straight, thin hair like the Vril society women. This is how deep the deception of the truth is and this is how much the white Gentiles are being deceived.

To this very day, the white Gentiles believe that the Aryans from Aldebaran are white because the black Aryans from Aldebaran appeared to the white Gentiles as "Familiars" or as white Gentiles to deceive the white Gentiles to do their bidding. In the Stargate SG1 movies, when the Asgards who are a representation of the Grey extraterrestrials appear to the white gentiles, the Asgards appear to them as white pagan Vikings to be "familiar" to the white Gentiles. It was these black Aryans from Aldebaran that created the white Gentiles. This is the story of "Yakub", the big head scientist who was one of the black Aryans that created the white Gentiles. These black Aryans appear to the white Gentiles that they had created as white Gentiles to be familiar to the white Gentiles. When the Fallen Angels had no more used for their genetically engineered creatures that they created, the creatures were to be destroyed. They were brute beast made to be destroyed when no longer needed by the Fallen Angels. Jesus and the people of God had no dealings with the Samaritans and the pagans tares the Samaritans created. Leviticus 19: 31, Leviticus 20: 6, Leviticus 20: 27, 2 Peter 2: 12, John 4: 7-9, Stargate SG1-Thor's Hammer, Thor's chariot and Ezra 10: 2-3

When the Olympians were forced away from the earth by the Titans, the young white Gentile race that they had created for their personal use was to be destroyed. The Anunnaki were also forced away from the earth by the Titans. They were cast into "Outer-Darkness" which is "Outer-Space" because "outer-space" is "outer-darkness". The Aryans from Aldebaran says they were the Anunnaki that dwelled in Sumer that was forced away from the earth. When the Anunnaki left the earth, their created subservient creatures that they created for their private purpose that did not go with them to the star system Aldebaran were to be destroyed. The subservient creatures that did not go with the Aryans to Aldebaran were not destroyed but were given an opportunity to mix with the people of the earth to become human beings. Matthew 8: 12 and Matthew 13: 30

After bringing the white race that they had created to the star system Aldebaran after the first world, the pure blooded, black, Aryans said that they had to separate themselves from the subservient race because the subservient race was degrading the pure, black Aryan race.

The Aryans told Maria Orsic that the subservient race that they created was brought back to the planet earth to be away from the pure black Aryan race in the star system of Aldebaran because the subservient white race was degrading the pure black race of Aryans. Because of that, the pure blood black Aryans returned the white beings who had been genetically devolved by nuclear war in the first world back to the earth and instead of returning back to Aldebaran, the pure blood black Aryans stayed on the earth and became the Sumerians and the Anunnaki. These pure black Aryans loved the white beings that they had created, and they refused to kill the brute beast that was made to be destroyed. They returned the brute beast that they had made back to the earth to become human, so the brute beast that was made to be destroyed could not degrade the pure blood black Aryans but could be transformed into human beings. Google Maria Orsic and read it for yourself. This is the story of the "Tares" and the "Wheat" recorded in the Holy Bible. 2 Peter 2: 12 and Matthew 13: 24-30

Once the white race was returned to the planet earth, the old black Africans wanted to mix with the young white race to produce children with lighter skin and curly hair not realizing that this was degrading their race and devolving their people on an evolutionary scale as well as on a spiritual level. This fascination with the white Gentiles hair that the old black African dominion had and even the black Aryans from Aldebaran had, is why the Vril society women worn their hair long as they could grow it. The old black African race requested that the young race be not destroyed but allowed to live on the planet earth with the Human Beings to mix with the Human Beings to become Human because they were white. The white race is the "Tares" spoke of in the Holy Bible that were put on the people of the old black African planet by the pure black Aryans from Aldebaran to grow and mix with the colored-people of the earth or the seed of men to become Human Beings but the Holy Bible has recorded that the Tares "mingled" with the seed of men but did not join with them or adhere to one another just as iron does not mix with clay even in the last gentile dominion of "iron and clay" which is the dominion we live in today. Mathew 13: 24-30 and Daniel 2: 43

Pure blooded, white Germans that thought they were Aryans were not superior to the colored-people of the earth but was lacking what they needed to survive. They were to mix with the people of the earth or the seed of men to become genetically complete. Pure blooded, white Aryans are genetically incomplete and cannot be made whole or right without the genes from the colored-people or the human beings of the earth. The purity of the white Aryans race is a death sentence to the white Aryans because the white Aryans must mix to become human to survive. That is why the pure-blooded white Gentiles that think they are Aryans called themselves colored-people or called themselves Human Beings to deceive all in Heaven that the joining of the white race and the human race had occurred and all on the planet earth now were human beings knowing that they were still white. If the pure-blooded, Gentiles who call themselves Aryans are so superior to the colored-people of the earth, why are pure-blooded white Gentiles calling themselves colored-people or calling themselves Human Beings? The word "Hu-man" means colored-man because "Hue" or "Hu" means color. Hebrews 11: 40

Pure blooded, white Gentiles were selected in Germany by the demons to come forth to be used in the aliens genetic engineering experiment to produce the perfect vessel to house disembodied ancient spirits. The demons were told not to touch God's people, so the demons felt if they used only pure blood white Gentiles that they had created with no godly DNA in them, God would not mind what they did to their created creatures who were made to be destroyed by the demons' experiments. Psalm 105: 15 and 2 Peter 2: 12

# 30

## The Invasion of the Earth

The aliens telepathically communicated with the white Gentiles to deceive them and instruct them to open a doorway from another dimension into our dimension by the use of powerful electromagnetic forces in the Philadelphia Experiment, so the aliens could enter our dimension. Communicating with these demons is where Maria Orsic, Nikola Tesla, Albert Einstein, De Vinci, Bill Gates, Stephen Hawking and all other white Gentiles received their vast knowledge from.

When the confused and deceived scientists that were lost in their own conceit calling themselves geniuses because of the knowledge that they had received continued experimenting with high electromagnetic fields on the ship in the Philadelphia experiment, opening doorways to another dimension, the alien removed all of the electromagnetic equipment from the vessel as a warning to them to stop their experiments. These extraterrestrials are from another dimension in the future and they are here in the past, our present, collecting DNA from the white Gentiles to construct more vessels to house more disembodied ancient cast-out demons that could not be collected in the future because of the worse plague the world will ever see that the white Gentiles will cause in the future because of the abuse of alien technology today. These extraterrestrials lied to the white Gentiles about the cause of the white race regression or devolvement this time to prevent the white Gentiles from changing the future that could also alter the extraterrestrials agenda on the earth.

Last time, it was Nuclear radiation that devolved the white Gentiles. We were given a second chance this time in the world we live in today to make better choices to defeat the aliens this time that could not be defeated last time or in one reality life time because of the aliens' superiority and method of attack.

The pure, black Aryans said that after the nuclear radiation died down from the last world, they returned to the earth and occupied Samaria in this world and planted the white race here on the earth again. In the movies titled, X-Men, the white Gentiles says that nuclear radiation will mutate them into evolved beings in ascended bodies with power and abilities far beyond those abilities of normal men. They are wrong. Nuclear radiation will devolve the white race into the Morlocks.

Now, it will not be nuclear radiation that devolve the white Gentiles on an evolutionary scale this time but will be the "Mark of the Beast". The white race has developed a way to destroy the people of the earth this time without nuclear bombs that would have fallout that will devolve the white race but now the white race has developed another way to get the effects of a nuclear blast without the fallout that will devolved the white race. The white race says that they can let heavy tungsten iron tubes fall to the earth at great speeds that once these heavy tubes hit the earth, it will have the same effect on the planet crust as a nuclear bomb but without the radiation. Because of this, the regression of the white race will not come from nuclear radiation this time but will come from the Mark of the Beast.

The mark of the beast that will cause the worse plague the world will ever see will be made from the abuse of alien technology. It is this mark of the beast tattooed on your flesh to buy or sell and not nuclear radiation that will mutate the white Gentiles and devolved the white Gentiles into the primitive creatures of their past. It is this mark tattooed on the flesh to buy and sell that will mutate and cause great, unbearable pain that will burn like fire and to stop the pain, all with the mark will have to "gnaw" or bite or chew on flesh. It is this mark that will turn the white Gentiles into a beast or the walking dead zombies that today's movies are made about. Revelation 13: 16-17, Revelation 14: 9-11, Revelation 16: 2 and Revelation 16: 10

The Greys are not here for observation as they have stated, and the Greys are not the white Gentiles in the future. The Greys are deceiving the white Gentiles. The Greys, working with the Anunnaki, created the white Gentiles to remove DNA and body parts to create more vessels, containers and bodies to house more disembodied ancient spirits in the beginning and it is this same agenda that the Greys are implementing in the latter-days of the white Gentiles dominion. Once abducted by the Greys, the Greys give the white Gentiles evolutionary development examinations by checking their hair, nails, fingers and toes, reproductive organs as well as the orb or aura or electro-magnetic energy that is around a living body that is generated by a living body to determine if the white Gentiles are at their fullness or maturity and if that abducted individual is at his or her maximum level of evolutionary development, eggs and sperm is extracted from that individual and is used to construct more vessels to house more disembodied ancient spirits. The white Gentiles were brute beast made to be destroyed for this purpose. 2 Peter 2: 12

Abductees have reported that the Greys have said that the Greys have the right to abduct and do whatever they please to the Gentiles because the Greys created the white Gentiles for this cause. The white Gentiles will not evolve into a space-traveling race in the future with high technology but will be "Cut-Off" from the Tree of Life and regressed into the Paleolithic beings of their beginning and there will be no place found for the great white throne in the future. Because there is no future for the great white Gentiles, the Greys are here in the past, our present, not observing but collecting DNA from the white Gentiles that could not be collected in the future because of the regression. Romans 11: 22 and Revelation 20: 11

In 1947, Kenneth Arnold witness the arrival of the first reconnaissance forces of the invaders of the earth. Later in 1952, the invading forces arrived and flew over Washington D.C. to announce their presence on the earth. July 19, 1952, a large UFO hovered over the White House and another one hovered over the Capital. On July 26, 1952, the UFO'S returned and a large UFO hovered over the White House lawn at 1700 feet. Key figures in the government were possessed and taken over by unseen forces. From that day forward, the government has denied the existence of the aliens and the UFO'S that the aliens use.

In 1958, Major Donald Keyhoe explained that the UFO'S were real and are here on the earth and the government was concealing and suppressing all information about the invasion. Those who deny the UFO'S existence are those who are possessed by the aliens and instructed by the aliens to deny the aliens existence on the earth. The alien forces were so advanced that while the people of the earth were waiting for the aliens to land their saucers and fight a ground war with the people of the earth to take over the earth, the aliens took over the people of the earth bodies.

Once in the powerful, the super-rich and the leaders of the people of the earth bodies, the aliens controlled the earth. The invaders knew that the people of the earth were preparing to defend their planet, but could they defend their bodies. Could the people of the earth control their thoughts, emotions and sexual pleasures that would be door ways for the disembodied invading forces to enter the people of the earth bodies to control the earth.

The invading forces were so advance that not only did they have an army, a navy and an air force to attack the body and the physical, solid land but they also had parts of their forces that were invisible that could attack an enemy spirit to take over the body. Once in the body, the invaders would control the land. Because the people of the earth did not believe in possessions or believe that other spirits could possessed their body, the people of the earth would never see the invaders coming. The enemy within would never be seen coming and the people of the earth would be totally unaware of the enemy presence in their vessels.

# 31

# Possession

The government and the people of the earth till this very day do not understand that we are containers, vessels, or bodies that are designed to house spirits. Depending on your spirit and your desires will determine what outside invading spirit seek shelter in your container, vessel or body. The Holy Bible has instructed us how to summon positive or godly spirits to your container, vessel or body and how to resist and prevent evil negative spirits from possessing your container, vessel or body. The Holy Bible says, "If the Spirit of Him who raised Jesus from the dead dwells in you, He who raised Jesus from the dead will also give life to your mortal bodies through His Spirit who dwells in you". The Holy Bible has recorded to be sober, vigilant because your adversary the devil walks about like a roaring lion, seeking whom he may devour. Resist him, steadfast in the faith, knowing that the same sufferings are experienced by your brotherhood in the world. Romans 8: 1-11 and 1 Peter 5: 8-9

Because of this possession, the Holy Bible tells us, for though we walk in the flesh, we do not war according to the flesh. Because of the nature of our enemy and his ability to enter our bodies, our weapons of warfare are not carnal or guns and bombs but mighty in God for pulling down strongholds or possessions. We must cast down arguments or thoughts in our heads and every high thing or reasoning that exalts itself against the knowledge of God. We must control our thoughts or bring every thought into captivity to the obedience of God to ensure that we are not being influence by the invaders thoughts and will. 2 Corinthians 10: 3-5

Because we do not wrestle against flesh and blood, but against principalities, against powers, against the rulers of the darkness of this age, against spiritual hosts of wickedness or invisible, evil, invaders in the heavenly places or in the sky, we must put on the whole armor of God. Stand therefore, having girded your waist with Truth, having put on the breastplate of Righteousness, having shod your feet with the preparation of the Gospel of Peace because the invader wants violence and chaos and above all, taking the Shield of Faith with which you will be able to quench all the fiery darts or the hot, sexual thoughts of the wicked one. Take also the Helmet of Salvation, and the Sword of the Spirit, which is the Word of God, praying always with all prayers and supplication in the Spirit being watchful to this end with all perseverance and supplications for all the Saints or those who are Sent and for Me, the one who is delivering this profound Truth to you, that utterance may be given to me that I may open my mouth Boldly to make known the Mystery of the Gospel, for which I am an ambassador in chains, that in it or in my position as Ambassador to the Gentiles from the people of God, I may speak Boldly, as I ought to speak or as you agreed last time at judgment that you would allow me to speak to deliver the Truth to you, so you could be saved. Do not renege on this agreement. Last time at judgment, the Gentiles sent the latter-day deliverer to themselves this time, in the latter-days, after the fullness of the Gentiles came in at the end of the age after December 21, 2012, so you would not be deceived by the false prophet. Last time at judgment, the Gentiles assertion was that they were deceived by the false prophet. The Holy Bible has recorded that the latter-day deliverer would come after the fullness of the Gentiles comes in. The fullness of the Gentiles came in at the end of the age and the end of the age was on December 21, 2012. The Gentiles must be wise in their own Conceit (undesired self-importance, pride and vanity), if the Gentiles are to be saved, this time. Do not make it difficult for the latter-day deliverer to reveal the Mystery of the Gospel to you. Ephesians 6: 11-20, Revelation 19: 20 and Romans 11: 25-26

Do not be an idiot (a person with sub-normal intelligence that is out of touch with reality) and ignore prophecy. We all will go before a judgment again. At that judgment, you will again ask those who were Sent to you this time for help. Those that are Sent to you this time shall judge the world and all that's in the world even judge the fallen angels at judgment this time. For the Gentiles benefit, allow those who are Sent who you will call Saints because the Saints are only those who are Sent to reveal the Mystery of the Gospel to you and be the judge of the things that pertain to this life from the largest of things to the smallest matters, so you can be saved. It is preferred that you go to the Saints having a matter against another before you go to the law of the unrighteous for judgment. For we shall all stand before the judgment seat of Jesus who is the Lamb in Heaven who is the color of brass (brown) that has been burn in a furnace (dark brown to black) with hair like sheep wool (nappy hair). 1 Corinthians 6: 1-3, Romans 14: 10-12 and Revelation 1: 14-15

For we must all appear before the judgment seat of Jesus, that each one may receive the things done in the body, according to what he has done, whether good or bad. This judgment, this time, shall be without mercy. Do not believe today's Christians saying that by the blood of Jesus, all of the white Gentiles sins are wiped away. Knowing, therefore the terror of the Lord, we will try to persuade men. We are well known to God and I also trust that we are well known in your conscience because it is you Gentiles, who Sent the latter-day deliverer and that is recorded in the Gentiles DNA, so their ethics, integrity and morality is worthy enough for them to be judged to remain grafted on the Tree of Life. 2 Corinthians 5: 10-11 and James 2: 13

Jesus was Sent only to the house of Israel. The Holy Bible says, every one of the Brethren or the Brothers who believe is justified from all things from which you could not be justified by the law of Moses. This justification by belief is for those who were under the laws of Moses only. The white Gentiles were never under the laws of Moses. Only the people of God were under the laws of Moses. This justification by belief only apply to the Brethren who are the people of God. Matthew 10: 5-6, Matthew 15: 24 and Acts 13: 38-39

The white Christian gentiles must understand that by the belief in Jesus they are not saved. They must understand that by the blood of Jesus they are not saved. Their sins are not washed away for life when they accepted Jesus in their lives. They must know that we shall be judged for everything that we have done and thought in the flesh. It is said that at judgment, if your sins out-way a bird feather, you will not be saved. For we must all appear before the judgment seat of Jesus, that each one may receive the things done in the body according to what he has done, whether good or bad. 2 Corinthians 5: 10, Romans 2: 16, Romans 14: 12, Galatians 6: 7, Romans 2: 6 and Ephesians 6: 8

Simeon, in the beginning, revealed that God wanted to take out of the white Jews and white Gentiles a people for God's name and for that cause, the words of the prophets or the Books of Simion are written. The end of the dominion will be declared from the beginning of the dominion and in the beginning of the dominion it was Simeon who revealed this to the white Jews and to the white Gentiles. At the end of the dominion, it will be Simeon and only Simion that will reveal this again to the white Jews and to the white Gentiles. You better believe, this time. God and a lot of souls in Heaven wants the Gentiles to survive but that will be totally up to the Gentiles. The Gentiles must do what is in their hearts to prove or disprove if the Gentiles are worthy. God wants the Captain Kirks from the Star Trek series and the Captain Jean Luc Picards from the Star Trek New Generation series and the Captain Kathryn Janeways from the Star Trek Voyager series or all white Gentiles who share these characters honesty, fair-play, morals and justice for all traits to be with the people of God again in the future. There are Gentiles that are destined or ordain to believe this time because they believed last time. The Gentiles or the Captain Kirks, the Captain Jean Luc Picards and the Captain Kathryn Janeways that believed last time are "Ordain" or "Appointed" to believe again this time. They shall receive eternal life. Those who are contacted are those who asked to be contacted last time at Judgment to support the message to save themselves and their people. Great One, the president that is contacted in the latter-days is the one who asked to be contacted last time at Judgment to save his people and for that cause, he was maneuvered to the presidency. The "Deliverer" message to the Gentiles is that God wants to take out of the Gentiles a people for God's name. It is these "ordain" Gentiles that God wants to take out of the Gentiles. Simion will deliver that message to the Gentiles in the latter-days. Do not let the false prophet, the skeptics or no one else prevent you from receiving that message. Acts 15: 14-15, Isaiah 46: 10 and Acts 13: 48

The Books of Simion are the Books of Records that are referred to as the Books of Remembrance that are written for Kings and all in Authority, so Kings and all in Authority are not dishonored and their kingdoms are not destroyed by deceptions. Ezra 4: 14-15 and Malachi 3: 16

The message to Kings and all in Authority is that Kings and all who are in Authority (the Illuminati) must have a Sanctuary for the people of God so the people of God can live quiet and peaceful lives in godliness and reverence for this is good and acceptable in the sight of God our Savior who desires all men to be saved and to come to the knowledge of the truth. There at the Sanctuary prayers, supplications and "intercessions" will be made for all men including Kings and all who are in Authority (the Illuminati). There at the Sanctuary interventions, mediations and arbitrations will be made for Kings and all in Authority (the Illuminati). 1 Timothy 2: 1-4

Resist the devil and he will flee from you and from the earth. Do not join the devil to receive technology. James 4: 7

John Lear, a retired airline captain and a former CIA pilot and son of the inventor of the Lear Jet, said that in his studies of the UFO phenomenon, the aliens refer to earthlings as containers. John Lear said that he was at a lost why the aliens would refer to us as containers. What John Lear and the government do not understand is that the aliens' agenda is not about building pyramids on the earth as the Ancient Astronauts Theorists purpose but is about immortality and to create more containers for disembodied spirits to live in. This is why the invasion of the earth was so successful. The people of the earth could not conceive that an invading superior force would take over or possess our bodies first to control the earth and control the people of the earth and because of the people of the earth lack of understanding about who and what the people of the earth are, the people of the earth would never see the invaders coming. The people of the earth till this very day are still waiting for the invaders to land their flying saucers and fight a ground war with the people of the earth not knowing that the aliens are here in the people of the earth and the earth was taken without one shot be firing. Once the invaders were in the leaders and super rich of the people of the earth, the people of the earth sold the invaders the earth and the invaders made the leaders of the earth feel that the invasion of the earth and the taking over of the earth was "nothing personal but was strictly business". The Grey aliens consider us as containers because we are vessels and bodies that were designed to house spirits.

The Holy Bible has recorded that the Prince of the Power of the Air or those who control the air in their UFO'S were also those or the spirit who now work in or have possessed the children of disobedience or possessed wicked people. Ephesians 2: 2

Understand that the Holy Bible says that the same evil, demonic spirit that is in a possessed body of the children of disobedience that must be exorcised out of the body by a man of God or a Catholic Priest are the same evil, demonic spirits that are in the pilots and passengers aboard a UFO. It is by this possession that the alien invasion is suppressed so thoroughly. Because the only way to defeat the aliens is found in the Holy Bible, those who are possessed by the invaders will not want government and religion to come together to understand the nature of our invasion. They will not want to connect the UFO phenomenon to the evil demons spoke of in the Holy Bible.

Not even the aliens could stop the white Gentiles regression. The regression will continue unless the white Jews and white Gentiles steer events in another direction to prevent what is prophesied to come to pass. They must receive the Truth and act accordingly. The final level of this regression was portrayed in the 1968 movie titled, "Planet of the Apes" with Charlton Heston. Prophecy does not say that Apes will inherit the earth but says the "Meek" who are the "Slaves" who were persecuted and scattered will inherit the earth. The Holy Bible says the "Dead" or the "Negro" shall be raised first to be with the Lord. Negro and Necro are the same word and Necro means Dead. All who see the white Jews and white Gentiles in the future will say, "It is hard to believe that this is the man that made kingdoms shake". To receive farther evolutionary growth, the white gentile beings will be judged to determine if they are worthy to continue to exit with the colored people or the human beings of the earth. Matthew 5: 5, Revelation 21: 1-5, 1 Thessalonians 4: 16-17 and Isaiah 14: 16

In the beginning, the white Jews as the Greeks and the white Gentiles as the Romans were in darkness in caves and identified as cave-men. The people of God who were living in palaces and great kingdoms like Egypt, Babylon, Assyria and Persia did not believe that God could take the cave-men and evolve them on an evolutionary scale to the point where they would be given dominion on the earth against the will of the old black African dominion because the old black African dominion was so powerful and advance that anything that they wanted to do, they could do it, but it was true. Those who sat in "Darkness" suddenly received a great "Light". Genesis 11: 6 and Matthew 4: 16

The ancient ruins that are being found today are proof of the old black African dominion technology but still, the impossible was done and cave-men were evolved into intelligent Homosapien beings and given dominion on the earth. The white Gentiles who were in "Darkness" suddenly received a great "Light" and the kingdom of God was taken away from God's people and given to the white Gentiles. Matthew 4: 16 and Matthew 21: 43

The people of God did not believe that this could be done so they ignored God's orders. They were broken-off from the Tree of Life because they did not believe that God could do it. To be saved this time, the white Jews and white Gentiles must believe that this can be done and that it happened to the old black African dominion because of disbelief and if the white Jews and white Gentiles do not "Behold" everything that have happened and make that public declaration proclaiming who are the true people of God, the same or worst will happen to the white Jews and white Gentiles because of disbelief. If God did not spare His natural branches on the Tree of Life because of disbelief, take heed white Jews and white Gentiles that God will not spare you either. Romans 11: 20-22

The white Jews and white Gentiles proclaimed in their hearts or in the movie titled, "Independence Day" that from the day of the "War of Armageddon" forward that they will declared that the white Jews and white Gentiles are no longer under the laws of God but will be "independent" of God's laws. They said in their movie that all of the white Gentiles shall join together and fight God and from that day forward, the fourth of July would not just be an American holiday but a holiday for all white Jews and white Gentiles throughout the world who have declared themselves independent from God and God's laws. In that movie, the white Gentiles portrayed God as an extraterrestrial monster with dread-lock hair or nappy hair and not as Jesus, the Lamb in Heaven, who shall be given everything and be the judge of the white Gentiles that is the color of brass (brown) that has been burned in a furnace (dark brown to black) with hair like sheep wool or nappy dread-lock hair. He who comes with dread-lock nappy hair will not be the monster but will be Jesus, the Lamb in Heaven. Revelation 1: 14-15

The extraterrestrial monster that the Gentiles portrayed Jesus, the Lamb in Heaven, as in the movie "Independence Day" is the same type of extraterrestrial beings or interdimensional beings that invaded the earth that the white Gentiles are working with underground in Antarctica and in underground military bases in America to receive technology from. These are the same demons that the white Gentiles have said in their hearts and minds and in their Stargate SG-1 movies that they will work with who they will call the "Asgards" to fight the return of God, the Son of God and the ancient people of the earth. These demons control the earth and the governments of the earth have joined forces with these demons to fight God for the people of God inheritance on the earth.

The interdimensional beings do not want to lose control of their feeding ground where they obtain whatever they need to construct more vessels to house more disembodies ancient spirits in and the white Gentiles wants an extended thousand-year Reich on the earth and neither of the two want God to return and establish God's kingdom on the earth and give the people of God total dominion of the earth forever. Daniel 2: 44 and Daniel 7: 27

To prevent this, the government of the earth have sold the people of the earth out to the invaders for advance technology, so if the interdimensional beings do not win the fight against God to control the earth, the elite white Gentiles could leave the earth in space ships before God returns to escape God's judgment. The government brag about how they were given UFO's that they back engineered to create their own version and how their secret space program is hundreds of years ahead of NASA space program and their technology is hundreds of years ahead of what is given to the people of the earth. What they don't say is the price that was paid for that UFO technology and what they gave the extraterrestrials in exchange for UFO technology.

The Greys who are interdimensional beings only agenda is to obtain new vessels for ancient disembodied spirits to dwell in forever. Wealth to them is not about money and technology because they already own everything until Jesus return, and they possess the ability to do the impossible because they operate outside of our laws of physic. If Robots, Cyborgs and nanno technology in flesh bodies were the answer to constructing advance vessels to house spirits in, the Greys can create the best of robots and cyborgs, but the Greys are here to construct flesh and blood vessels to house ancient disembodied spirits. Do not believe Hollywood that says in their movies that robots, cyborgs and synthetic individuals with computers for brains will be better than flesh and blood bodies. Flesh and blood bodies are living machines or machines that were created and are alive that surpass all other types of machines that can be created. At full compacity, living machines can out-think computers and out perform any created mechanical device.

# 32

# He who will come with dread-locks

For the Greys, their agenda is about "Life Immortal" or the ability to continue to live and dwell on the earth and experience feelings and emotions and all that life has to offer. This is why these demons were cast out of Heaven and later for the same reason as the "Cast-Out" ones, the "Fallen-Ones" abandon their heavenly stations to descend down to earth to take on flesh and blood bodies to live again and enjoy all the things of life that mankind and humanity enjoys. The only thing that interdimensional beings who are on a quest for immortality need and want to complete and fulfill their mission and cause is more vessels, containers or bodies to implant disembodied ancient spirits in to continue to live life in. The payment for the Greys advance technology were bodies and souls. The cost for the government to have advance UFO technology was far too high. People and animals were abducted and experimented on to produce an appropriate container for a specific ancient spirit. Combinations of people and animals were created to house spirits that would be appropriate to live in such a vessel. Because of the war in the future when Satan is imprisoned for a thousand years in the "pit" and then cast into the Lake of Fire, Satan now is building his army of monsters to fight that war. Revelation 20: 1-3 and Revelation 20: 10

Hollywood is deceiving the white Gentiles to believe that the demons that invaded the earth whose image was in the movie "Independence Day" will be resisted and an all-out effort to fight the demons would be launched when in actuality, the government of the world has joined with these demons and is working with these demons underground in Antarctica and in underground military installations in America for advance technology. It may be interesting to know that in these underground government installations where the government is working with the extraterrestrials, they are cloning and creating more vessels to put ancient disembodied spirits in. This is the Grey extraterrestrials agenda. Some of these vessels, containers or bodies that they are creating are monstrous. Monsters like a half man and half spider combination are being created to house disembodied ancient spirits. The white Jews and the white Gentiles have exchanged God's truth about who are the true people of God for the lie that the white Jews and the white Gentiles are the people of God because they are white, and they are now worshipping and serving the "Creature" or the Grey extraterrestrials for technology instead of serving the Creator. Romans 1: 25

Him, who is coming to the earth to take over the earth and to judge the people of the earth who the white Gentiles and the extraterrestrials monsters underground in Antarctica are preparing to fight who shall be called the "Lamb" who shall judge the earth and all nations who shall set up a kingdom that will never perish who shall rule the earth and the universe forever is the color of brass (brown) that has been burned in a furnace (dark brown to black) with hair like sheep wool (nappy hair) and not the extraterrestrial monster seen in the movie "Independence Day". Revelation 1: 14-15, Revelation 5:

6, Revelation 5: 12, Revelation 12: 11, Revelation 13: 8, Revelation 19: 9 and Daniel 7: 27

The "Lamb" will have power and authority over the Scorpions and Serpents who are really Insectoids and Reptilians in their true nature. These Insectoids and Reptilians are the extraterrestrials monsters that the government is working with in underground facilities. While the Insectoids have a base underground in Antarctica, the Reptilians have a base at the bottom of the ocean. With all of their technology, they are no match for the Lamb in Heaven. These demons shall be cast-out and away from the earth. Luke 10: 19, Mark 16: 17, Isaiah 26: 21 and Isaiah 27: 1

The Gentiles screamed, "Wake up the mighty men of the Gentiles". Let all the men of war draw near. Beat your plowshares into swords or turn your farms and farming equipment into weapons. Let the genetically weak Gentiles that cannot be made whole or perfect without the genes from the people of God say that they are strong. Joel 3: 10 and Hebrew 11: 40

The white Gentiles proclaimed that they would retaliate against God. In the movie "Independence Day", the white Gentiles said in their "hearts" and in their "minds" or in their movie that they would use nuclear bombs to destroy God. Because God knows what is in the white Gentiles "hearts" and "minds", God has said that God will swiftly and speedily return their retaliation upon their own heads. It is there in the "Valley of Jehoshaphat where God will sit to judge all the nations. Revelation 2: 23, Jeremiah 17: 10, Joel 3: 4 and Joel 3: 12

For we all shall stand before the judgment sent of Jesus who is the Lamb in Heaven. Every knee shall bow to Jesus and every tongue shall confess to Jesus as God and each of us shall give account of himself to God. Romans 14: 10-12

Jesus, who shall judge all nations, who is the Lamb in Heaven is the color of brass (brown) that has been burned in a furnace (dark brown to black) with hair like sheep wool or nappy hair. Jesus is a hue-man or a human being and not a white-man or a white being. Jesus is not a white pagan gentile but is a black brother from the brethren. Revelation 1: 14-15

Remember, you cannot be a white man and a hue man or a human being at the same time. You are one or the other. To be a hue man or a human being, you must have a shade, color or tint. To be a hue man or a human being, you must have a hue in your complexion. White is the absent of all color or hue in the complexion.

If you identify yourself as being "White", which is saying you have no color because white is the absence of all color, you cannot identify yourself as being a "human being" which means you are a colored man or a man with a hue. You are either one or the other. The white Gentiles are saying today at Tulane University in New Orleans, La. that it is alright to be "White". They are wrong. The white beings were supposed to join with the human race to become human beings, but they failed to do so but they screamed to all in Heaven that the joining had taken place and all on the planet earth were human beings or people with a shade, color or tint knowing that they were still white.

Being white means, they are lacking something including color. Understand that no white, blonde hair, blue eye, white gentile Aryan is superior to the Human Beings or superior to the "Colored People". White, blonde hair and blue eye gentiles are the most "UNNATURAL" white being out of them all. They are the ones that cannot be exposed to the sun not even for a sun tan and the genetic regression starts with them first and starts earlier in their lives than in the other white Gentiles. They are a half of a step from being an

Albino which is the bottom of the genetic pool. They are unnatural because they cannot be exposed to the life-giving rays from the sun. Black is the top of the genetic pool. Black absorbs the life-giving rays from the sun. This is why the white, blonde hair, blue eye Aryans are calling themselves "Colored People" or calling themselves human beings because the "human race" is the most dominate and advance race on the planet earth and not the "white race".

The white, blonde hair, blue eye gentile is contrary to nature because they cannot be exposed to the life-giving rays from the sun for long periods of time without developing skin cancer and many other diseases. The sun which is the source of life for all on the planet earth is death to the white, blonde hair, blue eye, Aryan vampire gentile that must have large quantities of blood stored in blood-banks as well as stay in the dark to survive just like today's movies portray the vampires of their past. When the Grey aliens that controlled the white Aryan gentiles in Germany requested only pureblood Aryans be brought forth, it was "NOT" because they were superior to Humans but because their vessels were clean of any godly like DNA and that made their vessels suitable for the Grey aliens experiments in genetic engineering to produce a vessel that the Grey's could use to house more evil disembodied ancient spirits. The Grey's did not want any godly DNA in those created creatures' system because these creatures were made to be destroyed and with no godly DNA in them, the Grey aliens figured that God would not mine whatever they did to these created vampire creatures. Remember, the Grey's were warned not to touch God's anointed ones and do God's prophets no harm. The white Gentiles are the grafted branch that is contrary to nature that was made to be destroyed. (Google or You Tube "Rudolf of Germany, white people are not human"), 2 Peter 2: 12, 1 Chronicles 16: 22, Psalm 105: 15 and Romans 11: 24

In the 1996 movie titled "Independence Day", the white Gentiles said that "Mankind" or those who are not "human" or "men" but are the clones and replicas that were designed to look like "men" that were called "mankind" or a "kind of a man" would declare themselves independent from God and from humanity.

The white Jews and white Gentiles proclaimed," assemble yourselves and come all you heathens or those who do not believe in God together round about". Joel 3: 11

This is not a war against the Arabs, and God is on the infidel or heathen white Greek Jews and white Roman Gentiles side fighting the descendants of Abraham. This is a war between the heathens or those who do not believe in God against God and they are fighting God for the people of God who were "Slaves" and Oppressed, Persecuted and Scattered heritage to inherit the earth who were identified as the "Meek" and the "Dead" because of their condition. In the latter-days, at the end of the age, the ascendants of the slaves who are oppressed, persecuted and scattered are named Afro Americans and called "Negro" which means "Dead". The Holy Bible says, the "Dead" or the "Negro" shall be raised first to meet God in the air to forever be with God. Joel 3: 2, Matthew 5: 5 and 1 Thessalonians 4: 16-17

If you do not believe that God and the Son of God are the color of brass (brown) that has been burn in a furnace (dark-brown to black) with hair like sheep wool or nappy hair, you do not know or believe in God or the Son of God. This is a war against the Gentiles for scattering God's people and for wanting the people of God inheritance of a thousand-year reign with Jesus. Revelation 1: 14-15, John 16: 3, John 8: 19, 1 Thessalonians 4: 5, Joel 3: 2 and Revelation 20: 4

The white Jews and white Gentiles will be fighting God for the people of God who are scattered inheritance. Read it in the Holy

Bible. The Afro Americans who are the ascendants of the slaves and the slaves are God's first born and chosen people are the people of God that are being scattered today at the end of the age when God has promised to return and gather His people that are being scattered. Where are the Afro Americans that use to live in Los Angeles, California? Why were they scattered out? Joel 3: 2 and Exodus 4: 22

Remember, the white Gentiles wants an additional thousand years Reich on the earth with the Grey aliens giving them advance technology. They have exchanged the truth of God for the lie that they are the people of God because they are white and now they worship and serve the creature or the Grey aliens for technology rather than the Creator. They are now working with the Grey aliens underground in Antarctica and in their secret government underground military facilities doing all sorts of horrible inhuman things. Romans 1: 25

The Roman Catholic Christians of today and the white Hellenistic Greek Jews who are assuming the identity of the true people of God are the descendants of those pagan white Romans and pagan white Greek Jews who God was Zeus and are the ones who crucified Jesus. God will not be on their side against the Muslims who are the descendants of Ishmael who are the descendants of Abraham. The white gentile Christians are being deceived by the "False Prophet" who is the "False Brethren" who are the Accusers of the true people of God and they have assumed the true people of God identity to deceive the white Gentiles to believe different. It is this deception by the false prophet that will be the cause of the white Jews and white Gentiles destruction. The Holy Bible has recorded that the white Jews and white Gentiles were "Deceived" by the "False-Prophet" who are the false brethren who have assumed the identity of the true people of God. All Christians must know that they are being deceived by the false prophet. The "Accuser of the brethren" is the enemy. Anyone accusing the Brethren or the Brothers who are the true people of God who are the Afro Americans today of anything is the enemy to the white Jews and to the white Gentiles because the Brothers or the Brethren are the only ones who can bring the white Jews and white Gentiles to the path of Salvation. They are ordered by God to be for the Salvation of the white Jews and the white Gentiles from biblical days to "Present" till the end of the earth. Revelation 12: 10, 2 Corinthians 11: 26, Revelation 19: 20 Revelation 12: 10 and Acts 13: 47

Let the heathen be wakened and come up to the Valley of Jehoshaphat for there will God sit to judge all the heathens round about. Joel 3: 12

Now here is understanding. The Gentiles will be gathered together in a place called Armageddon, but the judgment of the heathen will take place in the Valley of Jehoshaphat. The battle and judgment will not occur in the mountains and hills of Megiddo but in the Valley of Jehoshaphat. The "False Prophet" who do not know the prophesies of the God of Abraham has suppressed this fact to deceive the white Roman gentiles who have dominion today. To deceive the white Gentiles who have dominion today about what the War of Armageddon is all about, the Valley of Jehoshaphat is never spoke of. Revelation 16: 16, Joel 3: 12 and Joel 3: 2

Once gathered in the mountains and hills of Megiddo in a place called Armageddon after the Gentiles sees the force that they will be fighting and understand what the war is all about, the white Gentiles who have dominion today will make a big decision to change their minds in helping the Synagogue of Satan and decide to join God and help the Arabs and the Valley of Jehoshaphat will turn into the "Valley of Decisions" where the white Gentiles decided to change their minds and join God. This prophecy of the "Valley of Decisions" has been suppressed by those who have assume the true people of God identity and do not know the prophesies of the God of Abraham. Revelation 16: 16, Joel 3: 2 and Joel 3: 14

It will not be good for the heathens in the Valley of Jehoshaphat. Multitudes of heathens will be there, and the Valley of Jehoshaphat will turn into the Valley of Decisions because the white Gentiles who have dominion today will change their minds after they find out what the War of Armageddon is all about and they will join God and the Valley of Jehoshaphat will turn into the Valley of Decisions because there the Gentiles who have dominion today will change their minds and join God. Joel 3: 2 and Joel 3: 14

Him who is called Faithful and True and in righteousness He judges and makes war will not be fighting the Arabs. He will be fighting those from the Synagogue of Satan and the Christians who crucified Jesus and the fight will be over the people of God who are scattered who are the Afro Americans today name, identity and heritage. The white Gentiles who have dominion today must understand that Jesus was not a Christian. Christianity did not come into existence until after Jesus was killed hundreds of years later. Christianity was started by those who killed Jesus and wanted the white Gentiles to worship the white Gentiles as a God. Jesus was against those who would be called Christians and those who would be called Christians are the ones who killed Jesus and Jesus people. Revelation 19: 11, Revelation 3: 9 and Joel 3: 2

# 33

## The Cross

The Christians worship the symbol of Satan when the Christians worship the cross. The "Cross" is a symbol of Satan and it is the symbol that Satan told God that would represent where Satan came from or where you will find Satan. God asked Satan "From where do you come from or where can you be found". Satan replies by saying "From going "to and fro" in the earth and from walking "up and down" in the earth". Job 2: 2

Here is understanding. Satan give God a symbol by which Satan will be identified and this symbol is where Satan comes from and where you will find Satan. Satan gives God a geometric symbol of two lines. Satan says his symbol would be going "to and fro" in the earth which in a horizonal line from front to back or left to right. Then Satan give another symbol of a vertical line from "up to down".

In geometry 101, we are taught that whenever you draw a horizonal line and a vertical line, somewhere in infinity these two lines will meet. The importance of these two lines is their point of intersection. Satan said at that intersection or at that "Cross" will be where you will find Satan. When you are driving down a street in your car, you are safe in the middle of the block but when you get to the corner or when you get to the "Cross" at the corner of the street, you better beware because there at the corner or at the "Cross" is where Satan would be or where you will get in an accident if you do not look both ways to prevent another car from running into the side of your car. As children growing up in the neighborhoods, the children were told never to play on the corners of the block at the "Cross" that you stayed in because on the corners of the block you stayed in or at the "Cross" there would be those that sold drugs, prostitutes and aggressive guys that would want to fight you for control of the neighborhood as well as, accidents from cars or motorbikes could hurt you.

At the "Cross" is where you will find Satan. None of the people of God would ever worship the symbol of the instrument that killed Jesus. Only those that were happy that Jesus was killed worshipped the instrument of Jesus death.

In biblical days, the Gentiles would use a "Cross" to say to the people of God that it was the "Cross" that stopped Jesus. If a love one of yours is killed by a 357-magna gun, would you worship the 357-magna gun as a symbol and reminder of your love one death or would you feel that you do not want to be around no guns because it was a gun that took your love one away? It is because of this truth that the author of this book has noticed that new age editions of the Holy Bible have changed the details of this symbol to "going to and fro" in the earth and from "walking to and fro" in the earth. This is a deception. Always use an older version of the Holy Bible to research the facts because new age versions of the Holy Bible are being changed and altered to suppress the truth. Job 1: 7, Job 2: 2

It was those who hated Jesus wagging their heads saying, "Aha! You who destroyed the temple and rebuilt the temple in three days when it took forty-six years to build, save yourself and come down from the cross"! They screamed, "Jesus saved others but cannot save Himself". It was these infidels and Heathens that worship the "Cross" which was the instrument of Jesus death. Jesus used the same magical building technics that the people of God used to build the pyramids. In three days, Jesus rebuilt the Temple by Himself when it originally took forty-six years for the temple to be built. Mark 15: 29-32 and John 2: 19-20

Today's white Vampires proudly wears black lip-stick and black finger-nail polish and a "Cross" around their necks to illustrate their dedication to Satan and evil. In the movies, when Vampires run from the cross, it is not because the cross is a symbol of something good or holy but because the "Cross" is the symbol of Satan, their supreme leader and those that are holding the Cross are saying, "Your leader Satan order you to depart".

The false prophet who is the false brethren that will be caught and thrown into the Lake of Fire which is the Sun when they try to leave the earth in space ships to escape judgment are those who are assuming the identity of the true people of God and have deceived the white Gentiles who have dominion today that they know the prophesies of the God of Abraham. 2 Corinthians 11: 26 and Revelation 19: 20

When the second Beast that will look like a lamb or look like one of God's people of peace but will speak like a dragon ready for war that most Israelites believes is "Barack Obama" that only look like a Lamb of God because he is not a "Israelite" or a "Hebrew" who is the ascendants of slaves because his mother was a white Gentile and his father a native African neither of which were the ascendants of the slaves in America and he ignored the people of God persecution and carried out the wishes of the white Jews and white Gentiles faithfully when he was in office and the false prophet who are the leaders of the white Christians and white Jewish religions who do not know the prophesies of the God of Abraham try to escape the earth in space ships to get away from judgment, they will be CAUGHT and their space ships will be thrown into the Lake of Fire or thrown into the Sun. Revelation 13: 11 and Revelation 19: 20

When Him who sat on the white horse who is called Faithful and True and in righteousness He judges and makes war arrives with His army from Heaven to rule the earthly kingdoms with a rod of iron, that rod of iron will be made of twelfth dimensional material. The people of God will be given two new elements that are not water, air, earth or fire but is something else from the twelfth dimension that has three of its dimensions visible in the third dimensional space time continuum, but nine dimensions of this twelfth dimensional material will be somewhere else that cannot be touched by no one who do not have a highly evolved body, or a body given immortality as the people of God bodies will be given when they are joined with the Lord. The Gentiles will fear and flee from these two new elements the way animals in the jungle fears and flee from fire. The rod of iron that Him who will rule the nations will have will be made from one of these two new elements. Revelation 2: 27, Revelation 19: 15 and Psalm 2: 9

The beast, the kings of the earth and their armies gathered together to make war against Him who sat on the horse. Revelation 19: 19

Another part of the identity of the false prophet is that religious order that will require all to take the mark of the beast or the mark that will turn you into a beast and worshiped the beast image. This is a reference to the leaders of the religious order of the white Gentiles who have dominion today that call themselves Christians who also to do not know the prophesies of the God of Abraham. Revelation 19: 20

    The white Christians do not worship God or the Son of God. They worship the white Gentiles as a God. They worship the image or the picture of the upright paleolithic beast or the beast that was made to walk upright as the son of God. The white Gentiles who are the Christians believe that God and the Son of God are white. No white gentile Christian from the local churches in America to the Basilica in Rome knows God or the Son of God because the white gentile Christians believes that God and the Son of God are white pagan gentiles. 1 Thessalonians 4: 5, John 16: 2-3, 1 Corinthians 10: 20 and Revelation 14: 9-10

    The Holy Bible has recorded that God and the Son of God are the color of brass (brown) that has been burned in the furnace (dark brown to black) with hair like sheep wool or nappy hair. The Shroud of Turin is a Lie and a Fake. Revelation 1: 14-15 and Daniel 7: 9

    The Holy Bible says in Daniel 7: 9 that the Ancient of Days who is the Most-High in the Throne Room of 25 thrones in Heaven has sheep wool or nappy hair. Like His Son, we know that He also has skin the color of brass (brown) that has been burned in a furnace (dark brown to black). Revelation 4: 4

    Remember, the Lamb in Heaven who is the color of brass (brown) that has been burned in the furnace (dark brown to black) with hair like sheep wool or nappy hair is He who is worthy to take the scrolls and open all of its seals. Revelation 1: 14-15 and Revelation 4: 8-10

# 34

# The white Created Creatures purpose for existing

The white Gentiles worship the image or picture of the white Paleolithic beast from Europe that was made to walk upright and turned into Homosapien as the son of God. They worship the image of this beast or they worship the picture of this beast that was called the upright beast or the beast that was made to walk upright as Jesus, the son of God. Revelation 13: 15, Revelation 14: 9 and Revelation 19: 20

"Rudolf of Germany", a white Aryan, says that white people are not human beings. Rudolf of Germany and the Ancient Astronauts Theorists believe that the white Gentiles are extraterrestrials from another planet that was put here on this planet to replace the human Beings because the white Gentiles are people of technology. They are wrong.

The white Gentiles are not from the planet earth. They are not extraterrestrials from another planet. They were created by the pure, black Aryans in the first world. The white beings are from the "test-tube" created in a laboratory. This is the story of "Yakub" the big head scientist, who was one of the fallen angels and black Aryans from Aldebaran that created the white beings. Nuclear war in the first world forced the black Aryans to leave the earth and take their creation with them to the Aldebaran star system because of the radiation on the earth. Once there, the pure, black Aryans told Maria Orsic that the servient white race was devolving because of the radiation that they were exposed to during the war before they were removed by the black Aryans and taken to Aldebaran as a servient race. (Google Maria Orsic and understand what she revealed.)

Once there, the white race was degrading the pure black Aryan race. After the radiation from the nuclear war in the first world died out and life was started again on earth in the world we live in today, the pure, black Aryans returned to the earth as the Sumerians and as the enemy who planted the white Gentiles on the earth to mix with the human beings to become human, so the white beings would not degrade the pure, black beings from Aldebaran. They are the "Tares" that were genetically created by the enemy who are the fallen angels or the pure, black Aryans and put on the planet earth to join with the people of the earth to become human beings because they were degrading the pure, black Aryans from Aldebaran. At the time of the Harvest of the earth, the white beings that did not mix to become human but remained white will be gathered into bundles identified as the "Tares" to be burn and those that did mix and became human beings will be gathered into God's barn. This is recorded in the Holy Bible and this is the message given to Maria Orsic of the Vril society that the Nazis did not understand. (You Tube- Rudolf of Germany) and Matthew 13: 24-30

The Aryans from Aldebaran said that in their star system, there were two races. One was an elder race that had the original men in it and the other was a servient race that was devolving because of nuclear radiation from a war in the first world. Like in the last world, in the world we live in today, it is the white beings that is threatening the world with nuclear destruction. Time is repeating itself because this world is being recorded over what happened in the last world and if nothing is changed or if different choices are not made, what happened last time will happen this time. It is because of this that events must be steered in another direction to prevent what happened last time from happening again this time.

Now, since the Aryans must be the elder race because the original man is a black man, the white beings were the servient race that was mixing with the mother race that the mother race said was degrading their race. When the Aryans from Aldebaran identified themselves as being a "Elder" race, they are saying that they are a black race. Being black with hair like wool or nappy hair is the proof of that race being an elder race because of the effects of the sun and the elements on their skin and hair for millions of years that darken their skin and dried-out their hair whereas a white race is a young race and their skin and hair reflects that. Having white Skin and oily hair is proof of that race not being expose to the sun and the harsh elements for a very long time. Dark skin that has been sun-tanned for millions of years and nappy hair that is dried-out is proof of that race being exposed to the sun for a very long time.

The white Gentiles have no planet to call their own because they were created in a test tube in a laboratory. The white Gentiles were created by the Fallen Angels to be used for body replacement parts and labor and they were to be destroyed when no longer needed. The black Aryans story of creating the white race in the first world and taking the white race with them to the star system named Aldebaran at the end of the first world is the story of "Yakub", the "big head" scientist and other Fallen Angels who created the white Gentiles for their personal reasons and these created beings were to be destroyed when no longer needed by the Fallen Angels. They were brute beast made to be destroyed. The black Aryans from Aldebaran returned to the earth after the radiation died down and planted the subservient white race on the planet earth to mix with the people of the earth to become human, so the black Aryans would not be degraded when mixing with the white race by losing their hue and becoming brown to yellow to white. This is the story of the "Tares and the Wheat" recorded in the Holy Bible. The "Tares" were to grow together with the people of the earth to become human. At the time of the Harvest of the Earth, the "Tares" that did not mix to become human will be gathered into bundles to be burn. The white race was made to be destroyed but spared for this one purpose. They were to mix with the people of the earth to become human beings. (You Tube- Yakub, the big head scientist), 2 Peter 2: 12 and Matthew 13: 24-30

The Fallen Angels who are today represented by the Grey aliens till this day are still rapturing the white Gentiles up in the air for evolutionary development examinations to determine if the white Gentiles are at their fullness or at their maximum level of evolutionary development and if so, sperm and eggs are taken from them to be used to make new vessels for disembodied ancient spirits to exist in somewhere else.

White Gentile women are impregnated and then the fetus is removed two months into the pregnancy by the Grey aliens to be raised by the Grey aliens for some unknown purpose somewhere else. White men are raptured on the Grey alien UFO's and sperm is removed from those that qualify to be used to construct more vessels for the Grey aliens purpose. These created white gentile beings had no planet because they were created out of a test tube in a laboratory for purposes of the fallen angels.

There is no missing link. There are only the experiments by Yakub and the other Fallen Angels to create a being that was not part of the Tree of Life that they could manipulate for their own needs. The evidence of that manipulation is found in the different craniums of the white Gentiles that are found throughout Europe marking the white beings' stages of development by the Fallen Ones to produce a living being for their use.

Because these replicated created creatures were not part of the Tree of Life but were biological beings created by the Fallen Angels, the Fallen Angels declared that they could do whatever they wanted to the creatures since these creatures were created in a laboratory. The Fallen Angels declared that these created paleolithic beings were brute beast made to be destroyed by extracting DNA from them to create more vessels for disembodied ancient spirits and when the Fallen Angels had no more use for them, the created creatures were to be destroyed. The Fallen Angels proclaimed these created paleolithic beings were created to be destroyed for the Fallen Angels needs or created for the Fallen Angels to remove their body parts and fluids. The white Gentiles were "CREATED" for this one purpose. They were brute beast made for this one purpose to be destroyed by the removal of body parts and fluids. 2 Peter 2: 12

The white Gentiles of today feel the same way about cloned individuals that they are creating for the white Gentiles purpose and needs to be used for bodily replacement parts and the extraction of DNA or "Stem Cells" and body organs to be used by the white Gentiles and the white Gentiles feels that when these replicated clones are no longer needed by the white Gentiles, these replicated clones could be put to death because they did not actually exist for real but were brute beast made to be destroyed by the white Gentiles when the white Gentiles have no more use for those that were replicated. This was the message given in the 1982 movie titled, "Blade Runner" with Harrison Ford. The white Gentiles have suggested that the rich white Gentiles could clone themselves and use the cloned creature for body replacement parts and the killing of the created creature will be of no importance because the created creature really was not designated to live but were created to be killed by the extraction of their body organs and fluids. They would be brute beast made to be destroyed. 2 Peter 2: 12

In the 2005 science fiction movie titled, "The Island", the white Gentiles said that in their future, cloning themselves for body replacement parts would be accepted. The white Gentiles of today's world says that these brute beasts that they will clone from themselves are being made or created to be destroyed by removing organs from them to be given to the original donor that these beings were created or cloned from. In the movie, the created clones that the white Gentiles in the future created wanted a full life span and independence from their creator and to be accepted and treated like all other human life forms on the earth were treated. The created up-right beast made to be destroyed by the falling angels in the beginning also asked for a full life span and an opportunity to live freely on the earth and mix with the people of the earth to become human beings. The created beings pleaded that they had a right to live just as much as those that they were created to look like because now, they were a kind of man that were created to look and act like man that is now a kind of a man that is called man-kind. 2 Peter 2: 12

These created white beings are the tares that were put on the planet earth that belongs to the people of the old black African dominion to be used by the Fallen Angels for body replacement parts, DNA extractions and for sex. This is why when the Grey's aliens abduct the Gentiles on the Grey's UFO'S, the Grey's who are working for the Falling Angels extract DNA from the Gentiles and give the Gentiles evolutionary development examinations by checking the Gentiles skin, hair, nails and reproductive system to determine if the Gentiles they have abducted are at their fullness or at their maximum evolutionary development stage at this time at the end of the age. When Zeus and the Fallen Angels that lived on Mt. Olympus who had abandon their heavenly posts to enjoy sex with mankind were defeated by the Titans who were the "Cast Out" ones and forced away from the planet, their created creatures that they made for their private use were to be destroyed. They were brute beast made for the Falling Angels agenda and were to be destroyed when the Falling Angels no longer needed them. Matthew 13: 24-30 and 2 Peter 2: 12

Because the created creatures were created to look like man, the people from the old black African dominion called them "mankind" or a "kind of a man" and they agreed with the created creatures request that the creatures be not destroyed but given a chance to mix with the human beings on the earth to become human. These created creatures were a new or young race of people whose skin had not been burned by the sun for millions of years and their hair had not been dried out from the heat of the sun for millions of years so the people of the old black African dominion on the earth wanted to mix with this new creation to share these young creatures new DNA to produce children with "lighter skin" and "curly hair".

To this very day, the people from the old black African dominion with dark skin and nappy hair still have a desire to mingle with the white Gentiles to produce children with lighter skin and curly hair. The old black African dominion was fascinated over the new race of people hair that was not dried out by the sun over millions of years of existence. Today, only the inferior, Lost Sheep, Negros are fascinated over the Gentiles oily, straight hair. These inferior lost-sheep are seen putting their hands on the white Gentiles head to touch and rub the white Gentiles hair. They are the integrationists who feel that they must be integrated with the white Gentiles to be happy. They are inferior parasites that cannot live and be happy and contented without the white Gentiles as their host.

Like the pure blood black Aryans from Aldebaran, the segregationists of the people of God wanted separation, isolation and exclusions as is order by God in the Holy Bible. Equal but separate was their desire because they felt that they could live without the white Gentiles and they wanted their own land, neighborhoods, doctors, churches and so on. They called the integrationists "parasites" for the white Gentiles because the integrationists could not live without the white Gentiles as their host providing for them. Now, at the end of the dominion, we see that the integrationists were wrong. Integrating in the white Gentiles societies degraded and destroyed the Afro Americans just as the pure, black, Aryans from Aldebaran had stated. The integrationists are responsible for all that have happened to the Afro Americans because they wanted white friends. The Holy Bible has ordered the people of God who are the ascendants of the slaves to be separate from the people of this world to be holy to the Lord just as the black Aryans from Aldebaran stated, but the integrationists wanted something else. Exodus 33: 16 and Ezra 10: 3

In the Holy Bible, Ezra, the priest stood up and said to the people of God, "You have transgressed and have taken pagan wives, adding to the guilt of Israel. Now therefore make confession to the Lord God of your fathers, and do His will, separate yourself from the people of the land and from the pagan wives". Therefore, let's make a covenant with our God to put away all these pagan wives and those children who have been born to them according to the advice of my master and of those who tremble at the commandment of our God and let it be done according to the law. God wanted His people to be separated from the people of the world to be a holy people to the Lord our God. God has chosen His people to be a special people unto God above all people that are on the face of the earth. This is what the segregationists of the people of God wanted. Those who wanted to integrate the people of God into the white Gentile society did not want the people of God to be special to God. The integrationists of the people of God transgressed against God's laws and the people of God that were integrated into the white Gentiles civilization were degraded and lost everything including their identity just as the black Aryans from Aldebaran had stated about themselves to Maria Orsic. Even now, the white Gentiles from Germany are trying to steal the black Aryans from Aldebaran identity. These white Gentiles are calling themselves Aryans and are saying that they are the pure, elder race that do not want to be degraded by mixing. The white Gentiles are not a "Elder" race and the proof of that is in their Skin. They are white meaning they have not been exposed to the sun and the elements for hundreds of thousands of years. The white beings must mix with the colored-beings to become "Human Beings" or people with a shade, color, or tint. The white beings only purpose for being on the earth was to become human beings by mixing. The white beings are claiming now at the end of the dominion that the mixing have occurred and all on the planet earth are colored-people or human beings knowing that they are still white without color. Ezra 10: 10-11, Ezra 10: 2-3, Deuteronomy 7: 3-4, Exodus 33: 16, and Deuteronomy 7: 6

Those Negros who were dead but are now born again and now, eyes have been opened are proud of their nappy hair knowing that the Lamb in Heaven who shall inherit everything and the God of the universe have hair like sheep wool or nappy hair. It is these integrationists that will stand against the white Gentiles at judgment this time and proclaim that the white Gentiles never wanted to integrate with them to become human beings no matter how hard they tried to integrate with the white Gentiles. Revelation 1: 14-15 and Daniel 7: 9

The white beings were supposed to mix with the human beings to become human. The white Gentiles only purpose for remaining on the earth after their gods had no more use for them was to mix with the people of the earth to become human beings. Remember, the white Gentiles were brute beast made to be destroyed when the fallen angels had no more use for them. Because of the request by the old black Africans to spare the white Gentiles, the white beings were given a dominion to determine if the white beings would comply and fulfill their only purpose for existing on the earth. This is why the white Greeks and the white Romans were given dominions to guarantee to them that no one would stand in their way or prevent them from fulfilling their purpose for existing on the earth and from joining with the people of the earth to become human beings. The white beings were not given dominion on the earth because they are better than the people of the earth but was given dominion on the earth to join with the people of the earth to become human beings. The only reason why these brute beasts who were made to be destroyed was not destroyed when their gods, the Olympians were forced away from the earth was to JOIN with the people of the earth to become human beings. They were "SPARED" for this one purpose. 2 Peter 2: 12

After giving the white Gentiles three dominions which were the Greek dominion, the Roman dominion and this last dominion we live in today identified as "Iron and Clay" which is a derivative of the Roman dominion to make that joining, the white Gentiles reneged on the agreement and said they would not join with the people of the earth to become human beings but would stay "White" but would tell all in Heaven that the joining had occurred and all on the planet earth were "Colored People" or "Human Beings". Daniel 2: 33-34 and Daniel 2: 41-44

Instead of fulfilling their only purpose on the earth by joining with the people of the earth to become human beings, the white gentile beings, in their dominions, made the people of the earth their servants and declared to the people of the earth that the white gentile beings who are the brute beasts that were made to be destroyed but was helped by the people of the earth were better than the colored people or better than the human beings of the earth.

Once the white Gentiles were given dominion on the earth to join with the people of the earth, the white Gentiles betrayed the people of the earth and used the power and authority given to them by God to join the people of the earth to become human beings to establish themselves as royalty over the people of the earth and they declared their leader to be the God of the earth and the only one with real power and called their leader "Caesar" and declared that Caesar was the only God for them. John 19: 15

The Greeks were given a dominion to make this joining, but they refused. The Romans were given a dominion to make this joining and they refused. The last gentile dominion of "Iron and Clay" that we live in today which is a combination of the iron as the strong white gentiles and the clay as the people of the earth was given the opportunity to make that joining and to make it easy, the iron was gathered together with the clay in this last dominion but the iron would not make that joining. As you saw the iron mixed with the clay, they or the white beings will mingle with the seeds of men, but they will not adhere to one another just as iron does not mix with clay. Daniel 2: 43

In all three dominions of the white gentiles second chance for salvation, the white Gentiles refused to make the joining with the people of the earth to become human beings. They declared that with the power and authority given to them in their dominions to make the joining with the people of the earth, they would use that power and authority to dominate the people of the earth and turn the people of the earth into their servants. Because of this betrayal by the white young Gentiles known as Esau by making the old race referred to as Jacob their servants, God has said that God hate the young race referred to as Esau and loves the old race referred to as Jacob. Romans 9: 12-13 and Malachi 1: 2-3

Remember, the "Deliverer" only mission is to deliver a profound truth to the white Jews and white Gentiles in the latter-days after the fullness of the Gentiles has come in at the end of the age or after December 21, 2012. His job is to reveal to the Gentiles the "Mystery of the Gospel" and for this purpose he must be given "Utterance to speak boldly". He will interpret the scriptures and reveal the secrets of the gospel that no one else on the planet knows. To save the Gentiles this time, the Gentiles insisted that the "Deliverer" be sent to them so they would know what was going on, so they would know what to do to be saved. The "Deliverer mission is only to deliver the "Mystery of the Gospel" to them. His mission is not to try to make the Gentiles accept the message or believe the message. The Gentiles must do whatever is in their hearts to prove or disprove if the Gentiles are worthy to continue to exist. Romans 11: 25-26, Ephesians 6: 19-20

The white Gentiles only purpose for existing on the earth is to join with the people of the earth to become human beings. If it was not for this purpose, the white beings would have been destroyed when their gods, the Olympians were forced away from the earth by the Titans. They were brute beast made to be destroyed when they were no longer needed by the Fallen Angels. The white beings refused to join with the human beings to become human, but they proclaimed to all in heaven that the joining had taken place and all beings on the planet earth were human beings from the human race that have a shade, color or tint in their flesh knowing that they were still white and without color. The white Gentiles are the Tares or bad seeds that is spoke of in the Holy Bible that were mixed in with the good seeds or mixed in with the people of God from the old black African dominion by the enemy or Fallen Angeles or the pure, black Aryans from Aldebaran. They were to grow together with the people of God to become Human, but they failed. Prophecy has it that at the time of the Harvest of the Earth, the Reaper will gather the tares into a bundle to be burn and the people of God will be gather together in God's barn. 2 Peter 2: 12, Matthew 13: 24-30 and Matthew 13: 37-43

The white Gentiles of today were genetically engineered from apes for servitude and body replacement parts by the Fallen Angels. The upright Beast named Paleolithic man who is the white Gentiles was genetically engineered from apes to walk upright for service and body parts replacement for the Fallen Angels who are represented by the Greys today. When they were no longer needed, they were to be destroyed. They were brute beast made to be destroyed. It is these brute beasts that were made to be destroyed that were put on the people of God planet and mixed in with the people of God from the old black African dominion that are the Tares that were put on the earth by the "enemy" or the "fallen angels" who were the beings from Aldebaran that will be gathered into bundles to be burn. 2 Peter 2: 12

The people of God from the old black African dominion were so obsessed with the white Gentiles hair that Jesus explained that if God would have gathered the white Gentiles together to be destroyed in the beginning, God would have also up rooted the wheat or the people of God that admired the created creatures so much because of the creatures' hair. It was decided that they both would grow together on the earth and at the time of Harvest at the end of the age, the tares or those who were still white and did not mix with the people of God to become Human beings would be gathered together to be burn and the wheat or the people of God who are the human beings would be gather into God's barn in New Jerusalem. The students at Tulane university in New Orleans, La says, "It is okay to be white". The students at Tulane University in New Orleans, La must know that it is not okay to be white. No, the white Gentiles are not from the earth, but they are not extraterrestrials that they think they are either and they are not people of technology. They are a subservient, brute beast called Paleolithic that were genetically engineered in test tubes from apes and placed on the people of God from the old black African dominion planet by the black Aryans from Aldebaran to mix with the colored-people to become human. These brute beasts are the Tares of this earth. These "Brute Beast" were made to be destroyed when the fallen angels no longer needed them. Matthew 13: 24-30, Matthew 13: 37-43 and Revelation 14: 15

It is this Paleolithic upright Beast that the white gentile Christians worship as the Son of God. The white Gentiles worship the image of this upright Beast or they worship the picture of this upright beast as Jesus, the Son of God. Revelation 14: 9-11

The white Gentiles will not get what was promise to them because they are worshipping the upright Beast as the son of God. Even if they have a good report and have lived a righteous life, they will not get what was promised if they are worshipping the upright white beast instead of the Lamb that is the color of brass (brown) that has been burned in a furnace (dark brown to black) with hair like sheep wool or nappy hair. If anyone worship the upright beast and his image or picture and receives his mark on the flesh shall drink of the wine of the wrath of God which will be poured out in full strength into the cup of his indignation or anger that the Son of God is black. He shall be tormented with fire that will burn and brimstone that will smell. Remember, a nasty, foul, repugnant, stinky, smelly sore that will smell worse than burning brimstone will develop on all who take the mark of the beast or the mark that will turn you into a beast. Hebrew 11: 40, Revelation 1: 14-15, Revelation 14: 9-11, Revelation 16: 2 and Revelation 16: 10

Understand, all of the white gentile Christians including their pastors and priests who have lived a righteous life will not get what was promised to those who live a righteous life if they believe that God and the Son of God are white. At judgment right now, the gentile Christians are screaming that they were deceived by the "False Prophet" who are the "False Brethren" who are the white Greek gentile Jews who deceived the white Christian Roman gentiles that they were the people of God that knew the prophecy of the God of Abraham. In the latter-days when they try to leave the earth to escape judgment in their spaceships, they will face a million-spaceship armada out in space. The decision will be made to reverse their coast and go around the sun to evade this unknown space fleet. It will be at this point, they will be cast into the Lake of Fire which is the Sun. Prometheus, from the government secret space program and SpaceX, a civilian operation must be told this prophecy. Hebrew 11: 39-40, Revelation 1: 14-15 and Revelation 19: 20

The people of the earth requested that the created replicant creature created in the image of man and called mankind or a kind of a man be allowed to live because they looked so much like man. All in Heaven said that the people of God were STUMBLING to make this request. The created creatures were given a dominion on the people of God planet earth to prove themselves worthy to continue to exist. It is because of this that salvation has come to the Gentles who are the created young creatures. They were to join with the people of the earth to become Human Beings. They failed. Romans 11: 11-12

When the Son of man comes, all the nations will be gathered before Him and He will separate them one from another. Then the

King will say to those on His right, "Come, you are blessed of my father. Come and inherit the kingdom that has been prepared for you from the foundations of the world. Matthew 25: 31-34

Then He will say to those on His left, "Depart from me, you cursed people. You shall go into the everlasting fire prepared for the devil and his angels. Matthew 25: 41

The Parable of the Tares and the Wheat is about the white Gentiles being planted on the people of God from the old black African dominion planet. Understand at this time, the white Gentiles will become a victim of their own iniquity. If they had joined with the human beings and became human, it would have been difficult to separate the Tares from the Wheat. The parable of the Tares and the Wheat is about the white Gentiles that were put on the people of the old black African dominion planet to grow and evolve with the people of the old black African dominion by joining with the people of the old black African dominion to become human beings but the white Gentiles refused to make that joining and they stayed white and now it will be easy for the Reaper at the time of Harvest to isolate the Tares who are the white Gentiles into bundles to be burned and easy for the Reaper to gather the Wheat into God's barn. Matthew 13: 24-30 and Matthew 13: 37-43

If the white Gentiles had joined with the people of earth from the old black African dominion to become human beings, it would have been difficult to separate them to be burn but not impossible because all things are possible with God. It would be harder to take the egg out of the cake once the cake is baked but it would be easy to take the egg out of the cake mix before mixing and baking while the egg is resting on the cake mix as well as to remove the cake mix that has become influenced or contaminated by the egg. If they had mixed with the people of the earth to become human beings, this would had been acceptable by God because this was their only purpose for being on the earth. Now, since the white Gentiles have remained white, it will be easy to identify them to be gathered to be burned along with their Uncle Tom admirers. Throughout the dominions of the white Gentiles, Uncle Toms have tried to mix with the white Gentiles to transform the white beings into human beings, but the white beings refused to do so. No, it is not okay to be white in the latter-days of the white Gentiles dominion of "Iron and Clay" at the time of the Harvest of the Earth when the Reapers will come forth to separate the "Wheat" from the "Tares" so the "Tares" could be burn and the "Wheat" gathered into God's barn. Matthew 13: 24-30, Matthew 13: 37-43 and Revelation 14: 15

If you are still white at the time of the Harvest of the earth, you must be with a human being who is an ascendant of a "Slave" and joined together in marriage or friendship to escape the "Reaper". The spirit of death will by-pass you just as the spirit of death by-passed the Egyptians that were with the Hebrews slaves in Goshen when the first born of Egypt were killed. At the end of the age when the fullness of the white Gentiles has come in, the white Gentiles must be wise in their own "Conceit" which is their undeserved self-importance and pride. "Great One", you must understand this. Romans 11: 25 and Matthew 13: 30

Understand, Prince Harry from the royalty of England in 2018 has married a black woman who is an ascendant of "Slaves". This was unprecedented, but it was acceptable by the royalty of England and even by the Queen of England. You must understand the importance and the dept of this marriage for the Queen of England to agree with this marriage and for Prince Charles of England to walk proudly in the wedding down the royal aisle to the alter with this ascendant of "Slaves" and present this ascendant of a "Slave" to the Prince of England in marriage. Prince Charles said that he was pleased to welcome this ascendant of the "Slaves" to the royal family in this way. This event was so important and significant that Prince Philip attended the wedding with a broken rib. Then, Negro spiritual gospel was sung in the castle of the royalty of England on the day of the marriage of the Prince of England to the descendent of a "Slave". The God of the "Slaves" was honored by song in the castle of England. The purity of the white Christian Catholic Gentiles has married a black woman who is a ascendant of the "Slaves" for some unknown reason that was not love but love could be there now because of the exposure of the two being together. Being an American actress is not the important detail or the identifying label about who prince Harry married. Prince Harry did not only marry an American actress but married an ascendant of the "Slaves". What is important here is that the presence of this one individual who is an ascendant of the "Slaves" could save all in the castle that are around her when the Reaper arrive if she and only if she knows God and believes and is saved. Remember, the "Deliverer" who shall be possessed by the spirit of Simon Peter who was called Simeon and called a Nig er (Nigger) will tell you how to save all in your house. Acts 13: 13-14

The royalty of England has joined with a ascendant of the "Slave" in marriage for this reason that was unknown to the public. If you are white, you must be joined with a human being that is a ascendant of the "Slaves" in marriage or friendship to be saved when the Harvest of the Earth comes at the end of the age when the fullness of the Gentiles has arrived, and the Reaper is sent to gather the Wheat from the Tares. The end of the age was on or around December 21, 2012. Nibiru, the winged globe from ancient times, is approaching. Remember, the Holy Bible has recorded that without us or the people of God, the white Gentiles will not receive nothing that was promised to them. Without us or the people of God, the white Gentiles will not be saved. Without us or the people of God, the white Gentiles will not be made whole or genetically perfect.

Because of this marriage to a ascendant of the "Slaves", the royalty of England in time will become genetically whole or perfect by mixing the DNA of the "Slaves" with the DNA of the royal family of England. Their skin, bone structure, immune system and life span will improve. "Great One" who is known as President, you must be wise in your own conceit. Black lives matter. You must know this to save all in your house or country. Matthew 13: 30, Hebrew 11: 39-40 and Romans 11: 25

There should not be one white being or person on the planet earth. All on the planet earth were supposed to be of one race called the human race that have human beings or people with a shade, color or tint in their complexion on it. That means everybody from yellow to red to brown to black are human beings because they have a hue in their complexion. The diminishing of this hue is the degrading and devolvement of the black race that the pure, black, Aryans spoke about to the Vril society. Only the white race is without this hue because white is the absence of all color. The degrading of the white Gentiles is not possible because they are already at the bottom of the genetic scale. The degrading went from black to brown to yellow to white. There is only one degrading left for the white beings. Anything removed from the white beings would be a diminishing or the destruction of the white beings. White mixing with white, in time, will produce albinos. To survive, the white beings must add to their genetic structure by mixing with the colored-people of the earth to become yellow to brown to black. Purity of the white race to remain white is a death sentence to the white race. The white race must mix to survive. The Holy Bible has recorded that without mixing with the people of the earth, the white race cannot be made whole or perfect. The white race has grown together with the human race and with the human beings and refused to make that joining to become human, but they proclaimed to all in Heaven and on Aldebaran that the joining of the white race with the human race had occurred and all on the planet earth were human beings knowing that they were still white. (Google or You Tube "Rudolf of Germany, white people are not human") and Hebrew 11: 40

In all of the science fiction movies about the future and space exploration, the white Gentiles are calling themselves human beings when they are still white. If you identify yourself as "White" you cannot call yourself a "human being" because white is the absent of the hue or color and a human being is one with a shade, color or tint. Hu-man means colored-man because "hue" or "hu" means color. When you want to add more color on your television set, you raise the "hue" or "hu" on the set.

Now, at the end of the dominion when the Reaper will come forth and separate the Wheat from the Tares, it will be easy to bind the white Gentiles into bundles to be burn with the people of the earth that are the cowardly, unbelieving, abominable, murderers, sexually immoral, sorcerers, idolaters and all liars who shall also have their part in the Lake which burns with fire. Matthew 13: 30, Matthew 13: 49, Revelation 14: 15, Matthew 25: 32-34 and Revelation 21: 8

When Him who sat on the horse who is called Faithful and True and in righteousness He judges and makes war arrive to gather or rapture the people of God in the air to be with the Lord, the white Gentiles have developed a plan to deceive the world. That plan is called the Blue Beam Project.

# 35

# Blue Beam Project

The Blue Beam Project was created by the government to deceive the people of the world into believing that when God return, it's really not God returning but the government trying to deceive the people to think that God is returning. So, whatever happens and whatever you see in the sky don't believe it because it is really our government with a laser light show and 3D holograms trying to deceive us.

This is why it was important and necessary for this book to be written because if this is the government plan for dealing with the return of God then the government needs a new plan and the government needs all of the information the government can get to know who and what they are dealing with.

The government has been told by the extraterrestrials how God will reveal new information about our history and how God would approach the earth to get the people of the earth attention.

The extraterrestrials tell the government that:

# THE BOOKS OF SIMION

First- There will be a reinterpretation of all archeology artifacts and biblical scriptures to reveal their true and hidden meaning. The Books of Simion are part of this new reinterpretation of the ancient biblical scriptures. Earthquakes will be created by God that will unearth new and unusual artifacts which will support the return of these aliens and Gods as well as reveal who are the true people of God. These artifacts will reveal knowledge of the old dominion and who are the people of the old dominion that are sacrificing so much for the people of the new white dominion to exist and why. The cover-up for this astronomical event is already in play. It is already being determined by all on the internet that these events will be the government trying to deceive the people of the earth. Because these events will unearth the truth and reveal that all religious doctrines have been misinterpreted and that knowledge now like in biblical days could turn the world upside down and this knowledge is the truth that has been hidden for generations but is now revealed to God's Saints (Sents) will prove that the government will not be behind these events to use the truth to deceive the people of the world. Acts 17: 6 and Colossians 1: 26

Second- There will be incredible signs in the sky as high as sixty miles in outer space that will be seen all over the world that will show images of God like, figures. In the United States, it will be Jesus. In India, it will be Krishna. In China, it will be Buddha and in the Middle East, it will be Allah. These figures will appear to be alive with full body motions, facial expressions and speech. The images will be as far out in space as sixty miles or more to prevent the government from deceiving the people of the world that what is being seen in space are laser lights and holograms. The holograms will be shown much closer to the earth and they will appear to all as holograms. What will be seen in deep space will look like something more than a hologram. It will look so real.

Third- These figures will speak or communicate with everyone on the planet through a form of telepathy deep inside of your mind. It will feel like your inner self is talking to you. These Gods will communicate with us through our hearts, minds and souls leaving no doubt concerning where the communication is coming from and who is sending the message. Abductees have reported that when raptured or taken aboard a flying vehicle referred to as a UFO for evolutionary development examinations, the abductors or alien that is referred to as the doctor will communicate with the abductees in this same manner. This is a form of communication that has never been experienced before by people that will speak to you from inside of you. Remember, the Kingdom of God is within you or is beyond the dream world of the fourth dimension that is in the universe in our minds. It is from this inner fourth dimensional universe in our minds where the communication will originate from. Luke 17: 21

Understand that the fourth dimension is not time as the white Gentile geniuses believes. The first dimension is when you move from up to down. The second dimension is when you move from left to right. The third dimension is movement from front to back. The fourth dimension is not time but when you move in and out of the first three dimension in sleep. The fourth dimension is where our consciousness goes when we are asleep or unconscious. Movement in the fourth dimension is just as important as movement in any other direction because failure to move in the fourth dimension for sleep and recuperation will cancel your ability to have movement in the other three lower dimensions. If you don't sleep, you will die.

Fourth- A global invasion of the earth or the return of God and the return of the people from the old black African dominion that were cast into OUTER DARKNESS which is outer space because outer space is outer darkness will happen next. When the kingdom was taken away from the people of God or when the new white

Gentile dominion started, the people of the old black advance African dominion was ordered to leave the earth to give the new dominion an opportunity to grow and evolve without being influenced by an advance culture. Matthew 8: 12 and Matthew 21: 43

They were cast into OUTER DARKNESS which is OUTER SPACE and they left a sign on the earth where they were going and would be until the fullness of the Gentiles had come in or until the Gentiles had reached their maximum level of evolutionary development in their second chance for salvation on the earth. The pyramids were constructed to reveal the star system that they went to in outer darkness until the fullness of the Gentiles comes in at the end of the age. After the end of the age or after December 21, 2012, they will be returning to the earth with the angels of God to establish the greatest kingdom to ever exist in the universe with the Gods. Matthew 13: 49

Massive mother ships will be seen hovering over the earth. Christians will believe that it is the rapture or judgment day. The government says that when these things start to happen, it is not aliens or the return of the Gods but only the government trying to deceive you to believe that it is aliens or the return of the Gods, so the government could have control over you. So, if you do not want to be controlled by the government, do not believe nothing that you see in the sky or hear in your heart or mind from a form of communication that you have never experienced before because it is a government trick that is done with laser lights, 3D holograms, computers and massive amounts of electromagnetic energy waves.

The Blue Beam Project is designed to deceive the people of the earth to trick them to believe that they are seeing illusions created from 3D holograms and a real invasion or the return of the Gods is not happening.

The government plan is that when these huge motherships appear in the skies, the government will shine 3D holograms and laser lights in the sky as well that the people of earth will see and believe that everything else in the sky are 3D holograms as well. If the government attempts this deception, all electrical and magnetic power generated on the earth will be neutralized. It will be "the day that the earth stood still".

The Blue Beam Project is actually an attempt by the government to confuse and disorientate the people of the world to render the people of the earth unable to see what is happening in the sky with 3D holograms and laser lights. Another thing that will be done to confuse and disorientate the people of the earth will be the bombardment of massive amounts of electromagnetic energy so the people will not be able to hear the telepathic voices in their minds that will be talking to the people or understand what the voices are saying because of the massive amounts of electromagnetic energy waves from the HAARP system that the government have that the government will use to bombard the people of the earth with to interfere with any telepathic communication or visions that you will be receiving from the Gods.

The massive light show and 3D holograms is to block your view of what is in the sky. The enormous amount of electromagnetic energy waves that they will use to interfere with gamma waves or any other type of telepathic communication between what's out there from communicating with us on the earth will cause all sorts of problems with our health including driving us crazy and even causing deaths.

We need another plan because the government plan will not work. The Sanctuary for the people of God is the only realistic option because the government plan is going to kill a lot of people and run a lot of people crazy bombarding the people with high amounts of electromagnetic energy to interfere with our thinking process to cause the people of the earth not to see what is in front of their eyes and not to hear what is said in our minds. The bombardment will have extremely negative side effects on the Gentiles. Remember, the Gentiles own actions will be the cause of their regression. At the Sanctuary where the people of God will live quiet and peaceful lives in godliness and reverence; supplications, prayers, intercessions and giving of thanks will be made for all men including kings and all who are in authority including the Illuminati for this is good and acceptable in the sight of God our savior who desires all men to be saved and to come to the knowledge of the truth. Only at the Sanctuary can the government and all who are in authority be saved. 1 Timothy 2: 1-4

What good would it do for the government to try to deceive the people of the world into believing that the return of the Gods and the return of the people from the old black African dominion is just an illusion that was created by the government for world control anyway other than destroying our brains, so we will not be of any use to the Creator once they land and walk the earth? How long do the government advisors think they can deceive the people of the world about something of this magnitude and what will the government tell the people of the world about an illusion when these ascended beings land and assume full control of the earth?

What else will be done to the people of the world in order for the governments of the world or the New World Order to maintain power and control over the people of the world and if the government of the world or the New World Order loses power and control, will the New World Order attempt to destroy the people of the world and the world to prevent the invaders from having their prize? Remember, the Scorch-Earth theory which is a last and final action of defeat to destroy everything including the people to prevent an enemy from having the land and the people. The Scorch-Earth Theory is used when all other options have failed, and defeat is inevitable. It is a way for the leaders of a nation to say to their enemy that if they lose, they will destroy the land and the people to prevent their enemy from having the land and controlling the people. Because the Blue Bean Project sounds like a Scorch Earth theory being implemented, the government needs more options. Because of who we are dealing with and the nature of the invasion of the earth, the government needs a dialog with the true people of God and because of that, the government needs an Ambassador from the People of God to the throne of the Gentiles that will be given utterance to speak boldly to reveal the mysteries of the Gospel to the Gentiles, so the Gentiles can be saved. Ephesians 6: 19-20

The New World Order has been deceived to believe that they will be able to intellectually resist the return of the Gods and put forth a reasonable defense because of the help of the Fallen Angels that the government refers to as Extraterrestrials. Maybe so, because the people of the world do not know what the New World Order knows. Maybe they do have a realistic plan that they think has a chance for working. If they do, they need to tell the people of the world soon because it has been written in Prophecy in the Holy Bible that the Beast and the false prophet will be caught and cast into an everlasting prison for eternity in the Lake of Fire and there was no place found for the great white throne in the future. The New World Order must be warned that because the Kingdom of God is within us, it will be easy for the Kingdom of God to babble the Gentiles minds and language, so they will not be able to communicate and understand each other as it was done to the old black African dominion in the beginning. Remember, the end of the dominion will be declared from the beginning or what happened in the beginning of the dominion will be what happens at the end. Revelation 19: 20-21, Revelation 20: 11, Luke 17: 21, Genesis 11: 7-9 and Isaiah 46: 10

The New World Order needs a plan that will guarantee safety and prosperity for all and that plan must include preserving the Gentiles on the Tree of Life. Only if the Gentiles receive the Truth in time and steer events in another direction to change the shape of the things to come can this be possible and if this is not possible, only at the people of God Sanctuary will the Gentiles be saved.

The scriptures say, "Touch not my Holy Ones". God's people will be protected by God. Even if they are killed, they will be born again and still inherit the earth. If the Gentiles kill the people of God, unimaginable horrors will await the Gentiles in life and in the afterlife. Horrors and torments that not even the Fallen Angels could endure will be waiting for all of those who kill the people of God. For those that say, "I don't care, and I don't mine dying", I pity you and your lack of understanding of all of the horrors and torments that will happen to you that you do not know about that exist in the afterlife or the existence after this life that will torment your soul for an eternity. Remember, your soul is energy and energy after death is not destroyed immediately but is judged, altered or transformed. If found worthy, it will be reborn. If it is found unworthy, its energy will be cast into the Lake of Fire which is the Sun to be used as fuel to burn in the Sun. The mighty of the white Gentiles who say that they don't care about judgment and they don't mine dying must be told that the terrible of the mighty shall be turned into prey and called the "Morlocks" because of their disfigurements and their regression on the evolutionary scale to be hunted and killed and after life, they shall be tormented forever in damnation in the Lake of Fire. Isaiah 49: 24-26

It may be cool to you now to die with what you call honor being patriotic and in defiance against God, but God is nobody to play with and you have no idea what will happen to you in the afterlife at Judgment for your actions today and you have no way of knowing that you will be sorry about thinking that you could endure punishment throughout eternity because of your patriotic actions today. If the Gentiles have any doubts about if there is an afterlife, they should confer or consult with a Catholic Priest or with today's Paranormal Researchers, so they could be informed that there is life or existence after death. Romans 14: 10, Hebrews 9: 27 and 2 Corinthians 5: 10

They will find out that there is a judgment somewhere because the lost souls that are contacted by Catholic Priests to force these lost souls to vacant a possessed container, vessel or body and the disembodied spirits that are contacted by Paranormal Researchers that haunts the dwellings that the vessel or body that the disembodied spirit used to possess when the body lived claims to be victims of a judgment and they are now trapped in a dimension that they cannot escape from once the soul that shared the vessel or body with them that they had possessed died and went on to judgment to determine if that soul would be reborn again in Paradise or Damnation.

These trapped spirits could not go forward to a judgment for Paradise or Damnation because their judgment has already happened, and they are now trapped in a dimension that they cannot escape from. The white Gentiles believes that when you die, you have a choice to not to follow the "light" but stay around the living because you felt that you did not die right. The white Gentiles must know that when you die, your soul is quickly moved through the fourth dimension to a place where you will rest in peace until your judgment. Then, you will be judged and depending on that judgment, you will either be reborn in Paradise or sent to "damnation" in the "Lake of Fire". Understand that we are 93% water and 7% minerals. When you die, your water is evaporated up into the clouds where a judgment takes place. If you are found worthy, you remain there in the clouds with the ascended water vapors until all is completed on the earth and the judgment of the earth come in. If you are found unworthy, you are rain down back to the earth to be drain into the pit of salty water of dead souls in the oceans. There in the pit of the ocean, you will rest until the judgment of the earth comes in. At the time of the judgment of the earth, the sea will give up the dead souls in it as well as death and Hades delivered up the dead who were in them to be judge. Revelation 20: 13

The Ghosts that are contacted in haunted houses by paranormal-investigators are not the original souls that use to occupy the body that was the resident of that home but are "Ghosts" or an image of the original person that use to live in the body. A Ghost of an individual is not the soul of the individual but is a copy or a ghost or an imitation of that person. A Ghost is the invader of the earth that possessed the body of the true individual that lived in the house and is imitating the original owner of the body.

Roger Morneau, an ex-Satan worshipper who was exposed to the upper elite in the Satanic cult revealed that the spirits that are contacted by mediums are not dead people that refused to go towards the "light" but were demons that were imitating the people that they once possessed. It is the ghost of that original person that could not go forward into the "light" but was trapped in the house when the individual who lived in the house died. It is these lost souls that proclaim that they will not move-on because they did not die right or did not have enough time in the possessed body to experience life because the "host" of the body did not die right or died too soon. There is no reincarnation when you die until after judgment day or after Jesus has reign on the earth for a thousand years. After that time and only after that time will the first "Resurrection" or reincarnation occur. (You Tube, Roger Morneau-A Trip into the Supernatural) and Revelation 20: 5-6

When you die, you will rest until judgment and at that time, if you are worthy, you will be reborn and live again. Those who say that they have been reincarnated are wrong. The knowledge of past lives that they have are not their memories but are the memories of the "Ghost" that have lived many lives in other individuals throughout time that have possessed them. Their knowledge of past lives is not proof that they have lived before but is proof that they are possessed by a "Ghost" that have lived in other bodies before. At seances, where ghosts are contacted to speak to the living, the ghost will deceive the living by telling the living that the ghost is the individual sort after in the séance. That ghost that speaks at seances is not your relative that you sort to speak with but is the spirit that possessed your relative when your relative was alive and now, since your relative has moved on to the next existence, this ghost is imitating your relative to have contact with the living to scan the living for the ghost next possession. The Gentiles must not be ignorant of this mystery but be wise in their own conceit. There is existence and a judgment after death. Because of this fact, you must fear God who can kill the body and the soul. At judgment, if you are found unworthy to continue to exist, your soul will be destroyed or cast into the Lake of Fire for eternity. There will be no reincarnation or coming back to live again at another time if you are found unworthy. Romans 14: 10, Hebrew 9: 27, 2 Corinthians 5: 10 and Matthew 10: 28

Attempting to destroy the earth or destroying the people of God or causing illusions to interfere with the plans of the Creator will not work and could be very detrimental.

# 36

# The Fullness of the Gentiles

The Gentiles are at their fullness or at their smartest right now. December 21, 2012 marked that the end of the age has arrived, and the fullness of the Gentiles has come in or the Gentiles are at their maximum level of evolutionary development, but that date is not the end, yet. The time given to the white Gentiles by God to have a dominion to grow and evolve in has been fulfilled. God has numbered your kingdom and finished it, or God has given the white race dominion and the white race had an allotted time to join the people of the earth to become human. With the fullness of the white Gentiles coming in on December 21, 2012, all that was promised to the white Gentiles have been fulfilled. The effort to save the white race is finished. The effort and the time given to the white Gentiles to save the white Gentiles is described as "Mene" in the Holy Bible. At the end of the age on December 21, 2012, the white Gentiles will be at their fullness or at their maximum level of evolutionary development on this level. To receive more growth or evolutionary development, the white Gentiles will have to be judged to determine if they are worthy. If the white Gentiles do not believe, the white Gentiles will be judged unworthy and the white Gentiles will not receive any more evolutionary development but will be "Cut-Off" from the Tree of Life and regressed. This is the goodness that was shown towards the young wild olive tree or the young white Gentile race. The white race must understand the severity of God towards the people of God because of disbelief as well as understand the goodness of God towards the Gentiles, grafting the white Gentiles on the Tree of Life and giving the white Gentiles dominion otherwise, the white Gentiles will be "Cut-Off" from the Tree of Life and become worse than the people of God are today that are identified as the "Dead". If God did not spare His own people because of disbelief, take heed white Gentiles that God will not spare you either. To be saved, in a public forum, the white Gentile must admit that the branches were broken off so that the white Gentiles could be grafted in. The truth must not be suppressed but must be revealed. Luke 21: 24, Romans 11: 25, Daniel 5: 25-26, Romans 11: 20-21, Romans 11: 22-25 and Romans 11: 19

The end will not come until after a stone cut without hands hits the kingdom. The Gentiles have that long to receive a lengthening of their kingdom by proving to God that they are truly evolved people that can find solutions for their problems without violence and bombs but with reasoning and understanding and still honors God for all that God have done for the Gentiles as the Gentiles did in the beginning. Before the stone that will be cut without hands hits the last white Gentile dominion described as "iron and clay" which is the dominion we live in today, the Gentiles must Behold or Consider therefore the goodness and severity of God. On the people of God that were cut off and fell, severity but towards the gentiles when the gentiles were grafted onto the Tree of Life in the place where those who fell and were cut off were, goodness and more goodness towards the gentiles if the gentiles continue in goodness OTHERWISE the gentiles also shall be Cut Off. Daniel 2: 34 and Romans 11: 22

This stone that will be broken off of a meteor will hit the earth and destroy everything including the memories of the dominions that came before it. The stone that will hit the earth will grow into a great mountain that will fill the whole earth. Daniel 2: 35

And in the days of these kings in the dominion of "iron and clay", which is the dominion we live in today, the God of heaven will set up a kingdom which shall never be destroyed, and the kingdom shall not be left to other people, but the people of God shall rule this kingdom. It shall break in pieces and consume all these kingdoms before it and it shall stand forever. Inasmuch as you saw that the stone was cut out of the mountain without hands or a stone cut out of a huge meteor, and it broke in pieces the iron, the bronze, the clay, the sliver, and the gold, the great God has made known to the king or president what will come to pass after this. The white Gentiles must know for a certainty that the dream is certain or is for-real and its interpretation is sure or is true. Daniel 2: 44-45

Only the true people of God can reveal this mystery to the white Gentiles to save the white Gentiles. In all matters of wisdom and understanding about which the President will examine those who are sent, the President will discover that those who are sent are ten times better than all the magicians, astrologers and geniuses who are in all of his realm. Daniel 1: 20

The spirit of the Holy God will be in them. Like in the days of your fathers, light and understanding and wisdom, like the wisdom of the gods will be found in them. They will have an excellent spirit, knowledge, understanding in interpreting dreams, solving riddles, and explaining enigmas as is demonstrated in the books of Simion. Daniel 5: 11-12

Kings promoted those who were sent and gave them many gifts and made them chief of the magicians, astrologers, Chaldeans, and soothsayers because their God is the God of gods, the Lord of kings, and the revealer of secrets since only the true people of God can reveal these secrets. They were promoted and given gold chains and much wealth and made third ruler in the kingdom. Daniel 5: 11-12, Daniel 2: 47-48, Daniel 5: 29 and Daniel 5: 16

Joseph, in Egypt and Daniel, in Babylon both were promoted and given gold, wealth and authority because of their excellent spirit, knowledge, understanding in interpreting dreams, solving riddles, and explaining enigmas like is revealed in the books of Simion. It was because of this promotion of Joseph and Daniel that Egypt and Babylon prospered when destruction was on their door step. Genesis 41: 37-45

It is recorded in the Holy Bible that in the last dominion of "iron and clay", the deliverer of the truth must be made the Ambassador from the people of God to the throne of the Gentiles that is given utterance to speak boldly as he ought to speak or as you agreed last time at judgment that you would allow him to speak to make known the "Mystery of the Gospel" to save the Gentiles. Do not renege on this agreement. Ephesians 6: 19-20

The people of God are commanded by God to be a light to the white Gentiles and to be for the white Gentiles salvation from biblical days to "Present" till the end of the earth. I can guarantee to you that those who are sent in the latter-days will obey that command from God and complete their mission. Acts 13: 47

Once the white Gentiles realizes who are the true people of God then the Gentiles will appreciate the books of Simion and only then will the Gentiles know for a certainty who is the "Deliverer". Anyone or race that deceives the white Gentiles who have dominion today that they are the people of God will be directly responsible for the white Jews judging themselves unworthy for eternal life and responsible for no place found for the great white throne in the future. Acts 13: 46 and Revelation 20: 11

The wisdom of God is in a mystery and only the true people of God can reveal that mystery to the Gentiles. 1 Corinthians 2: 7, Mark 4: 11, Ephesians 1: 9, and Colossians 1: 26-27

Only him who is sent by the Gentiles to reveal the truth to the Gentiles to save the Gentiles that is given utterance to speak boldly as he ought to speak because the Gentiles sent him to reveal the truth to them so they would know what is going on because Jesus said that the white Jews and white Gentiles did not know what they were doing will be able to reveal the Mystery of the Gospel to the Gentiles. Ephesians 6: 19-20 and Luke 23: 34

Only the true "Deliverer" will reveal the Mystery of the Gospel to the Gentiles. The Gentiles will know the "Deliverer" by the message that he delivers. No one else on the planet earth will interpret the Mystery of the Gospel and preach the gospel of the kingdom of God coming to the earth but him who was chosen. The Gentiles will know for a surety if what was delivered was indeed the truth that the disbelieving Jews in biblical days said if delivered by the brethren or brothers it could turn the world upside down. There is only one suppressed truth that is so profound that if revealed, it could turn the world upside down. The Gentiles will have no doubt about the delivered truth being what could turn the world upside down. Anyone trying to deceive the Gentiles in the latter-days that they are him who was sent will be killed by the Gentiles and afterward, the Fallen Angels will take his soul. False prophets and fake preachers beware. For the earnest expectation of the fallen creature "that controls the Gentiles" eagerly waits for the revealing of the sons of God to be delivered from corruption into the liberty of the children of God. Do not deceive the Gentiles or the Creature because both need the revealing of the sons of God to be deliver from corruption. Acts 17: 6 and Romans 8: 19-21

Now when the white Gentiles hear this, they will be glad and glorify the word of the Lord and as many as had been appointed to eternal life this time because they believed last time will believe again this time and the words of the Lord in the Books of Simion was published and spread throughout all the realm. Acts 13: 48-49

Higher evolved people would seek a solution that preserves instead of destroys at least for now. The choice is clear for a highly evolved race of people when asked by God to choose between Existence and Extinction.

The Gentiles are still calling all of the plays. The Gentiles are still in control. Everyone will follow the Gentiles lead. It is up to the Gentiles to make the best possible choices and decisions for all of us that are on the planet. God expects that the Gentiles will be defiant and fight and lose because of their conceit. This is prophecy. All in Heaven are waiting for things to happen this time as they did last time so all that happens to the Gentiles will be the Gentiles just due for killing the people of God. Revelation 6: 10-11 and Revelation 16: 6

Now, can the Gentiles do the impossible? Can the Gentiles steer events in another direction to change the shape of the things to come that is prophesied to happen to prevent the white Jews from judging themselves unworthy for eternal life because they want to be the people of God so bad, they have assumed the identity of the true people of God and to prevent no place found for the great white throne in the future? Are the Gentiles evolved enough to receive the

Truth and understand the Truth and if they are, they may be able to change the future. This is why the Gentiles were given a second chance in the world we live in today to make a difference from what happened last time. This is the message of the latter day "Deliverer". Like with the message that Joseph and Daniel delivered to Egypt and to Babylon, this message can save the Gentiles in the latter days if it is received. Acts 13: 46 and Revelation 20: 11

This is why it is so important that historians and archeologists do not suppress the Truth from the Gentiles especially at this time. The Gentiles must Behold or Consider everything that have happened and have the understanding of what happened to the old dominion that was before this dominion especially what happened to the old dominion because of disbelief and for doing the exact same thing that the white Gentiles are considering doing now. Romans 11: 21-22

This is why the Gentiles must know what happened in the past and by whom and why, so the Gentiles can make their final choices their best choices and decisions for all of the people especially for the Gentiles. If the Gentiles could somehow put aside their conceit or excessive self-pride which is a unrealistic high opinion of their own qualities or abilities that is not justified, to impress God with a superior evolved state of logic, reasoning and understanding about the changing of an dominion by God and understand what is actually going on here and accept the decree by God at least in the beginning until it could be determine the totality of the situation and understand what can be done and what cannot be done before all is sacrifice and lost since the Gentiles cannot do anything to prevent what the writer of this program call "Life" puts in his program because the Gentiles are just characters in an advance program written by God's own hand and most important, believe that God is God and is the one who created this program called "Life", the Gentiles could maintain their position on the Tree of Life and also receive a lengthening of their prosperity. The Gentiles must understand that a character in a story book called "Life" cannot demand that the writer of the book follow the character of the book demands and the Gentiles must know that the writer of the book can erase whoever he want to erase from the story of the book. Romans 9: 20-21

No, the Gentiles will not have dominion on the earth in the future, but they could receive a lengthening of their prosperity and afterwards, they would be a blessed branch on the Tree of Life and they would be permitted to travel in outer space and advance and grow just as all of the other branches on the Tree of Life are doing. Changing your ways and steering events in another direction by showing "mercy", "compassion" and a "love" for God and for God's people could prove that the white Gentiles are intelligent, evolved beings that do not have to be mixed in with the other people to become "human beings" but can stand on their own because of their morals, discipline and love for God and the true people of God. Love for God and God's people will cover a multitude of sins. 1 Peter 4: 8, Proverbs 10: 12

Since December 21, 2012 was the end of the age and marked that the fullness of the Gentiles has come in or the Gentiles are now at their maximum level of evolutionary development, the Gentiles must use their higher state of development to produce logic and reasoning that will bring a solution for all of the people of the earth including the Gentiles that will guarantee the people of the earth safety and prosperity and ensure that the Gentiles remains grafted on the Tree of Life. Violence and aggression against God will be futile.

If we are dealing with invaders or astronauts with advance technology from another world that are trying to invade our world then let's kick their ass and take their technology but if we are dealing with the return of God then we need another plan that will deliver peace, safety and prosperity for all of the people of the earth including the Gentiles.

Can anything be done to save the Gentiles? In the author of the Books of Simion opinion, the author would say yes, but the Gentiles must accept the fact that the people of God will inherit the earth. God want the next dominion for Himself and He wants to be joined with the people of God. The white Gentiles will not be given a Third Reich or an additional thousand years Reich on the earth. The Gentiles must not fight this. The white Gentiles will not have their way or win a fight against God. This is the message that the old black African dominion tried to leave in the ancient ruins for the white Gentiles to understand. As powerful as the old black African dominion was, it could not fight God. Knowing that in the War of Armageddon, in the Valley of Jehoshaphat, the Valley of Jehoshaphat will turn into the Valley of Decisions because there in the Valley of Jehoshaphat, the white Gentiles will decide to change their minds in helping the Synagogue of Satan and decide to help God and the people of God in Islam, it would be prudent if the Gentiles would decide to help the people of God now before they enter the Valley of Jehoshaphat. Daniel 7: 27, Revelation 21: 3-6, Joel 3: 2 and Joel 3: 14

I'm not suggesting anything to the white Jews or to the white Gentiles. The white Jews and white Gentiles must do what is in their hearts to prove or disprove if the white Jews and white Gentiles are worthy to remain grafted on the Tree of Life. Remember, the white Jews and white Gentiles will not be persuaded, convinced or won over by argument to accept the truth. The "Deliverer" mission is only to deliver the truth without offending the white Jews and white Gentiles, so they will at lease receive the truth that they wanted delivered. Only the Ambassador from the people of God to the throne of the Gentiles that is given utterance to speak "Boldly" as he ought to speak or as you agreed last time at judgment that you would allow him to speak to reveal the mystery of the gospel to the white Jews and to the white Gentiles to save the white Jews and white Gentiles will be permitted to tell the white Jews and white Gentiles anything else. Ephesians 6: 19-20

Can anything be done to preserve the Gentiles on the Tree of Life? The author of the Books of Simion would say yes. The Gentiles must admit what have happened to the Gentiles and what have happened to the people of God and the Gentiles must believe that God is God and if the Gentiles break away from sin and their iniquities and be righteous and if the Gentiles cease being greedy for profits and show mercy to the poor, the Gentiles could receive a lengthening of their prosperity as was done with King Nebuchadnezzar when his kingdom was coming to an end. Romans 11: 22 and Daniel 4: 27

Remember, it was Gordan Gekko in the 1987 movie titled "Wall Street" assertion that Greed was good, and that assertion deceived the Gentiles and it was that assertion that Crashed the Gentiles Housing Market and Collapsed the Gentiles Global Financial System in 2008 because of Greed. The Gentiles have been Warned that they are being Set-Up to be broken off from the Tree of Life by the Devil Advocates in the Devil Advocates courtrooms and in the Devil Advocates movies.

Now here is understanding for the Gentiles. It does not matter how hard you were on the people in your dominion in the past and it is not important who your creator was at this time. Don't get lost in the question about who creator was good and who creator was evil. The Holy Bible has recorded that the God of Gods spoke of in the Holy Bible is responsible for all things including good and evil. Isaiah 45: 7

This is the time to receive remission of your sins if the Gentiles are told the truth and act quickly. This is the time to "Repent" and be "Converted", that your sins may be "blotted out" so that times of refreshing may come from the presence of the Lord. What the Gentiles do from December 21, 2012 forward will determine the Gentiles fate. The Gentiles must "Behold" what have happened to the Broken Branch and to the Grafted Branch and believe that God is God and remember that mercy and charity will cover the multitude of sins. Acts 3: 19 and Romans 11: 22

The Gentiles must understand that in the past, it was the Gentiles dominion to do as they pleased to prove or disprove if the Gentiles were worthy to remain grafted on the Tree of Life and it is written in the Holy Bible that all who would not serve the Gentiles shall be broken and grinded into powder. The stone (Gentiles) that the builders (The Gods) rejected (did not want the Gentiles to be genetically engineered or created), the same has become the head of the corner (has been given a dominion on the earth to grow until their fullness comes in or until they reach their maximum level of evolutionary development at the end of the age on December 21, 2012). Matthew 21: 42-44, Romans 11: 25 and Luke 21: 24

This is the Lord doing or this was done by God to save the Gentiles. The Gentiles do not have dominion because they are better than all the other branches on the Tree of Life and definitely not better than the ascendance of the slaves who are the broken branch who is God's first born and chosen people. Matthew 21: 42 and Exodus 4: 22

The white Gentiles have dominion because they are the weakest branch on the Tree of Life therefore more time and consideration were given to the white Gentiles, so the white Gentiles could grow and remain grafted on the Tree of Life and become strong enough to grow with the other branches on the Tree of Life. To achieve this, the white Jews and white Gentiles were to join and mix with the colored-people of the earth to become human beings. 1 Corinthians 12: 14-27

It is because of this that the kingdom or dominion shall be taken away from the people of God and given to the people of the new dominion, so the people of the new dominion can bring forth the fruit thereof or grow and evolve on the earth because the Creator view us all on the earth as one body and the members of the body which we think to be less honorable, upon these God bestowed more abundant honor. It was not because of the strength of the Greeks and the Romans why the Gentiles have dominion but because of their weaknesses that they were given a dominion to grow in and become strong in and to do that, the Gentiles are sharing the roots of the Tree of Life or planet that belongs to the people of God of the old black African dominion because the white genetically created out of a test tube Gentiles have no roots or planet. The white Gentiles must believe this and say this or confess to this in a public forum to remain grafted on the Tree of Life otherwise, they too will be "Cut-Off". Matthew 21: 42-44, 1 Corinthians 12: 23-24, Romans 11: 17-19 and Romans 11: 22

The white Gentiles must believe this and SAY this or confess this in a public forum for all to hear and know to remain grafted on the Tree of Life. The white Gentiles must say this. Romans 11: 19

Disbelief of this will be the cause why the white Gentiles will be broken off or Cut Off from the Tree of Life and regressed back into the Paleolithic beast of their beginning. The old black African dominion did not believe that they could be broken off from the Tree of Life and regressed into the Negro of today, but it happened. Disbelief will get you broken off from the Tree of Life faster than a New York minute. The white Gentiles must know for a surety that if God spared not His own people for disbelief, take heed white Gentiles that God will not spare thee. Therefore, the white Gentiles must consider or behold and reveal everything that have happened and everything that have been said. They must consider the goodness of God when God gave them a dominion and consider the severity of God to take an advance and powerful race of people and reduce them to what is called dead or Negro because Negro and Necro are the same word and Necro means dead otherwise, the white Gentiles too will be broken off and reduced to the Paleolithic upright beast. Romans 11: 20 and Romans 11: 19-22

Out of all of the dominions that would be in the white Gentiles second chance, the Greek and the Roman dominion were the worse and the last Roman dominion of iron and clay was the worse of them all even if it was full of technology. Today's civilization and societies must not say that this last dominion of the white Gentiles second chance that we live in today that is referred to as "iron" and "clay" is progress, improvement, growth or advancement from what was in the past. This civilization did not evolve or move forward into a better society but retreated and regressed from what was considered a Golden age to an Iron age or something that is considered as worthless and an artificial processed material with little value. Remember, as important as iron is in this civilization for construction, iron is not used for currency as gold and silver which are considered as precious metals. What is done today with technology, computers and machines and equipment was done in the past with telekinesis powers of the mind or the ability to do or make anything that you can imagine happen or come true. That ability was taken away from the white Gentiles dominion until the white Gentiles proves themselves worthy to have such extreme and powerful abilities. That is why in the white Gentiles dominions, the people of the dominion were capable of only using 7% of their mental and physical capabilities. Jesus came into the world to demonstrate all of the mental and physical abilities we should have. Jesus said that we wouldn't need doctors because the people would be able to cure all manner of sickness and diseases and even have the ability to cast out demons. Jesus said we would not have to worry about nothing in this life and that includes what you would eat, what you would drink nor about your body. Today Ancient Astronaut Theorists wonders how the pyramids were built because they say that today's technology could not have built the pyramids. The pyramids were built by this mental and physical power that Jesus talked about and demonstrated to all. Remember, Jesus did the impossible when Jesus destroyed the Holy temple and rebuilt it in three days when it took forty-six years to build the temple. This is how the pyramids were built. That is the type of mental power that the old black African dominion had that surpass anything that this civilization and modern society could ever do or accomplish and still, they could not fight God or prevent from losing their dominion on the earth. Matthew 10: 7-8, Matthew 6: 25-34, John 2: 19-20, Matthew 26: 61 and Matthew 27: 40

In the next world when the Meek inherit the earth, the people of God will be given these abilities again and given a whole lot more. Remember, if the white Gentiles who are the grafted branch that is contrary to nature achieve all that they achieved in their dominion, think about what the "Broken Branch" who are the natural branches of the Tree of Life who are the people of God who are the ascendants of "Slaves" who are the "Afro Americans" today will achieve when they are grafted back into the Tree of Life and is joined with the creator and given immortality. Matthew 5: 5, Isaiah 14: 2, Isaiah 54: 3, Romans 11: 24, Revelation 21: 3-7

They will not be able to be killed because for them there will be no Death. No weapon formed against the people of God in the future will prosper or work or be able to kill them. They will be able to float like the clouds and fly to their windows like birds and anything that they imagine in their minds without doubt will come true. The Holy Bible has recorded that all who see the people of God in the future in their own dominion will say that the people of God are the seed that the Lord has blessed. Revelation 21: 4, Isaiah 54: 17, Isaiah 60: 8, Isaiah 61: 9, Matthew 10: 8, Matthew 17: 20, Matthew 21: 21, Mark 6: 13, Mark 11: 22-24, Mark 16: 17-18, Luke 9: 1-2, Luke 17: 6 and John 14: 12

There were two black kingdoms and two white kingdoms in the Gentiles second chance and the last or fifth kingdom in the Gentiles second chance was a kingdom mix with the white Gentiles and the people of God described as a kingdom mixed with iron and clay. The iron is the genetically engineered white gentiles created out of a process like the creation of iron and the clay are the natural people of the earth. The first kingdom in the Gentiles second chance was a black kingdom represented as Gold because God was there in that kingdom. It was called Babylon and that dominion was called the Golden Age. The Greek dominion was not identified as the Golden Age as the white Gentiles believe today. The second kingdom in the Gentiles second chance was a brown kingdom represented as Silver because even if God was not present there, the people of God from that kingdom were in contact with God. It was called Persia. The third kingdom in the Gentiles second chance was a white kingdom represented as bronze not gold or silver but bronze. It was called Greece. The Greek dominion was not the Golden Age. The Fallen Angels were there in the Greek dominion on Mt Olympus having sex with mankind. The fourth kingdom in the Gentiles second chance was a white kingdom represented as iron. It was not represented as nothing precious but of something artificially created. It was called Rome. The last and final kingdom in the white Gentiles second chance was a combination of both the black and brown kingdoms with the two white kingdoms to produce a kingdom of iron and clay or a kingdom with artificial created people and natural people of clay.

The last kingdom of "iron and clay" in which we live in today is the worst of all of the kingdoms in the white Gentiles second chance. As the Greek dominion and the Roman dominion came to an end, the last Gentile kingdom of "Iron and Clay" will also come to an end. This is the time to make a difference by receiving the truth, believing the truth and then steering events in another direction to prevent what is prophesied to come to pass to change the shape of the things that are prophesied to come. Daniel 2: 31-43 and Daniel 2: 37-39

# Black Magic

Even the technology of today with cars, planes, trains, computers, cell phones and limited space travel is no comparison to ancient Babylon. All of these things were present in ancient Babylon but in a more sophisticated and advance manner. The technology that we use today is to try to imitate what the old black African dominions were using without the instrumentalities that are used today. The machines and devices that we use today to accomplish and enjoy the gifts of science all was done, accomplished and enjoyed in the ancient black dominions without the bulky machines and devices but by mystical forces that was called "Black Magic". In ancient times to fly, the ancient people did not need to build bulky metal machines with engines to propelled them in the air but used the carpet that they were sitting on and with a thought or a magical spell, they were off flying in the air with no gas or pollution and flying in such a controlled flight that at high speeds, they could not fall off the carpet.

"Black Magic" was the term used to describe the ancient black dominions technology. It was a technology that did not need instrumentalities or devices to make it work. "Black Technology" which was "Black Magic" worked by the power of your "will" and by the power of your "belief" that connects to a dimension where God dwelled and by His assistance, all things are possible. Matthew 19: 26

In black technology, you can make food materialize instantly as Jesus and Jesus disciples did in biblical days and as the magicians are doing today. Matthew 14: 17-21

In the Holy Bible, Jesus says "Seek first the Kingdom of God and all things shall be added to you". Jesus says, "You would not have to worry about food or clothing because all these things will be given to you by magic from the power of God. Matthew 6: 25-32 and Matthew 6: 33-34

In Voodoo, which is a form of black technology, one can make an image of someone out of anything and place something from that person on the image which will contain the person DNA and believe without doubt that the image is the person because of the person DNA is on the image which is the essence of that person and whatever is done to the image will happen to the person that the image was made from because these cells in the DNA that are put on the carved object or image even if separated from the body are still connected to the body. This is called by science "Supersymmetry" in quantum physic. Supersymmetry enables particles to affect each other instantaneously across any distance. These cells are entangled with each other and will remain connected even if they were on opposite sides of the universe. What is done to the cells on the carved image will happen to the cells in the body that the cells were taken from if they are connected and directed by the power of belief. Voodoo or Black Magic has its basics and powers in quantum mechanics.

With black technology, you would not need any doctors because by magic, you will lay hands on the sick and the sick would be healed.

The God of Heaven gave the king of Babylon his kingdom, power, strength and glory. All the kingdoms after Babylon were inferior to Babylon including this last kingdom of "Iron and Clay" that we live in today. God was in ancient Babylon and it is because of this that ancient Babylon was described as a dominion represented by Gold which was known as the "Golden Kingdom" and the Golden Age. Black Magic was very powerful in Babylon. James 5: 14-16, Mark 6: 13, Mark 16: 17-18, Acts 28: 3-6, Acts 28: 8-9 and Daniel 2: 37-39

The white Gentiles till this very day are frighten by the thought of black Africans being able to use "Black Technology" which is "Black Magic". It was the ability to receive your desires without the use of machines and devices. The Magicians of today are proof that this power exist. The Magicians are in contact with devils and demons and they are defying our Laws of Physics by walking on water, floating in the air, passing through solid objects, teleporting from one place to the other and performing operations on people that are impossible to perform by the best of doctors. Chris Angel, who is one of the greatest Magicians ever to live and perform has cut off the head of witnesses or spectators and reattached it back in moments as well as cut a witness or spectator body in half and reattached it in front of people and cameras and there are many more magicians doing the same and better. The Magicians can look at a television or computer screen at an object being broadcast on the screen and by the power of "Magic" put their hand inside of the screen and pull out of the screen, the object that they were viewing. They can take one fish and turn it into many fish. They can put their hand inside of an ATM money machine and pull out money as well as make money appear out of thin-air. The Magicians are in contact with a technology by which all things are possible as were the old black African dominions when the old black African dominions used "Black Magic" or "Black Technology". It is because ancient Babylon was in contact with this technology by which all things are possible that ancient Babylon superseded all other dominions after it. All of the kingdoms after black Babylon were "inferior" to Babylon because black Babylon was represented as Gold and called, the Golden Dominion or the Golden Age. Daniel 2: 39

The Ancient Astronaut Theorists are "Envious" of the old black African dominions that were superior to the white dominions that came after them. All of what the old black African dominions did to make a name for themselves before they were "scattered" to make room for the white Gentile dominions, the Ancient Astronaut Theorists are saying were done by advance extraterrestrials from somewhere else because of the sophistication of the ruins as well as where the ruins are located, and the advance technology used to construct the ancient ruins that are being found today that can't be replicated by today's technology. Genesis 11: 4-8

Remember, in biblical days, Jesus used this power or used "Black Magic" to prove to disbelievers that the power of God exists when Jesus promised to destroy the "Temple of God" and in three days raise it up again when it took forty-six years to build the "Temple". The Temple was destroyed and in three days, Jesus raised up the Temple as He had stated when it took forty-six years to build. John 2: 19-20, Matthew 26: 61 and Matthew 27: 40

David Copperfield who is also one of the greatest Magicians to perform on stage has said that Jesus Christ was the best Magician ever or what he meant was that Jesus Christ was in contact with the greatest of forces in all of the universe known as God and the Holy Ghost. What we see the great magicians doing today is only a fraction of what the ancient blacks dominions were doing because the magicians are getting their power and abilities from fallen angels and demons, but the old black Africans dominions received their power and abilities from the mighty God of the universe to do anything that their minds could conceived. Daniel 2: 37

The Magicians and the old black African dominions were using a technology that is beyond our present-day laws of physics. It was a technology that made all things possible. The Magicians are proof that the laws of Physics that we are governed by today is not universal but is restricted to a certain time, a certain place and certain people by some unknown powerful supreme force. This defiance of our laws of Physics is witnessed when extraterrestrials are observed performing movements with their flying crafts and how they abduct people through solid objects that are beyond our laws of Physics. What puzzles the scientist of today when dealing with the aliens is not just all that they don't know that the aliens knows but all that the white gentile scientist cannot learn. The aliens have exposed the gentile scientists to knowledge that the gentiles can never understand or cope with. It's like trying to teach a dog to fly a Phantom jet. The dog does not have the capabilities or understanding to know what to do. His brain is not capable of understanding this type of advance knowledge. The gentile scientist brains are not capable of understanding the Laws of Physic on the aliens level.

This highly evolved technology or use of extreme power from unseen powerful forces was not given to the white Gentiles in the white Gentile dominions as it was in the old black African dominions. The white Gentile dominions were given "Science" with its limited understanding and abilities to serve them and solve their problems for them. The old black African dominions were told to "believe all things" can be done with the power of "Black Technology" or with the power of "Black Magic" but the white Gentiles dominions were told to believe only what you can prove can be done by the power of "Science". 1 Corinthians 13: 7

Babylon and Persia were compared to precious metals because God was present in those kingdoms, but Greece and Rome were not compared to precious metals because God was not there in those kingdoms. Greece was compared to bronze because Fallen Angels were there in the Greek dominion on Mt. Olympus, but the fifth kingdom was not compared to anything precious but compared to iron because God nor the Fallen Angels were there in the fifth dominion. Only representatives from the Fallen Angels known as the Grey extraterrestrials were there in the fifth kingdom and they were there only to monitor the white Gentiles evolutionary development to determine if the Gentiles had reached their fullness or their maximum level of evolutionary development and to obtain organs and DNA from their creations before the return of God to the earth at the end of the age when the fullness of the Gentiles had come in. When the Gentiles were raptured or abducted aboard the extraterrestrial flying crafts, they were given these evolutionary examinations to determine where the Gentiles were on the evolutionary scale or to determine if the fullness of the Gentiles had come in. It is interesting to know that those of the white Gentiles dominion of bronze and of iron were not called Men. The Bible said that the artificial replicated people created out of a test tube of the Roman dominion represented as iron were supposed to mix with the seed of men who are represented as the clay to become human beings, but conceit prevented the white Gentiles from doing so. Daniel 2: 43

Because the white Gentiles do not have any Roots or do not have a planet but are sharing the people of God from the old black African dominion planet, the Gentiles must not boost in their movies about the strength and power of the Greeks and the Romans to try to make the people of God jealous. Romans 11: 17-19 and Romans 11: 11

It may be interesting to know that because the kingdom of God was taken away from the people of God and given to the white

Gentiles who are the Greeks and Romans for a season, the people of God from the old black African dominion were cast into Outer Darkness or cast into Outer Space. Outer Space is Outer Darkness. That is how much more advance the people of God from the old black African dominion is to the white Gentiles of our past and of today. The people of God from the old dominion left a map of pyramids detailing where they were going until the fullness of the Gentiles came in when they would be allowed to return. Pyramids were built in formation that were identical to the constellation of Orion's belt which indicated where the people of the old black African dominion went when they were cast into Outer Darkness which is Outer Space. Matthew 21: 43 and Matthew 8: 12

All of the ancient ruins of the mighty black African Olmecs shows the weeping or crying the people of God did when the kingdom of God was taken away from them and given to the white Gentiles who are the Greeks and Romans of our past and present. At Puma Punku, there is a statue that has three tears coming down from his eyes. The same tears can be found coming from the serpent at Serpent Mound in Ohio because the serpent is one of the symbols or representations of the Olmecs. Matthew 21: 43 and Matthew 8: 12

The faces on the Olmec heads that are found in South America with their wide noses and thick lips are the faces of the West African people of today. In Zecharia Sitchin book titled, "The Lost Realms", Zecharia Sitchin points out in figure 138 of the book, the comparison of the faces on the colossal Olmec heads with those of today's West Africans. One of Nigeria leaders, General I.B. Banagida is an identical genetic match to the Olmec heads that are found in South America at La Venta, Mexico as is the head of Christopher Judge, an Afro American actor on the SG-1 Stargate series. Because of envy, the Ancient Astronaut Theorists and today's white Gentile historians wants the world to believe that the Olmec heads are the heads of

Mexican Indians or the heads of extraterrestrials. It is the African Olmecs that built all that is found in South America including all of the pyramids. (The Lost Realms, chapter 12, page 273)

One of the rare academic studies admitting that the Olmecs were Negroid Africans was "Africa and the Discovery of America" by Leo Wiener, professor of Slavic and other languages at Harvard University. Here the professor proves that Africans were in America before anyone else and that Africans were not only the original inhabitants of the Americas but also the original inhabitants of England, Germany, China, Russia and everywhere else on the earth because the Africans are the original People of the world and it is because of their sacrifice for others that the white Gentiles were given a dominion on the earth. The Olmecs were here on the earth when the earth had only one super continent named, "Pangea". (The Lost Realms, chapter 12, page 272)

The people of God were broken off from the Tree of Life, so the Gentiles could be grafted in and share the roots that belong to the broken branch to help the Gentiles and God has said that God will not let this action to save the Gentiles be a stumble for the people of God. After the Gentiles have had their chance for salvation, the people of God will inherit the earth. Romans 11: 11

Jesus said that all of this was marvelous in God's people eyes because it verified and strengthened God's people faith in the promise made to them by God that said after the Gentiles have had their second chance for salvation in their own dominion, the Meek or the people of God who were sacrificing everything to give the Gentiles a dominion afterwards would inherit the earth, receive ascended bodies and be joined to God. Matthew 21: 42, Matthew 5: 5, Romans 11: 11-12, Romans 11: 24, Daniel 7: 26-27 and Revelation 21: 4

Evolving the Paleolithic creatures into homosapiens was proof that the promised that God made to His people to evolve them into Gods was possible. God's people were told to believe this and have faith that this will happen. This is the faith that Jesus will find when He returns to the earth. The people of God do not have faith in the lie that the white Jews and white Gentiles are the people of God. The people of God have faith in prophecy that when Jesus return, the people of Jesus will be joined with God and given immortality. This will be revealed to the white Gentiles by the last "Apostle", "Preacher" and "Teacher" to the white Gentiles. Luke 18: 8 and 2 Timothy 1: 9-11

# 38

## The Deliverer

All of the screams about how lousy and evil the white Gentiles dominion was are not important and is not the determining factor in whether the Gentiles remain grafted on the Tree of Life or is broken off from the Tree of Life at this time. This is the last opportunity to win time for the kingdom if the Gentiles are told the truth and understand what they must do to lengthen their prosperity. The white Gentiles will have only one chance to change the shape of the things to come after the fullness of the Gentiles comes in or after December 21, 2012 when the "Deliverer" will deliver the profound message that the white Gentiles asked to be delivered to them in the latter days, so they would know what is going on, so they would know what to do. This is the "Precipice" point that was spoke of in the 2008 science fiction movie titled "The Day the Earth stood Still" for "mankind" to understand that it too must change to prevent total destruction. This is the time to hear the truth and act accordingly to steer events in another direction to change the shape of the things that are prophesied to come. Romans 11: 25-26

Because only those who are worthy can evolve on the Tree of Life, the Gentiles must do what is in their hearts and minds to determine if they are worthy to remain grafted of the Tree of Life. Last time at judgment, knowing that the Gentiles would be living a lie wrapped up in their conceit, they asked their friends to deliver a message to them in the latter-days that could steer them in the right direction. Remember, Jesus said that the white Jews and white Gentiles did not know what they were doing because they have no idea what is really going on. Luke 23: 34

Because they knew that the truth would be suppressed, and the Gentiles would be "Deceived" by the "False Prophet", those at judgment who were for the Gentiles promised their friends that this time, they would send a message to them in the latter-days to inform them of what was going on. This is the message of salvation that the white Gentiles asked for that was promised by the people of God before the world begun to be delivered to the white Gentiles to save the white Gentiles regardless of whatever was going on at that time. To guarantee this message delivery, the white Gentiles sent their best friend in the future to make that delivery in our present without offending them in the process, so they would at lease receive the message. The people of God have fulfilled their promise to the white Gentiles to deliver the message in the latter days no matter what was going on and the people of God have obeyed their God by being for the salvation of the Gentiles from biblical days to "PRESENT" till the end of the earth because God want to take out of the white Gentiles a people for God's name and for this cause, the words of the prophets or the Books of Simion are written. Revelation 19: 20, 2 Timothy 1: 9, Acts 13: 47 and Acts 15: 14-15

It is recorded in the Holy Bible that the white Gentiles must behold the goodness of God to the Gentiles when the Gentiles were grafted on the Tree of Life and later when the Gentiles proved themselves unworthy to grow with the other branches on the Tree of Life were given a second chance for salvation in the world we live in today and the Gentiles must behold the severity of God on God's own people because of "Disbelief" and the Gentiles must "Believe" that if God spared not His natural branches on the Tree of Life because of "Disbelief" take heed white Gentiles that God will not spare the white Gentiles for "Disbelief". The white Gentiles must believe that God is God and all that is written and delivered did happened as is recorded in the Holy Bible. Romans 11: 11-12 and Romans 11: 21-22

Simon who was surnamed Peter who was called a "Nig er" (Nigg er) and called Simeon will reveal to the Gentiles to save the Gentiles and all in the Gentiles house or kingdom that "Charity" which is the collection of money, provisions, material and help to God's people in need as well as a "Tolerate Attitude" with impartial "Love" for God's people as a Christian Virtue will cover not "a" sin but the "multitude" of sins in the white Gentiles dominion. Acts 11: 13-14, Acts 13: 1 and 1 Peter 4: 8

The white Gentiles must remember that we all will go before a "Judgment" and the judgment will be without "Mercy" for those who have shown no "Mercy". James 2: 13

Since the end of the dominion will be declared from the beginning of the dominion and in the beginning of the dominion it was Simon who was surnamed Peter and called Simeon and called a Nig er (Nigg er) when Simon was being called "Simeon" the Nig er who declared all of this to the white Jews and white Gentiles, at the end of the dominion it will be Simeon, the Nig er and only "Simion", the Nigg er who again will declare all of this to the white Jews and white Gentiles again because God want to take out of the white Jews and white Gentiles a people for God's name and because of that, the words of the Prophets or the "Books of Simion" are written. Isaiah 46:10, Acts 10: 5, Acts 13: 1 and Acts 15: 14-15

The Holy Bible has recorded that by Simon who was surnamed Peter who was called "Simeon" and called a Nig er (Nigg er) mouth only will the white Jews and white Gentiles hear the truth and Believe. Peter's Basilica in Rome was built to received him who would be possessed by the spirit of Simon Peter that would deliver the last important profound message to the Gentiles to save the Gentiles. Remember, the ancient prophets are subject to the Prophets or the ancient Prophets will be in the latter-day Prophets. Acts 15: 7, Acts 15: 14-15, Acts 13: 1 and 1 Corinthians 14: 32

After the fullness of the Gentiles come in at the end of the age after December 21, 2012, the "Deliverer" who will be "Simion" will come and Simion will be the last "Apostle", "Preacher" and "Teacher" of faith and truth to the white Jews and white Gentiles. There will be no one else that will come forth and deliver the message of salvation to the white Gentiles. There will be no white Neo as was stated in the 1999 science fiction movie titled "The Matrix" nor will it be a white "John Connor" as stated in the 1984 science fiction movie titled, "Terminator" or no one else that come to save "Mankind" in these latter days. The Holy Bible has stated by Simon who was surnamed Peter who was called "Simeon" and called a "Nig er" (Nigg er) mouth only will the white Gentiles hear the truth and believe. Do not be deceived. It is because of this that utterance must be given to "Simion" that he may open his mouth boldly to reveal the mystery of the gospel to the white Jews and white Gentiles who have dominion today as he ought to or as you white Gentiles agreed last time at judgment that you would allow him to that the white Gentiles should be fellow heirs of the same body of people of the planet earth and partakers of God's promise in our Lord through the gospel of which I became a minister according to the gift of grace of God given to me by the effective working of God's power. This is a holy calling not given according to my works but according to God's own purpose and grace which was given to me before the world began to which I was appointed a "Preacher", an "Apostle, and a "Teacher" to the white Gentiles concerning the gospel. Romans 11: 25-26, 1 Timothy 2: 7, Acts 15: 7, Ephesians 6: 19, Ephesians 3: 6-7 and 2 Timothy 1: 9-11

To Me, who am less than the least of all the "Saints" or those that are "Sent" this grace was given that I should preach among the white Jews and white Gentiles the unsearchable riches of God and to make all see what is the fellowship of this mystery which from the beginning of the ages has been hidden in God who created all things through Jesus to the intent that now the manifold wisdom of God might be made known to the Gentiles. A Saint is not a white Gentile that has lived a righteous life. A Saint is only those who are Sent. The word Saint is a mispronunciation of the word Sent. No white Gentile was selected last time at judgment to be Sent this time to the white Gentiles. The coming of "Simion" is written in Prophecy and the white Gentiles will know beyond any doubt if the message that "Simion" will deliver is indeed the message that the disbelieving Jews said in biblical days could turn the world upside down. Because of the importance of this delivered truth and the identity of the latter day "Deliverer", the white Gentiles must search the scriptures to find out whether these things are so. Utterance must be given to the latter-day "Deliverer" so he can speak boldly to make known the latter-day message as he ought to speak to save the Gentiles. All of this is "Prophecy". Ephesians 3: 8-10, Acts 17: 6, Acts 17: 11 and Ephesians 6: 19-20

If the white Gentiles are to save themselves, they must know that "Mercy" will triumph over "Judgment" and we all shall go before Judgment to receive blessings or curses for our actions today. James 2: 13

Because the people of God fate and the white Jews and white Gentiles fate are intertwined and "Double" will happen to the white Jews and white Gentiles that happened to the people of God, the people of God are asking the white Jews and white Gentiles to show "Mercy" now and in so doing, the Gentiles will be saving the people of God and saving themselves. Revelation 18: 6-8

# The End of the Dominion

Now at the end of the dominion, let's make certain that the Truth that the white Gentiles wanted delivered to them this time that would explain everything that have happened, so this time the white Gentiles would know what to do to be saved was delivered indeed.

At judgment last time, the white Gentiles were found "unworthy" to remain grafted on the Tree of Life and live with the people of the earth that are called Human Beings. They asked the people of God that came out of the tribulations with them to ask their Father in Heaven to give the white Jews and white Gentiles another chance for Salvation. The people of God that came out of the tribulations with the white Jews and white Gentiles felt "Sorrow" for them and brought the white Gentiles request to their Father in Heaven. Everyone in Heaven said that the people of God that came out of the tribulations with the white Gentiles were "Stumbling" to make that request. Romans 11: 11

The request was granted, the world was rewound over what happened last time so if nothing is changed this time what happened last time will happen again this time. The memory of the last world is in our DNA and is brought to our attention in the Déjà vu experience. It is the experience of experiencing a situation now that you have experience before just as it is happening now. This Déjà vu experience is so profound that you will stop and acknowledge it by saying, "I have done this before just as it is happening now". Last time the white Gentiles were broken off from the Tree of Life and regressed into the Paleolithic beast that was called the "Morlocks".

The people of God were told to be "Meek" in the white Gentiles second chance for salvation and afterwards, the people of God would inherit the earth. Matthew 5: 5

In the womb of the universe, the white Gentiles betrayed the people of God by fighting with the people of God to be born first to receive a second chance that was promised to the white Jews and white Gentiles and to also receive what was promised to the people of God to inherit the earth who were responsible for the white Jews and white Gentiles second chance. Genesis 25: 22-23

Because of this, no one in Heaven or Hell trust the white Gentiles now. Their fate is almost a certainty this time because of what they did in the beginning before the world was started and everything that the white Gentiles have done on the earth to maintain their dominion against the word of God.

At judgment last time, the white Jews and the white Gentiles knew the state their minds would be in at the end of the age and they feared that they would be on the same path as before. A path that led them to destruction and damnation. To guarantee their survival or to at least increase their chances in surviving, they requested that in the latter days of the dominion that a message was sent to them, so they would know what was happening, so they would know what to do to survive. Knowing that they would be barbaric at that time and full of hatred and would probably reject any message to them from the people that they hated, they sent their best friend in the future to deliver the message and their best friend promised to deliver the message without offending them no matter what was going on at that time against the people of God. He promised that he would not give in to the hate of that time but would remember the order from God to be a light for the Gentiles and remember the promise he made to his friends in the future, so they would be saved and deliver the message of Salvation to the white Jews and to the white Gentiles because God wants to take out of the white Jews and white Gentiles a people for God's name and for that cause, the words of the prophets or the Books of Simion are written. No one else on the planet will deliver this message to the white Jews and white Gentiles to save the white Jews and save the white Gentiles in the latter days. This is the only message that will come to save "Mankind". The message has been delivered, the promised has been fulfilled. Acts 13: 47 and Acts 15: 14-15

Now, no one can tell the white Gentiles what they must do to be saved. The white Jews and the white Gentiles must do what is in their hearts to prove that they are worthy to live with the people of the earth. Only the "Deliverer" will be allowed to deliverer a Profound message to the white Jews and to the white Gentiles and only the Ambassador from the people of God to the throne of the Gentiles will be allowed to tell them more about being saved to tip-the-scale in their favor. The "Ambassador" must be given utterance to speak boldly as he ought to speak to reveal the mystery of the gospel to the white Jews and to the white Gentiles. No harm must ever come to the "Deliverer or to the Ambassador" to prevent God from giving the white Gentiles and white Jews blood to drink for it will be their "Just Due" for betraying him that they sent so they could be saved. The end of the age is the precipice point that the white Jews and white Gentiles said would compel them to accept the truth and act accordingly. Ephesians 6: 19-20 and Revelation 16: 6

Understand that everything that is happening throughout the world including in Antarctica and everything that is happening in outer space is about the return of God. All living beings, may they be advance beings or less advance beings are preparing for the return of God. We on earth were given the holy scriptures that contained prophesies of what happened last time and what will happen this time if different choices are not made. It was imbedded in our DNA to honor the holy scriptures and to search for the "Mystery of the Gospel" in the holy scriptures so we would know what was going on, so we would know what to do to survive.

After the fullness of the Gentiles comes in or after the End of the Age or after December 21, 2012, the "Deliverer" will come and deliver a message so Profound that it will turn away ungodliness in all who hears and receive it. Romans 11: 25-26

Look for him and help him if you can and be watchful to this end with all perseverance and supplications for all the Saints or for all who are Sent. If the white Gentiles are to be saved this time, the "Deliverer" must be given Utterance to speak Boldly as he ought to speak or as it was agreed last time at judgment that he would be allowed to speak to save the Gentiles by making known the Mystery of the Gospel. Ephesians 6: 19-20

The author of the Books of Simion, an ascendant of the "Slaves", who are God's first born and chosen people who is a friend has risked everything to deliver this message to the Gentiles, so the Gentiles would know what is going on, so the Gentiles would know what to do to be saved. Exodus 4: 22

"Great One" known as President, the author of the Books of Simion is asking the Federal Government, the Jews and the Gentiles to research what have been written in the ancient scriptures, the books of Simion and in the Holy Bible and then do whatever they think is best to prove if the Gentiles are worthy or not worthy to remain grafted on the Tree of Life. The "Deliverer" and the people of God will accept the Jews and the Gentiles latter-day choices as being what is right and what is just no matter what those choices are. Only at judgment, this time, will the Jews and the Gentiles have to answer for their choices and actions of today.

# Black Lives Matter

If the white Jews and white Gentiles are to be saved this time, events must be steered in another direction to prevent what is prophesied to come to pass. The people of God are the only ones who can show the white Jews and white Gentiles the path to Salvation. They are under orders from God to be a light for the Gentiles and to be for the salvation of the Gentiles from biblical days to "Present" till the end of the earth. It is for this cause that the white Gentiles who have dominion today must know who IS RAEL (REAL) and who is not. Anyone who is assuming the people of God identity to deceive the white Gentiles who have dominion today is the enemy to the white Jews and to the white Gentiles. Acts 13: 47

Black lives do matter. The righteous of them are in direct contact with the Most-High or the God of Abraham and the way they see things and their wisdom and understanding about things and world affairs is what that can save the Gentiles. It is because of this that the throne of the Gentiles must have an Ambassador from the people of God revealing the Mystery of the Gospel to the Gentiles that is given utterance to speak "Boldly" if the white Gentiles are to be saved, this time. Ephesians 6: 19-20

In the Holy Bible, Jesus said that the people of God who are the ascendants of the slaves who are those who are being scattered who are the Afro-Americans today are the "Salt" and the "Light" of the earth. The Afro-Americans are the "Salt" of the earth because without them the world is tasteless, plain, uninteresting and very boring. Destroying the Afro Americans music industry and replacing it with ignorant, vulgar, "Rap" and "Hip-Hop" which was elementary rhyming of the low-life removed the "Salt" and the "Light" from the Gentiles and cast the Gentiles in farther darkness. They are the "Light" of the earth because only through them can a "Light" which is the knowledge of God be in the world and only through them can "Salvation" come to the Gentiles. Only the true people of God can be for the "Salvation" of the Gentiles. No other race of people on the planet earth can be a "Light" for "Salvation" to the Gentiles other than the people of God. No other race on the planet earth could have delivered this message of "salvation" to the white Jews and white Gentiles. The white Jews and white Gentiles will know for a certainty that what was delivered was indeed the truth that the disbelieving Jews in biblical days said would turn the world upside down. Anyone assuming the identity of the people of God to deceive the Gentiles to prevent "Salvation" from coming to the Gentiles is the enemy to the Gentiles. This is why the white Roman Gentiles who have dominion today must know who Is Rael (Real) and who is not if the white Gentiles are to be saved, this time. This is Prophecy and if the white Gentiles are to be saved this time, Prophecy must not be ignored. Matthew 5: 13, Acts 13: 47 and Acts 17: 6

Remember, the Holy Bible has recorded that those who are Sent to save Kingdoms are Ten Times Better than everyone else in all matters of Wisdom and Understanding. Kings promoted them and gave them great gifts and made them chief over all others in the kingdom by making them third ruler in all of the realm. Only those who have a secret agenda to see the Gentiles Cut Off from the Tree of Life will want the People of God left out of the Gentiles latter day decision making that will determine if the Great White Throne is found in the future. Daniel 1: 20, Daniel 5: 11-12, Daniel 2: 48, Daniel 5: 16 and Daniel 5: 29

Remember, those who are Scattered are not the enemy. They are the true people of God who can help the Gentiles. The ACCUSER of the Brethren is the enemy or anyone accusing those who are scattered as being the enemy to the Gentiles is the true enemy of the Gentiles. Revelation 12: 10

The accuser of the Brethren who are those who have assumed the identity of the true people of God and are deceiving the white Gentiles that they are the people of God that knows the prophesies of the God of Abraham are the Enemy. They are the "False Brethren" who is the "False Prophet" because they deceived the white Gentiles that they knew the prophesies of God. Last time at judgment, the white Gentiles assertion was that they were deceived by the "False Prophet" who are the "False Brethren" who are those that have assumed the identity of the true people of God and are now deceiving the Gentiles that have dominion today that they are the true people of God. 2 Corinthians11: 26 and Revelation 19: 20

This is the Truth that must be interpreted from the Holy Bible and delivered to the Federal Government, so the Federal Government will know what to do to save the Great White Throne. This is why the Federal Government needs a representative or an Ambassador from the true people of God revealing the "Mystery of the Gospel" to the federal government to save the Great White Throne. This Ambassador must be given utterance to speak "Boldly" as he ought to speak to reveal the "Mystery of the Gospel" to the white Gentiles to save the white Gentiles. This is "Prophecy". Ephesians 6: 19-20

The white Jews and the white Gentiles will know the latter day "Deliverer" by the message that he delivers. There is only one Truth in the world today that is being suppressed that the disbelieving Jews said in biblical days that if that Truth was delivered, it could turn the world upside down. The white Jews and white Gentiles will know for sure if that suppressed Truth that could turn the world upside down was indeed delivered in the latter days to save the Gentiles. Acts 17: 6

In the latter days of the last Gentile kingdom of "Iron and Clay", the Afro Americans are those who are being scattered. They are the true riches and glory in the Gentile kingdom. They are the most important race of people in the Gentile kingdom. They are God's first born and chosen people who will inherit the earth and the only ones that can be for the "Salvation" of the Gentiles. Daniel 2: 36-44, Genesis 11: 4, Jeremiah 23: 2-3, Jeremiah 50: 17, Mark 14: 27, John 16: 32, Exodus 4: 22 and Acts 13: 47

Double will happen to the white Gentiles and the white Jews at judgment this time that happened to the Afro Americans. That's double the curses or double the blessings. This is the great Mystery. The riches and glory of this biblical mystery among the Gentiles is that God will be in the Afro Americans and their hope for glory in the world to come. It is because of this that their "Lives and Opinions do Matter" and must not be ignored if the white Jews and white Gentiles are to be saved at this late hour, this time. Revelation 18: 6-7 and Colossians 1: 26-27

The Sons of Perdition or the Sons of Hell or the Hellenistic white Greek gentiles who are assuming the identity of the true people of God and deceiving the white Gentiles who have dominion today are the enemy and if the white Jews and white Gentiles who have dominion today are to be saved, there must be a falling Away from that man of sin. This is Prophecy. Revelation 2: 9, Revelation 3: 9 and 2 Thessalonians 2: 3-4

Everything that the white Jews were afraid of giving to the true people of God in biblical days must be given to the people of God today to show sorrow for killing Jesus to prevent the white Gentiles who have dominion today from believing in Jesus and to prevent the white Gentiles who have dominion today from gathering together those who are scattered and giving them a nation. There must be a Gathering of those who are Scattered, and they must be given a nation and the white Gentiles who have dominion today must join with them to become Human to share with them the world to come. The white Jews can keep their nation, but a nation must be given to those who are scattered if the Jews and Gentiles are to be saved. "Sorrow" must be shown for the killing of Jesus to preserve the white Jews nation and lie that they are the people of God. "Sorrow" must be shown. A Penance must be paid. John 11: 48-54

There must be a Revealing of the Sons of Perdition who are those who are assuming the identity of the true people of God and there must be a Falling Away from that man of sin. This is Prophecy. 2 Thessalonians 2: 3-4

There must be a Gathering of the true people of God because they are the "Salt" and the "Light" for the Gentiles. God has set them and only them to be a "Light" for the Gentiles that through them and only them, can "Salvation" come to the Gentiles. The "Mystery" and the "Glory" of this "Mystery" is that only the people of God can be for the "Salvation" of the Gentiles. Matthew 5: 13, Acts 13: 47 and Colossians 1: 26

It is because of this that the people of God must not be scattered but must be gathered together as a nation. In biblical days, the white Jews who are assuming the people of God identity and are deceiving the white Gentiles were afraid that the white Roman Gentiles who have dominion today would find out who were the true people of God and then take away the white Jews place as the people of God and their nation and then gather together the people of God that are "Scattered" and give the people of God the title of the people of God and a nation. John 11: 48-52

Jesus was killed to prevent Jesus from revealing the true people of God to the white Gentiles that have dominion today so the white Gentiles who have dominion today could not take away the white Jews place and nation and give that place and nation to those that are scattered. John 11: 53-54

The white Gentiles who have dominion today and the white Jews both must "Behold" everything that have happened, or they will be "Cut-Off" from the Tree of Life. Roman 11: 21-22

# 41

## The Ambassador

Right now, at the end of the age or the end of the millennium or after the fullness of the Gentiles comes in at the end of the age or after December 21, 2012, the people of God are the most important people in the world to the Gentiles. Determining on how the true people of God are treated will determine the future of all of the Gentiles. Double will happen to the Gentiles at judgment that happened to the people of God. That's double the blessings or double the curses. This is why the Gentiles must know who IS RAEL (REAL) and who is not. The future of the great white throne will be determined by if the Gentiles know who IS RAEL (REAL) and who is not. Those who deceived the white Gentiles who have dominion today that they are the people of God will be the cause why there is no place found for the great white throne in the future. Revelation 18: 6-7, Revelation 2: 9, Revelation 3: 9 and Revelation 20: 11

There must be an Ambassador from the people of God to the throne of the Gentiles that will be the most important Ambassador that the Gentiles have that will be given utterance to speak BOLDLY as he ought to speak or as it was agreed last time at judgment that he would be allowed to speak to reveal the Mystery of the Gospel to the Gentiles if the Gentiles are to be saved this time. He will deliver a truth to the Gentiles about the Mark of the Beast and if the Gentiles receive the truth and act accordingly they could prevent the worse plague the world will ever see and save a billion lives.

God will not send the knowledge to save the Gentiles to no one else but to the Ambassador from the people of God to the throne of the Gentiles that is not an Ambassador in chains but is given utterance to speak boldly as he ought to speak. That was the plan and the deal that the Gentiles made with those who stood up for the Gentiles last time at judgment that the Gentiles chose to be sent to the Gentiles this time that the Gentiles would call Saints (Sents) because their utterance will inform the Gentiles of what the Gentiles must do to survive and save billions. The Gentiles must not renege on this agreement.

Only if the Gentiles honor God by giving the people of God a nation and have an Ambassador from the people of God nation to the throne of the Gentiles will the knowledge of how to save the Gentiles be delivered to the Gentiles. To be saved, the white Jews and white Gentiles must turn the world upside down and acknowledge the true people of God as a nation. This is the revealing of the Mystery of the Gospel and this is Prophecy. Prophecy says that the Gentiles must have an Ambassador from the people of God nation to the throne of the Gentiles that is given utterance to speak "Boldly" as he ought to speak to reveal the Mystery of the Gospel to the Gentiles. If there must be an Ambassador from the people of God to the throne of the Gentiles, then the people of God must be given a nation that the ambassador from the people of God will represent. If the Gentiles are to be saved, prophecy must not be ignored. The ambassador from the people of God to the throne of the Gentiles must not be an ambassador in chains that is restricted from acting or from speaking "Boldly" if the Gentiles are to be saved. This is Prophecy. Ephesians 6: 19-20

Anyone who advises the Gentiles to ignore Prophecy and not to do this is the enemy to the Gentiles and has a secret agenda to see the Gentiles cut off from the Tree of Life and regressed. If the people of God are not given a nation and the giving away of the people of God jobs, homes, neighborhoods and civil rights to illegal immigrants by the New Ten Kings or Banks is not discontinued immediately, the second collapse of the Gentiles global financial system will occur causing the Gentiles to adopt a new financial system that will require all to be marked on their right hands or foreheads before anyone can buy or sell. Revelation 13: 16-17

Because that tattooed mark will be made from the abuse of alien technology, that tattooed mark on the hand or forehead before anyone can buy or sell will turn into a foul sore that cannot be healed. That sore will spread over the entire body causing great pain that will burn like fire. To receive temporary relief from the pain, those with the Mark of the Beast tattooed on their flesh will have to gnaw or bite and chew on flesh aggressively. This is a description of the walking dead zombies that today's movies that are titled "Night of the Living Dead" and the "Walking Dead" are made about. Revelation 16: 2, Revelation 14: 9-11 and Revelation 16: 10

In those latter days when this plague has come upon the Gentiles, the Gentiles will seek death and will not find it. They will desire to die and death will flee from them. Revelation 9: 6

This tattooed mark on the flesh to buy and sell shall spread over the body causing great pain that will burn like fire and it is this that will transform the Gentiles into the primitive regressed beings that will be called the Morlocks who will be referred to as the "Walking

Dead". Because of the great pain that will burn like fire and because of the regression from homo sapiens to the Paleolithic creatures of their beginning that will be cursed with foul smelling sores and great pain and called the "Morlocks", the Gentiles will desire to die, and death will flee from them. Revelation 9: 6

These regressed creatures that will be cursed by God will not find death when they lose a limb or is seriously wounded nor, will they heal and become better but will continue to survive mutilated and wounded under great pain and suffering never getting better and never finding relief from their discomfort. Because of these conditions that cannot be healed and the multitudes of different pain causing problems throughout their body that all will be causing great pain and discomfort until they slowly die from their injuries, they will desire to die quick and fast, but death will flee from them and only pain and suffering will be their lasting and constant companions until death comes. A third of "Mankind" will be killed by this plague and two other plagues that will strike the earth. Revelation 14: 9-11, Revelation 9: 6, Revelation 9: 15 and Revelation 9: 18

Only if the New Ten Kings or Banks invest in the people of God will the Gentiles global financial system be saved. Only the people of God with their reckless spending habits can stimulate and save the Gentiles financial system now.

The white Gentiles must understand that this would be the lengthening of the Gentiles kingdom. Understand that God will give the Gentiles extra time to prove that they are worthy if the Gentiles honor God by honoring the people of God by finally giving the people of God a nation and "Beholding" and "Revealing" everything that have happened and everything that is being suppressed in a public forum because God wants to take out of the white Jews and white Gentiles a people for God's name and for this cause, all is done or will be allowed to be done and the words of the prophets or the "Books of Simion" are written to reveal this to the Gentiles. Once the white Gentiles realizes who are the true people of God, the white Gentiles will realize the importance in the truth that is written in the Books of Simion that only the true people of God can deliver to the Gentiles. The white Jews and white Gentiles will only have their trust in who are the true people of God and the true people of God interpretation of the gospel to help the white Jews and white Gentiles make their final latter-day choices. The white Gentiles must "Behold" all of this to prevent from being "Broken Off" or "Cut Off" from the Tree of Life and regressed into the "Morlocks". Romans 11: 22 and Acts 15: 14-15

# 42

# The Penance

Only if the Gentiles demonstrate that they honor God and honor the people of God for what the people of God have done for the new white gentile race will God give the Gentiles extra time to bring this into reality because a Penance must be paid and God will give the Gentiles extra time to pay that Penance because God wants to take out of the Gentiles a people for God's name and for this cause, all will be allowed to be done and it is the words of the prophets that are written or the Books of Simion that will reveal this to the Gentiles. The written word is powerful. All that is written will come to pass. As it is written, is as it shall be done. Acts 15: 14-15

The dividing and giving away of the Gentiles nation to the Gentiles neighbors will not save the Gentiles global financial system no matter how much the minimal wage is increased. The dividing and giving away of the Gentiles nation to their neighbors is the "writing on the wall" concerning the destruction of the Gentiles nation. (Peres) Daniel 5: 28

# THE BOOKS OF SIMION

The Holy Bible has recorded that the destruction of the Gentile dominion in the latter days was about "Housing" and how the Gentiles were living Luxuriously while the New Ten Kings or Banks gave the people of God jobs, homes, neighborhoods and civil rights to illegal immigrants. Revelation 18: 6-8

Anyone who say that what is revealed is not the truth must explain the presence of the "Watchers". The "Watchers" are not the Greys. The Greys who are here now abducting or rapturing the Gentiles in the air on the "Greys" UFO'S for evolutionary development examinations to determine if the Gentiles are at their fullness now since the fullness of the Gentiles did come in at the end of the age or on December 21, 2012 are not the Watchers because they are not here just watching but are implementing a secret agenda to obtain more vessels, containers and bodies. The Greys have lied to deceive the white Gentiles when they have said that they are the white Gentiles in the future and are here to watch and observe history.

The true Watchers are watching and recording everything to be used this time at judgment for or against the Gentiles. Melchizedek is a Watcher. Melchizedek is without father, without mother, without descend having neither the beginning of days nor the end of life but made like the Son of God, abideth a priest continually. Melchizedek is still walking the earth right now watching and recording everything. The Watchers and the Greys presence here on the earth cannot be explained or ignored and their presence here on the earth is proof that something else is going on that involves the evolutionary development of the white Gentiles because the Gentiles are given evolutionary development examinations when the Gentiles are abducted or raptured up in the air aboard the Greys UFO'S. Aboard the UFO, samples of the Gentiles hair, skin, body fluids and reproduction systems are extracted and examined to determine their development at this point. Hebrew 7: 3

The fullness of the Gentiles means, the Gentiles are at their maximum level of evolutionary development. To receive farther evolutionary development, the white Gentile Beings will have to be judged to determine if the white gentile Beings are worthy to continue to exist with the Human Beings on the planet earth. Romans 11: 25 and Luke 21: 24

The white gentile Beings were given the Greek dominion, the Roman dominion and the dominion we live in today described as "iron and clay" which is a derivative of the Roman dominion to join with the Human Beings to become part of the Human Race but they stayed white and they proclaimed to all in Heaven that the joining of the white Beings with the colored Beings or the Human Beings had taken place and now all on the planet earth were part of one race called the Human Race with people that have a shade, color or tint in their complexion. White is the absent of all color. The White Beings and the Human Beings are not the same. Only the colored Beings are Human Beings because Human Beings means Colored Beings because Hu or Hue in the word "Human" means color. Daniel 2: 36-45

If the Gentiles are to be saved this time, the rebirth of the true people of Israel must be allowed to come to pass. To be saved, the white Jews and white Gentiles must make the Afro-Americans great again. Remember, God and the Creature both are waiting eagerly for the revealing or the manifestation of the Sons of God. The people of God must not be turned into Rappers and Hip-Hoppers. The people of God must be allowed to manifest into the Sons of God if the Gentiles are to be saved. Romans 8: 19

This is the Mystery that has been hidden for generation but is now made known to God's saints and the "Saints" are only those who are "Sent". To them, God will make known what are the "Riches and Glory" of this mystery among the Gentiles which is God in His people and God's people "Hope" for glory in the world to come. It is because of this that the people of God are the most important race of people in this last gentile dominion. The people of God who are the Afro-Americans today lives do matter and the way they see things and their understanding about what is going on is very important for the survival of the Gentiles. They are the "Riches and the Glory" of the mystery in the Holy Bible among the Gentiles. This is why the Gentiles must know who Is Rael (Real) and who is not. It is because of this that the Gentiles must not leave the Afro-Americans out of the latter-day decisions making for the Gentiles. Colossians 1: 26-27

Because of the way the people of God were treated by the Gentiles in the Gentiles dominion, a Penance must be paid. Only if the Gentiles honor God by honoring the people of God by giving the people of God a nation and have an Ambassador from the people of God to the throne of the Gentiles that is given utterance to speak "Boldly" and acknowledging the people of God royalty equal to that of the white Gentiles and are willing to share and give to the people of God will the Gentiles kingdom be lengthen and the reign of the people of God in the world to come be delayed because God wants to take out of the Gentiles a people for God's name. Acts 15: 14-15

Simion will reveal this to the Gentiles in the latter-days as Simeon did IN the BEGINNING because the End of the Dominion will be declared from the Beginning of the dominion and it was Simeon who declared this to the Gentiles IN the BEGINNING and at the END, it will be Simeon and only Simion who will declare this to the Gentiles again. It is for this cause that the words of the Prophets or the Books of Simion are written. The revealing of this "Mystery" is part of the "Riches and the Glory" that is among the Gentiles. The people of God that will reveal this "Mystery" to the Gentiles to save the Gentiles is part of the "Glory" that is among the Gentiles in the people of God that no one else on the planet have and they are now among the Gentiles if the Gentiles are mature enough, intelligent enough and evolved enough on an evolutionary scale to understand and then use prophecy to steer events in another direction to prevent all that is prophesied to come to pass. This is the revealing of the Mystery of the Gospel and this is Prophecy. Halleluyah, therefore let it be known to the Gentiles that the "Salvation" of God has been written, sent and delivered to the Gentiles and they will hear it. Acts 15: 14-15, Isaiah 46: 10 and Acts 28: 28

# 43

# The Plan for Salvation

It must be known to the Gentiles that if they help the people of God and "Behold" everything that have happened, they will be helped because in so doing, they will change the shape of the things that are prophesied to come and prevent the Gentiles from being "Cut-Off" from the Tree of Life and no place found for the great white throne in the future but the Gentiles are not commented to that end or that choice of actions. The Gentiles will not be persuaded, convinced, encouraged, influenced or won-over by argument to accept the delivered truth.

The Deliverer mission is only to deliver the truth. The "Deliverer" mission is not to try to make the white Jews and white Gentiles accept the delivered truth. This time, the "Deliverer" delivered the truth to the white Jews first because the white Jews in the future are the ones who organized the Gentiles and the people of God to request from God to give the white Jews and white Gentiles a second chance. Because the white Jews judged themselves unworthy for eternal life last time because they wanted to be the people of God so bad that they assumed the identity of the true people of God and said in their hearts that they did not care about the consequences, the white Jews sent the latter day "Deliverer" and they wanted the "Deliverer" to come to them "First" before he turns to the white Gentiles so the white Jews could be there to back him up when he goes to the white Gentiles to deliver the message that would save the white Jews and the white Gentiles. Acts 13: 46, Romans 1: 16, and Romans 2: 10

This was the plan made by the white Jews, white Gentiles and the people of God last time at judgment. The people of God have fulfilled their side of the agreement. The white Jews and white Gentiles must not renege on this agreement. The white Jews and white Gentiles must know that they will stand before judgment again with the people of God and it will be very bad for the white Jews and white Gentiles if at that judgment it is reported that the white Jews and white Gentiles reneged on the agreement that they made with the people of God. 2 Corinthians 5: 10 and Romans 14: 10

The white Jews and white Gentiles are still in command. We all will follow the white Jews and white Gentiles lead. The Gentiles must do whatever they think is best. To prove that the Gentiles are worthy or not worthy to survive, the Gentiles must do whatever is in the Gentiles hearts and minds. The Deliverer and all who are "Sent" (Saint) will accept the Gentiles final choices as being what is "right" and "just" no matter what their final choices are. The "Deliverer" mission is not to walk on water nor to do miracles to prove his point nor is his mission to convince the white Jews and white Gentiles through reason and logic and nor is his mission to judge the white Jews and white Gentiles but his mission is to only deliver the message that God wants to take out of the white Jews and white Gentiles a people for God's name without offending the white Jews and white Gentiles and for this cause, the words of the prophets in the books of Simion are written. Only at judgment this time will the Gentiles have to answer for their choices and actions. The white Jews must not stir up the white Gentiles against the people of God who are the Afro Americans today as they did in the past and like they are doing now in America. Acts 15: 14-15, and Acts 14: 2

Honoring God by honoring the people of God and having an Ambassador from the people of God nation to the throne of the Gentiles that is given utterance to speak and act "Boldly" could steer events in another direction and prevent the white Jews from judging themselves unworthy for eternal life and prevent no place found for the great white throne in the future. It is written in the Holy Bible that the white Jews and white Gentiles will hear and receive the truth from him who is sent and believe and be saved. Ephesians 6: 19-20, Revelation 20: 11, Acts 15: 14-15, Acts 14: 1 and Acts 15: 7

Salvation or the knowledge to save the Gentiles from harm has been delivered to the Gentiles as was promised. The Promise has now been fulfilled. Therefore, let it be known to the Gentiles that the "Salvation" of God has been "Sent" to the Gentiles in the Books of Simion and the Gentiles will hear it. The Gentiles must "Glorify" God by honoring God by honoring the people of God because God has granted the Gentiles a second chance or repentance to life or the opportunity to receive repentance to life if the Gentiles honor the people of God. Acts 28: 28 and Acts 11: 18

Until the return of God, the white Gentiles of today's dominion are the shepherds of God's flock. Shepherd the flock of God which is among you, serving as overseers, not by compulsion but willingly, not for dishonest gain but eagerly, nor as being lords over those entrusted to you but being examples to the flock and when the Chief Shepherd appears, you will receive the crown of glory that does not fade away. 1 Peter 5: 2-4

Now, the "Plan for Salvation" for the white Jews first and then to the white Gentiles is "Wash" yourselves clean. Put away the evil of your doing from the eyes of God. Cease to do evil. Learn to do good. Seek justice. Rebuke the oppressor. Defend the fatherless. Plea for the widow. Isaiah 1: 16-17

It is necessary that the "Word of God" or the "Plan for Salvation" should be spoken to the white Jews first because the Jews in the future are the ones who sent the Word of God to themselves in our present but since the white Jews last time rejected the "Word of God" because they want the identity of the people of God so bad that they have assumed the people of God identity and now because of this, have judged themselves unworthy of everlasting life, behold, the "Word of God" last time was delivered to the white Gentiles who have dominion today because God wants to take out of the white Gentiles and the white Jews, who are also gentiles, a people for God's name. This is the message that the "Deliverer" or "Simion" will deliver to the white Jews and to the white Gentiles at the end of the age after the fullness of the Gentiles comes in or after December 21, 2012 which was the end of the age. Acts 13: 46, Acts 15: 14-15, Romans 11: 25-26

Understand, "Mankind" must seek the Lord even the white Gentiles who are called by God's name or who call themselves Jews. Acts 15: 17

The white Jews and white Gentiles who are Ordained or Appointed to eternal life this time because they believed last time will believe again this time. It is these white Jews and white Gentiles that God wants to take out of the Gentiles for God's name and for that cause, the Words of the Prophets or the Books of Simion are written. Acts 13: 48 and Acts 15: 14-15

The Gentiles are now at the "Precipice" point spoke of in the 2008 science fiction movie titled, "The Day the Earth Stood still", for the Gentiles to understand what is really going on and to change and steer events in another direction to prevent the white Jews from judging themselves unworthy for ever-lasting life because they want to be the people of God so bad that they are assuming the true people of God identity and to prevent no place found for the great white throne in the future. Acts 13: 46 and Revelation 20: 11

It is now up to the Gentiles to change as they said they could and would and save the kingdom or destroy it however the Gentiles see fit. A drastic, collaborative evolution of our thought patterns must be performed or a radical alteration of our thought patterns and actions must be achieved if events are to be steered in another direction to change the shape of the things that are prophesied to come to prevent no place found for the great white throne in the future.

It is now the responsibility of every Gentile that comes in contact with the truth to guarantee the survival of the great white throne by revealing the truth and everything that is being suppressed. This action is specifically written in prophecy to be done by the white Gentiles. The white Gentiles who are the Grafted Branch must "Behold" and "Reveal" everything that have happened to prevent from being "Cut-off" from the Tree of Life and regressed into the Paleolithic creatures of their beginning that will be called the "Morlock". Romans 11: 22

Now since an Afro American has reached out to help the great white throne, how many Gentiles will join him to save the great white throne. Those that are assuming the identity of the people of God who deceived the white Gentiles who have dominion today that they were the people of God that knew the prophesies of the God of Abraham have not brought the message of "Salvation" to the white

Gentiles who have dominion today to save the Gentiles and we are at the end of the age.

They have deceived the white Gentiles who have dominion today that only hydrogen bombs can guarantee the white Gentiles survival and salvation. They are wrong. Bombs and technology cannot help the Gentiles now. The white Gentiles who have dominion today must understand this. Bombs and technology cannot stop the regression of the white Gentiles genes that is making them weak, frail, impotent sexually and mentally unbalance. It is because of this that the white Gentile man feel that he must have a gun with him at all times for protection. The regression has definitely started in the white Gentiles.

# 44

# The Regression

Look at the Afro Americans today and be WARNED. They are God's first born and chosen people and the pyramids builders of the past and look at them now after their regression into the Negro because of disbelief. Exodus 4: 22 and Romans 11: 20

Their regression was so complete that today's Gentiles and the ascendants of the "slaves" cannot believe that the ascendants of the "Slaves" ancestors built the pyramids in Egypt. The "slaves" built Pharaoh's treasure cities "Pithom and Raamses including the Ramses statues that are seen in Luxor today and everything else in Egypt. The slaves did not believe that the regression could happen to them, but it did. Exodus 4: 22, Exodus 1: 11, and Romans 11: 20

The regression will happen to the white Gentiles if the white Gentiles do not steer events in another direction. The regression of the white Gentiles will be so complete that in the future, all who see the white Gentiles will ask themselves if this is the man that made nations to shake. Isaiah 14: 16

Only if the Gentiles hear the truth and act accordingly will the Gentiles be saved. This is the message that the old black African dominion left in their ancient monuments for the new white Gentile dominion to understand.

Even with bombs and extreme technology, technology and bombs that were a thousand times more advance than the Gentiles technology and bombs are today and still, the old black African dominion could not fight God. This is the knowledge and warning that the old black African dominion left for the new white Gentile dominion to comprehend in their ancient ruins that are found all over the world today that cannot be duplicated or copied by today's technology. Before the old black Africans were scattered, they built extraordinary cities and towers or pyramids whose tops are in the heavens like Machu Picchu and the others ancient structures built high in the mountains to make a name for themselves, so the new white Gentile dominion would know who they were and what they were capable of and still, they could not fight God. Genesis 11: 4

The Mayans, the Incas or no other native Mexican Indian built none of the ancient structures found in South America and found all over the world. The only pyramids that native Indians built were pyramid shape "Teepees" tents for their dwellings made from animal hides. When these extraordinary cities were built who tops were in the heavens like Machu Picchu, the Indians of today's world from the new white Gentile dominions had not been created yet. Many years after the old black African were scattered and cast into "Outer-Darkness" which is "Outer-Space", the local Indians moved into the old black Africans abandon structures and cities thousands of years later and claimed, "squatter's rights" to the ancient ruins. Matthew 8: 12

The ancient city ruins found at Machu Picchu in Peru and all of the other ancient structures that are found all over the world all were built by the old black African dominion before they were scattered to make room for the new white Gentile dominion which was the Greek dominion and the Roman dominion. The Holy Bible has recorded that the kingdom of God was taken away from the people of the old black African dominion and given to a nation bearing the fruit of it or given to a new dominion and the people of that new dominion. Genesis 11: 4 and Matthew 21: 43

Jesus explained this to His people when He said, "The stone which the builders rejected has become the chief cornerstone" which means, the genetically engineered people that were created by the "Falling Angels" that were made to be destroyed when no longer needed that were called the "Tares" of the earth that God rejected has been given evolutionary growth and a dominion to prove themselves worthy to continue to exist by joining with the people of the earth to become human beings. Jesus said that this is the Lord's doing. Jesus said that this action towards the white Gentiles was marvelous in the people of God eyes because it verified and proved the promised God made to the "Meek" who are His people to inherit the earth and be joined with God and given god-like abilities that will allow them to float like the clouds and fly like the birds to their windows as well as given ever-lasting-life wherein they will not be able to be killed after the white Gentiles have had their dominions. Matthew 21: 42, 2 Peter 2: 12, Matthew 13: 24-30, Matthew 5: 5, Revelation 21: 3-4 and Isaiah 60: 8

Evolving the white Gentiles into homosapiens and giving the white Gentiles dominion making the white Gentiles the head of the corner or the rulers of the planet for a time was marvelous in the people of God eyes because knowing that God evolved the created white creature from Paleolithic to homosapiens and gave them a dominion on the earth proved that everything that was promised to the people of God after the white Gentiles have had their dominions on the earth were possible.

The white Gentiles must "Behold" the goodness and severity of God. The white Gentiles must behold what happened to the old black African dominion being broken-off from the Tree of Life because of "disbelief" or not believing that God could take dominion away from them and the white Gentiles must behold the goodness of God who evolved them from paleolithic into homo sapiens and gave them a dominion to grow in and become human beings or the white Gentiles also will be broken-off. Disbelief about what God can do will get you "Cut-Off" from the Tree of Life in a New York second. The white Gentiles must "Believe" that it happened to the old black African dominion and know for a certainty that the same or worse will happen to the white Gentiles if they do not believe that what happened can happen. Romans 11: 20 and Romans 11: 21-22

The white Gentiles must know that the people of God will be grafted back into the Tree of Life and supersede the accomplishments that the white Gentiles achieved in the white Gentile dominions. For if you white Gentiles were cut out of the olive tree which is wild by nature and were grafted "contrary to nature" into a good olive tree and achieved what the white Gentiles achieved in their dominion, how much more shall the people of God achieve in their dominion who are the "natural branches" when they are grafted back into their own olive tree? Romans 11: 23-24

The old black Africans that were before Babylon, the black Babylonians and the black Persians whose dominion came before the white Greek and the white Roman dominions built all of the ancient structures that are found today to make a name for themselves before they were scattered to make room for the new white Gentile dominions. Genesis 11: 4

The world was taken away from the old black Africans and given to the white Gentiles. The old black Africans from the old dominion were cast into "Outer-Darkness" which is "Outer-Space" because "Outer-Space" is "Outer-Darkness". None of these structures were built by native Indians or extraterrestrials from another dimension. The extraterrestrials that were in our past are here now in our present, but they are not building anything because construction and building is not their agenda. The extraterrestrials agenda now and in the past, is about the quest for "immortality" in obtaining new vessels, containers or bodies to house more disembodied ancient spirits to continue to exist in the three-dimensional-universe somewhere else in the universe. The extraterrestrials that are under the ice in Antarctica and the tall white aliens that say they are from the Pleiades as well as the "Greys" are the same extraterrestrials that were in the past and they are not building anything. They are the Falling Angels spoke of in the Holy Bible. Matthew 21: 43 and Matthew 8: 12

# 45

# The Deception

Woe to the inhabitants of the earth and the sea. The devil has come down from outer-space to you having great wrath because he knows that he has a short time to complete his agenda and be gone before the Lord God and God's Angels returns to the earth after the end of the age or after December 21, 2012. Revelation 12: 12 and Matthew 13: 49

They have deceived the white Gentiles of the earth by appearing to them as "Familiars" or as white Gentiles to appear "familiar" to the white Gentiles to deceive the white Gentiles so they could continue their secret agenda on the earth and this deception was made possible because of the white Gentiles greed for new technology. The Holy Bible has warned us not to communicate with these "familiar ancient spirits" who have cloned Gentile looking bodies to deceive the Gentiles because eventually, they will defile the white Gentiles of the earth. Leviticus 19: 31

The aliens that say they are from the Pleiades are deceiving the white Gentiles and are appearing to the white Gentiles as "Familiars" or appearing to the white Gentiles as white Gentiles. The white

Gentiles have no idea how the Pleiadeans really look. They are appearing to the white Gentiles as charming beings and is influencing the white Gentiles in a sweet way. The Holy Bible has warned the white Gentiles about the sweet influences of the Pleiades. Job 38: 31

The white race is a young race created by the fallen angels for bodily replacement parts and to house disembodied ancient cast out spirits. The white race is not an ancient race in some other part of the Galaxy. The white Race is a young race that is wild by nature because it is young, and it was grafted contrary to nature into an old, ancient, and cultivated Tree of Life here on the earth. The white race is the "Tares" that were put on the people of God planet to grow with the people of God to become human beings. Because of this grafting into a cultivated Tree of Life here on the earth, the white Gentiles here on the earth are the highest evolved white Gentiles in the universe. All others white Gentiles anywhere in the universe are still young and wild by nature. There are no other white Gentiles anywhere else in the universe that are more evolved than the white Gentiles here on the earth. There are no ancient white Gentiles flying in advance UFO'S from the Pleiades. White Gentiles do not control the Pleiades. The Holy Bible has recorded that God controls all of the stars constellations in Heaven including the Bear, Orion and the Pleiades and all of the chambers in the southern part of the universe. When the fullness of the Gentiles came in at the end of the age when the white Gentiles were at their maximum level of evolutionary development here on the earth, the white Gentiles were no more evolved than the Hatfields and the Mc Coys or the Cowboys and Gangsters of their past. Romans 11: 24, Matthew 13: 24-30, Job 38: 31, Job 9: 9, Amos 5: 8, Romans 11: 25 and Luke 21: 24

These ancient spirits in cloned gentile bodies deceived the German people in World War 2 to imitate them and to adopt a rigid work ethic to carry out the aliens secret agenda on the earth.

Everything about the Nazis was of alien origin. The Nazis were helped or controlled by aliens from somewhere else. (Dr. Hermann Oberth, top German Nazi in World war 2 and NASA space scientist till 1972)

In 1961, Betty and Barney Hill were abducted by aliens that said they were from the Zeta Riticuli star system many light-years away from earth. Barney Hill reported that the aliens were dressed like Nazis. They were alien beings in Nazis uniforms or the white Germans Nazis were in aliens uniforms because the aliens would not come here to dress up like German soldiers but German soldiers would dress like their conquerors in admiration. In World War Two, those that the Germans conquer in Europe later dress-up in uniforms like their German conquerors. Nazi Germany rocket scientists admits that they were the puppets of the aliens that had invaded the earth and the aliens directed them in their rocket program which was part of the aliens agenda to control the earth. When the Nazis commanders that were possessed by these ancient evil spirits retreated to Antarctica at the end of World War Two, they had been ordered to return to their masters and to return all alien technology. (Dr. Hermann Oberth, top German Nazi and NASA space scientist 1972)

No white Gentile from Germany built none of the ancient structures in Antarctica. No white German built any UFO'S. The UFO'S were for the aliens. If the white German Nazis would have had "one" working UFO identical or even close to what the aliens have, the white German Nazis would have won the war by controlling the skies. The saucer shape crafts that the Germans built trying to imitate the aliens never flew in the skies for their protection because their shape like saucers were contrary to the use of jet or rocket engines. With jet or rocket engines, the German flying saucers shape crafts could not complete with the allied forces fighting against them because the saucer shape crafts were not aerodynamic in its flight. Because the aliens use a different power source that moves their crafts in the sky that do not require aerodynamics for their flight, the saucers built by the Germans that were powered with turbo engines and jets could not perform like the aliens saucers did and the saucer shape crafts that the Germans built with turbo and jet engines were not aerodynamic enough to dog-fight in the skies with the allied flying forces that were built for aerodynamic flying.

All of the UFO'S that attacked Admiral Byrd naval fleet in 1947 in Antarctica were flown and built by aliens from somewhere else. There is no ancient German Nazi base in Antarctica but there is an ancient alien base in Antarctica that manipulated the Germans because of the Germans desire for advance technology. The "Swastika" is an alien symbol that the Germans copied and used and so did others like the Hindu who used the symbol of the swastika to ward-off evil spirits or to identify evil spirits when the Hindu heard the aliens telepathic message and listened and then imitated and copied what they saw in visions.

The aliens who helped the Germans because the Germans had sold the people of the earth out for technology to the aliens and were helping the aliens do the aliens secret agenda on the earth against the people of the earth said that they never trusted the Germans and would not give the Germans advance weapons in fear that the Germans would use them on the aliens too to steal the aliens technology that was being operated on the earth. When the aliens did not give the Germans a secret weapon to win the war, the Germans tried to imitate the aliens' technology and flying vehicles. They failed.

The aliens told the Germans to kill the Hebrew Jews as the American government is being told today to kill the Afro Americans who are the original Jews so the black Hebrew Israelites who are the original Jews could not inherit the earth that the aliens presently control. Because the white Greek gentiles were passing off as the people of God calling themselves "Hebrew", Hitler was deceived and went after them instead of the true people of God.

When Hitler, who studied biblical prophecy, realized that the Greek gentile white Jews passing-off as the people of God would be the cause of the Germans economy crashing as is predicted to happen soon in this last dominion when the Gentiles global financial system today collapse again because of "greed" that was suggested to them by Gordon Gekko in the 1987 movie titled "Wall Street" and that suggestion crashed the white Gentiles housing market and collapsed the Gentiles global financial system in 2008 and will be the cause that the white Gentiles global financial system collapse again causing the Gentiles to development another financial system using the Catholic church money whereas everyone will have to be marked on their hand or forehead to buy and sell and that tattooed mark on the flesh will cause a foul "sore" that cannot be healed that will spread over the entire body that will cause great pain that will feel like burning fire and that sore will start the worse plague the world will ever see killing billions and transforming all with the "mark" into the walking "Zombies" that today's movies are made about that must "Gnaw" or bite and chew on flesh to get relief from the pain and also the Greek gentile white Jews will stir-up the white Roman Gentiles who have dominion today and make their minds evil against the "Brethren" or the people of God who are the true "Hebrews" who are called the "Brothers" till today because the correct pronunciation of the word "Hebrew" is "Hey Bro" referring to the "Brethren" or "Brothers" and be the cause of the white Gentiles being broken-off from the Tree of Life and regressed and no place found for the great white throne in the future destroying Hitler's dream of a Third-Reich or an extended thousand-year reign, Hitler went after the white Greek Jews. That is how important prophecy was to Hitler. Revelation 13: 16-18,

## THE BOOKS OF SIMION

Revelation 16: 2, Revelation 16: 10, Revelation 14: 9-11, Acts 14: 2, Romans 11: 22 and Revelation 20: 11

It was because Hitler did what was best for Germany instead of doing what was best for the extraterrestrials that controlled Germany by not knowing who were the true people of God and stopping them from inheriting the earth and that would have satisfied the extraterrestrials that control the earth but went after the "false brethren" because the white Jews would be the cause why Germany economy collapse and be the cause why Hitler's dream of a "Third Reich" could not be brought into reality that Germany did not receive the promised secret weapon to win the war. Hitler screamed to his extraterrestrials conquerors that he was dedicated and loyal to them but was "deceived" by the "false brethren" who are also the "false prophet" who lied about being the true people of God but it was no use. The Germans were abandoned by the aliens and once the aliens were removed from the German equation, the collapse of the Third-Reich was imminent. Instead of fighting the alien invading force as the Holy Bible instructs us to do, the Germans joined with the invaders of the earth to obtain advance technology to rule the earth under the guidance of their alien conquerors. The aliens are also deceiving the white Gentiles now that are working with the aliens under the ice in Antarctica as well as deceiving the white Gentiles that are working with the aliens in under-ground military facilities in America. These ancient spirits are superior to us in their nature and in their technology and they will defiled the Gentiles. Leviticus 19: 31

At judgment last time, the white Gentiles assertion was that they were "deceived" by the "false prophet" who is also the "false brethren" who are those who have assumed the identity of the true people of God and deceived the white Jews and white Gentiles that they knew the prophesies of the God of Abraham. It is because of this "deception" that kept the white Jews and white Gentiles ignorant about what was really going on that the white Jews and white Gentiles at judgment last time sent the latter day "Deliverer" to themselves this time to reveal a truth that was so profound that it could turn the world upside down and if the white Jews and white Gentiles are to be saved, that conversion must come to pass. Remember, Jesus said that the white Jews and white Gentiles did not know what they were doing because the white Jews and white Gentiles have no idea of what is going on because they are being "Deceived". Revelation 19: 20, 2 Corinthians 11: 26, Acts 17: 6 and Luke 23: 34

Understand that the white Jews and white Gentiles who are "Offended" by this revelation are those who are possessed by the invaders. The Holy Bible says, "Woe to the world because of "offenses! For offenses must come if the white Jews and white Gentiles are to be saved, this time but "woe" or be cautious of that man by whom the "offenses" comes for he is the one who is the enemy to the white Jews and white Gentiles". Matthew 18: 7

# 46

# The Aliens and the Beast that will come out of the CERN Particle Accelerator and Collider

The aliens technology and their nature of existence are so much more evolved higher than our nature and technology that they can do things that we would consider impossible to be done or achieved by our laws of physics. In their flying crafts, they can perform operations on your body that is impossible to be perform by our laws of physics. They can remove your head, brain, arms, legs, hearts, eyes or your spinal column completely from the body and return them or reattach limbs with no scar tissue. When the Reptilians or Insectoids appear for your evolutionary development examination who will identify himself as the "Doctor", they can manipulate your feelings and emotions to the extreme. They can turn your fear level up to an unbelievable level to a point where you can't move or speak and is so frighten that you will retreat deep into your inner-self to escape for your protection when they are in the room and this is done for their protection if you have the slightest thought of violence as well as manipulate your sexual desire level to a point that you will consent to sex or consent to anything else while they have you in this horrible situation on their UFO. They can remove your spirit from the body and put you somewhere else while your body is handle like clothing taken off.

Before your abduction, there is nowhere to hide or no escape because they can identify your soul resonance or vibrational pattern while you are on the earth and they are deep in outer-space and they can hear your brain waves and then like with their UFO'S, transport you or their UFO'S through solid objects even through deep underground steal bomb proof shelters to bring you to their flying ships in the air or deep in space.

Excuse me, there is one place or the only place to hide where their power will not work where you could be safe and that is on Holy Ground identified as "Sanctuary". Because only in religion is there a way to stop the invaders and force the invaders from the planet as well as force the invaders from our bodies that the invaders will not want religion and government to come together to form an understanding of what is happening on the earth. The name of the Lord is a strong tower. The righteous runs to it and are safe. Proverb 18: 10

To save the earth and the people of the earth, the white Gentiles who have dominion today must understand this. This is what the invaders don't want you to know and understand. Understand, the same evil spirits that must be exorcised out of a demon possessed body by a man of God or a Catholic priest are the same evil spirits or entities that are flying in the gigantic UFO'S in the skies or is working with the government under the ice in Antarctica as well as working with the government in underground government military facilities. The prince of the power of the air who control the air in their UFO'S are the same spirits that now works in the children of disobedience. Ephesians 2: 2

We were given a second chance in the world we live in today to defeat a superior enemy from another dimension that could not be defeated last time or in one reality life time. We must receive the truth and act accordingly.

Only the "Word of God" can force the invaders from the body or force the invaders from the earth. The "Word of God" is our only weapons. The thought of the "Word of God" and help from our "Heavenly Father" and His Son our "Heavenly Brother" will instantly end your abduction experience and return you to the place where you were abducted from. If you don't believe in God and is not protected by the "Full Armor of God", you don't have a chance. This is why the aliens and those possessed by the aliens will not want government and religion to come together because only in religion is there the knowledge and a method to defeat the disembodied aliens.

These aliens can exist without bodies and can possess or inhabit another vessel, container or body by way of an unknown method and process that we on our present day evolutionary development cannot understand. Their technology can create vessels, containers or bodies that they can possess by putting their essence or spirits in to continue to exist. The Prince of the power of the air or those who control the skies in their gigantic UFO'S defying gravity utilizing the power of the air are the same evil spirit that now work in or has possessed the children of disobedience. Ephesians 2: 2

It is because of this that our weapons of our warfare to fight these advance disembodied invaders whose first-wave of attack was spiritual in nature having the ability to take over our planet by first taking possession of our bodies are not carnal but mighty through God to pulling down of strong holds or possessions and casting down arguments in our minds and every high thing or thought that exalts itself against the knowledge of God, bringing every thought into captivity to the obedience of God to prevent possession. This is how to save our lives and save our planet from these advance invaders that could not be defeated last time or in one reality life time. Be sober, be vigilant because your adversary the devil walks about like a roaring lion, seeking whom he may devour. "Resist" him, steadfast in the faith of God. "Resist" the devil or the invaders and the devil or the invaders will flee from you or from the earth is the knowledge in the Holy Bible of how to "fight" the aliens this time and this is our only hope to force the aliens from the body and from the earth. Do not join with the aliens for technology but give no place in your body or the earth for the devil and his forces to dwell. The Germans in World War Two did not understand this in World War Two and they were deceived and became the puppets of the invaders for technology. 2 Corinthians 10: 3-5, 1 Peter 5: 8-9, James 4: 7 and Ephesians 4: 27

The white Gentiles who uses deception as a virtue will not be able to deceive these ancient beings to obtain their technology. These ancient beings have already deceived the white Gentiles to believe that these ancient spirits in gentile looking bodies are young white Gentiles from somewhere else and they will defile the white Gentiles in the end as they did to the Germans in World War Two because of the Gentiles greed and hate for the people of God. Leviticus 19: 31

We were given a second chance in the white Gentiles second chance for salvation to defeat an invader that could not be defeated last time or in one reality life time because of their method of attack. While the Gentiles were waiting for the aliens to land their UFO'S and fight a ground war with the Gentiles to take over the earth, the aliens took over or possessed the Gentiles bodies and the white Gentiles had no idea what was happening. The white Gentiles never saw the invaders coming. This was the theme that was stressed in the 1997 movie titled, "The Devils Advocates", where the people from the Synagogue of Satan who made the movie and deceived the white

Gentiles bragged that the white Gentiles would never see the devil or the invaders coming. The Holy Bible has warned us that the devil or the invaders have come down to the earth with great wrath because they know that their time to complete their agenda with the white Gentiles is short in the latter days. They must be gone before the return of the "Most-High". Revelation 12:12

The proof that these disembodied aliens have possessed the world government leaders and are now in control of the governments of the earth is that now, it is against the aliens' National Security to report on anything that involves the alien agenda. The "Men-In-Black" some of which are aliens themselves and others are possessed by these disembodied aliens are enforcing the aliens' national security to be silent about the aliens agenda on the earth and to ignore the aliens presence throughout the world. The soldiers of the invaders will be possessed government soldiers and possessed city policemen in government and police uniforms following the inhuman orders from their commanders who will be aliens themselves or possessed by aliens to do the aliens agenda on the earth. This was the message put in the 1988 science fiction movie titled, "They Live". These soldiers and policemen will do all sorts of inhumane attacks on the people of the earth and their explanation will be that they were just following orders. Because these aliens can possess people and things, they will possess soldiers, policemen and computers by artificial intelligence and force soldiers, policemen and computers to do their bidding. The artificial intelligence or the alien intelligence inside of the computer will be part of the mind of Satan and it is this entity that will control the computer. There is no such thing as artificial intelligence. The intelligence in the computers is not artificial or false or fake but is real and it is part of the cosmic mind of Satan that electronics have connected to.

These invaders who could not be defeated last time or in one reality life time method of attack will be so advanced that the white Jews and white Gentiles will never see them coming. The negative thoughts in the white Jews and white Gentiles minds that they will believe are their own thoughts will be the aliens who have possessed them suggestions to them to do the aliens bidding. Because they will be unaware that they are possessed by a demonic force, they will believe that the aliens suggestions to them in their minds are their own thoughts of a given situation. This is why the Holy Bible has warned us to cast down arguments and every high thing that exalts itself against the knowledge of God in our minds bringing every thought into captivity to the obedience of God. For though we walk in the flesh, we do not war according to the flesh or for though we are flesh and blood beings, we will not be in war with flesh and blood beings but beings who can possess flesh and blood beings and make flesh and blood beings do their bidding. For the weapons of our warfare are not carnal or guns, bombs and missiles but mighty in God for pulling down strong holds or possessions. 2 Corinthians 10: 3-5

The governments of the earth that was supposed to protect the people of the earth is now protecting the aliens and are denying that the aliens are here. Government and commercial aircraft pilots that report seeing UFO'S in the air are laugh-at, ignored, dismissed and degraded by the government to prevent their opinion and observation of a UFO from being heard and believed. Like Germany in World War Two, the governments of the world today have sold-us-out to the invaders for technology and are aware of all abductions of people of the world and cattle mutilations by the aliens throughout the world. Even with these disembodied aliens leaving "Crop-Circles" throughout England and throughout the world that have coded messages within the "Crop-Circle" that cannot be explain, the governments of the world are denying that these disembodied aliens exist. The aliens have possessed people in England and have them saying that they are the ones who are making the "Crop-Circles" knowing that the "Crop-Circles" are not made with boards pressing down on the crops crushing and destroying them in the process but are made some other way bending the crops in a manner that do not crush or destroy the crops in the process. To farther deceive the people of the world to conceal the aliens' presence on the earth, the "News Media" of the government has not called these possessed people liars.

The Holy Bible was written to inform us about these advance disembodied spiritual invaders and how to resist the devil this time. It is written in the Holy Bible to submit to God who is another more powerful spiritual force. Do not submit and join the devil to receive technology. Resist the devil and he will flee from you as well as flee from the earth. Remember, these invaders are the same entities that can possess our bodies and only a man of God or a Catholic priest reciting the "Words of God" can exorcise or force the invading spirit out of a possessed body. The weapons of our warfare against these invaders are not carnal or our weapons against these invaders are not guns, bombs and missiles but mighty in God or the "Words of God" for pulling down strongholds or possessions. That includes possessions of the body as well as possession of the earth. James 4: 7 and 2 Corinthians 10: 3-5

To defeat these aliens that will be in your body trying to encourage you to give them strength by doing their bidding, we must put on the Full Armor of God that you may be able to withstand in the evil day having done all to stand.

1. Stand therefore having girded your waist with "Truth".

2. Put on the breast-plate of "Righteousness".

3. Shod your feet with the preparation of the "Gospel of Peace".

4. Above all, take the "Shield of Faith" with which you will be able to quench all the fiery darts or suggestions to do evil of the wicked one.

5. Take the "Helmet of Salvation" and the "Sword of the Spirit" which is the "Word of God". The "Word of God" is our only weapon to fight these superior ancient alien invaders because of who they are and their nature of existence. You must understand this to save ourselves and save the earth. Remember, the same evil spirits that must be exorcised out of a demon possessed body is the same evil spirit that are in those beings that fly in the UFO'S in our skies. You must understand that once possessed, no weapon or medicine can force the invaders from the body. Only the "Word of God" spoken by a man of God or a Catholic priest can force the invader from the body in a hurry. Resist the invaders with the "Word of God" and the invader will flee from you and flee from the earth. This is what the invaders do not want you to know and understand. Ephesians 6: 11-17 and James 4: 7

    This was revealed to the government in the 2015 movie titled, "The Atticus Experiment" when the government tried to control a possessed individual and weaponized the demon within her. In the fall of 1976, a small psychology lab in Pennsylvania became the unwitting home to the only government confirmed case of possession. The US military assumed control of the lab under orders of national security and soon after implemented measures aimed at controlling and weaponizing the entity. The details of the explicated events that occurred are now being made public after remaining classified for nearly forty years. The government discovered that only the "Word of God" could control the entity in the possessed body. What the government did not understand is that the same entities that are in a possessed body are the same entities that are flying in the air in the gigantic UFO'S that are identified in the Holy Bible as the "Prince of the Power of the Air" and they have possessed the children of disobedience. Because these demonic invaders have been ordered by God not to touch God's anointed ones, only God's anointed ones can help the Gentiles save the Gentiles and save the earth. Ephesians 2: 2 and 1 Chronicles 16: 21-22

We must pray always with all prayer and supplication in the Spirit being watchful to this end or watchful about what thoughts comes in your mind and watchful for those who will deliver the message to you with all perseverance and supplication for all the Saints or those who are Sent and for "Me" who is delivering this important profound message to you, that "Utterance" may be given to "Me" that I may open my mouth boldly to make known the "Mystery of the Gospel" for which I am an "Ambassador" in chains that in this position I may speak boldly as "I ought to speak" or as you agreed that I would be allowed to speak last time at judgment when you asked that this message be delivered to you this time before judgment. Do not renege on this agreement. Ephesians 6: 18-20


Understand, we wrestle not against flesh and blood beings like ourselves but against principalities or royalty from another dimension and time, against powers or against those that possess god-like extreme powers, against the rulers of darkness of this world and against spiritual wickedness in high places or against the Cast-Out-Ones who were spirits in Heaven that were "Cast-Out" as well as those elementals who were the controlling force of the sun, the rain, and the wind who abandon their heavenly post to descend down to the three-dimensional-universe to take on human shape and form and obtain bodies full of feelings and emotions to enjoy and to have sex with mankind. In other words, the elementals that were not cast-out of Heaven but "Fell" from grace when they abandon their heavenly stations or duties were like the fog that you see that descends from heaven and rest on the ground in the grass early in the morning. It is elements like the fog, wind, rain and fire that abandon their stations or duties of being fog, wind, rain and fire and took on human shape and became solid, flesh and blood bodies to have sex with mankind. These elementals were identified as the Fallen Angels because they fell from grace or fell from their heavenly stations or duties to take bodies to enjoy the feelings and the desires of life as mankind. Ephesians 6: 12 and (The book of Enoch)

It is these cast-out ancient spirits that have possessed the controllers at the Geneva-based CERN particle-accelerator and collider and have interest them to try to retrace the beginning of the universe and since the beginning of the universe started in Heaven when the cast-out ones departed Heaven to live in the three-dimensional-universe that they called Hell and Earth, retracing that action back to the beginning could allow those principalities, powers and rulers of darkness who were cast out of Heaven and told that they could never return or told that there was no place found in Heaven any longer for them because they fought with Michael and His Angels, an opportunity and a way to return back to that heavenly dimension without permission and in defiance. Retracing the origin of the universe is of no practical use to no one on the earth of flesh and blood but that knowledge is useable to Abaddon, the king over fallen-ones in the bottomless pit and those spiritual forces who were kick-out of Heaven and now wants to force their way back into Heaven in defiance. Beware of the door-ways and portals that are being open at the Geneva-based CERN particle-accelerator and collider. Only Satan or the angel from the bottomless pit name Abaddon will want the god-particle or the particle that holds all matter in place, so Satan could undo the work of God by undoing all matter. Everything that is being done at the CERN particle-accelerator is of Satanic origin. Because we are at the end of the white Gentiles dominion, the white Gentiles who are control by Satan want to threaten God by demanding more time or a third Reich or an extra thousand-year dominion from God and if God refuse, they want to threaten God by undoing all of God's creations. Once again, the god-particle is of no importance to life on this earth. It is insane to tapper with the glue that holds all matter together. Only those that wants to destroy all that God has created will want to have the particle that can destroy all matter. They want the god-particle to threaten God by undoing all that was created if God refuse their requests. Revelation 12: 7-9

All in Heaven knows what the Gentiles have in their hearts to do if they could. The "Deliverer" mission is to reveal this to the white Jews and the white Gentiles, so the white Jews and white Gentiles would know what to do to be saved. Now, since the Gentiles knows that all in Heaven knows their desires, different choices must be made to steer events in another direction to prevent what is prophesied to come to pass. To save the white Jews and white Gentiles, this time-line must not be allowed to continue and here is why.

These door-ways and portals that the Geneva-based CERN particle-accelerator are opening are portals into infinity or portals into the bottomless pit. It is prophesied that the white Gentiles would open a black-hole that will be called the bottomless pit and smoke arose out of the pit like the smoke of a great furnace. The sun and the air were darkened because of the smoke of the pit. Now, understand that a Star fallen from heaven to the earth or a fallen angel will be given the key to the bottomless pit and it is "he" who will open the bottomless pit or give the white Gentiles the knowledge to do his bidding. Revelation 9: 1-2

Out of the smoke, aircrafts appeared that swarmed like locusts and came upon the earth and to them was given power as the scorpions or the extraterrestrials whose true nature is insectoids of the earth have power. The extraterrestrials who are insectoids and reptilians by their nature control the earth now. They were commanded not to harm the grass of the earth or any green thing or any tree but only those men who do not have the seal of God on their foreheads. They were not given authority to kill them but to torment them for five months. The torment was like the torment of a scorpion when it strikes a man. The shape of the locusts or aircrafts was like horses prepared for battle. On their heads were crowns of something like gold and their faces were like the faces of men or inside of the crafts through the transparent dome, beings with faces like men will be seen. They had hair like women's hair or hair like the Marvel comic character known as "Thor" that is in today's Marvel movies and their teeth were like lions' teeth. It must be noted that godly hair is not long hair like women hair or like the hair that Thor has in the Marvel comics. The bible says that Thor hair is Satanic hair. The Holy Bible has recorded that godly-hair is hair like sheep-wool or nappy hair. They had war armor on or breastplates like breastplates of iron and the sound of their wings was like the sound of chariots with many horses running into battle or like the sound of Huey Cobra gunships flying into battle. They had tails like scorpions and there were stings or guns in their tails. Their king over them was the angel of the bottomless pit whose name is Abaddon or Apollyon. Two-hundred million of them will come out of the bottomless pit like a plague and they will kill a third of mankind. The rest of mankind who were not killed by these plagues did not repent of the works of their hands that they should not worship demons and idols of gold, silver, brass, stone, and wood, which can neither see nor hear nor walk and they did not repeat of their murders or their sorceries or their sexual immorality or their thefts. It is this fallen angel that will control the military and control gunships like the "Huey Cobras". Revelation 9: 3-11, Revelation 1: 14-15, Revelation 9: 15-16, Revelation 9: 18, and Revelation 9: 20-21

In the 2009 science fiction movie titled "Avatar", the white Gentiles said that in the future, they would be the demons that possessed bodies that would fly in their scorpion aircrafts led by the Dragon to attack the people of the Tree of Life. In the movie, they proclaimed that they would go to the "Halleluyah mountains which was a reference of the mountains of the God of the Holy Bible because Halleluyah means, "Praise Yah", the God of the Holy Bible and would burn down the Tree of Life that the movie called the "the Tree of Souls". In the movie Avatar, the principal God or deity that the people prayed to name was Eywa or Ay-Wah or A-Wah which is the ancient Hebrew name of the God of the Holy Bible whose ancient Hebrew name is Yah-A-Wah. This movie was blasphemous, profane, sacrilegious and irreligious to God and the future that God has promised for the earth. In the Stargate SG-1 series titled "The Ark of Truth", the white Jews and the white Gentiles have said in their hearts or in their movies that they would create a weapon that would kill all ascended beings. A weapon that would kill anyone on a higher level of evolutionary development than the young white race would be killed. That is like the Paleolithic man planning on killing the homosapiens because the homosapiens are more evolved than the Paleolithic beings. To have this in your mind and in your heart or in your movies is blasphemous, profane, sacrilegious, and irreligious to God. (You Tube-How to spell Jesus' real name in ancient Hebrew)

## Dominions

The Holy Bible has recorded that the ancient cities and towers or pyramids whose tops were in the heavens were all built by the people of the earth from the old black African dominion that was before the white Greek and white Roman dominions and not built by extraterrestrials or Mexican Indians. Genesis 11: 4

The Holy Bible has recorded that black Babylon that was represented as "Gold" and black Persia that was represented by "Silver" were superior to the white Greek and white Roman dominion that were represented as "bronze" and "iron" as well as superior to the last white Gentile dominion represented as "iron and clay" that we live in today. From the Babylon dominion down to the "Iron and Clay" dominion, the dominions did not get better in time but got worse and descended to the lowest level as time went on. The dominions descended from a time where God lived with the people and all things were possible with God to a time where all had to count on technology with its limited abilities and attributes. Daniel 2: 36-43 and Matthew 19: 26

The old black Africans requested that the young white Gentiles who were made to be destroyed be spared and allowed to live on the planet earth and join with the people of the earth to become human beings because the old black Africans wanted to share the new white Gentile race young DNA to produce children with lighter skin and curly hair. After the white Gentiles were grafted on the planet, the people of the old black African world refused to share with the beast that was made to walk up-right. They call the up-right beast barbarians and savages, but they still wanted to have sex and children with the barbarian savages to add straight or curly hair and lighter skin to their DNA. To this very day, the people of the old black African dominion still want to have sex and children with the white Gentiles who say that the people of the old black African dominion "lives do not matter" just to produce children with lighter skin and curly hair. It is for this cause that the beast that was made to be destroyed was not destroyed but was grafted on the Tree of Life. 2 Peter 2: 12 and Romans 11: 11-18

Two black African dominions which were Babylon and Persia would not make the joining because they did not want to share power with these recently replicated creatures but still wanted to have sex with them to produce children with lighter skin and curly hair so the Lord God gave three dominion to the white Gentiles which were the Greek dominion, the Roman dominion and the dominion we live in today referred to as the dominion of "iron and clay" to make that joining so there would be no excuses to prevent the white Gentiles from joining with the people of the earth to become human beings because God wants to take out of the white Gentiles a people for God's name but once given a dominion, the white Gentiles acted just as or worse than the black Africans did and refused to join with the people of the earth to become human beings but chose to take a position of superiority over the people of the earth because the white Gentiles were given dominion.

The white Gentiles proclaimed that they were given dominion on the earth over the black Africans because they were better and more advance than the black Africans and because the white Gentiles were a people of technology. They are wrong. The white Gentiles who are the beasts that were made to be destroyed only purpose on the earth is to join with the people of the earth to become human. They refused but screamed to all in Heaven that the joining had taken place and now all on the earth were human beings knowing that they were still white. This is the truth that will be delivered to the Gentiles in the latter days, so the white Gentiles would know what is going on and know what to do to survive. It is because of this and the knowledge that God wants to take out of the Gentiles a people for God's name that the words of the prophets or the Books of Simion are written. Acts 15: 14-15

The Holy Bible has recorded that it was nothing that the old black Africans could not do and still, they could not fight God. The old black African dominion technical abilities were so great that today's Ancient Astronaut Theorists believes that advance extraterrestrials from another dimension with god-like abilities were responsible for all of the ancient ruins that the old black African dominion created to make a name for themselves before they were scattered so the new white Gentile dominion would know who they were and what they were capable of and still, they could not fight God. Genesis 11: 4 and Genesis 11: 6

The Ancient Astronaut Theorists and the white Gentile historians do not understand. That is why it is necessary that the throne of the Gentiles have an Ambassador from the people of God interpreting ancient texts and revealing the "Mystery of the Gospel" that is given "Utterance" to speak "Boldly" as he ought to speak or as it was agreed last time at judgment that he would be allowed to speak to save the Gentiles. Do not renege on this agreement. Ephesians 6: 19-20

This is the message left in the ancient ruins of the old black African dominion that illustrated their extreme technical abilities. Regardless of what they did and tried with their advance abilities, dominion and the kingdom of God was taken away from them and given to the young white Gentiles. The old black African dominion was cast into "Outer-Darkness" which is "Outer-Space" because "Outer-Space" is "Outer-Darkness". There will be weeping and gnashing of teeth. Matthew 21: 43 and Matthew 8: 12

The ancient ruins at Tiwanaku in Bolilvia, Gobekli Tepe in Turkey as well as Serpent Mound in Ohio, USA all have the tears falling from the eyes of the statues to illustrate the weeping of the eyes and the gnashing of the teeth by the old black African dominion because God ended their dominion and gave a dominion to the white Gentiles which were the Greek dominion and the Roman dominion as well as this last dominion of Iron and Clay that we live in today. It may be interesting for you to know that the same deteriorated African stone statues that are found in Warco Wasi, Peru are also found in Malibu, California. The date of construction of these ancient monuments in Peru and California are unknown but it is believed to be hundreds of thousands of years old because of the weathering and the deterioration of the monuments. The old black African dominion was everywhere on the planet earth. Mountains were carved in their image. Hubble telescope has even caught the image of a Negro or African face deep in space formed by the stars. In a cluster within a star-forming region in the small Magellanic Cloud deep in outer-space is a portrait of a Negro face. What this portrait is, is a large portion of the universe including stars and even galaxies are brought together to form the shape of a Negro face. This imagine that is in the shape of a Negro face encompass hundreds of light years in distance and in dimensions. Only the creator of the universe could have put this image in the cosmos. (You Tube- Black alien face discovered on Hubble photo)

It was the old black Africans that occupied the ancient continent of Lemuria in the Pacific Ocean as well as occupied the ancient continent of Atlantis in the Atlantic Ocean. The old black African dominion was here when the planet earth had only one huge supercontinent named Pangea 200 million years ago. The planet earth belongs to the old black Africans.

The white Gentiles bombs and technology will not work against God no more than the advance abilities of the old black African dominion worked for them. Therefore, let it be known to you white Gentiles that the "Salvation" of God in the knowledge that bombs can't help you has been sent and delivered to the white Gentiles and if they hear it and receive it, they will know what to do by selecting alternative actions to be saved. Acts 28: 28

Absolutely nothing is more important than preventing the white Jews from judging themselves unworthy for everlasting life because they want to be the people of God so bad that they are assuming the identity of the true people of God and nothing is more important than preserving the white Gentiles on the Tree of Life to prevent no place found for the great white throne in the future. Acts 13: 46 and Revelation 20: 11

The Kingdom of God is now at hand. The opportunity to become part of the kingdom of God is now available. Hear and receive the word of God and repent so your sins could be blotted-out and you be granted admission to Paradise in the world to come. Acts 3: 19

Do not be a fool and say that you are not interested in the world to come and you are only interested in the world we live in today. Know that the world we live in today purpose for existence was to determine who would live in the world to come which will be the greatest Kingdom ever to exist in three-dimensional-space anywhere in the omniverse. The existence of the world to come and the people of the world to come that shall dwell in New Jerusalem and dwell at the "Outer-Court" of New Jerusalem that shall be identified by all other beings in the universe as the seed that the "Lord" has blessed are more important than anything that can be imagined and desired in the world we live in today. We now have the opportunity to be part of this great Kingdom by our choices and actions in the world we live ion today. Isaiah 61: 9

Know for a certainty, that we all shall die and enter the realm of our existence after life where we shall all be judged, and this judgment shall be without mercy. There in the after-life or the existence after this life, God who knows what is in our minds and hearts will give to each one of us according to our works. 2 Corinthians 5: 10, James 2: 13, Revelation 2: 23, Jeremiah 17: 10 and Romans 2: 6

Fear this and know that we shall go before God, the Lamb in Heaven, who can kill the body as well as kill the spirit. Do not be deceived to believe that energy cannot be destroyed but only be altered. Your soul which is entirely energy can be destroyed. Fear Him who can kill the body and the soul because if your body is destroyed, your soul can always be reincarnated into another body but if your soul is destroyed, there will be no coming back by reincarnation to live again in another body at another time. Matthew 10: 28 and Luke 12: 4-5

It is also important for the white Gentiles to know that the "Lamb" in Heaven who shall do the judgment is the color of brass (brown) that has been burned in a furnace (dark brown to black) with hair like sheep wool or nappy hair. If the white Gentiles die believing that the Son of God who is the "Lamb" in Heaven that shall inherit everything and judge us all is white, they will go to Hell because they do not know God or the Son of God. Revelation 1: 14-15, John 16: 3 and John 8: 19

All white Gentiles must know that as many as receive Him, Jesus as the Son of God, the Lamb in Heaven that is the color of brass (brown) that was burned in a furnace (dark brown to black) with hair like sheep wool or nappy hair), to them He gave the right to become children of God. To those Gentiles who believe in Jesus who is the Lamb in Heaven that is the color of brass that was burned in a furnace with hair like sheep wool, to them He gave the right to become children of God. If you believe that Jesus who is the "Lamb" in Heaven is white with hair like eagle feathers or straight hair, you do not know God or the Son of God. To them this time at judgment, the "Lamb" will say, "You never knew me" and "I never knew you", "depart from Me". John 1: 12, Revelation 1: 14-15, John 16: 3, John 8: 19 and Matthew 7: 23

To those who believe in and worship the image or picture of the up-right Paleolithic white beast or the Paleolithic white beast that was made to walk up-right as Jesus, the son of God, to them they shall drink of the wine of the wrath of God which is poured out full strength into the cup of their indignation which is their anger, resentment and outrage that Jesus who is the "Lamb" in Heaven is black with hair like sheep wool. They shall be tormented with fire and brimstone in the presence of the "Holy Angels" and in the presence of the "Lamb" who is black with hair like sheep wool or nappy hair. Revelation 14: 9-11 and Revelation 1: 14-15

After death, there will be a judgment. Those that are found worthy will be reborn in paradise in the world to come as well as those that are not worthy will be reborn in the world to come as the cursed Morlocks or cast into the Lake of Fire for ever-lasting torment and damnation. Romans 2: 16, Romans 14: 10-12, Galatians 6: 7, Ephesians 6: 8 and Revelation 20: 4-10

This entering of Paradise once your life here on the earth is complete and you are found worthy to exist in God's kingdom will not be in thousands of years after your death but in a day. Time passes different in the afterlife than the way time passes here in the three-dimensional universe. The review of your life and your judgment in the existence after this life will come in a day in our space-time notwithstanding the time this judgment will take in the afterlife. Time in the afterlife is much different than time is in the three-dimensional universe if time exist there at all. It could be longer or shorter or however the controller of the afterlife deems fit. Jesus told the thief that believe in Jesus when Jesus was on the cross being crucified that, that day when they died, he would be with Jesus in Paradise. Luke 23: 43

# 48

# The Promise has been fulfilled. The Message has been delivered.

Everything in the Matrix of this life in this world have been set in order for the return of God. Isaiah 44: 7

The "Message" of "Salvation" to save the Gentiles in the latter-days has been delivered as promised. The order from God to His people to be a light for the Gentiles from biblical days to "Present" till the end of the earth has been obeyed. Acts 13: 47

The Sons of Perdition have been revealed as ordered by God before His return. To give the white Jews and white Gentiles their chance to fall away from that man of sin before the return of God so God could take out of the white Jews and white Gentiles a people for God's name, the words of the prophets or the Books of Simion have been written and delivered. 2 Thessalonians 2: 3-4 and Acts 15: 14-15

The End of the dominion has been declared from the Beginning of the dominion meaning what happened in the beginning of the dominion will be what happens at the end of the dominion. In the beginning of the dominion, Simeon revealed to the white Jews and white Gentiles that God wanted to take out of the white Jews and white Gentiles a people for God's name and now at the end of the dominion, Simion has declared this to the white Jews and white Gentiles again. The End of the dominion has been declared from the beginning of the dominion as was prophesied in the Holy Bible. Isaiah 46: 10, Isaiah 41: 22, Isaiah 41: 26, Isaiah 43: 9 and Acts 15: 14-15

The "Mystery of the Gospel" that reveals that the "Slaves" and the ascendants of the Slaves are God's first born and chosen people and the Sons of Perdition who are those that are assuming the identity of the true people of God have been revealed and this had to be done first before the return of God to give the white Jews and white Gentiles a chance to fall away from the Sons of Perdition who is that man of sin and then join with the true people of God who are the ascendants of the slaves to prove that the white beings were worthy to continue to exist with the human beings because God wants to take out of the white Gentiles a people for God's name and for that cause, the words of the Prophets or the Books of Simion are written. Exodus 4: 22, 2 Thessalonians 2: 3-4 and Acts 15: 14-15

It must be known to the Gentiles that if they help the people of God now and behold or reveal everything that have happened, they will change the shape of the things to come and prevent the Gentiles from being Cut-Off from the Tree of Life and no place found for the great white throne in the future, but the Gentiles are not committed to that end or that choice of actions. The white Gentiles must do whatever they think is best to prove or disprove if the white Gentiles are worthy to remain grafted on the Tree of Life. The "Deliverer and all who are sent will accept the Gentiles final choices as being what is right and just no matter what those choices are. Only at judgment this time will the white Gentiles have to answer for their choices of today. Honoring God by honoring the true people of God by giving a nation to the people of God and having an Ambassador from that nation to the Throne of the Gentiles that is given utterance to speak 'Boldly" will steer events in another direction and prevent no place found for the great white throne in the future. It is written in the Holy Bible that the white Gentiles and white Jews will hear and receive the truth from him who is sent and believe and be saved. Romans 11: 22, Revelation 20: 11, Ephesians 6: 19-20, Acts 14: 1 and Acts 15: 7

Salvation or the knowledge to save the Gentiles from harm has been delivered to the Gentiles as was promised. The Promise has now been fulfilled. It is now up to the Gentiles to change as they said that they could and would and save the kingdom. A radical alteration of our thought patterns and actions must be performed if events are to be steered in another direction to change the shape of the things to come to prevent no place found for the great white throne in the future.

It is now the responsibility of every gentile that comes in contact with the truth to guarantee the survival of the great white throne by revealing the truth and everything that is being suppressed. Now, since an Afro American has reached out to help the great white throne, how many Gentiles will join him to save the great white throne? Absolutely nothing is more important than preventing the white Jews from judging themselves unworthy for everlasting life because they are assuming the identity of the true people of God and nothing is more important than preserving the white Gentiles on the Tree of Life to prevent no place found for the great white throne in the future. Acts 13: 46 and Revelation 20: 11

The Message has been delivered. The people of God have obeyed God by being for the salvation of the Gentiles from biblical days till "Present" and the promise made to the Gentiles to deliver a truth to them in the latter-days have been fulfilled. The End of the dominion has been declared from the beginning. The Mystery of the Gospel and the Sons of Perdition have been revealed. Everything has been set in order for the return of God. Revealing this unknown truth is how the last two witnesses of God or the prophets and Sents (Saints) will be identified. Do no harm to the Prophets or to the Sents (Saints) to prevent God from giving the Gentiles blood to drink and to prevent the Gentiles from receiving their Just-Due. Acts 13: 47, Isaiah 44: 7, Isaiah 41: 22, Isaiah 41: 26, Isaiah 43: 9, Isaiah 46: 10, Revelation 11: 3-14, and Revelation 16: 6

The Promise from the Lord God to send to the Gentiles prophets, wise men and scribes or those who would write books declaring the End from the beginning and how God wants to take out of the Gentiles a people for God's name and it is for this cause and purpose that the Words of the Prophets or the Books of Simion are written have been fulfilled. The words of the prophets or the Books of Simion have been written and delivered as was promised. The true people of God have been a light for the Gentiles in the last Gentile kingdom of Iron and Clay. The Sons of Perdition have been revealed. This is prophecy, and this is the revealing of the Mystery of the Gospel. This is how the last two witnesses of the white Gentiles second chance or prophets from God will be identified. Do no harm to the prophets or to those that are Sent that will be called Saints to prevent God from giving the Gentiles blood to drink and to prevent the Gentiles from receiving their "Just-due". In the past, those who were sent to save nations by revealing the Mystery of the Gospel were "Promoted" and given great wealth and made third ruler in the realm. They were given utterance to speak boldly as they ought to speak. Now, all have been set in order and all shall come to pass. The Kingdom of God is at hand and the Kingdom will come to the earth and all of us who are worthy will experience Paradise. Matthew 23: 34, Acts 13: 46-47, Acts 15: 14-15, 2 Thessalonians 2: 3-4, Revelation 11: 3-6,

IVORY SIMION

Revelation 16: 6, Genesis 41: 37-45, Daniel 2: 47-48, Daniel 5: 11, Daniel 5: 16, Daniel 5: 29, and Ephesians 6: 19-20

Knowing the terror of the Lord, we will try to persuade men in the latter days to seek God. We who are sent are well known to God and I also trust that we are well known to you in your consciences because it was you Gentiles that sent the message to yourself in the latter days so this time you would know what to do. 2 Corinthians 5: 11

Understand, this dominion we live in today is about to end just as the Greek dominion and the Roman dominion ended. God Himself and His Son will rule the next dominion forever and they want the people of God to serve them. The people of God will be transformed into a new race of Gods that can't be killed that can float like the clouds and fly like the birds to their windows as God made Moses a God over Pharaoh. They will control the universe forever. All who do not serve them will be destroyed. Nothing can change this. Daniel 7: 26-27, Revelation 21: 3-4, Isaiah 60: 8, Exodus 7: 1 and Isaiah 60: 12

Now, the Gentiles have a great part in this new world. No, New Jerusalem will not be given to the gentile Christians, but the Gentiles will be given the "Outer Court" of New Jerusalem and they will be running in and out of New Jerusalem for 42 months. A day with the Lord is like a thousand years to us. 42 months with days that are a thousand years long will have the Gentiles with the people of God for almost an eternity. They will be exposed to the glory of God and the Son of God. There with the people of God, they will be given god like abilities. Abilities that will elevate them above all others in the universe. They will receive evolutionary growth, spiritual advancement and universal domination all of which are things that the white Gentiles could have never achieved on their own. Revelation 11: 2 and 2 Peter 3: 8

It is them who will sneak leaves from the Tree of Life out to the nations on the outside to heal all diseases and ailments. Remember, the nations on the outside will be suffering from the worse plague the world will ever see. That is why the Greys extraterrestrials are here from the future in the past or our present collecting uncontaminated DNA from the white Gentiles that could not be collected in the future because of the plague. Revelation 22: 2

And this shall be the plague with which the Lord will strike all the people who fought against Jerusalem:

Their flesh shall dissolve while they stand on their feet.

Their eyes shall dissolve in their sockets and their tongues shall dissolve in their mouths. Zechariah 14: 12

Listen to me carefully and clearly, you do not want to be in the Valley of Jehoshaphat fighting God for the people of God who are scattered, who were slaves and persecuted who are the Afro-Americans today inheritance. There, God will enter into judgement with them who want the heritage of Is Rael (Real). This is not a fight against the Arabs or Muslims and God is on the white Christian Gentiles and white Greek Jewish gentiles side. God will be fighting those who have assumed the identity of the people of God and wants the people of God inheritance. God will be fighting those who wants the heritage of Is Rael (Real) or wants the heritage of those who are Really the true people of God. The true people of God are the Slaves or the ascendants of the Slaves because the Slaves are God's first born and are those who are Is Rael (Real). Understand, the Slaves are God's first born and are those who are Is Rael (Real). The race that was slaves in Egypt is the same race that was slaves in America brought to America on slave ships in bondage to be sold. The Afro Americans are the ascendants of the Slaves brought to America on slave ships in bondage to be sold. You have been Alerted. The Deliverer that you sent to yourself mission is to alert you to the things that shall come to pass so you could make your latter-day choices wisely. Joel 3: 2, Exodus 4: 22, Deuteronomy 28: 68, Chapter 3 in this book and African American History commission Act titled H. R. 1242

The white Gentiles that are with the people of God at the Outer Court will be exposed to the Trees of Life and Knowledge that will expand their consciousness. With this expanded consciousness they will communicate with higher forms of beings throughout the universe in their travels with the people of God. They will drink from the River of Life to live forever without any ailments or diseases. The people of God will receive an ascension that will evolve them into a new race of Gods that can't be killed. There will be no death for the people of God and there will be no death for the Gentiles that are with the people of God while they are drinking from the River of Life. Revelation 22: 1-2 and Revelation 21: 4

In New Jerusalem, they will be exposed to all of the godlike powers that the people of God will have that they will share with their Gentiles friends. All who see the Gentiles at the Outer Court will say that the Gentiles there with the people of God in New Jerusalem are "also" a seed that the Lord have blessed. Isaiah 61: 9

The white Gentiles will not explore the universe with Spock, a descendant of Satan, but will control the universe with the people of God forever. Do not let Hollywood that is controlled by the false prophet from the Synagogue of Satan deceived you again. Those from the Synagogue of Satan must remember the channeled message to them from the future that they put in their movie that stated, "the needs of the many out way the needs of the few or the one". Those from the Synagogue of Satan must allow this future for the Gentiles, the Jews and the people of God to come to pass. Yes, this also apply to the white Gentiles that are called by God's people name or call themselves Jews. This is for all of "Mankind" or those who were made to look like men to be with God. It is because of this that the white Jews must not stir up the white Gentiles against the brethren or the brothers poisoning the Gentiles minds against the brothers who are the Afro Americans today as they did in biblical days. This future for the Gentiles, the Jews and the people of God out way any need that the white Jews may have for themselves. The needs of the many out way the needs of the few or the one. (Star Trek the Wrath of Khan), Revelations 2: 9, Revelation 3: 9, Revelation 19: 20, Acts 15: 17 and Acts 14: 2

The world shall be divided among the tribes of Is Rael (Real). The white Gentiles that are with the people of God shall share this inheritance with the people of God. They shall be to Is Rael (Real) as native-born or special gentiles who can be trusted who loves God and loves the people of God who shall be treated and is honored like a child of Is Rael (Real). It shall be that in whatever tribe the stranger dwells, there Is Rael (Real) shall give him his inheritance. The future for the white Jews and white Gentiles is not with Spock and the people of Satan but will be with the people of God. Space flight in the future will be with the people of God who will control the universe forever. There, with the people of God will the Gentiles become the police of the universe enforcing the will of God. They will represent a Force and Power greater than the Federation and they will not be called Starfleet but will be called the children of God. Please, do not forfeit this glorious future. Do not let your second chance for salvation be in vain. Absolutely nothing in this world today can compare with what God has for you and those in the future who love Him and believes. Remember, we all shall die one day and go before a judgement to determine who will be reborn in paradise or damned to Hell. Death is not the end but is the beginning of the rest of your true journey that will determine where you will be throughout eternity. It is the

Deliverer mission to bring this knowledge to your attention so you could make your latter-day choices wisely. Ezekiel 47: 21-23, Daniel 7: 27 and 2 Corinthians 5: 10

Eye has not seen, nor ear heard, nor have entered into the heart of man the things which God has prepared for those who love Him. Right now, on our present level of evolutionary development, we can't imagine the joys and the physical and spiritual gifts that the Lord God has prepared for those who loves Him in His dominion. 1 Corinthians 2: 9

God will make all things new or new laws of physics will be created that allows the impossible to be done. The people of God will be able to float like the clouds and fly like the birds to their windows. They will be immortals that cannot be killed. There will be no death for them. They will also be able to bring the dead back to life as Jesus did. Revelation 21: 5, Isaiah 60: 8, Revelation 21: 4 and John 11: 43

They will have the power over life and death throughout the universe. For the people of God, death will be swallowed up in their victory. They will control Hades where the souls of the dead are tormented. Hades shall be the new maximum-security insulation throughout eternity for those who cannot live in God's new world. Once there, there is no return. You will never come back. For the nations and kingdoms that will not serve the people of God shall be destroyed and the people of those destroyed nations will be sent to Hades never to return again. 1 Corinthians 15: 54-55 and Isaiah 60: 12

You Gentiles do not want to be nowhere else in the universe with the most advance technology other than at the "Outer Court" of all of this glory and power. The Gentiles can either be part of this glory and power or they can be controlled by it. The Controllers or the Controlled? Well, we all know how the Gentiles feel about being in control. So, that choice should be easy. No technology nowhere in the universe will be better than the evolutionary gifts and the miracles experience there at the "Outer Court" of the throne of the God of the universe and the throne of the Son of the God of the universe. With the most advance technology, there still will be limitations or things that you cannot do with technology. Whereas with God and those Gentiles at the Outer Court of New Jerusalem, all things will be possible. There, the Gentiles will be exposed to a supernatural power that is operated by your will and belief that do not need instrumentalities to function. All you need to do is imagine it, believe in what you imagined, and have faith in your belief that it will come true and it will come true. Revelation 11: 2, Revelation 22: 1, Matthew 19: 26

Jesus said: "If you have faith as a mustard seed, you will say to this mountain, move from here, and it will move; and nothing will be impossible for you". Matthew 17: 20

Jesus said: "If you have the faith as a mustard seed, you can say to this mulberry tree or to a mountain, 'be pulled up by the roots and be planted in the sea,' and it will obey you, it will be done". Luke 17: 6 and Matthew 21: 21

In the future, in New Jerusalem and after seeing the glory of God and the glory of the Son of God, the people of God will have complete faith to do the impossible. They will truly believe. Now, let me tell you something, the Gentiles at the Outer Court will also believe. This ability will be given to all who believes in God and believes in the Son of God. Jesus said: "If you can believe; all things are possible to him who believes". No technology in the universe will surpass this spiritual gift that will be given to the people of God in New Jerusalem and given to the Gentiles at the Outer Court. You

Gentiles do not want to be nowhere else in the universe other than at the Outer Court of New Jerusalem. Mark 9: 23 and Revelation 11: 2

There will be no more death, nor sorrow, nor crying and no pain there ever. All who are there shall drink from the fountain of the water of life. There will never be doctors or hospitals there in New Jerusalem and there at the Outer Court. Drinking from the fountain of the water of life, you will never get sick, damaged or aged. The streets in New Jerusalem shall be made of pure gold like transparent glass and the stones alone the side of the streets will be diamonds, rubies, peals and many others. There will be a river there that if you drink from that river you will regenerate yourself to maintain your youth and trees on both sides of the river that if you eat fruit from these trees it will expand your consciousness making you smarter and wiser. Revelation 21: 4, Revelation 21: 6, Revelation 21: 21 and Revelation 22: 1-2

Every living being in the universe will want what is given to those on the earth in New Jerusalem and at the Outer Court of New Jerusalem. Because of that, God will turn His people into a new race of Gods to protect what will be on the earth. The Gentiles shall share in this glory and be protected forever by the grace of God. To help control the universe, the Gentiles will be given godlike powers that will elevate them above all others in the universe. They will also be close friends with a new race of Gods that cannot be killed. They will not be friends with Spock and the descendants of Satan but friends with the people of God. Their backup will not be Spock and the power of Satan but will be the people of God who will be transformed into a new race of Gods powered by the God of the universe and the Son of the God of the universe.

Listen, you don't want to be nowhere else in the universe flying in the best of star ships better than the Enterprise and forfeit your gifts at the Outer Court. The orb ships of light given to the Gentiles to enforce the will of God shall supersede all other star ships in the universe. These orbs of light have no engines or movable parts to break down and they will transcend time and space. They will even travel through black holes to enter other universes. The inside of these orbs of light will always be larger than the orb itself. All inside of these orbs of light will exist in another reality that will allow their bodies to be beyond the physical dimensions of space. Extreme heat or cold from traveling through suns and isolated area of the universe will have no effect on them as well as the twisting and stretching effect that will happened going through a black hole will have no effects on them either. No other ships in the universe will equal or come close to the orbs of light given to the people of God to travel in Outer-Darkness or Outer-Space.

Inside, these orbs of light will be operated by the will of the individual in control and the environment inside of the orb of light will be anything imagine by the controlling operator. It will be powered by supernatural forces that will permit it to reach warp 100 or any unimaginable warp speed without over heating as well as traveling and teleporting through time and parallel dimensions. Because the orbs of light will be generated from outside of our time and space from the spiritual realm of the $12^{th}$ dimension where the kingdom of God use to be, no destructive force in this physical universe will be able to affect it or harm or penetrate it. Three dimensions of the orbs you will be able to see like the height, width, and length but nine dimensions of its existence will be somewhere else that cannot be seen or touched. It will be untouchable by anything in this universe. The weaponry aboard the craft will be whatever the operator can imagine or see in his mind. From a single isolated pin-pointed shot to total planetary destruction will be available to the operator and a lot more. Inside God's orbs of light, all things will be possible. Inside God's orbs of light, the operator will be invincible, and all passengers will forever be safe and comfortable in their space flights. Matthew 19: 26

All who are there in New Jerusalem and at the Outer Court shall inherit all things and the God of the universe shall be his God and he shall be God's son. Revelation 21: 7

Nothing the white Gentiles have imagined in all of their science fiction movies concerning life in the future compare with what God has prepared for those at New Jerusalem and at the Outer Court of New Jerusalem. Star Trek, Star Wars or no other imagined reality of the future comes close to what will be given to those in New Jerusalem and at the Outer Court of New Jerusalem. The Kingdom of God is at hand and in the future, the Kingdom of God will be on the earth with man in New Jerusalem. Revelation 21: 3

The Holy Bible has recorded that the Gentiles will bring all of their mighty forces of guns, ships, planes, and missiles to the Lord our God as well as all of their gold and silver to be part of God's new world. These are things that they will play with in their leisure time because their real power will be in the spiritual gifts given to them by the people of God that will make all things possible. No technology or wealth will be equal to the gifts that God has instore for you in the future at the Outer Court. You will freely give up all of your technology and wealth and scream, "Lord God of Israel, these things of mines, I do not want anymore. Father in Heaven, please give me your spiritual gifts and blessings". Isaiah 60: 9-11

Because the wisdom of God is in a Mystery and only God's elect knows that Mystery behold, I tell you that Mystery. We all shall be changed in a moment or in the twinkling of an eye. The "Dead" or the Negro shall be raised incorruptible. Remember, Negro and Necro are the same word and Necro means "Dead". Negro should be pronounced the same way you pronounce "Negative" because "Neg" and "Nec" have the same sound. So, when the corruptible Negro has put on incorruption and his mortal body has put on immortality, then shall be brought to pass the saying that is written: "Death is swallowed up in victory". When the Slaves or Afro Americans tribulations on this earth are complete and they have proven themselves to be worthy to replace the Cast Out Ones and the Fallen Angels and is joined with God in Heaven on the earth at New Jerusalem, "Death" shall be swallowed up or absorbed, conquered and controlled in their victory on the earth to be the race chosen to join with the God of the universe. Not only will they not be able to be killed, but they will also be able to bring the dead back to life as Jesus did with Lazarus. They will have the power and authority over Life and Death throughout the universe. The white Gentiles at the Outer Court will be best of friends with this new race of Gods that cannot be killed. Do not be deceived by the false prophet in Hollywood that is controlled by the Synagogue of Satan who are those that say they are Jews but are not. The white Gentiles will not be with the Vulcans or the descendants of Satan but with the descendant of the God of the universe. Remember, the ascendants of the Slaves who shall inherit everything are God's first born. It is the Deliverer mission to reveal this Mystery of the future to you so you could make your latter-day choices wisely. As important as this Mystery is and the importance of the Outer Court for the white Gentiles, the false prophet has never brought this knowledge to the white Gentiles for their examination and study so the Gentiles could determine for themselves if what is recorded in the Holy Bible and ancient scriptures have any merit. The false prophet has given them hope in a future full of sickness and struggles with science and technology to combat their sickness, ailments and discomforts. Science and technology cannot compare with miracles and a reality whereas all things are possible. This is a reality that is beyond science and technology because this reality is above and outside of science and technology laws of physics. With science and technology there will always be limitations but with God's new reality, all things are possible. With the people of God, a future awaits the white Gentiles in paradise full of miracles and everlasting life with no sorrow, no crying, no sickness, no pain or death. The Gentiles must be given the right to choose how they would like to spend eternity. This time, you will have your choice. 1 Corinthians 2: 7, Mark 4: 11, 1 Corinthians 15: 51-52, 1 Corinthians 15: 53-55, Revelation 3: 9, Exodus 4: 22, Matthew 19: 26 and Revelation 21: 1-4

It is because of this future that the Gentiles wanted so bad and the people of God wanted so bad to share with the Gentiles by joining with them so the white Gentiles could become human and become one race with the people of God called the Human race that everything was rewound and started over to give the Gentiles a second chance to share in this glory. Lying by calling yourself human beings to deceive all in Heaven that the joining of the white beings and the colored beings have taken place and all on the earth are human beings or people with a shade, color or tint, because hu-man means colored-man because "hu" means color, while you are still white and screaming that "Black lives do not matter" is not the way. Grant you, you can do whatever you want to do. The deliverer is not making any suggestions because the white Jews and the white Gentiles have to do what is in their hearts to prove or disprove if the white Jews and white Gentiles are worthy to remain grafted on the Tree of life. The Deliverer is only revealing the Mystery of the Gospel and is asking the Gentiles to make their latter-day decisions wisely. It is for this cause that the Books of Simion are written.

Nothing in the universe have ever been as great of a thing as what the people of God did for the white Gentiles when the people of God agreed to a second chance for the Gentiles. This time at judgement, the white Gentiles can ask from one end of Heaven to the other concerning the days that are past, which were before you in the first world and since the day that God created man on the earth in this world we live in today, whether any great thing like this has happened before or anything like this has been heard and they will be told that nothing in the universe in as great as what the people of God did for the white Gentiles. The white Gentiles owe the people of God. Are the white Gentiles evolved enough to acknowledge a debt? Deuteronomy 4: 32

The Deliverer mission was to bring this to mind so you would have your choice this time because last time you were deceived by the false prophet and at judgement your assertion was that you did not know or was not given a choice to be part of this great kingdom. Revelation 19: 20

Last time, the people of God said that they could not tell you because you threatened to kill those who revealed the suppressed truth. Your response was that regardless of the consequences, you were ordered by God to be for the salvation of the Gentiles. Acts 13: 47

You stated that the people of God disobeyed an order from God to save their own lives. You stated that the people of God were only interested in saving their own lives and not concern with saving the Gentiles. The people of God responded by saying "This time, no greater love has no one than this, than to lay down his life for his friends". John 15: 13

This time, the people of God promised their friends that they would deliver the message to save the white Jews and white Gentiles no matter what was going on at the time without offending the Gentiles. This time, the message to save the white Jews and white Gentiles was delivered regardless of the consequences. This time, the order from God to be for the salvation of the Gentiles from biblical days to "present" till the end of the earth has been obeyed. Acts 13: 47

This time, you will have your choice. You can remain in iniquity or you can "Fall Away" from the Sons of Perdition who do not believe in Jesus, Son of the God of Is Rael (Real). Every spirit that does not confess that Jesus, the Son of God did come in the flesh is not of God. This is the spirit of the anti-Christ or anti-God which you have heard was coming and is now already in the world in Jerusalem occupying Israel today. The anti-Christ is in Jerusalem today right now passing off as the people of God. 1 John 4: 3

The white Roman gentiles who have dominion today have put white Greek gentiles in the holy land that do not believe in Jesus who are identified by the holy bible standards as the anti-Christ and Sons of Perdition or sons from Hell. The anti-Christ is in Jerusalem right now. 1 John 4: 3 and Chapter 4, this book, the Books of Simion

God has promise that the Kingdom would not come until you have had your chance to choose to remain in iniquity or fall away from that man of sin who opposes and exalts himself above all that is called God or that is worshiped. Simion has revealed to you the identity of the Anti-Christ and the Sons of Perdition. Simion has brought you the message that God wants to take out of the white Jews and white Gentiles a people for God's name. Since the end of the dominion shall be declared from the beginning and since in the beginning Simeon, the Nig er declared that God wanted to take out of the white Jews and white Gentiles a people for God's name, so it was done in the latter-days by Simion, the Nigg er. It was for this cause that the Books of Simion are written and delivered. This time, Simion has given you the opportunity and the right to have a choice that you said you did not have last time because you were deceived by the false prophet. Now, this time, the choice is yours. 2 Thessalonians 2: 3-4, Acts 15: 14-15, Isaiah 46: 10 and Acts 13: 1 and Revelation 19: 20

So, until we meet again on the other-side, your friend will say to his friends, you will remember, understand and "Believe" and I know that friends will celebrate with friends after all is completed in this world and we are joined together in paradise in the world to come. Until then, a friend will say to his friends, "Take Care and God Bless". Acts 15: 7

The Promise to friends has been fulfilled. The Order from God has been obeyed. The Message to save the white Jews and white Gentiles has been written and delivered.

It is finished. All is done.

# ABOUT THE AUTHOR

The Author of the Books of Simion makes no claims of having any special knowledge other than the knowledge that the Author has read in books. The Author of the Books of Simion also makes no claims of receiving or having any divine wisdom other than having his own common sense.

Other books written by the Author are:

1. The War between Men and Women.
2. The History of the Afro Americans.
3. The Broken Branch and the Grafted branch.
4. The Matrix.
5. Prophecy.
6. The Crash of the Housing Market.
7. Aliens and the Invasion of the earth.
8. The Second Chance for Salvation.
9. Evolution and Creation.
10. The Old Dominion and the Olmec Calendar
11. The Kingdom of God is at Hand.

www.ingramcontent.com/pod-product-compliance
Lightning Source LLC
Chambersburg PA
CBHW030314100526
44592CB00010B/428